HOUSING, HOMELESSNESS, AND SOCIAL POLICY IN THE URBAN NORTH

Edited by *Julia Christensen, Sally Carraher, Travis Hedwig, and Steven Arnfjord*

Housing, Homelessness, and Social Policy in the Urban North brings together leading scholars on northern urban housing across the Canadian North, Alaska, and Greenland. Through various case studies, the contributors examine the ways in which housing insecurity and homelessness provide a critical lens on the social dimensions of northern urbanization. They also present key considerations in the development of effective and sustainable social policy for these areas. The book kickstarts a conversation between multiple stakeholders from different cultural and national regions across the North American north. It asks key questions including these: What are the common problems of, and responses to, housing insecurity and homelessness across these northern regions? Is a single definition of "homelessness" even possible, or desirable? And if not, can a shared language around how to end the housing crisis and homelessness in our northern regions still occur?

The contributors explore how experiences of northern towns and cities inform an overall understanding of urban forms and processes in the contemporary world, and speak directly to the emerging body of literature on cities. Highlighting key limitations to federal, state, and provincial policy, *Housing, Homelessness, and Social Policy in the Urban North* raises important implications for developing policy that is responsive to northern realities.

JULIA CHRISTENSEN is an associate professor of geography and planning at Queen's University.

SALLY CARRAHER is an associate professor of anthropology at the University of Alaska Anchorage.

TRAVIS HEDWIG is an associate professor of health sciences at the University of Alaska Anchorage.

STEVEN ARNFJORD is an associate professor of social work and the director of Ilisimatusarfik's Centre for Arctic Welfare at the University of Greenland.

Housing, Homelessness, and Social Policy in the Urban North

EDITED BY JULIA CHRISTENSEN,
SALLY CARRAHER, TRAVIS HEDWIG,
AND STEVEN ARNFJORD

UNIVERSITY OF TORONTO PRESS
Toronto Buffalo London

© University of Toronto Press 2024
Toronto Buffalo London
utorontopress.com

ISBN 978-1-4875-5108-7 (cloth)   ISBN 978-1-4875-5420-0 (EPUB)
ISBN 978-1-4875-5289-3 (paper)   ISBN 978-1-4875-5375-3 (PDF)

Library and Archives Canada Cataloguing in Publication

Title: Housing, homelessness, and social policy in the urban north / edited
  by Julia Christensen, Sally Carraher, Travis Hedwig, and Steven Arnfjord.
Names: Christensen, Julia (Writer on homelessness), editor. | Carraher,
  Sally, 1981– editor. | Hedwig, Travis H., editor. | Arnfjord, Steven, editor.
Description: Includes bibliographical references and index.
Identifiers: Canadiana (print) 20230538940 | Canadiana (ebook) 20230538975 |
  ISBN 9781487551087 (cloth) | ISBN 9781487552893 (paper) | ISBN 9781487554200
  (EPUB) | ISBN 9781487553753 (PDF)
Subjects: LCSH: Housing – Canada, Northern. | LCSH: Housing – Alaska. |
  LCSH: Housing – Greenland. | LCSH: Homelessness – Canada, Northern. |
  LCSH: Homelessness – Alaska. | LCSH: Homelessness – Greenland. |
  LCSH: Canada, Northern – Social policy. | LCSH: Alaska – Social policy. |
  LCSH: Greenland – Social policy.
Classification: LCC HD7287 .H65 2024 | DDC 363.51097 – dc23 | 363.5/1 – dc23

Cover design: Val Cooke
Cover illustrations: Pro_Studio/Shutterstock.com, Jacob Boomsma/istockphoto.com,
Evgeniya Uvarova/shutterstock.com, stockphoto52/istockphoto.com

We wish to acknowledge the land on which the University of Toronto Press
operates. This land is the traditional territory of the Wendat, the Anishnaabeg, the
Haudenosaunee, the Métis, and the Mississaugas of the Credit First Nation.

This book has been published with the help of a grant from the Federation for the
Humanities and Social Sciences, through the Awards to Scholarly Publications
Program, using funds provided by the Social Sciences and Humanities Research
Council of Canada.

University of Toronto Press acknowledges the financial support of the Government
of Canada, the Canada Council for the Arts, and the Ontario Arts Council, an agency
of the Government of Ontario, for its publishing activities.

Canada Council   Conseil des Arts
for the Arts   du Canada

ONTARIO ARTS COUNCIL
CONSEIL DES ARTS DE L'ONTARIO
an Ontario government agency
un organisme du gouvernement de l'Ontario

Funded by the   Financé par le
Government   gouvernement
of Canada   du Canada

Canadä

Contents

Introduction 1

Section One: The Canadian North

Regional Introduction: The Canadian North 15
JULIA CHRISTENSEN

1 It's a Tough Game: Navigating Housing Monopolies in
Yellowknife, Northwest Territories 25
LISA FREEMAN AND JULIA CHRISTENSEN

2 Responding to Homelessness in Yellowknife: Pushing the Ocean
Back with a Spoon 49
NICK FALVO

3 An "Urban" Issue, and the Issue with "Urban": Contextualizing
Homelessness in Whitehorse 79
ALEX NELSON

4 Homelessness, Mobility, and Migration from the James Bay
Region 105
CAROL KAUPPI, MICHAEL HANKARD,
AND HENRI PALLARD

5 A Different Kind of "Ecological Refugee": Land Claims,
Migration, and Inequalities in Northern Labrador 139
JOSHUA MOSES

6   Making Place Home: The Contradictions of Inuit Housing
    in a Liberal Democracy   157
    FRANK TESTER

Section Two: Alaska

    Regional Introduction: Alaska   181
    SALLY CARRAHER AND TRAVIS HEDWIG

7   Northern Voices on Homelessness: Engaging the Public
    and Promoting Inclusivity for Homeless Alaskans in Public
    Discourse   191
    SALLY CARRAHER AND TRAVIS HEDWIG

8   Differing Meanings of Housing First: Lessons Learned
    from a Single-Site Program Evaluation in Anchorage,
    Alaska   211
    TRAVIS HEDWIG

9   Alaska Is a Very Small Town: Moving towards an
    Understanding of Homelessness in the Urban North   227
    CLARE J. DANNENBERG

Section Three: Greenland

    Regional Introduction: Greenland   247
    STEVEN ARNFJORD AND JULIA CHRISTENSEN

10 In Search of Security: Women's Homelessness in Nuuk,
    Greenland   255
    STEVEN ARNFJORD AND JULIA CHRISTENSEN

11 Welfare Colonialism and Geographies of Homelessness
    in Nuuk, Greenland   277
    JULIA CHRISTENSEN, STEVEN ARNFJORD,
    AND MARIE-LOUISE AASTRUP

Conclusion   301

Epilogue: Homelessness across the Arctic in the Shadow of
COVID-19   315

Contributors   327

Introduction

Urbanization and homelessness in circumpolar Arctic communities have both been the focus of recent media and research attention. These two phenomena, however, have been examined only separately, with little attention given to the ways in which they interact – for example, the role of rural-to-urban movement in rising visible homelessness in the urban North, or the particular challenges and opportunities presented to northern towns and cities in their efforts to address housing insecurity and homelessness through social policy. Meanwhile, devolution, resource development, infrastructural improvements, and climate change continue to boost the economic and political significance of the circumpolar North, and demographic change suggests that Arctic urbanization is gaining momentum. The social dimensions of the urban North, and in particular the ways in which marginalization and exclusion within these spaces are structured and experienced, is of critical importance.

This book assembles the leading scholarship in housing, homelessness, and social policy in urban locales across the Canadian North, Alaska, and Greenland. Specifically, the chapters in this volume examine the ways in which housing insecurity and homelessness provide a critical lens on the social dimensions of northern urbanization, and also present key considerations in the development of effective and sustainable social policy for these areas. Through various case studies and reflections across northern urban contexts, chapter contributors explore the myriad ways in which northern urban places foster new forms of community building, health, and social services provision, as well as social inclusion for people experiencing homelessness. At the same time, the northern urban regions and community contexts included in this book have significant differences in terms of governance, scale, settler-Indigenous relations and social welfare provision – differences that provide useful and insightful comparisons in our efforts to identify commonalities and ways forward.

Northern towns and cities are regionally significant, not just as centres for administration, employment, and education, but also as important hubs for diversified housing opportunities, health and social services, social networks, political organization, and much more. At the same time, housing insecurity and homelessness are on the rise in urban centres across the Canadian North, Alaska, and Greenland.[1] What these phenomena reveal about the social dimensions of urban life and processes of political-economic constraint in northern regions has not been well examined. The rising significance of towns and cities to northern life presents unique challenges and opportunities regarding the development of social policy and programs for the provision of emergency shelter, supportive and transitional housing, and health and social services for northern people experiencing the varied forms of socio-structural and spatial exclusion and disenfranchisement commonly associated with homelessness.

With interest increasing in both the dynamics of rural-to-urban migration and urbanization in the North, it is critical that scholars and policymakers begin to understand the diverse processes and forms of social marginalization in northern communities. Alongside the growing concentration of social and economic resources in Arctic urban centres, a picture of increasing disparity and marginalization has appeared in certain sectors of these northern populations. The specific social, health, economic, political, and infrastructural challenges encountered in northern areas compound the dynamics and consequences of such disparity and marginalization. Underlying these challenges is the landscape of chronic housing insecurity across the Canadian North, Alaska, and Greenland since the introduction of state-sanctioned modern housing programs. While this volume was in a state of post-review revision, the onset of the COVID-19 pandemic brought matters of housing insecurity and homelessness under renewed scrutiny, particularly in the North (see the Epilogue in this volume). In particular, the critical relationship between housing and public health underlined the lack of new-build affordable housing, deterioration of existing housing stock, stagnant wages, low vacancy rates, disproportionately high average rental costs, and other material and structural inequalities that

---

1 Julia Christensen et al., "Homelessness across Alaska, the Canadian North and Greenland: A Review of the Literature on a Developing Social Phenomenon in the Circumpolar North," *Arctic* 70, no. 4 (2017): 349–64, https://www.jstor.org/stable/26387309.

create the preconditions for housing insecurity and homelessness in the North.

The Urban North

Researchers have begun to take up discussions of urban forms and processes in the circumpolar Arctic, and the most recent Arctic Human Development Report identified urbanization as a growing trend across the Arctic.[2] Although these towns and cities are relatively small in size, they still "act" like major cities in that they play important roles in regional administration and increasingly in the global economy. We are witnessing what urban planner Torill Nyseth has called the emergence of a new type of small-scale urban development.[3] When urbanization is typically discussed in the context of the North, however, it is often framed as a process brought about by economic and educational opportunities. The concentration of such opportunities in towns and cities, however, has not occurred by chance, nor has it been experienced evenly or equitably. Urbanization has in many ways been a process under way for decades in northern regions through state-sanctioned centralization or concentration policies that were often part and parcel of larger colonial strategies to bring northern peoples off the land and into the wage economy.[4] Challenges associated with administering services in northern areas – particularly in education and health care, the dynamics of resource-dependent economies, and globalization – all play a role in the present-day focusing of opportunities in northern regional centres.[5]

Alongside the spatial and material dimensions of northern urbanization, however, are the social dimensions. These are characterized by the increased concentration of institutionalized health, education, and

2 Joan Nymand Larsen and Gail Fondahl, *Arctic Human Development Report: Regional Processes and Global Linkages* (Copenhagen: Nordic Council of Ministers, 2015).

3 Torill Nyseth, "Arctic Urbanization: Modernity without Cities," in *Arctic Environmental Modernities: From the Age of Polar Exploration to the Era of the Anthropocene*, ed. Lill-Ann Körber, Scott MacKenzie, and Anna Westerståhl Stenport (London: Palgrave Macmillan, 2017), 59–70.

4 Frank Tester and Peter Kulchyski, *Tammarniit (Mistakes): Inuit Relocation in the Eastern Arctic, 1939–63* (Vancouver: UBC Press, 2011); Matthew Farish and P. Whitney Lackenbauer, "High Modernism in the Arctic: Planning Frobisher Bay and Inuvik," *Journal of Historical Geography* 35, no. 3 (2009): 517–44, https://doi.org/10.1016/j.jhg.2009.02.002.

5 Susanne Dybbroe, Jens Dahl, and Ludger Müller-Wille, "Dynamics of Arctic Urbanization," *Acta Borealia* 27, no. 2 (2010): 120–4, https://doi.org/10.1080/08003831.2010.527526.

social services, the criminal justice system, the child welfare system, and emergency shelter supports in northern urban centres. These urban institutional geographies are deeply implicated in the rural-to-urban mobility of northern homelessness, and contribute to the visibility of homelessness in northern urban locales, all the while reproducing the narrative that homelessness is predominantly an urban phenomenon.[6] This narrative leads to an important form of erasure that this volume seeks to challenge, particularly in the context of rural and Indigenous communities, many of which actively contest definitions of homelessness imposed by outsiders – a phenomenon that contributes both to the relative invisibility of homelessness in rural communities and to the lack of access to programs and services that require adherence and compliance to culturally rigid definitions.

Yet despite the rapid urbanization of northern regions, the North itself does not figure at all in conceptual discussions of urbanization. Many northern towns and cities are not oriented towards one another in a network of circumpolar urban locales,[7] but rather to the South in what can be understood to be pathways embedded in historical and/ or contemporary colonial relations.[8] Thus, the complex rural-urban geographies of homelessness are significant in the ways they illuminate these socio-structural, administrative, and institutional networks. This collection seeks to build or strengthen relations between Arctic urban locales and to facilitate a cross-contextual exchange that focuses on housing, homelessness, and social policy.

To the people who live in the Canadian North, Alaska, and Greenland, it is not difficult to see that the chronic housing crisis and homelessness are increasingly dire. However, it is difficult to define, assess, and effectively address both the root causes and the immense consequences of housing insecurity and homelessness. There are indeed many conversations happening within local, territorial, provincial, and state governments; within communities and among service providers for whom the northern housing crisis is a fact of daily life; and in the media. To date, however, there has been little talk across northern communities and regions about how housing and homelessness have been emerging in

---

6 Julia Christensen, "'They Want a Different Life': Rural Northern Settlement Dynamics and Pathways to Homelessness in Yellowknife and Inuvik, Northwest Territories," *Canadian Geographer* 56, no. 4 (2012): 419–38, https://doi.org/10.1111/j.1541-0064 .2012.00439.x.

7 Nyseth, "Arctic Urbanization."

8 In the west Nordic region, however, which includes Greenland, Iceland, and the Faroe Islands, the Arctic Circle Assembly arguably has strengthened an urban network.

northern contexts in patterned ways, how governments, organizations, and communities are dealing with housing and homelessness, and how these varied approaches are working (or failing).

This book is an attempt to remedy this problem by kickstarting a conversation among multiple stakeholders from different cultural and national regions across the North. What are the common problems of, and responses to, housing insecurity and homelessness across these northern regions? What is the full scope of the problem, and how do we even begin to speak about housing and homelessness in a shared language? Is a single definition of "homelessness" even possible, or desirable? And if not, can a shared language around how to end the housing crisis and homelessness in our northern regions still occur? The experiences of northern towns and cities have much to inform an over-all understanding of urban forms and processes in the contemporary world, and speak directly to the emerging body of literature on small and medium-sized cities. They also highlight key limitations to federal, state, and provincial policy and raise important implications for developing policy that is responsive to northern realities.

Assembling the Research on Housing and Homelessness in the Urban North

The chapters in this book emerged out of a workshop on "Housing and Homelessness in the Urban North," held in Yellowknife, Northwest Territories, Canada, in the spring of 2018. The workshop brought together the experiences and perspectives of leaders from northern regional and community governments, Indigenous leaders, community leaders, service providers, and researchers from Canada, Alaska, and Greenland. All workshop participants and chapter authors have come to know the northern housing crisis and northern experiences of homelessness in different ways. In the workshop, we encouraged a conversation that included a wide range of personal experiences and theoretical stances, which we discussed, unpacked, and critiqued at the workshop and in the writing and editing process of the book that followed. From this multivocal conversation, an appreciation for the diversity of experiences and perspectives has emerged, as well as the realization that four broad themes cross-cut experiences with housing and homelessness in the Canadian North, Alaska, and Greenland. These themes are: 1) definitional challenges across and within the three regions; 2) lack of recognition by policymakers of the scope and scale of homelessness in northern regions; 3) governance and organizational challenges to assessing and addressing housing insecurity and homelessness; 4) a reliance by policymakers and service providers on definitions, programs, and approaches developed and applied in southern and/or more conventionally urban contexts; and 5) the significance, power, and consequent vulnerability of personal relationships, and the precarity this presents for governance, organizations, and communities.

The book is organized into regional sections, beginning with the Canadian North, then Alaska, and finally Greenland. A brief introduction to the geographic and social context of housing and homelessness is provided by authors living and working in each of these northern regions. Presenting the chapters in this way provides a tangible sense of how similar threads of housing and homelessness are picked from the diverse geographic, social, and politico-economic fabrics of each region. It also allows for the common patterns in each region to come into view. We now turn to a brief introduction of the workshop themes as they relate to the chapters in this book.

Definitional Challenges: What Counts as "Homeless"?

Although in many ways the social geography of the North is similar across North America, important differences exist in governmental provisioning of housing, housing assistance, and related social and health services between the United States, Canada, and Greenland. For example, in all three jurisdictions, much (if not all) of the policymaking, governance, and, ultimately, oversight for housing programs is located in towns and cities, and is rarely available in rural settlements. Each region, however, takes different approaches to managing and allocating these resources, and faces different challenges related to addressing chronic housing stock shortages. Furthermore, there is no single definition of "homelessness," what it means to communities, and who counts as "homeless," even within each northern region, let alone across them. These definitional complexities are illustrated in Chapter 6, where Frank Tester discusses this challenge in relationship to a lack of Inuit consultation and participation in the design of housing for Inuit communities in the eastern Canadian Arctic, tracing the disconnect to a conflict over how home is (mis)understood in Inuit cultural contexts. In Chapter 3, Alex Nelson confronts the geographical imagination of Whitehorse, Yukon, as a rural oasis that conflicts with representations of homelessness as a distinctly urban issue, presenting challenges for how northern homelessness is conceptualized.

At the Yellowknife workshop, we were able to discuss these definitional challenges, and learned of some important concepts and meanings by people living and working across the three northern regions. One of these is a broad acknowledgement of the direct relationship between homelessness and each region's limited and often overcrowded housing stock. In many northern urban centres, there is a low vacancy rate, and the rental housing that exists is controlled by a few public and private housing providers who ultimately decide who they do and do not want living in their properties – often discriminating against Indigenous residents and the poor. For example, in Chapter 1, Lisa Freeman and Julia Christensen discuss the consequences of constrained public and private housing markets in Yellowknife and their effects on the implementation and sustainability of local Housing First programs – programs that offer unconditional, long-term housing for the chronically homeless as quickly as possible. In the Alaskan context, Travis Hedwig (Chapter 8) addresses the competing meanings of Housing First, using an example from Anchorage to examine tensions in Housing First philosophy that create challenges for practice from a tenant perspective. Collectively, the contributions of these three authors engage with the notion of program fidelity in the ways in which Housing First is adapted and applied in northern contexts.

The Complete Picture of Housing and Homelessness in the Urban North

Workshop participants also stressed that homelessness is a complex set of circumstances experienced differently by everyone, and thus requires dynamic and flexible solutions that address more than just housing. Specifically, people experiencing homelessness in the North are simultaneously dealing with the high cost of living overall, the uneven flows of resources (including financial and human capital) between rural and more urban settlements in the northern geography, and issues of loneliness and disconnection from family, home community, and culture, as well as discrimination in the local housing market. Northerners living in rural settlements face particular sets of challenges to accessing stable housing, employment, and supportive services.

People living in group homes, temporary housing, transitional housing, and supportive housing face numerous problems beyond finding permanent housing or employment. In Chapter 8, we learn that, although Housing First (and related) programs in Alaska are supposed to create pathways out of homelessness by providing stable housing and offering optional supportive services, yet residents struggle with the intense loneliness that comes from separating themselves from friends and family still living on the streets where drinking and drug use are common. Furthermore, residents there are forced to abide by restrictions on whom they can see and when approved visitors may come to see them, despite the fact that these residents are rent-paying tenants. These complexities of homelessness are underlined in Chapter 1, where Freeman and Christensen discuss the challenges in adapting supportive housing programs to fit context realities and cultural needs. Even within a single locale, there are gendered experiences with homelessness and particular obstacles faced by youth, homeless families, and Indigenous peoples. In Chapter 10, Steven Arnfjord and Julia Christensen trace the intersectional lived experiences of homelessness in Nuuk, Greenland, illuminating the diverse "face" of homelessness and underlining the need for supports designed with a variety of different needs in mind.

Several workshop participants discussed the idea that "homelessness is about making a home" and that making a "home" extends beyond securing stable long-term housing. In Yellowknife, the largest urban centre in the Northwest Territories, many people experiencing homelessness come from other, more rural parts of the territory, and can find themselves disconnected from their original homes and families. This has additional cultural implications for Indigenous people who find themselves separated from their homelands or from important familial and community relations. At the same time, urban environments can offer opportunities for the development of new and important social networks or reunification with relocated family members. In Chapter 2, Nick Falvo notes the high number of rural migrants to the city who find themselves living homeless on the street, and conversations abound in popular discourse about how these people "need to go home." The narrative of the northern city as a place that is not for those who are struggling is one that runs through many of the chapters. In fact, collectively these chapters seem to suggest that northern urban places are imagined differently than those in the South, where it is taken for granted that cities are a logical meeting place for those reliant on social support services. Conversely, the accounts from northern towns and cities begin to paint a picture of a northern urban identity that is rooted in a self-image of prosperity and self-reliance.

At the same time, homelessness in northern regions must also be understood as it relates to migration and mobility. Nelson (Chapter 6) describes how Whitehorse sits within a broader regional geography of homelessness in Yukon, while Carol Kauppi, Michael Hankard, and Henri Pallard (Chapter 7) and Moses (Chapter 8) collectively reveal the ways in which Indigenous peoples' connections to ancestral lands, colonial disruptions and subsequent land claims, and recent histories of forced settlement and resettlement have shaped mobility, migration, and homelessness in places such as James Bay and northern Labrador.

Governance and Organizational Challenges

Responding effectively and ethically to homelessness in the North requires solutions that address the complete picture of homelessness, from addressing the structural insufficiencies of housing stock, to housing and social assistance programs that are unevenly provided across rural-urban networks, to addressing loneliness and other deep privations and discrimination experienced by different groups of homeless people. To quote two workshop participants, people working in northern government and organizations tasked with addressing homelessness are essentially "trying to push the ocean back with a spoon," while only being afforded enough personnel, time, and resources to manage homelessness from the "corner of someone's [already full] desk."

Outside limited provisioning from governments in the United States, Canada, and Greenland, funding to address homelessness in the North does also come from non-profit and other private sources, such as industry. These funding and service-provision arrangements present their own sets of dilemmas, several of which are discussed in Chapter 11, where Christensen, Arnfjord, and Marie-Louise Aastrup describe the ways in which an absence of social policy around homelessness has led to a reliance on the non-profit sector for services and support, rendering these programs vulnerable to shifts in funding or the prioritization of causes. In the Northwest Territories, some private funding is provided by the extractive industries, but this form of investment is highly uneven and generally lacks government oversight. Non-profit organizations sometimes can leverage private funding, but they are often located – and therefore only able to provide services and resources – in urban areas. In northern urban areas such as Anchorage or Yellowknife, non-profits have the means to implement projects and provide services, often long term. In rural settlements, however, even when funding might be available and local people qualify for assistive programs, there is usually no office to administer available resources. For example, in Alaska, people in rural communities might be eligible for Veterans Affairs Supportive Housing vouchers or other assistance, but simply cannot access these supports because no office exists to administer them in small settlements (see the analysis by Sally Carraher and Travis Hedwig in Chapter 7). The non-profit sector is also markedly absent outside northern urban centres, which both causes and is an effect of the reproduction of homelessness as an urban phenomenon.

Although many people are dedicated to addressing homelessness and related issues in their respective regions and communities, there is a lack of coordination among service providers at different levels of government and in the non-profit sector. In Greenland, the absence of policy to address education and economic opportunities in small settlements is characteristic of a kind of passive approach to urbanization in the North, which Christensen, Arnfjord, and Aastrup (Chapter 11) describe as the "the total absence of social policy." As Clare Dannenberg (Chapter 9) concludes, homelessness and related issues, as well as community capacity for addressing homelessness, are not the same from one community to the next, particularly in the urban North. To address homelessness holistically requires gaining a fuller picture of all the varied communities affected, from the most urban places such as Anchorage or Yellowknife out through the network to hub towns and the smallest rural settlements across the North. This includes assessing capacity for the provision of services and resources as well assessing what people in different communities and different socio-economic demographics are actually experiencing in terms of homelessness, housing shortages, crowding, family and community ties, and their ability to access supports.

Relationships as Strengths and Vulnerabilities

During the workshop, many people identified times when an individual relationship with someone in government, a non-profit organization, or within the community proved critical to addressing successfully issues related to homelessness. One participant who has worked to address homelessness in the eastern Canadian Arctic during her time in the Nunavut government asked the room with a concerned uncertainty, "what happens when you go?" Simply put, there is never a guarantee the next person who is assigned to a position or job will have the same level of concern or skill for working humanely and effectively to help address and prevent homelessness. It also highlights the need to increase local participation and capacity, develop contingency plans to maximize existing community assets, and find ways to generate local interest, excitement, and momentum around addressing a problem of shared concern.

The value of personal relationships is further illustrated by Freeman and Christensen in Chapter 1, where they demonstrate the significance of positive working relationships between Housing First providers and the private rental market. Without such relationships, the Housing First program could not operate, and yet there is but one major private rental company in Yellowknife, leaving the program in a precarious situation if relationships were to fail.

Finally, the importance of relationship building cannot go unrecognized in terms of generating public acceptance of programs related to homelessness. Too often people who have experienced living homeless are left out of public, industry, and agency discourses about how to address homelessness. As stated above, this results in an incomplete picture of how people experience homelessness differently and how it is related to many other facets of life in the northern context. As Sally Carraher and Travis Hedwig (Chapter 7) discuss, including in public discourses people who are experiencing homelessness provides an opportunity for non-homeless community members to connect with homeless people in humanizing ways. Carol Kauppi, Michael Hankard, and Henri Pallard (Chapter 4) contextualize the stories of two individuals against their study of mobility, migration, and homelessness of Cree people in the James Bay region. In Chapter 5, Joshua Moses shares the stories of two young people in northern Labrador to illustrate the ways in which Inuit youth are caught in governance structures that do not reflect their needs or adequately embrace their potential, producing ontological as well as material experiences of homelessness.

Learning about people's lived experiences helps those privileged enough never to have been homeless better understand the complete picture of homelessness. It is our hope that this book kindles more of these kinds of conversations, within as well as across the Canadian North, Alaska, and Greenland. Our aim is to encourage more people, organizations, and whole communities to identify, understand, and address northern homelessness by working directly in solidarity with both homeless and non-homeless community members, service providers, and researchers.

Conclusion

Homelessness, especially as it manifests in the Canadian North, Alaska, and Greenland, is not just an urban issue. Yet it is in northern towns and cities where complex regional geographies of housing insecurity and social determinants of health are made most visible. Still, the story of each individual northerner who experiences homelessness is different, and a one-size-fits-most approach to ending homelessness is neither feasible nor desirable. While we take a decidedly urban lens in this volume, our intention is to use the urban visibility of northern homelessness as a way to bring into analytical focus the meshwork of social, institutional, and administrative relationships that exist between rural and urban northern communities, as well as between northern towns and cities and those in the southern United States and Canada as well as Denmark. The study of housing insecurity and homelessness in northern urban centres thus can shed critical light on the factors that contribute to homelessness in both rural and urban areas in the North, and help scholars identify possible solutions or ways forward.

Our intention with this volume is to push back against the tendency to impose decontextualized understandings of homelessness on northern regions and to advance a richer, grounded, and more nuanced understanding of homelessness across the Canadian North, Alaska, and Greenland. In so doing, we hope to lay the conceptual foundation for interventions and strategies to alleviate housing insecurity and homelessness through an emphasis on community strengths, context, and cultures. We also seek to reveal the complexities and contradictions of, and the possibilities for, community building in the increasingly urban North. The rise in visible homelessness in the North is representative of the roots of social challenges to urbanization. And yet the proliferation of community engagements in efforts to address homelessness and social exclusion in northern urban centres speaks to the range of opportunities and new forms for outreach and support that can arise through northern urbanization. These opportunities also deserve our attention.

SECTION ONE

The Canadian North

Regional Introduction: The Canadian North

JULIA CHRISTENSEN

Homelessness in the Canadian North

The Canadian North is characterized by vast amounts of land, relatively small populations, and considerable distances between communities, most of which are connected only by transportation routes through air or water. Much of the region was governed by Canada at arm's length until the Second World War, when both the resource-rich "hinterland" and its placement along the Arctic coast brought the region's economic and geopolitical potential to national attention.[1] This was largely accomplished through northern settlement and housing policy intended to extend the Canadian social welfare state northward and assimilate northern peoples through culturally imbued health and social programming.[2] Today, northern territorial governments play a key role in the provision of public and subsidized housing, and, as in the rest of the Canada, universal health care is also available.

Combined, the northern territories – Yukon, Northwest Territories (NWT), and Nunavut – account for a population of 108,000 across a landmass of almost 4 million square kilometres, over a third of Canada's total landmass. Yukon is the most urbanized of the three, with over 130 localities, settlements, hamlets, towns, and one city – the capital, Whitehorse, with a population in 2016 of 25,085.[3] The next largest town, Dawson, had a population of only 1,375. The NWT has a total

1 Frances Abele, "Canadian Contradictions: Forty Years of Northern Political Development," *Arctic* 40, no. 4 (1987): 310–20, https://doi.org/10.14430/arctic1788.
2 Julia Christensen, *No Home in a Homeland: Indigenous Peoples and Homelessness in the Canadian North* (Vancouver: UBC Press, 2017).
3 Statistics Canada, *Population and Dwelling Count Highlight Tables, 2016*, Census (Ottawa, 2016).

of thirty-three communities, again with only one city, the capital, Yellowknife, with a population in 2016 of 19,569.[4] Five other communities had populations in 2016 between 1,202 (Fort Simpson) and 3,528 (Hay River); the remaining twenty-seven had populations under 1,000. The largest of Nunavut's twenty-eight communities is Iqaluit, the territorial capital, which had population of 7,740 in 2016.[5] Nunavut's population is concentrated less in the capital than is the case in Yukon and the NWT, with ten other communities having populations between 1,324 (Gjoa Haven) and 2,842 (Rankin Inlet).

Homelessness first appeared as a policy issue in the Canadian North in the late 1990s. Although chronic housing need has been documented in northern communities for decades, the social concern around homelessness has largely focused on northern urban centres. In all three northern territories, the consensus by advocacy and support groups is that homelessness is on the rise.[6] A lack of adequate and affordable housing in northern communities, higher poverty rates than elsewhere in the country, and the prevalence of intergenerational trauma associated with colonialism have been highlighted repeatedly by advocacy groups as underlying the increase in the number of northerners living on the streets and/or relying on emergency shelters. At the same time, despite their many similarities, the three territories have distinct geographies that distinguish their experiences with homelessness.

Single adults, youth, women who have experienced domestic violence, and low-income households are highly represented among people living homeless in the Canadian North.[7] Overarching these

---

4 Statistics Canada, *Census Profile, 2016 Census* (Ottawa, 2016).

5 Ibid.

6 Inuvik Interagency Committee, *Inuvik: Homelessness Report* (Inuvik, NWT: Inuvik Interagency Committee, 2003); Inuvik Interagency Committee, *Homelessness: State of Response in Inuvik, NWT* (Inuvik: Inuvik Interagency Committee, 2006); Yellowknife Homelessness Coalition, *Planning for Phase III of the Community Plan to Address Homelessness in Yellowknife* (Yellowknife, NWT: Yellowknife Homelessness Coalition, 2007); Yellowknife Homelessness Coalition, *Yellowknife Homelessness Report Card 2008* (Yellowknife, NWT: Yellowknife Homelessness Coalition, 2009); Yukon Anti-Poverty Coalition, *A Home for Everyone: A Housing Action Plan for Whitehorse* (Whitehorse, YT: Yukon Anti Poverty Coalition, 2011); Judie Bopp and YWCA Yellowknife, *You Just Blink and It Can Happen: A Study of Women's Homelessness North of 60* (Yellowknife, NWT: Yellowknife YWCA, 2007), https://assembly.nu.ca/library/Edocs/2007/001483-e.pdf.

7 Yukon Health and Social Services, *Safe at Home: A Community-Based Action Plan to End and Prevent Homelessness in Whitehorse, Yukon* (Whitehorse, YT: September 2017), http://www.hss.gov.yk.ca/pdf/Safe_at_Home-Report.pdf; Christensen, *No Home in a Homeland*; Rose Schmidt et al., "Trajectories of Women's Homelessness in Canada's

characteristics, however, are the disproportionate numbers of Indigenous northerners affected by homelessness;[8] anecdotal accounts indicate that hidden forms of homelessness, particularly "couch surfing," are even more pervasive than visible homelessness, especially outside urban locales. Meanwhile, in urban locales, northerners who experience homelessness engage in innovative strategies such as constructing makeshift tents, camps, and sleeping in warm stairwells or utilidors to find warmth and shelter.[9] The prevalence of hidden forms of homelessness combined with other coping strategies adds to the difficulty of a comprehensive assessment of northern homelessness.

Core Housing Need

The research literature on homelessness in the context of the Canadian North reveals a wide range of key themes. Chief among these is the high rate of core housing need in both rural and urban communities, which includes affordability, adequacy, and suitably of both the private market and public housing stock. The prevalence of core housing need across the North is one that several scholars have blamed on state-organized northern settlement schemes, the introduction of modern housing programs, and the subsequent volatility of northern housing policy in the early to mid-twentieth century.[10] Furthermore, the transition to settlement life, combined with the social and economic circumstances that brought Indigenous peoples into northern settlements, has undermined traditional Indigenous livelihoods and prioritized participation in the wage economy.[11]

In all three territories, private market housing tends to be concentrated in urban centres, whereas smaller communities tend to rely more on publicly subsidized housing options. However, as Yukon Health and

---

3 Northern Territories," *International Journal of Circumpolar Health* 74, no. 1 (2015), https://doi.org/10.3402/ijch.v74.29778.

8 Yukon Health and Social Services, *Safe at Home*; Christensen, *No Home in a Homeland*; Schmidt et al., *Trajectories of Women's Homelessness*; Nathanael Lauster and Frank Tester, "Culture as a Problem in Linking Material Inequality to Health: On Residential Crowding in the Arctic," *Health & Place* 16, no. 3 (2010): 523.

9 Yukon Health and Social Services, *Safe at Home*; Christensen, *No Home in a Homeland*.

10 Frank Tester and Peter Kulchyski, *Tammarniit (Mistakes): Inuit Relocation in the Eastern Arctic, 1939–63* (Vancouver: UBC Press, 2011); Christensen, *No Home in a Homeland*; Lauster and Tester, "Culture as a Problem."

11 Lauster and Tester, "Culture as a Problem."

Social Services[12] and studies by Nick Falvo[13] suggest, increasing unaffordability in the private rental market, combined with a limited number of public housing units in urban centres, has led to a particularly
bleak picture of low-income housing availability in the larger centres.
Rose Schmidt and colleagues[14] identify the shortage of housing as a
critical factor in the incidence of homelessness in Canada's North, citing in particular the very low rental vacancy rates in the larger centres.

Rural-Urban Geographies of Homelessness in Northern Canada

In all three territories, rural-to-urban movement plays a significant role
in homeless geographies and experiences. Northern settlement geography, in combination with uneven economic and infrastructural development and the uneven concentration of key institutional services in
larger centres, contributes to distinct patterns of rural-to-urban movement in the lives of homeless northern people. Although homelessness
in the Canadian North is often portrayed as confined to people already
living in larger centres, many northern residents who are experiencing
homelessness in cities and towns came from small rural communities.
In an earlier study,[15] I suggested that uneven and fragmented social,
institutional, and economic geographies have resulted in a unique landscape of vulnerability to homelessness in the Canadian North. Frank
Tester[16] argues that historical settlement policy in the North resulted
in rural settlements that were not anchored in sustainable economies,
creating distinct rural-urban disparities.

   Another factor framing the significance of rural-to-urban movement
in northern homeless geographies is that emergency shelter services in

---

12 Yukon Health and Social Services, *Safe at Home*.
13 Nick Falvo, *Homelessness in Yellowknife: An Emerging Social Challenge* (Toronto:
    Canadian Homelessness Research Network Press, 2011); Nick Falvo, "Who Pays,
    When, and How? Government-Assisted Housing in the Northwest Territories
    and the Role of the Federal Government," in *How Ottawa Spends, 2011–2012*, ed.
    Christopher Stoney and G. Bruce Doern (Montreal; Kingston, ON: McGill-Queen's
    University Press, 2011), 243–61.
14 Schmidt et al., *Trajectories of Women's Homelessness*.
15 Julia Christensen, "'They Want a Different Life': Rural Northern Settlement Dynamics
    and Pathways to Homelessness in Yellowknife and Inuvik, Northwest Territories,"
    Canadian Geographer 56, no. 4 (2012): 419–38, https://doi.org/10.1111/j.1541-0064.2012
    .00439.x.
16 Frank Tester, "Iglu to Iglurjuaq," in *Critical Inuit Studies: An Anthology of Contemporary
    Arctic Ethnography*, ed. Pamela Stern and Lisa Stevenson (Lincoln: University of
    Nebraska Press, 2006): 230–52.

the Canadian North are limited to the larger centres, and even in those centres the number of emergency shelter options is small. The research literature shows, moreover, that emergency shelters in the three capital cities function more as long-term accommodation than as short-term emergency housing – with reports of clientele staying in shelters for upward of five years.[17] This has to do, in large part, with the lack of available affordable housing and of effective support services for northerners with problems of mental health, substance abuse, or other factors that might limit their ability to access sustainable employment and housing. The small number of available shelter options also means that, if an individual loses privileges at a shelter, the result is likely to be immediate street homelessness. Several shelters also implement sober-only policies, or will not allow people to stay if they are visibly intoxicated. These circumstances, along with other situations that result in an individual's being denied access to a shelter, will result – particularly in the winter months – in the person seeking access to a holding cell at the local detachment of the Royal Canadian Mounted Police.[18]

Indigenous Experiences of Homelessness

One of the most troubling characteristics of homelessness in the Canadian North is the high representation of Indigenous peoples among those experiencing homelessness. One factor is racism, which is reported in the housing and employment markets in both Whitehorse[19] and Yellowknife.[20] The Yukon Anti-Poverty Coalition[21] found that Indigenous respondents to its homelessness survey were nearly four times more likely to be homeless than the non-Indigenous, while my own research[22] in the NWT revealed anecdotal evidence that 90–95 per cent of those living homeless in that territory were Indigenous. This speaks both to a higher incidence of poverty and to core housing need among Indigenous people, as well as to other factors related to social determinants of health that also contribute to homelessness,

---

17 Kate Mechan, *Enriching Our Understanding of Homelessness: What We Know in Whitehorse* (Whitehorse, YT: Yukon Anti-Poverty Coalition, 2013); Julia Christensen, "Homeless in a Homeland: Housing (In)Security and Homelessness in Inuvik and Yellowknife, Northwest Territories" (PhD diss., McGill University, 2011).
18 Mechan, *Enriching Our Understanding of Homelessness.*
19 Yukon Anti-Poverty Coalition, *A Home for Everyone.*
20 Christensen, *No Home in a Homeland.*
21 Yukon Anti-Poverty Coalition, *A Home for Everyone.*
22 Christensen, "Homeless in a Homeland."

including spiritual homelessness.[23] Research points to the combined effects of colonial settlement and social policy and the intergenerational effects of colonialism on Indigenous peoples, and to the specific role that these geographies have played in framing the overrepresentation of Indigenous people among the northern homeless.[24] The intergenerational impacts of colonialism are tied particularly to the prevalence of poor mental health, addictions, family violence, children in foster care, and incarceration among northern Indigenous individuals and families, all of which play a role in the factors contributing to homelessness.[25]

At the same time, however, research suggests that the phenomenon of Indigenous homelessness is also reproduced through culturally inappropriate social policy. I have argued,[26] for example, that public housing policy in the NWT actively works against Indigenous family cohesion and homemaking by imposing strict rules that prevent family members from being able to help one another in times of housing need. Elsewhere, I have suggested that Indigenous homelessness is experienced not only in the lack of housing but also through ongoing traumas associated with colonialism, and that its alleviation requires Indigenous self-determination in housing policy and provision.[27] These reflections are further supported by the work of Métis scholar Jesse Thistle and the Canadian Observatory on Homelessness's Definition of Indigenous Homelessness in Canada,[28] which articulates Indigenous homelessness as more than a lack of shelter, and links historical displacement and cultural loss with experiences of spiritual homelessness and lack of shelter.

23 Julia Christensen, "'Our Home, Our Way of Life': Spiritual Homelessness and the Sociocultural Dimensions of Indigenous Homelessness in the Northwest Territories (NWT), Canada." *Social & Cultural Geography* 14, no. 7 (2013): 804–28, https://doi.org/10.1080/14649365.2013.822089.

24 Christensen, "Our Home, Our Way of Life"; Julia Christensen, "Indigenous Housing and Health in the Canadian North: Revisiting Cultural Safety," *Health & Place* 40, no. 1 (2016): 83–90, https://doi.org/10.1016/j.healthplace.2016.05.003; Tester, *Iglu to Iglurjuaq*.

25 Katherine Minich et al., "Inuit Housing and Homelessness: Results from the International Polar Year Inuit Health Survey, 2007–2008," *International Journal of Circumpolar Health* 70, no. 5 (2011): 520–31, https://doi.org/10.3402/ijch.v70i5.17858.

26 Christensen, "Indigenous Housing and Health."

27 Christensen, *No Home in a Homeland*.

28 Jesse Thistle, *Definition of Indigenous Homelessness in Canada* (Toronto: Canadian Observatory on Homelessness Press, 2017).

Women's Experiences of Homelessness in Northern Canada

In addition to Indigenous homelessness in the Canadian North, gendered experiences of housing insecurity frame hidden and visible homeless geographies in all three northern territories. Schmidt and colleagues[29] estimate that upwards of a thousand women are homeless in the three territorial capitals. For homeless women, in particular, trauma and family violence are significant factors framing the personal life crises that, combined with housing insecurity, lead to homelessness.[30] Nancy Poole and Judie Bopp[31] argue that the nature of the experience of northern homeless women with mental health and addiction issues is often lost on service systems that tend to be blind to gender and the ways in which it frames trauma, violence, and post-traumatic stress disorder. Key in the challenge of addressing northern women's homelessness, according to Schmidt and colleagues,[32] is that most such individuals are not living rough but, rather, are included in the definition of the hidden homeless. Schmidt and colleagues also suggest that migration from rural communities to the capital cities for social, economic, and employment opportunities plays a significant role in homeless geographies. Once in the city, however, many women still face a lack of financial, social, and cultural resources, as well as unaffordable or limited housing.[33]

Overview of Key Themes from the Section on the Canadian North

Research on homelessness in the Canadian North points sharply to the urgent need for more affordable housing options, in conjunction with support to access and maintain this housing. In general, the literature on homelessness in the Canadian North collectively identifies the need for collaborative approaches, intergovernmental and interagency cooperation and improved communication, and specific actions aimed at diversification across the northern housing spectrum: emergency shelters, transitional housing, housing with long-term supports, rental

---

29 Schmidt et al., *Trajectories of Women's Homelessness.*
30 Judie Bopp, *The Little Voices of Nunavut: A Study of Women's Homelessness North of 60* (Cochrane, ON: Four Worlds Centre for Development Learning, 2007).
31 Nancy Poole and Judie Bopp, "Using a Community of Practice Model to Create Change for Northern Homeless Women," *First Peoples Child & Family Review* 10, no. 2 (2015): 122–39, http://www.ncbi.nlm.nih.gov/pmc/articles/PMC4959877/.
32 Schmidt et al., *Trajectories of Women's Homelessness.*
33 Christensen, "They Want a Different Life."

housing, and affordable home ownership. Significant strides have been made in the area of transitional and supportive housing in Whitehorse and Yellowknife, but more development is needed in this area across other northern communities.

Despite promising developments in the areas of Housing First and supportive and transitional housing in northern Canada, the absence of a diverse and complete housing spectrum poses significant challenges to the success of such housing programs, particularly if they are not offered as a long-term housing solution. In the following chapter Lisa Freeman and I highlight the constrained housing landscape in northern Canada, and argue that a limited housing spectrum in Yellowknife presents a range of challenges for the implementation of supportive housing and Housing First programs. In general, we illustrate some of the significant barriers to housing accessibility and affordability in northern regional centres. The dominance of territorial governments and the limited number of private rental housing providers of affordable or subsidized housing further compound the problems of the northern housing landscape.

The limited housing spectrum is not the only challenge to the northern housing landscape. Both Nick Falvo (Chapter 2) and Alex Nelson (Chapter 3) give attention to the role that rural-urban disparities and inequities play in the reproduction of homelessness in the urbanizing centres of Yellowknife and Whitehorse, respectively. The poorer education outcomes, high unemployment, low income, and higher rates of violence in settlement communities are linked inextricably to the rise of homelessness in regional centres. Funding for homelessness, however, tends to focus on urban places, effectively ignoring the rural-urban interconnections that frame the northern regional geography of homelessness. Policymakers continue to approach northern homelessness as a largely urban phenomenon – a tendency, Falvo argues, that results in the perpetuation of in-migration of housing-insecure northerners to towns and cities and ultimately fuels homelessness in these centres.

As Carol Kauppi, Michael Hankard, and Henri Pallard (Chapter 4) and Joshua Moses (Chapter 5) point out, however, rural-urban disparities are only part of the overall picture of mobility and movement and the role they play in northern geographies of homelessness. Absolute or visible homelessness arises in northern regional centres because of a lack of affordable, accessible housing and additional, culturally appropriate supports for people who migrate into northern urban places.

Finally, the role of Indigenous people in the design, provision, and administration of housing in the Canadian North is a call echoed across the chapters in this section of volume. In the context of Nunavut, for example, Tester argues (Chapter 6) that, in order to make housing a home, Inuit must be engaged directly in the creative and culturally informed design, planning, and construction of housing. Across northern Canada, it is clear that the solutions to chronic housing need lie in housing policy and programs that better respond to the needs and realities of northern residents.

1 It's a Tough Game: Navigating Housing Monopolies in Yellowknife, Northwest Territories

LISA FREEMAN AND JULIA CHRISTENSEN

In 2016, an unassuming three-storey building opened off of the main street in Yellowknife, Northwest Territories (NWT), a city of approximately 20,000 inhabitants. The plain exterior – boxy with siding in shades of taupe and grey – was misleading: inside Lynn's Place, a supportive housing program was in operation with the objective to provide eighteen fully furnished units for women and their children looking for stable and safe housing after leaving emergency shelters. In addition to shelter, residents are offered a variety of wraparound programs such as financial, literacy, parenting, and life-skills training, aimed at promoting well-being, self-determination, and, ultimately, independence. The same year, the City of Yellowknife launched its inaugural Housing First program, emphasizing rehousing people with acute housing need into already-existing private rental apartments scatted through the city.

One of the original aims of Lynn's Place and other supportive housing and Housing First initiatives in the city was to promote a sense of forward momentum through and (eventually) out of the program and onto other home rental or ownership options. This goal, however, proved to be misaligned in many ways with the needs of residents. Moreover, local housing dynamics also suggest that an emphasis on "graduation" from Lynn's Place and other transitional housing programs like it might clash with the existence of public and private housing "monopolies" in the community and the obstacles they present to housing accessibility for low-income residents. In fact, a strong emphasis on moving out of Housing First evoked the kinds of Housing First infidelity that Hedwig explores in Anchorage (see Chapter 8) – infidelity that is exacerbated by the limited resources and housing stock that Housing First programs can work with in northern urban centres.

Like other supportive housing initiatives in southern Canada, Lynn's Place offers single-room accommodation for women with or without children who need safe and supportive housing. For many of the women at Lynn's Place, however, these individual rooms are not ideal living arrangements. According to anecdotal stories shared during our research, many women expressed wanting to live communally, share living space, and interact more regularly with other tenants, using the common-use spaces as regular gathering places to connect with each other and in many ways replicating familial living arrangements.

Not only does the story of Lynn's Place emphasize the need for individual agency in terms of designing affordable housing from a northern perspective; it also exposes the lack of options on the spectrum of affordable rental housing in Yellowknife. The difficulties of accessing affordable rental housing in the city, and across the circumpolar North, are well known,[1] but difficulties are rarely framed as a result of the lack of a housing spectrum. In this chapter, we argue that the limited Yellowknife rental housing spectrum leads to greater vulnerability for low-income tenants in need of accessible and affordable housing. We suggest that, to create more affordable housing in Yellowknife, the city's lack of a housing spectrum must first be addressed.

This chapter emerges from community-based research in collaboration with Alternatives North, a social justice, anti-poverty non-profit

---

1 Julia Christensen, "'They Want a Different Life': Rural Northern Settlement Dynamics and Pathways to Homelessness in Yellowknife and Inuvik, Northwest Territories," *Canadian Geographer* 56, no. 4 (2012): 419–38, https://doi.org/10.1111/j.1541-0064 .2012.00439.x; Julia Christensen, "Indigenous Housing and Health in the Canadian North: Revisiting Cultural Safety," *Health & Place* 40, no. 1 (2016): 83–90, https:// doi.org/10.1016/j.healthplace.2016.05.003; Turner Strategies, *Everyone Is Home: Yellowknife's 10-Year Plan to End Homelessness* (Yellowknife, NWT: 2017), https:// www.yellowknife.ca/en/living-here/resources/Homelessness/everyone-is-home ---yellowknife-10-year-plan-to-end-homelessness-final-report-july-2017.pdf; Frances Abele, Nick Falvo, and Arlene Haché, "Homeless in the Homeland: A Growing Problem for Indigenous People in Canada's North," *Parity* 23, no. 9 (2012): 21–3, https://www.homelesshub.ca/resource/homeless-homeland-growing-problem -indigenous-people-canadas-north; Nick Falvo, *Homelessness in Yellowknife: An Emerging Social Challenge* (Toronto: Canadian Homelessness Research Network Press, 2011), http://hdl.handle.net/10315/29376; Peter C. Dawson, "Seeing Like an Inuit Family: The Relationship between House Form and Culture in Northern Canada," *Inuit/Studies* 30, no. 2 (2006): 113–35, https://doi.org/10.7202/017568ar; Mary Beth Levan et al., *Being Homeless Is Getting to Be Normal: A Study of Women's Homelessness in the Northwest Territories* (Yellowknife, NWT: YWCA Yellowknife and the Yellowknife Women's Society, 2007), http://ywcacanada.ca/data/publications/00000011.pdf.

in Yellowknife since 2017.[2] The purpose of this work was to speak with housing providers, non-governmental organizations (NGOs), housing advocates, and policymakers in government about housing security and affordability in the context of non-renewable resource development. From November to May 2018, we conducted semi-structured interviews across NGOs and government, with thirty housing and service providers, advocates, municipal politicians, city staff, members of the NWT Legislative Assembly, staff of the government of the NWT, and other government officials.[3] These interviews gave us a glimpse of the affordable housing landscape for marginalized tenants in Yellowknife, the multijurisdictional approaches taken by multiple governments to address poverty, housing, and homelessness, and challenges that housing providers and advocates face in trying to secure any type of temporary or permanent housing for low-income individuals. In May 2018, we also organized two arts-based workshops with local housing advocates and service providers in Yellowknife. The intent of these workshops was to gather ideas for a public outreach document and to gain feedback on our research.

The original scope of our research did not include an explicit focus on supportive housing and Housing First or on the dynamics of public and private housing monopolies in the city, and yet these were very important threads that emerged over the course of our interviews and workshops. Time and again, we listened to research participants discuss challenges they faced when trying to provide housing to those in acute need, their frustration with lack of co-ordination between different levels of government, and the many challenges they experienced with regard to funding. In addition, respondents repeatedly underlined the prevalence of the intergenerational effects of colonial trauma and the significant role such effects play in shaping the particular support needs of northerners experiencing homelessness. These new threads in our work directed us to the effects that public and private housing monopolies have on housing advocates, service providers, and decisionmakers, and the particular constraints this housing landscape

---

2 Our collaboration was funded by Resources and Sustainable Development in the Arctic, a northern social sciences research network funded by the Social Sciences and Humanities Research Council that looks at the dynamics of resources and sustainable development in the Arctic.
3 Alongside this research, we facilitated the creation of a publicly accessible document (poster/pamphlet) on affordable housing in Yellowknife. This consisted of two co-design workshops facilitated by the graphic design studio AndAlsoToo and on-going consultations with community stakeholders.

presents for the implementation of contextually and culturally relevant Housing First programs.

In this chapter, we focus on Housing First in Yellowknife to demonstrate how the lack of a housing spectrum in the city negatively affects low-income tenants and complicates the program's implementation and outcomes. First, we discuss the pragmatic and philosophical underpinnings of the Housing First model. Second, we outline the barriers to housing in Yellowknife and the territory more generally. The final sections of our chapter focus explicitly on stories and perspectives shared by our research participants. We discuss the landscape of private and public housing "monopolies" as well as the benefits and challenges experienced during the inaugural Housing First program in Yellowknife. Overall, we explore how the persistence of private and public housing monopolies places significant limits on the success of supportive and transitional housing models such as Housing First when they are implemented in northern communities. In sum, we suggest that such models need to be reconceptualized and adapted to northern contexts to reflect constraints on the northern housing spectrum. In particular, we identify a set of concerns related to the delivery of Housing First in a context of limited public and private rental housing markets, one that is left highly vulnerable to policy shifts in both markets.

Housing First

The philosophy of Housing First, as established by Sam Tsemberis and Pathways to Housing in 1992,[4] is based on the premise that it is necessary to secure long-term housing for chronically homeless individuals before addressing the issues (like addictions and mental health) that often underly chronic homelessness.[5] The idea is that providing a person first with housing creates a foundation on which recovery can begin.[6] Moreover, the philosophy is based on a consumer-driven movement, in

---

4 Sam Tsemberis, Layla Gulcur, and Maria Nakae, "Housing First, Consumer Choice, and Harm Reduction for Homeless Individuals with a Dual Diagnosis," *American Journal of Public Health* 94, no. 4 (2004): 651–6, https://doi.org/10.2105/ajph.94.4.651.
5 Ibid.; Maritt Kirst et al., "The Impact of a Housing First Randomized Controlled Trial on Substance Use Problems among Homeless Individuals with Mental Illness," *Drug and Alcohol Dependence* 145, no. 1 (2015): 24–9, https://doi.org/10.1016/j.drugalcdep.2014.10.019.
6 Deborah K. Padgett, Leyla Gulcur, and Sam Tsemberis, "Housing First Services for People Who Are Homeless with Co-Occurring Serious Mental Illness and Substance Abuse," *Research on Social Work Practice* 16, no. 1 (2006): 74–83, https://doi.org/10.1177/1049731505282593.

contrast to the continuum-of-care approach, which places housing as contingent upon treatment.[7]

The core elements of Housing First include providing immediate permanent housing for chronically homeless individuals in scattered sites, harm reduction with respect to mental health and addiction treatment, and on-going access to wraparound support.[8] The model relies heavily on an assertive community treatment (ACT) team that provides around-the-clock support, is located off-site, and works directly with housing specialists.[9] These supports are not limited to addiction and mental health treatment, but also include support for employment, family relations, interactions with housing providers, and recreational opportunities. Although essential for a successful Housing First program, the level of treatment and supports available to participants could be constrained by the availability of community resources and funding.[10]

---

7 Ibid.; Kirst et al., "Impact of a Housing First Randomized Control Trial"; Ana Stefancic and Sam Tsemberis, "Housing First for Long-Term Shelter Dwellers with Psychiatric Disabilities in a Suburban County: A Four-Year Study of Housing Access and Retention," *Journal of Primary Prevention* 28, no. 3 (2007): 265–79, https://doi .org/10.1007/s10935-007-0093-9; Vicky Stergiopoulos et al., "Effect of Scattered-Site Housing Using Rent Supplements and Intensive Case Management on Housing Stability among Homeless Adults with Mental Illness: A Randomized Trial," *JAMA* 313, no. 9 (2015): 905–15, https://doi.org/10.1001/jama.2015.1163; Paula Goering et al., "The At Home/Chez Soi Trial Protocol: A Pragmatic, Multi-Site, Randomised Controlled Trial of a Housing First Intervention for Homeless Individuals with Mental Illness in Five Canadian Cities," *BMJ Open* 14, no.2 (2011): 18, https:// doi.org/10.1136/bmjopen-2011-000323; Joshua Evans, Damian Collins, and Jalene Anderson, "Homelessness, Bedspace and the Case for Housing First in Canada," *Social Science & Medicine* 168, no. 1 (2016): 249–56, https://doi.org/ 10.1016/j .socscimed.2016.06.049. I. Atherton and C.M. Nicholls, "'Housing First' as a Means of Addressing Multiple Needs and Homelessness," *European Journal of Homelessness* 2, no. 1 (2008): 289–303, https://www.feantsaresearch.org/en/publications/european -journal-of-homelessness?journalYear=2008; Geoffrey S. Nelson et al., "Systems Change in the Context of an Initiative to Scale up Housing First in Canada," *Journal of Community Psychology* 47, no. 1 (2018): 7–20, https://doi.org/10.1002/jcop.22095.
8 Padgett et al., "Housing First Services."
9 Tom Baker and Joshua Evans, "'Housing First' and the Changing Terrains of Homeless Governance," *Geography Compass* 10, no. 1 (2016): 25–41, https://doi.org /10.1111/gec3.12257; Stefancic and Tsemberis, "Housing First for Long-Term Shelter Dwellers."
10 Stefancic and Tsemberis, "Housing First for Long-Term Shelter Dwellers"; Jeannette Waegemakers Schiff, Rebecca Schiff, and Alina Turner, *Housing First in Rural Canada: Rural Homelessness & Housing First Feasibility across 22 Canadian Communities* (Calgary: University of Calgary, Faculty of Social Work, 2014), https://www .homelesshub.ca/resource/housing-first-rural-canada-rural-homelessness-housing -first-feasibility-across-22-canadian; Ana Stefancic et al., "Implementing Housing

Housing First has clear and defined stages for program implementation, including an individual needs assessment, feasibility studies, fit, and baseline requirements.[11] For the most part, the assessment procedure identifies individuals who are "high acuity" – in other words, in the most need of housing. Once individuals are selected, the foundations and structures of Housing First are established, including policy alignment, funding, and identification of required resources (such as host agencies). Following this, housing is secured and wraparound services are set in place.[12]

Started in New York City, Housing First has been successful in major cities across North America, including Toronto and Vancouver.[13] The literature emphasizes the importance of adhering to the specific stages of implementation of the Housing First model to ensure success.[14] However, many foundational components of the Housing First model rely heavily on resources primarily found in

First in Rural Areas: Pathways Vermont." *American Journal of Public Health* 103, no. 2 (2013): 206–9, https://doi.org/10.2105/AJPH.2013.301606.

11 S. Kathleen Worton et al., "Understanding Systems Change in Early Implementation of Housing First in Canadian Communities: An Examination of Facilitators/ Barriers, Training/Technical Assistance, and Points of Leverage" *American Journal of Community Psychology* 61, nos. 1–2 (2018): 118–30, https://doi.org/10.1002/ajcp .12219.

12 Padgett et al., "Housing First Services"; Iain Atherton and Carol McNaughton Nicholls, "'Housing First' as a Means of Addressing Multiple Needs and Homelessness," *European Journal of Homelessness* 2, no. 1 (2008): 289–303; Eric Macnaughton et al., "Navigating Complex Implementation Contexts: Overcoming Barriers and Achieving Outcomes in a National Initiative to Scale Out Housing First in Canada," *American Journal Of Community Psychology* 62, nos.1–2 (2018): 135–49, http://dx.doi.org/10.1002/ajcp.12268.

13 LeeAnn Shan and Matt Sandler, "Addressing the Homelessness Crisis in New York City: Increasing Accessibility for Persons with Severe and Persistent Mental Illness," *Columbia Social Work Review* 7, no. 1 (2016): 50–8, https://doi.org/10.7916 /D82J6C8K; Stephan W. Hwang et al., "Ending Homelessness among People with Mental Illness: The At Home/Chez Soi Randomized Trial of a Housing First Intervention in Toronto," *BMC Public Health* 12, no. 787 (2012): 1–16, https://doi .org/10.1186/1471-2458-12-787; Michelle L Patterson, Akm Moniruzzama, and Julian M Somers, "Community Participation and Belonging among Formerly Homeless Adults with Mental Illness after 12 Months of Housing First in Vancouver, British Columbia: A Randomized Controlled Trial," *Community Mental Health Journal* 50, no. 5 (2014): 604–11, https://doi.org/10.1007/s10597 -013-9672-9.

14 Todd P. Gilmer et al., "Development and Validation of a Housing First Fidelity Survey," *Psychiatric Services* 64 no. 9 (2013): 911–14, https://doi.org/10.1176/appi .ps.201200500.

larger cities, such as a diversified housing stock and a large support service network.[15]

Even so, the Housing First model has been successful in rural and suburban areas and in smaller regional cities through not necessarily replicating the urban model.[16] A study in Vermont identified the challenges and key adaptions required to make Housing First successful in rural regions. Ana Stefancic and colleagues[17] note that rural areas lack a comprehensive social service network to provide the wraparound services required for a successful Housing First program. In response to this constraint, the Vermont-based initiative implemented a telehealth component instead of in-person support.[18] This adaptation created a model that worked for rural communities without compromising the philosophy of Housing First.

Similarly, a study of twenty-two rural Canadian regions/cities outlined some of the challenges (and solutions) of implementing Housing First.[19] The authors premise their analysis on the important distinctions between rural and urban homelessness, and they illustrate "distinct dynamics from urban regions, particularly related to the availability of social infrastructure, the impacts of macro-economic shifts, housing markets, and migrations."[20] Limitations can include underdeveloped social service infrastructure, unqualified staff, limited emergency shelter space, and limited availability of rental housing stock. In Newfoundland and Labrador, Housing First programs face challenges in workers' isolation from peers; in rural New Brunswick, Housing First participants had a choice of moving to a different city with more housing options or staying in a city with few. Unfortunately, not all adaptations are long-term solutions, but they do help with program implementation in the

15 Sam Tsemberis, "Housing First: The Pathways Model to End Homelessness for People with Mental Illness and Addiction Manual," *European Journal of Homelessness* 5, no. 2 (2011): 235–40.
16 Stefancic and Tsemberis, "Housing First for Long-Term Shelter Dwellers"; Waegemakers Schiff et al., *Housing First in Rural Canada*; Jeannette Waegemakers Schiff, Rebecca Schiff, and Alina Turner, "Rural Homelessness in Western Canada: Lessons Learned from Diverse Communities," *Social Inclusion* 4, no. 4 (2016): 73–86, https://doi.org/10.17645/si.v4i4.633; Paul Cloke, Rebekah C. Widdowfield, and Paul Milbourne, "The Hidden and Emerging Spaces of Rural Homelessness," *Environment and Planning A: Economy and Space* 32, no. 1 (2000): 77–90, https://doi.org/10.1068/a3242.
17 Stefancic et al., "Implementing Housing First in Rural Areas."
18 Ibid.
19 Waegemakers Schiff et al., "Rural Homelessness in Western Canada"; Waegemakers Schiff et al., *Housing First in Rural Canada*.
20 Waegemakers Schiff et al., *Housing First in Rural Canada*, 4.

short term. The authors of this study make several recommendations that could benefit rural and northern Housing First programs, including changes to funding for staffing and social services, increasing shelter beds, and creating more non-market rental housing options.[21]

The federal government has prioritized funding Housing First programs through the Homelessness Partnership Strategy (HPS), which has benefited rural communities across the country. This funding has enabled rural areas and smaller cities such as Yellowknife to initiate their own Housing First programs – Yellowknife's program was launched in September 2016. Although transitional and supportive housing programs had been on offer in Yellowknife since the Bailey House opened its doors to single men in 2009, the launch of the inaugural Housing First initiative was welcomed by housing providers, government workers, and politicians alike.[22] It was a joint project between the HPS and Yellowknife's Community Advisory Board (CAB) intended to address the need for affordable housing for Yellowknife's most vulnerable individuals. The former provided a set amount of federal funding, while the CAB administered the program and (initially) coordinated with the Yellowknife Women's Society, supported by other non-profit organizations.

In 2017, the City of Yellowknife endorsed a 10-Year Plan to End Homelessness, which built on previous experience at Lynn's Place, the Bailey House, and the Housing First program, with emphasis on a Housing First approach to addressing homelessness in the community. The plan proposed an expanded Housing First project to be implemented through engagement with private sector business, including developers, builders, and landlords, and stressed that, "ultimately, government will not solve the affordable housing crisis without partnerships and innovation for a made-in-the-North approach with the private sector."[23] In particular, the plan required eighty-five scattered site units to be accessed through existing private rental housing stock in order to address immediately a number of acute cases of homelessness in the community, with an additional eighty new place-based units of Permanent Supportive Housing to be constructed.

---

21 Ibid.
22 Randi Beers, "Yellowknife's Housing First eyes expansion and graduating 1st clients out of program," *CBC News*, 25 June 2018, https://www.cbc.ca/news/canada/north/yellowknife-housing-first-update-1.4717121.
23 Turner Strategies, *Everyone Is Home*, 35.

By December 2017, Yellowknife's Housing First project reached its goal of housing twenty formally homeless individuals.[24] It did so by following the main premises of the Housing First model, while also being highly dependent on a good working relationship with North-view Properties, a real estate investment trust (REIT), the primary private property management company in Yellowknife. Although this suggests some promising and productive developments where collaboration between the public, private, and non-governmental sectors is concerned, it also highlights the precarious nature of supportive housing programs in such a constrained housing landscape. As we shall see, however, Yellowknife's Housing First initiative experienced challenges faced by rural communities and small cities across Canada. Ultimately, the success of the Yellowknife's 10-Year Plan hinges upon enhanced cooperation and collaboration with the private rental housing sector, which presents potential problems when considering the dominance of one provider in the community and the ways the private rental housing landscape is vulnerable to economic fluctuations.

The Landscape of Housing Insecurity in Yellowknife

The barriers to affordable housing in the Canadian North are well known.[25] The construction of new housing units is challenging due to the high costs of materials, high demand for a limited number of skilled, local construction workers, high transportation costs, and complexities around land zoning and development. In northern urban or

---

24 Canadian Mortgage and Housing Corporation, *Northern Housing Report 2018* (Ottawa, 2018), http://publications.gc.ca/collections/collection_2018/schl-cmhc/NH12-263-2018-eng.pdf.

25 Christensen, "They Want a Different Life"; Julia Christensen, *No Home in a Homeland: Indigenous Peoples and Homelessness in the Canadian North* (Vancouver: UBC Press, 2017); Canadian Mortgage and Housing Corporation, "Housing Need among the Inuit in Canada, 1991," *Socioeconomic Series* 35 (Ottawa, 1997); Peter C. Dawson, "Examining the Impact of Euro-Canadian Architecture on Inuit Families Living in Arctic Canada," *International Space Syntax Symposium* 4, no. 21 (2003): 1–16; Inuit Tapiriit Kanatami, "Backgrounder on Inuit and Housing" (Ottawa, 2004); Nunavut Housing Corporation and Nunavut Tunngavik Inc., *Nunavut Ten Year Inuit Housing Action Plan: A Proposal to the Government of Canada* (Inuvik: Government of Nunavut, September 2004); Pamela Stern, "Wage Labor, Housing Policy, and the Nucleation of Inuit Households," *Arctic Anthropology* 42, no. 2 (2005): 66–81, https://www.jstor.org/stable/40316647; Frank Tester, "Iglutaasaavut (Our New Homes): Neither 'New' nor 'Ours': Housing Challenges of the Nunavut Territorial Government," *Journal of Canadian Studies* 43 no. 2 (2009): 137–58, https://doi.org/10.3138/jcs.43.2.137.

regional centres, as Nick Falvo[26] suggests, increasing unaffordability in the private rental market, combined with a limited number of public housing units, has led to a particularly bleak picture of low-income housing availability. Rose Schmidt and colleagues[27] identify the shortage of housing as a critical factor in the incidence of homelessness in Canada's North, citing in particular the very low rental vacancy rates in larger centres such as Yellowknife.

Visible homelessness first began to emerge in Yellowknife in the late 1990s,[28] and has continued to grow in the years since. Point-In-Time (PIT) counts and the City of Yellowknife's Homelessness Report Cards show that between 3 and 5 per cent of the community's residents stay in emergency shelters or sleep outside, although very little data exist on the rates of hidden homelessness in the community. The vast majority of people experiencing homelessness are single adults, or adults whose children are not currently in their care, as well as youth.[29] In addition, many single adults' experiences with shelter living are chronic in nature, with many citing emergency shelter stays of more than five years.[30] Yellowknife's 10-Year Plan to End Homelessness also describes the prevalence of chronic homelessness, which suggests that housing inaccessibility and inadequate health and social supports perpetuate chronic homelessness.[31]

As the capital city and main administrative, economic, and political hub of the territory, Yellowknife draws many people from across the region for work, services, and housing.[32] While the homeless population is growing in Yellowknife, many of the city's homeless come from smaller, more geographically isolated, rural settlement communities.[33] The territorial economy is largely dependent on non-renewable resource development, with booms and busts in response to fluctuations in the extractive resource industry. Since the mid- to late 1990s,

26 Falvo, *Homelessness in Yellowknife*.
27 Rose Schmidt et al., "Trajectories of Women's Homelessness in Canada's 3 Northern Territories," *International Journal of Circumpolar Health* 74 no. 1 (2015), https://doi.org/10.3402/ijch.v74.29778.
28 Christensen, "They Want a Different Life."
29 Turner Strategies, *Everyone Is Home*.
30 Christensen, *No Home in a Homeland*.
31 Ibid.
32 Levan et al., *Being Homeless Is Getting to Be Normal*; Abele et al., "Homeless in the Homeland"; Community Partnership Forum, *Homeless in Yellowknife: Community Partnership Forum April 26–27, 2016* (Yellowknife: Northwest Territories Housing Corporation, 2016), a359227.pdf (gov.nt.ca).
33 Christensen, "They Want a Different Life."

resource extraction has focused primarily on diamond mining. The significance of extractive-industry-induced economic variability cannot be overlooked when examining the housing landscape and its effects on the city's most marginalized residents. Meanwhile, the city's population continues to grow, increasing by 80 percent between 1986 and 2016.

Although a lack of affordable, adequate housing across northern communities is behind the rise in visible homelessness in Yellowknife, a wider-reaching northern housing crisis has been ongoing since the first modern housing programs in the Canadian North in the 1950s and 1960s.[34] A federal northern resettlement policy was implemented shortly after the Second World War, when the Canadian government embarked upon a period of welfare state reform that included a more interventionist approach to northern Indigenous people.[35] Part of that approach involved encouraging the centralization of Indigenous people into settlements, which the government believed would be the first step towards their full integration into both Canadian society and the wage economy.[36] Not surprisingly, these policies of centralization and housing provision were significant drivers of social and cultural change, and also increased vulnerability for northern Indigenous peoples by creating reliance on the federal and territorial governments for shelter that too often was, and remains, inadequate in terms of both quality and quantity.[37]

The relative geographic isolation of northern rural settlements is compounded by the fact that, because most were not formed around a sustainable economic base, there is a critical shortage of formal sector employment opportunities.[38] By contrast, most employment opportunities in Yellowknife reflect the structure of the territorial economy and are reliant on non-renewable resource development and the territorial and federal governments. The uneven development of the northern

---

34 Frank Tester, *Iglutaq (In My Room): The Implications of Homelessness for Inuit – A Case Study of Housing and Homelessness in Kinngait, Nunavut Territory* (Kinngait, Nunavut: Harvest Society, 2006).

35 Frank Tester and Peter Kulchyski, *Tammarniit (Mistakes): Inuit Relocation in the Eastern Arctic, 1939–63* (Vancouver: UBC Press, 1994); Robert M. Bone, *The Geography of the Canadian North* (Oxford: Oxford University Press, 2003); Community Partnership Forum, *Homelessness in Yellowknife.*

36 Bone, *Geography of the Canadian North.*

37 Tester, *Iglutaq (In My Room)*; Tester and Kulchyski, *Tammarniit.*

38 Peter Collings, "Housing Policy, Aging, and Life Course Construction in a Canadian Inuit Community," *Arctic Anthropology* 42, no. 2 (2005): 50–65, https://www.jstor.org/stable/40316646; Tester, "Iglutaasaavut"; Bone, *Geography of the Canadian North.*

economic landscape, Abele[39] argues, has been accelerated by major resource development projects, such as diamond mines and gas pipelines, creating a highly variable, and vulnerable, "boom-bust" economy.

Northern resettlement policy combined with the economic nature of non-renewable resource development, therefore, have shaped a geography of economic and social disparity between northern rural settlements and urban centres. This same rural-urban disparity is reflected in the geography of northern housing. For example, Yellowknife is one of only five NWT communities with a functional housing market.[40] In the city, housing stock is more diverse, with private ownership and private rental housing being the main forms of housing tenure. In contrast, public housing dominates the housing stock in most northern rural settlements and is the primary source of affordable housing in regional centres such as Yellowknife. Thus, the rural-urban disparity in housing types is also present within Yellowknife itself: affordable housing provided largely by public housing, with little, if any, regulation of the private rental market to ensure its affordability and accessibility. This is a particular barrier for single adults, who are shut out of public housing due to a lack of single-person units.

Inaccessibility of public housing, high cost of living, housing unaffordability, and employment insecurity all characterize life in Yellowknife for many single adults who experience homelessness.[41] The city's 10-Year Plan to End Homelessness strongly emphasizes the need for permanent social housing, where movement out of such housing is not necessarily seen as the end goal, acknowledging that many people who experience homelessness would benefit from ongoing support. As one of us has argued,[42] "there is a tremendous need for not only public housing units for single adults, but also for additional supportive housing programs that combine needed social supports, such as counselling or skills development, with housing." Greater collaboration and coordination between the various levels of government in the territory – municipal, territorial, Indigenous, and federal – are required.

39 Frances Abele, *Education, Training, Employment, and Procurement: Submission to the Joint Panel Review for the Mackenzie Gas Project* (Yellowknife, NWT: Alternatives North, 2006), https://alternativesnorth.ca/oil-and-gas/.
40 Christensen, "They Want a Different Life"; Northwest Territories, *Homelessness in the NWT: Recommendations to Improve the GNWT Response*, (Yellowknife: Government of the Northwest Territories, 2005).
41 Christensen, "They Want a Different Life."
42 Ibid., 17.

Yet even though multiple governmental and non-profit agencies are addressing affordable housing, housing and service providers in Yellowknife continue to face many challenges, including jurisdictional obstacles and funding constraints. Canada Mortgage and Housing Corporation (CMHC) provides the territorial government significant funding for housing, but little is directly channelled from the federal government to the municipal government or to NGOs. Although funding opportunities have shifted since the implementation of Canada's National Housing Strategy in 2018, many housing and service providers we interviewed cited lack of funding or "too many hands in one pot" as a primary challenge to providing affordable housing.

Public and Private Housing Monopolies in Yellowknife

The lack of a housing spectrum in Yellowknife can be understood in part as the result of a public and private housing monopoly. The Northwest Territories Housing Corporation (NWTHC), a department of the territorial governmental, is the main public or social housing provider, while, as noted, Northview Properties is the primary private property management company offering rental apartments. Unfortunately, for low-income tenants, there are few other options. The limited kinds of rental housing present serious obstacles to supportive and transitional housing programs, rendering them vulnerable to ongoing fluctuations in the local, resource-dependent economy as well as changes in the overall local housing market, such as the introduction of condominium housing. These dimensions are explored in further detail below.

The NWTHC was created to oversee the construction, maintenance, and governance of housing throughout NWT communities and in regional hubs such as Yellowknife. It receives and manages funding from CMHC, and operates several housing programs across the territory. An interviewee explained that, "technically, the NWTHC has a mandate to provide opportunities for suitable and affordable housing in the territory. It has operations and programs and services across the housing continuum, including support for homeless persons, all the way up to ... transitional housing, to public housing, market housing, affordable housing in kind of a leased-owned manner, all the way up to rental incentives for developers to develop more market housing."

Despite the NWTHC's dominant and extensive role in providing public housing to territorial residents, several housing advocates we interviewed were quite critical of its housing conditions and governance. They raised concerns about the quality and condition of NWTHC housing, providing detailed accounts of houses that were not built for the northern climate, or describing homes in ill-repair with major mould infestations. Many noted that NWTHC houses did not reflect the need for multifamily dwellings or the cultural or contextual needs of Indigenous communities. In terms of governance, several housing advocates and services providers described the NWTHC as having a reputation for being inflexible, punitive, and unsupportive of tenants. One housing advocate noted that "there is no alternative community voice or Indigenous voice to present an alternative model." Many research participants were critical of the NWTHC's policy changes around housing subsidies and welfare, which they view as detrimental to individual tenants.

Rental arrears with the NWTHC, in particular, were a contentious issue, and were viewed as a barrier to accessing affordable housing in Yellowknife. There are multiple reasons people go into rental arrears in public housing. According to our research, some tenants refuse to pay rent for political reasons in response to (colonial) policies and the fiduciary responsibility of the Crown towards Indigenous peoples. Others take leave from the community to hunt, fish, or trap, and do not pay their rent while away. We also heard accounts of women stuck with full rent when leaving an abusive partner and subsequently in arrears.[43] Regardless of how arrears are accrued, once they are on record it is an uphill battle to find alternative housing in Yellowknife. Since individuals with rental arrears can no longer access public housing, they look to private market rentals, which, in Yellowknife, leaves very limited affordable rental housing options.

The primary option is Northview (formerly Northern Properties), which has a significant presence across northern Canada and is the largest property management company renting apartments in Yellowknife. Northview owns a range of properties, from low-rise apartment buildings to townhomes. According to CMHC's 2022 Northern Housing Market Report, the average rental rates in the city were $1,564 for a one-bedroom, $1,806 for a two-bedroom, and 2,095 for a three-bedroom, making the Yellowknife rental market the most expensive in the country.[44] Not surprisingly, many of these units are inaccessible for people on income assistance, and nearly impossible to access if you are in rental arrears with the NWTHC.

---

43 See also Christensen, *No Home in a Homeland.*
44 Canadian Mortgage and Housing Corporation, *Northern Housing Report 2022* (Ottawa, 2022), https://assets.cmhc-schl.gc.ca/sites/cmhc/professional/housing -markets-data-and-research/market-reports/northern-housing-report/northern -housing-report-2022-en.pdf?rev=48c601e2-31ad-4428-b4f4-0b90a26919e0.

Several housing advocates and service providers noted a complex yet challenging relationship with Northview, claiming it has blatantly discriminated against low-income and homeless individuals in the past by refusing to rent to them. One advocate noted: "the private market landlord that is a monopoly has declared they won't rent to anyone on income support in spite of the fact that it's against human rights. No one's challenged this so they still don't rent to [people on disability]." Another housing advocate called the discrimination a policy whereby there is "one major landlord...who rents most of the [rental] stock, and [has] stopped taking income support tenants." The advocate's organization was now operating a Housing First program, giving it more access to such rental housing, but was very clear in stating that Northview would "not accept income support for their rentals, because it was unpredictable about when they would receive payment ... So they would have units sitting empty rather than take tenants [that were on income support]."

Furthermore, the dominant presence of a single private rental company means that it is easy for tenants to burn their bridges if they have a negative experience with the REIT. Christensen[45] has described the ways in which the housing landscape in Yellowknife creates a high degree of precarity for low-income residents. She describes, for example, several instances where tenants were evicted during a crisis point in their personal lives and then struggled to rent again from the company later on once they were in a better personal situation.[46] Similarly, public housing tenants described several instances where they were not given a second chance to access public housing due to a negative first experience. Our research corroborates these observations, further illuminating the difficult housing situation for low-income, marginally housed individuals in Yellowknife.

The public and private housing monopoly is challenging, both for individuals in search of rental housing and for support providers trying to find adequate accommodations for clients. The lack of a housing spectrum presents a huge barrier in the provision of affordable housing in the city. On one hand, there is publicly funded affordable housing, although limited in number, accessibility, and suitability; on the other hand, there is a private property management company with a bottom line based on market values. For low-income tenants, this is not an easy housing landscape to navigate. Moreover, due to the threadbare nature

45 Christensen, *No Home in a Homeland*.
46 Ibid.

of the affordable housing market, it is very easy to find oneself shut out of both public and private rental options.[47]

The creation of supportive housing and the implementation of programs such as Housing First thus become increasingly important in the context of a city with a limited housing spectrum and a public and private rental housing monopoly. The success or failure of a program such as Housing First relies on the already-established landscape of affordable housing landscape in Yellowknife, which is limited at best. When Yellowknife started its first Housing First program in 2016, government officials, housing advocates, and service providers were excited and hopeful, but, as we explore in the remainder of this chapter, the lack of a housing spectrum constrains the program's ability to address housing insecurity in the community in challenging and significant ways.

The challenges of relying on one private rental property management seem insurmountable, but this is the reality of housing affordability in Yellowknife. Despite the many stories of challenging situations with Northview, however, there were also positive stories related to the Housing First project, where housing providers collaborated and felt supported by Northview.

Supportive Housing Programs and Housing First

Like other small Canadian municipalities, Yellowknife launched its inaugural Housing First project with federal funding through the Homelessness Partnership Strategies (HPS). The program was implemented following the formula of the Tsemberis Pathways to Housing as closely as possible.[48] Assessments of potential tenants were conducted, and only individuals with the highest acuity were admitted. Wraparound services from local service agencies were secured and scattered site housing in rental apartments was procured. After an exciting and successful first year, Housing First in Yellowknife accomplished its goal of housing twenty individuals.

Even with paying attention to implementation procedures outlined by the Pathways approach to Housing First, Yellowknife's program faced a few challenges, although it is important to note that these were not unlike those experienced by other smaller cities and municipalities

47 Ibid.
48 Ana Stefancic et al., "Early Implementation Evaluation of a Multi-Site Housing First Intervention for Homeless People with Mental Illness: A Mixed Methods Approach," *Evaluation and Program Planning* 43 (April, 2014): 16–26, doi: 10.1016/j.evalprogplan.2013.10.004.

that have implemented Housing First programs. Challenges were related to the lack of affordable housing options and a small social service network. As well, the program encountered discrimination in the rental market, specific difficulties maintaining housing for highly vulnerable tenants, and incompatibilities between Housing First principles and the cultural context of the North. A significant portion of Yellowknife's marginally housed people self-identify as Indigenous, and we encountered several anecdotes of racism in private market housing as a major barrier to secure housing and thus to the overall success of the Housing First program.[49]

Another challenge faced by Yellowknife's Housing First program was the difficulty of maintaining housing for highly vulnerable tenants. Housing the most vulnerable, chronically homeless, or "hard-to-house" individuals is a foundational component of the Housing First model. As one housing provider noted, however, the assessment scale focusing on the most vulnerable tenants makes it challenging to establish long-term secure housing (without continued interventions from wraparound services). In addition, it was noted that the focus of Housing First on the most vulnerable tenants might leave many other potentially successful tenants out of the program and without supportive housing. In other words, the concept of hard-to-house might take on a different meaning in Yellowknife's housing landscape, where the limited housing options affect a broader range of individuals in need of housing than in the much larger and more diversified urban housing landscapes where Housing First was developed.

Still another challenge experienced by Housing First providers in Yellowknife involved a disjunction between the program's primary goal and the local cultural context. Housing First emphasizes the need for individuals to live alone in their own apartment, but some Housing First participants faced difficulties living on their own in a one-bedroom apartment, resulting in violent outbursts, noise complaints from neighbours, and damage to the apartment unit or building. This approach to housing, as several of our research participants noted, did not always fit the cultural needs of tenants and was often in direct contradiction to the way they live, or wish to live, their lives. For example, many individuals would welcome relatives or street-involved friends into their apartment to socialize or spend the night. This welcoming of others fostered an important sense of community, but often led to challenges with the landlord and ultimately to potential eviction. In addition, many

---

49 Turner Strategies, *Everyone Is Home*; Christensen, *No Home in a Homeland*.

participants wanted to live more communally and collectively, something that is not facilitated by the one-individual-per-unit structure of the Housing First program. As mentioned earlier, other supportive or transitional housing programs in Yellowknife, such as Bailey House and Lynn's Place, also emphasize a single-individual-per-unit model, which is not necessarily the preferred living situation for tenants and in fact might perpetuate or worsen a sense of social isolation.

The success of Yellowknife's Housing First program rests on the ability of housing support providers to navigate the local housing landscape. Although Yellowknife experienced challenges similar to other smaller Canadian municipalities that have implemented Housing First, such as limited housing options and a small social service network, the program persevered. Overcoming difficulties relating to discrimination, housing hard-to-house clients, and the cultural context of the North relies heavily on relationship building between Housing First staff and landlords. As a result, housing support providers in Yellowknife, as discussed below, focus on building successful and collaborative working relationships with staff in the city's only private property management company. Although these relationships appeared strong over the course of our research, there was nevertheless a constant fear among housing support providers that, if the economy shifted and private rental market housing became in greater demand, rents would increase, collaborating with the Housing First program would be less desirable, and Housing First tenants would be evicted.

Building and Brokering Relationships

The limited housing spectrum in Yellowknife is a primary challenge faced by the city's Housing First program. Several research participants spoke about the precarity involved in relying on one private market company for the provision of housing units for Housing First. If, for example, a tenant was evicted from Northview properties, it would be very difficult to find an alternative housing option.

Building relationships with property management staff was therefore seen to be integral to the success of the program. According to one research participant, "it has been a nice relationship to have with [the] major landlord. It's kind of a three-way tenant program – tenant, support, landlord triangle – it kind of all works to keep them housed."

This type of working relationship highlights the important role that support providers play in securing housing for Housing First clients. It demonstrates the extra work required by support providers, who also provide wraparound services for Housing First clients, to ensure their clients are securely housed. In the context of Yellowknife's limited housing spectrum and the presence of one major rental landlord, building healthy and collaborative relationships with Northview properties is essential for the success of the Housing First program.

The case of a support provider who worked with at-risk youth is a key example of how good relationships with property management staff kept tenants housed. During our interview, the support provider kept mentioning how "brokering" with property management really worked to maintain secure housing for hard-to-house individuals. The support provider told us a story of a tenant who "trashed a unit," causing $20,000 in damages, yet the tenant did not get evicted but rehoused – indeed, this tenant had to be rehoused three times. The support provider attributed this success to the good relationship with Northview: "They're a profit business. And maybe because it's [name of worker]. He's new and he's so personable that if there's an issue I'll go over to his office and problem solve. I don't think its pure economics. Because he really likes what he's doing." Thus, brokering and building relationships is critical to the sustainability of the Housing First program in Yellowknife.

The potential precarity of relationships with the only private property management company in town raises serious questions, however, about the longevity of the program. As one housing provider noted:

It's really person-based, and that's the unfortunate thing. And, I mean, right now we have a great relationship with the manager, and when we were initially starting up, the manager … was advocating for Housing First in Yellowknife. But if someone comes in who's not supportive of our program, then we can very easily lose the units. And it's not sustainable because of the funding model. We have to rely on funding coming in to support our tenants and support our staff.

Unfortunately, the status of this relationship could change without notice: "That's kind of out of our hands. They do what they need to do. We're not in the business of competing with them … But we can't tell anyone what they can set their prices at." At the moment, this the relationship is working, but, as another interview participant indicated, it is not necessarily sustainable: "having all your eggs in one basket [is a] difficult thing."

Although successful and thriving in many ways, Yellowknife's Housing First program faces three significant challenges: funding, support for wraparound services, and lack of rental options. These challenges reflect obstacles faced by rural communities implementing Housing

First programs across Canada, as noted by Jeannette Waegemakers Schiff and colleagues.[50] Yellowknife, like other smaller cities and rural municipalities, has a limited network of social service providers, a significant lack of affordable rental options, and precarious funding arrangements. As a result, a substantial part of the responsibility for ensuring the success and longevity of the Housing First model rests on the shoulders of those administering the program and providing wrap-around services for clients.

Funding – more specifically, the allocation of funding – was noted as a major concern by many of our research participants. In particular, those working in non-profit organizations and in the municipal government had concerns about the centralization of federal funding within the territorial government and how that affected policy and programming decisions. Several non-profit support providers expressed the desire to see the municipal government in greater control of funding, suggesting it would allow for more contextually appropriate programming. At the same time, these same support providers acknowledged that more municipal involvement in funding allocation would mean more resources for Yellowknife over some of the territory's smaller communities. While Yellowknife is where housing needs are most visible, an unequal distribution of housing programs and support services can further exacerbate urban homelessness.

Other challenges are found in the ways supportive housing and Housing First programs are funded. Housing providers we spoke to expressed frustration at the federal and territorial funding models, which operate on a fiscal-year basis. This means that the final months of each fiscal year are spent on reporting, completing proposals for new funding, and generally demonstrating the program's success – all time, housing advocates argue, that could be better spent on longer-term planning.

Funding sources also present challenges in other ways. For example, research informants described a disconnect between the expectations of funding agencies for housing tenants to "graduate" from supportive housing or Housing First, despite the long-term needs of tenants and the lack of available private or public rental options. In the words of one housing provider we interviewed, "I often think there is no sense calling it 'transitional' housing, because in Yellowknife and all across the territory there is really nowhere to transition to. Even if they could afford to rent an apartment, many of our clients have had previous experiences

---

50   Waegemakers Schiff et al., *Housing First in Rural Canada.*

with the main landlord in town, and some have arrears with the Housing Corporation. There's nowhere else to go, really."

As mentioned above, it is also difficult for non-profit housing providers to push back against funding agencies since they are in a precarious situation as being dependent on government funding while also wanting to advocate on their clients' behalf. "I'm both an advocate and a service provider," one informant told us, "and that's really hard because we don't have an advocacy office here ... I'm going to lose my funding sometime because I'm a mouthpiece and saying too much against the hand that feeds you."

Evaluating the challenges of Yellowknife's inaugural Housing First program provides some tangible "lessons" for the future of housing policy in the city and throughout the territory. This research raises key questions about the role of non-profit and private market housing providers in securing the housing necessary for Housing First programs in northern municipalities, as well as in other small and medium-sized cities in Canada. Both private and non-profit providers play a significant role in creating and maintaining affordable housing in Yellowknife. However, they do not have consistent funding for the operation of Housing First and are not represented at the decision-making table in either the territorial or the federal government. "We're very vulnerable in that way. So, you know, a couple of things that were noted and we're mindful of, and we're just seeing if we can advocate our way forward."

Yellowknife's Housing Spectrum: Challenges and Ways Forward

In April 2019, the federal government announced Reaching Home: Canada's Homelessness Strategy, to replace the Homelessness Partnering Strategy.[51] The new strategy supports the goals of the 2017 National Housing Strategy – specifically, the aim to reduce chronic homelessness nationally by 50 per cent by 2027–28.[52] To support these efforts in the Canadian North, the strategy plans to implement a specific territorial homelessness funding stream to increase federal homelessness investments in the capitals of each territory, while offering more flexibility on how funding can be used to address the unique homelessness

---

51 Employment and Social Development Canada, "Government of Canada announces funding to address homelessness in the Northwest Territories," 29 August 2019, https://www.newswire.ca/news-releases/government-of-canada-announces-funding-to-address-homelessness-in-the-northwest-territories-872156420.html.

52 Employment and Social Development Canada, *National Housing Strategy: A Place to Call Home* (Ottawa: Government of Canada, 2018).

challenges in the North. At first glance, this announcement is a step in the right direction for Yellowknife, but the National Housing Strategy has promoted Housing First in earnest, an approach that, as we have explored in this chapter, has encountered significant challenges in Yellowknife – challenges that are likely to be encountered in the two other territorial capitals, Whitehorse and Iqaluit, as well. Careful consideration needs to be given to these challenges in order to ensure that Canada's (new) Homelessness Strategy is both effective and sustainable in the context of northern urban centres such as Yellowknife.

As we have illustrated in this chapter, the housing landscape in Yellowknife presents a range of challenges for the implementation of supportive housing and Housing First programs, and in general illustrates some of the significant barriers for housing accessibility and affordability in northern regional centres in Canada. Our interviews with housing support providers revealed the benefits of maintaining a positive working relationship with Northview, the city's main private property management company. Indeed, the level of NGO-private collaboration here is encouraging. At the same time, it is concerning that the success of the Housing First program is largely contingent upon such relationships. What happens, for example, if a relationship sours or if those filling the key roles in the relevant organizations move on to other jobs or communities?

The history of Northview also indicates that there can be quick policy change on the part of the REIT – it was only in 2014 that Northview announced it would not be renting to tenants on income support.[53] The 2019 Northern Housing Report from CMHC indicated that Yellowknife's housing market is cooling as the local diamond mines approach the end of their lifespan and the territory's economic future looks increasingly bleak. Providing units for Yellowknife's Housing First initiative might be a productive use of Northview's resources now, but what might happen during a time of relative economic boom?

Relatedly, the increase in condominium units on the Yellowknife housing market also requires some consideration in terms of its possible impact on Northview's activities, not to mention on the private rental housing landscape as a whole. For example, the influx of condominium units could result in a decrease in Northview's market value, which in turn could affect the REIT's willingness to increase or renovate

---

53 *CBC News*, "Northern Property tightens rules for renters on income support," 9 May 2014, https://www.cbc.ca/news/canada/north/northern-property-tightens-rules -for-renters-on-income-support-1.2638266.

its units. At the same time, many condominium owners in Yellowknife are renting their units out, which could lead to a significant dent in Northview's professional, employed tenants.

What is clear is that supportive housing and Housing First programs are filling very important gaps in the Yellowknife housing spectrum. At the same time, there is a significant need for additional supportive housing options, including ones that are permanent or long term without expectations for transitioning to other, more independent housing options. We need to recognize that the current prioritization of Housing First by municipal, territorial, and federal governments creates a ready environment for the creation and proliferation of supportive housing programs. In a very limited housing landscape such as that found in Yellowknife, much depends on the policy priorities not only of government, but also of the private rental market. With the anticipated expansion of funding for supportive housing in northern capital cities under Canada's Homelessness Strategy, there will be intensified need for apartments through public-NGO-private partnerships. As such, the implementation of the Strategy rests on precarious ground: if priorities change for Northview, the consequences could be bleak for those Yellowknifers currently benefiting from supportive housing and Housing First.

At the same time, there is also an urgent need to broaden housing options for low-income residents who do desire a more independent living arrangement. In the words of one key informant, "we need more options for people to transition to." Our research interviews with NWTHC representatives indicated an unwillingness to involve the territorial government in regulating the private rental market. However, placing caps on rents would go far in ensuring the availability of affordable housing stock for low-income residents.

Research informants also provided a range of additional housing options that could, if supported, broaden the local housing spectrum. These options were included in a foldout poster resource produced as one outcome of this research: housing advocates encouraged more forward thinking about the possibility of tiny homes, creating community-based housing (such as housing co-operatives), building more supportive housing, and rezoning land for affordable housing. These suggestions are tangible. In the context of a city with a limited housing spectrum, however, insecure funding for housing, and intergovernmental disputes regarding housing policy, it might be an uphill battle.

Nevertheless, the Housing First program in Yellowknife provides a glimmer of hope. It is a program that, despite multiple challenges, has successfully housed some of the city's hardest-to-house residents.

Perhaps this inaugural Housing First program could be used as both a guiding light and a cautionary tale for future affordable housing initiatives in Yellowknife. It demonstrates that funding can be procured, that the network of social service providers in the city is strong enough to implement wraparound services, and that building relationships among support providers, governments, and private landlords is essential for securing housing for some of Yellowknife's most vulnerable individuals. But if programs like Housing First (and other supportive housing models) are to flourish and grow into sustainable long-term housing options, attention needs to be invested into building sustainable collaboration between Housing First providers – public, NGO, and private – diversifying the limited rental housing spectrum, and addressing chronic housing need in northern rural communities. An integrated territorial approach to northern housing is required to address the urban manifestations of northern housing insecurity and homelessness. Although Reaching Home: Canada's Homelessness Strategy is promising in its commitment to a territorial funding stream, the emphasis on northern capitals signals a continued policy focus on homelessness as an urban issue. As the chapters in this volume collectively convey, homelessness in the urban North needs to be approached at broader scales in order to account adequately and effectively for the complex ways in which rural and urban life intersect in northern geographies of homelessness.

2 Responding to Homelessness in Yellowknife: Pushing the Ocean Back with a Spoon

NICK FALVO

Yellowknife, the capital of the Northwest Territories (NWT), is known for its strong reliance on the mining sector, a large Indigenous population, cold weather, and very expensive housing. It also has a considerable amount of absolute homelessness. Homelessness, however, never exists in a vacuum, and the present chapter has three underlying messages. First, structural factors throughout the NWT contribute to homelessness in Yellowknife. Second, there have been considerable funding initiatives over the past several years responding to homelessness in Yellowknife; they have involved the federal, territorial, and municipal governments. And third, in light of the structural factors contributing to homelessness in Yellowknife, attempting to *respond* to homelessness without *preventing* it is akin to pushing the ocean back with a spoon.

I begin the chapter by discussing several of the structural drivers of homelessness in Yellowknife, including unemployment, poverty, physical and sexual violence, and Yellowknife's housing market. I then briefly discuss the "face of homelessness" in Yellowknife, largely with the help of findings from the city's 2018 Point-in-Time (PIT) homelessness count. This followed by an outline of funding initiatives by the federal, territorial, and municipal governments, and a review of ongoing challenges. I end the chapter with several policy recommendations.

Method

This chapter updates a 2011 report that relied on key informant interviews and consultation with several non-governmental organizations. Since preparing that report, I have been part of a four-person consulting team that helped develop Yellowknife's 10-Year Plan to End Homelessness. To prepare the chapter, I asked my contacts in Yellowknife for advice on new material on homelessness in Yellowknife. I read the material that has surfaced since 2011, incorporated a discussion of the city's "10-Year Plan to End Homelessness,"[1] and sent a draft of the chapter to twenty-five well-placed local experts for review.

Structural Factors and Migration

Women are forced from their homes and communities into the city and regional centres by poverty, lack of access to services, overcrowded housing, and epidemic rates of violence, internal and external to the Indigenous community.[2]

– Arlene Haché

The quote above is from a long-time advocate and service provider in Yellowknife. Although she is writing specifically about women, the migration of which she writes is relevant to all NWT households. Indeed, most people experiencing absolute homelessness in Yellowknife are not originally from Yellowknife. Most come from other NWT communities with lower levels of educational attainment, higher rates of unemployment, lower income levels, and higher rates of violent crime. In some cases, a person from a community outside Yellowknife ends up in Yellowknife after being discharged from the North Slave Correctional Complex, a prison situated in the city. In other cases, people (particularly women) leave communities for Yellowknife in the hope of escaping physical and sexual violence.[3] In order to understand homelessness in Yellowknife, it is therefore crucial to consider all of these factors.

---

1 City of Yellowknife, *Everyone Is Home: Yellowknife's 10-Year Plan to End Homelessness* (Yellowknife, July 2017), https://www.yellowknife.ca/en/living-here/resources /Homelessness/EVERYONE-IS-HOME---YELLOWKNIFE-10-YEAR-PLAN-TO -END-HOMELESSNESS-FINAL-REPORT-JULY-2017.pdf.
2 Arlene Haché, "Decolonizing the North," in *Beyond Shelters: Solutions to Homelessness in Canada from the Front Lines*, ed. James Hughes (Toronto: James Lorimer, 2018), 197.
3 Julia Christensen, "'They Want a Different Life': Rural Northern Settlement Dynamics and Pathways to Homelessness in Yellowknife and Inuvik, Northwest Territories," *Canadian Geographer* 56, no. 4 (2012): 419–38, https://doi.org/10.1111/j.1541 -0064.2012.00439.x; Julia Christensen, "'Our Home, Our Way of Life': Spiritual Homelessness and the Sociocultural Dimensions of Indigenous Homelessness in the Northwest Territories (NWT), Canada." *Social & Cultural Geography* 14, no. 7 (2013): 804–28, https://doi.org/10.1080/14649365.2013.822089; Julia Christensen, *No Home in a Homeland: Indigenous Peoples and Homelessness in Canada's North* (Vancouver: UBC Press, 2017).

Indigenous Peoples

The overrepresentation of Indigenous peoples among persons experiencing homelessness throughout Canada has been well documented. Yale Belanger, Olu Awosoga, and Gabrielle Weasel Head have attempted to quantify it.[4] Jesse Thistle has tried to define it.[5] And Julia Christensen has discussed it in the context of the NWT.[6] Just over half of people living in the NWT are Indigenous – that is, First Nations, Inuit, or Métis (table 2.1). According to Canada's 2021 census, 50.6 per cent of the NWT's population is Indigenous. Among Canada's provinces and territories, only Nunavut has a higher proportion of Indigenous peoples (86.7 per cent). For Canada as a whole, the figure is just 5.0 per cent.[7]

In all NWT regions but Yellowknife, Indigenous peoples outnumber non-Indigenous peoples (table 2.2). According to the results of Yellowknife's 2018 PIT Count, 90 per cent of persons experiencing absolute homelessness in Yellowknife were Indigenous.[8]

Table 2.1. Population, by Indigenous Identity, Northwest Territories, 2021

	Number of Persons	Per cent of Population
Northwest Territories	41,070	100
Total Indigenous	20,035	50.6
First Nations	12,315	31.5
Métis	2,890	6.7
Inuit	4,150	10.6
Non-Indigenous	20,345	49.4

Source: Northwest Territories, Bureau of Statistics, "Indigenous Profile: 2021 Census" (Yellowknife, November 2021), https://www.statsnwt.ca/census/2021/Indigenous%20 Profile_2021.xlsx.

---

4 Yale D. Belanger, Olu Awosoga, and Gabrielle Weasel Head, "Homelessness, Urban Aboriginal People, and the Need for a National Enumeration," *Aboriginal Policy Studies* 2, no. 2 (2013): 4–33, https://doi.org/10.5663/aps.v2i2.19006.
5 Jesse Thistle, *Definition of Indigenous Homelessness in Canada* (Toronto: Canadian Observatory on Homelessness, 2017).
6 Julia Christensen, *No Home in a Homeland*.
7 Statistics Canada, *Canada's Indigenous Population* (Ottawa: June 2023), https://www .statcan.gc.ca/o1/en/plus/3920-canadas-indigenous-population.
8 Turner Strategies, *2018 Yellowknife Point-in-Time Count at a Glance* (Yellowknife: City of Yellowknife, 2018).

52   Nick Falvo

Table 2.2. Indigenous and Non-Indigenous Population, Northwest Territories, by Region, 2018

	NWT	Beaufort-Delta	Sahtu	Dehcho	South Slave	Tlicho	Yellowknife
Indigenous	22,278	5,315	1,836	2,830	4,049	2,926	4,983
Non-Indigenous	22,242	1,358	709	598	3,276	250	15,851

Source: Northwest Territories, Bureau of Statistics, "2018 Summary of Community Statistics" (Yellowknife, June 2018), https://www.statsnwt.ca/community-data/NWT%20 summary%20of%20Community%20Statisitcs%202018.pdf.

Socio-economic Disparities across the NWT

There are important variations in education outcomes across the NWT, with Yellowknife having the highest percentage of residents ages 25 to 64 who have completed high school, and the Tlicho region having the lowest (table 2.3). Yellowknife's rate of 85.5 per cent is almost identical to the rate for Canada as a whole (86.5 per cent).[9]

There is also considerable variation in the official unemployment rate across NWT regions (table 2.4). Yellowknife's official unemployment rate is the lowest of any region – as of 2016, less than one-third the rate in the Tlicho region.

Similarly, average income across regions varies (table 2.5), perhaps not surprising in light of variations in education outcomes. Average annual income for an individual is considerably higher in Yellowknife than it is in any other NWT region.

Likewise, rates of poverty, according to Statistics Canada's low income measure, vary across regions (table 2.6), mirroring rates of unemployment and average income levels discussed above. Yellowknife's poverty rate is the lowest in the territory.

Rates of violent crime in many ways mimic other socio-economic disparities. The rate for Yellowknife is the lowest in the NWT; the rate for the Beaufort-Delta region the highest (table 2.7).

---

9 Statistics Canada, *Education in Canada: Key Results from the 2016 Census* (Ottawa, November 2017), https://www150.statcan.gc.ca/n1/daily-quotidien/171129 /dq171129a-eng.htm.

Table 2.3. Share of Population (%) with High School Diploma, Northwest Territories, by Region, 2018

NWT	Beaufort-Delta	Sahtu	Dehcho	South Slave	Tlicho	Yellowknife
72.6	59.0	57.3	57.3	71.9	40.5	85.5

Source: Northwest Territories, Bureau of Statistics, "2018 Summary of Community Statistics" (Yellowknife, June 2018), https://www.statsnwt.ca/community-data/NWT%20 summary%20of%20Community%20Statisitcs%202018.pdf.

Table 2.4. Unemployment Rate (%), Northwest Territories, by Region, 2016

NWT	Beaufort-Delta	Sahtu	Dehcho	South Slave	Tlicho	Yellowknife
10.6	15.6	16.0	23.8	10.9	20.9	5.9

Source: Northwest Territories, Bureau of Statistics, "2018 Summary of Community Statistics" (Yellowknife, June 2018), https://www.statsnwt.ca/community-data/NWT%20 summary%20of%20Community%20Statisitcs%202018.pdf

Table 2.5. Median Annual Personal Income ($ per year), Northwest Territories, by Region, 2021

NWT	Beaufort-Delta	Sahtu	Dehcho	South Slave	Tlicho	Yellowknife
56,800	40,800	40,400	36,000	56,400	36,000	71,500

Source: Northwest Territories, Bureau of Statistics, "NWT Income" (Yellowknife, June 2021), https://www.statsnwt.ca/census/2021/NWT%20Income.xlsx.

Table 2.6. Percentage of population in poverty, Northwest Territories, by Region, 2021

NWT	Beaufort-Delta	Sahtu	Dehcho	South Slave	Tlicho	Yellowknife
11.1	21.9	17.8	15.3	8.4	12.0	7.3

Source: Northwest Territories, Bureau of Statistics, "Poverty Estimates by Region" (Yellow-knife, 2021), https://www.statsnwt.ca/census/2021/MBM%20from%202021%20Census.xlsx.

Table 2.7. Violent Crime Rate (per 1,000 population), Northwest Territories, by Region, 2021

NWT	Beaufort-Delta	Sahtu	Dehcho	South Slave	Tlicho	Yellowknife
121	215	127	279	96	165	72

Source: Northwest Territories, Bureau of Statistics, "Crime Incidences and Rates by Detailed Type of Offense" (Yellowknife, 2021), https://www.statsnwt.ca/justice/police -reported-crime/Comm_Incidents_2021.xlsx.

Housing in the North

Housing is more expensive in the NWT than in most other parts of Canada. First, construction costs are higher, largely because of the costs associated with transporting work crews and supplies to rural communities (especially on the Arctic coast). Further, once housing is built, it deteriorates more quickly in the NWT than it would in most other Canadian jurisdictions. As Luigi Zanasi notes: "The [northern] climate results in housing deteriorating faster. Large temperature differentials between outside and inside houses in winter lead to large amounts of condensation, resulting in mould and premature rot. Movement due to permafrost freezing and thawing also takes a toll on houses."[10]

Further, operating costs for housing are usually higher in the NWT than in southern Canada. This is due largely to the need for higher energy consumption in a colder climate and higher energy prices. Zanasi notes: "In Nunavut and the Northwest Territories, the cost of drinking water and sewage disposal is extremely high as houses depend on trucked water delivery and sewage tank pumpouts."[11]

In light of the very high costs involved in building, operating, and replacing housing infrastructure in the NWT, the federal government spends considerably more on housing per capita in the NWT than in southern Canada. However, no recent quantification has contrasted the precise size of this difference. The Northwest Territories government also spends a considerable amount on housing:[12] the NWT Housing Corporation (NWTHC) Annual Report for fiscal year 2016/17 reported that 67 per cent of its budget came from the territorial government, 23 per cent from the federal government, 7 per cent from rent, and 3 per cent from other sources.[13] It is not clear, however, how much of the territorial contribution is truly own-source funding, as the NWT receives several types of federal transfers, some of which are earmarked for specific initiatives, some of which are not.

10 Luigi Zanasi, "Discussion Paper on Expiry of Federal Funding for Social Housing: Implications for the Territorial Housing Corporations" (Whitehorse, YK: NWT, Nunavut and Yukon Housing Corporations, 2007), iii.
11 Ibid., 21.
12 Ibid.
13 Northwest Territories Housing Corporation, *NWTHC Annual Report 2016–17* (Yellowknife, 2017).

Table 2.8. Households in Core Need (per cent of housing stock), Northwest Territories, by Region, 2021

Housing Problem	NWT	Beaufort-Delta	Sahtu	Dehcho	South Slave	Tlicho	Yellowknife
Not affordable	15.8	9.4	8.6	11.2	11.2	13.0	21.5
Not adequate	13.7	14.0	23.3	22.4	14.1	40.9	8.2
Not suitable	7.9	10.5	10.5	8.8	4.3	27.3	6.1
In core need	13.2	19.2	17.3	22.7	8.9	18.4	10.5

Note: Affordable housing is defined as shelter costs (e.g., rent or mortgage payments, utilities, heat, insurance & property taxes) being less than 30 per cent of household income. Adequate housing must have running water, an indoor toilet, bathing and washing facilities and must not require major repairs. Suitability is defined as having the appropriate number of bedrooms for the characteristics and number of occupants as determined by the National Occupancy Standard requirements. Core need indicates households that have affordability, adequacy and/or suitability issues, and a total household income below the core need income threshold.

Source: Northwest Territories, Bureau of Statistics, "Households in Core Need" (Yellowknife, 2021), https://www.statsnwt.ca/census/2021/Core%20Need.xlsx.

Compared with other regions of the NWT, Yellowknife appears to have the most expensive housing; by contrast, other NWT regions (with strong reliance on the social renting sector) do not have major affordability challenges per se, largely because tenants in social housing receive a subsidy. Yet, Yellowknife appears to have the highest-quality housing stock of all NWT regions, with just 8.2 per cent of households reporting that their unit was in need of major repairs (table 2.8). The logical "take away" from this is that regions outside Yellowknife require major investment in repair and renovation, while Yellowknife households need rental assistance – possibly in the form of financial assistance for housing, and possibly in the way of better rent regulation by the territorial government.

Employment Insurance

Residents of the NWT are eligible for a variety of income assistance programs, some of which are funded and administered by the federal government, others by the territorial government. These include child benefits, workers' compensation, seniors' benefits, and social assistance. Although this chapter does not provide an exhaustive overview of these programs, it is worth discussing income-assistance options available to persons without paid employment in Yellowknife, especially since recent research finds a strong link between income assistance and demand for emergency shelter beds.[14]

Residents of the NWT who have been recently employed are eligible for employment insurance (EI). Rules governing EI are strict, however, and benefits for those who qualify are modest, especially considering the high cost of the living in the NWT. Typically, EI recipients receive just 55 per cent of their average insurable weekly earnings, up to a maximum amount. As of January 2019, the maximum yearly insurable earnings amount was $53,100, meaning that a recipient could receive a maximum weekly benefit of $562.[15]

As of September 2018, in order to qualify for regular benefits in Yellowknife, a person must have worked at least 700 insured hours in the previous 52 weeks. Once approved for regular EI benefits, the recipient can receive benefits for a maximum of 36 weeks.[16] These stipulations reflect changes to EI implemented by the federal government in October 2014 – changes that apply to all three territories. Prior to these changes, workers must have worked just 420 insured hours to qualify for regular benefits, and they could receive benefits for up to 45 weeks.[17]

EI is typically a source of income for persons who are actively searching for work and who, until very recently, were earning income from employment. Once a person's EI eligibility runs out, they may apply for Income Assistance (IA). Because of the program's design and reliance upon labour market participation for eligibility, EI itself is generally not a source of income for persons experiencing absolute homelessness.

---

14 Ron Kneebone and Margarita Wilkins, "Shrinking the Need for Homeless Shelter Spaces," *SPP Research Papers* 9, no. 21 (2016): 1–16, https://doi.org/10.11575/sppp .v9i0.42590.

15 Canada, "EI Regular Benefits: How Much You Could Receive" (Ottawa: Employment and Social Development Canada, January 2019), https://www.canada.ca/en/services /benefits/ei/ei-regular-benefit/benefit-amount.html.

16 Canada, "Employment Insurance (EI)" (Ottawa: Employment and Social Development Canada, August 2018), https://www.canada.ca/en/employment -social-development/programs/ei.html.

17 Meagan Wohlberg, "Federal government cuts EI benefits to northern capitals," *Northern Journal*, 25 February 2014, https://norj.ca/2014/02/federal-government -cuts-ei-benefits-to-northern-capitals/.

Income Assistance

Unemployed residents who are not eligible for EI can apply for Income Assistance. Relative to comparable social assistance programs in other Canadian jurisdictions, benefit levels for IA recipients in the NWT are rather substantial, keeping in mind the NWT's very high cost of living. Including tax credits, a single employable adult in the NWT can receive a maximum of just over $25,000 annually from the IA program and a person with a disability a maximum of just over $26,000 annually. In general, the larger the family unit, the higher the household benefit levels.

Rules pertaining to IA receipt are strict. Unless the potential recipient has a bona fide disability or is age sixty or older, the applicant is required to demonstrate being "productive" every month – specifically, to participate in what the NWT government refers to as *Productive Choice* activities. Activities that count include: employment, career planning, caregiving, parenting, wellness, education and training, and volunteer work. Ongoing monitoring of these activities is done by Client Service Officers (CSOs) who refer recipients to programs and decide whether specific activities meet the Productive Choice expectations of government policy.

Typically, an IA recipient will fulfil Productive Choice requirements by attending several programs and counselling sessions throughout the month, where staff administering the programs sign the recipient's time log.[18] A person can be suspended from IA receipt for sixty days for failing to uphold Productive Choice requirements (e.g., missing appointments). IA recipients do not receive transportation or childcare funding to attend programs or counselling.[19]

The NWT, like all Canadian provinces and territories, has rules stipulating what kind of non-IA income a recipient is allowed to receive throughout the year. A single adult in the NWT who is considered employable may keep up to $200 per month from earned income, as

---

18 A blank version of a Productive Choice Time Log can be accessed at https://www
.ece.gov.nt.ca/sites/ece/files/resources/ia_-_form_i_-_productive_choice_time_log
.pdf.

19 For general information on IA, see Northwest Territories, Education, Culture and Employment, "Income Assistance Program," https://www.ece.gov.nt.ca /en/services/income-security-programs/income-assistance. For a handbook for applicants, see https://www.ece.gov.nt.ca/sites/ece/files/resources/income _assistance_handbook_-_aug_2019.pdf.

well as 15 per cent of all additional income beyond the $200.[20] Many IA recipients therefore must engage in monthly income reporting to their CSO, which requires considerable documentation. Each IA recipient typically must provide documentation showing all deposits into their bank account for the past thirty days. Since many IA recipients do not do online banking, it is common for an IA recipient to have to walk physically into a branch of their financial institution in order to acquire this paperwork, and some financial institutions charge a fee for this. Any one deposit from an unknown source over $100 generally has to be justified to the CSO (notwithstanding the fact that the CSO typically will "claw back" that same amount from the person's monthly IA benefits anyway. For such deposits, a letter of explanation is required, demonstrating if it was a gift or income from employment – and if so, from whom.[21]

Monthly IA payments to recipients are often late, in part due to the need for CSOs to review documentation. This sometimes results in recipients paying their rent late, which can result in late fees if they rent from a for-profit landlord. This makes for-profit landlords more reluctant to rent a unit to an IA recipient.

Rules and procedures still in place for IA receipt likely contribute unnecessarily to increased homelessness. Indeed, the rules likely contribute to fewer people collecting IA, which means less income for some people experiencing homelessness.[22]

In April 2018, the "rent cap" for single IA recipients without dependants was removed. Previously, this group had been allocated a maximum of $900 per month for rent from IA funds, making it very difficult to find rental housing, as noted below. But now, each IA recipient household is provided with a rental allowance large enough to secure a housing unit that meets nationally accepted suitability standards.[23] It is

---

20 For more on these rules and how they compare across the provinces and territories, see Anne Tweddle and Hannah Aldridge, *Welfare in Canada, 2017* (Ottawa: Maytree, November 2018).

21 There are allowances for some earned income, depending on family size. For more on asset limits, see ibid.

22 For social assistance analysis that finds an association between strict rules and less receipt, see Ronald D. Kneebone and Katherine White, "Fiscal Retrenchment and Social Assistance in Canada," *Canadian Public Policy* 35, no. 1 (2009): 21–40. For analysis that finds a negative association between household income for very low income households and use of homeless shelters, see Kneebone and Wilkins, "Shrinking the Need for Homeless Shelter Spaces."

23 Specifically, the standards in question are the National Occupancy Standards determined by Canada Mortgage and Housing Corporation.

not unheard of for a single employable IA recipient without dependants to have the rent for a $1,500 per month one-bedroom housing unit fully covered by the rental portion of the person's IA benefits. No diagnosed disability is required. This has been received very positively by many people in the community, notwithstanding the fact that for-profit landlords still generally prefer to rent to tenants who are employed.

People living in emergency shelters are eligible for some IA benefits, but not the portion intended to cover the cost of housing; they may be eligible for other portions, however, especially if they do not receive other forms of income. Assuming no additional income sources, it would not be unreasonable to expect a single adult without dependants or a diagnosed disability staying in a Yellowknife homeless shelter to receive $300–$350 monthly in IA benefits.

Yellowknife's Housing Market

Renting an apartment in Yellowknife is expensive: average monthly rent is even higher than in Vancouver or Toronto (table 2.9).

Cost factors discussed above are a major reason for the high cost of rent, but another reason likely stems from the fact that one private landlord owns nearly three-quarters of the city's rental units and might be in a monopoly situation.[24] It should be further noted that many non-profit housing options in the city are not available to persons experiencing absolute homelessness. Instead, access to most such units is determined by a "points system" that results in persons with disabilities getting faster access to units. A household in arrears with public housing gets fewer points and therefore remains on the waiting list for much longer than other households.

All bachelor and one-bedroom apartments administered by the Yellowknife Housing Authority – which administers the lion's share of public units in the city – are designated for persons who either have a physical disability or are over age sixty. To quote from a 2011 report: "No single, unattached person, unless in one of those two categories, has ever or will ever get into a public housing unit administered by the Yellowknife Housing Authority, under the current system."[25]

---

24 Nick Falvo, "10 Things to Know about Yellowknife's Northern Property Conundrum" [Blog], *Northern Public Affairs*, 23 May 2014, http://www.northernpublicaffairs.ca /index/falvo-10-things-to-know-about-yellowknifes-northern-property-conundrum/.

25 Nick Falvo, *Homelessness in Yellowknife: An Emerging Social Challenge* (Toronto: Canadian Homelessness Research Network Press, 2011), 11.

Table 2.9. Average Monthly Market Rent ($ per month), by Private Apartment Type, Yellowknife, Edmonton, Toronto, and Vancouver, 2021

City	Bachelor	1-Bedroom	2-Bedroom
Edmonton	879	1,038	1,271
Toronto	1,217	1,439	1,680
Yellowknife	1,234	1,564	1,802
Vancouver	1,302	1,434	1,830

Source: Canada Mortgage and Housing Corporation, "Housing Market Information Portal," https://www150.statcan.gc.ca/t1/tbl1/en/tv.action?pid=3410013301.

The Face of Homelessness Today

In April 2018, 338 persons were found to be experiencing absolute homelessness on the night of Yellowknife's PIT Count (table 2.10). Approximately nine out of every ten of these people self-identified as Indigenous. Also, more than two-thirds of homeless persons in Yellowknife reported being from a different NWT community, with Behchokǫ̀, Hay River, and Inuvik being the top three source communities.[26]

Governance

In the NWT, the federal, territorial, and municipal governments all play important roles with respect to homelessness.

The Federal Role

Federal funding for homelessness comes from a program called the Homelessness Partnering Strategy (HPS). Locally, this is administered by the City of Yellowknife, which serves the role of Community Advisory Board (CAB) – a formal role often played by a municipal government in order for the community in question to receive HPS funding. The CAB's formal membership includes one representative from the NWT government and one from Service Canada, but neither of these officials has voting rights. This body decides which specific initiatives

---

26 Turner Strategies, *2018 Yellowknife Point-in-Time Homeless Count.*

Table 2.10. Homeless Population Relative to Total Population, Yellowknife and Selected Cities, 2018.

City	Homeless Population	Total Population	Homeless Population as a % of Total Population
Calgary	3,117	1,462,927	0.2
Edmonton	1,636	1,386,788	0.1
Vancouver	2,181	2,542,278	0.1
Whitehorse	195	21,732	0.9
Yellowknife	338	19,569	1.7

Note: Figures pertaining to homelessness include both sheltered and unsheltered individuals; Vancouver figures pertaining to both homelessness and total population refer to Metro Vancouver.

Sources: Each city's 2018 Point-in-Time Counts; Statistics Canada, 2016 Census of Canada.

will receive HPS funding designated for Yellowknife (in accordance with HPS directives). Strictly speaking, Yellowknife's CAB is an ad hoc committee of Yellowknife City Council. The CAB's major focus is on how HPS funding will be allocated locally.[27]

The Territorial Role

The NWT government has a Minister Responsible for Addressing Homelessness, a role that is always one of several ministerial roles held by the same individual. For example, at the time of writing, the role was held by the same individual who was simultaneously Minister Responsible for the NWTHC, Minister Responsible for the Workers' Safety and Compensation Commission, and Minister Responsible for Youth. At

---

27 A considerable amount of background material can be found online about HPS funding. HPS directives for 2014–19 can be found here: https://www.homelesshub .ca/resource/homelessness-partnering-strategy-directives-2014-2019. For a general overview of the role of a CAB, see Canadian Housing and Renewal Association, https://chra-achru.ca/en/community-advisory-boards-community-entities-cabsces . For the Terms of Reference for the City of Yellowknife's CAB, see https://www .yellowknife.ca/en/city-government/resources/Current_Committees_of_Council /Community_Advisory_Board_on_Homelessness/Community-Advisory-Board -on-Homelessness-Terms-of-Reference.pdf. And for the web link for the City of Yellowknife's CAB, see https://www.yellowknife.ca/en/city-government /community-advisory-board-on-homelessness.asp.

the bureaucratic level, there is one staff person who is the territorial government's lead on homelessness. Again, at the time of writing, that person's title was Manager of Homelessness and Community Planning. In September 2018, the government announced its intent to: 1) develop a homelessness strategic plan; 2) integrate work currently happening on the homelessness file across territorial departments; and 3) create five- to ten-year goals pertaining to homelessness. Further, a Homelessness Projects Officer has been hired to administer the various territorial homelessness funding streams and to engage with communities on potential programs.[28]

The Municipal Role

Municipal funding for homelessness is determined by Yellowknife City Council. One municipal staff person is the lead on homelessness; at the time of writing, that person's title was Homelessness Specialist.

Funders' Table

A Funders' Table was struck in 2018 and held its first meeting in May of that year. It is expected that this body's main goal will be to help coordinate all three of the above funding sources, identify overlaps and identify gaps. The City of Yellowknife is taking the lead on this initiative.

Homelessness Commission

The City of Yellowknife recently struck a Homelessness Commission, which was one of the recommendations of Yellowknife's 10-Year Plan (discussed below). The membership of this relatively small body includes the Mayor of Yellowknife, the Chair of the Community Advisory Board, the City Administrator (ex officio), a Yellowknives Dene First Nation representative, the minister responsible for the NWTHC, the president of the NWTHC (ex officio), and an Indigenous Elder.[29] The commission's main function is to champion the 10-Year Plan, both by

28 *CBC News*, "N.W.T. gov't announces intention to develop homelessness strategic plan," 26 September 2018, https://www.cbc.ca/news/canada/north/nwt-homelessness-plan-announcement-1.4840040.
29 City of Yellowknife "Homelessness Coalition," 2021, https://www.yellowknife.ca/en/city-government/homelessness-commission.aspx.

lobbying and by providing high-level direction. While the implementation of an Interagency Council was explicit recommendation made in the 10-Year Plan, this plan did not proceed. Instead, the Terms of Reference for the Community Advisory Board (CAB) on Homelessness were amended in 2021 to play a greater role in the coordination of local homelessness services.

Funding Initiatives

An assortment of funding initiatives coming from the federal, territorial, and municipal governments is directed at persons experiencing homelessness in Yellowknife.

Federal

Housing First for Singles is an initiative administered by the Yellowknife Women's Society and has twenty spaces. Its focus is on persons experiencing chronic homelessness; participants typically have been homeless for at least six consecutive months before entering the program. Housing with professional staff support is provided in private apartment units. The program benefits from HPS funding (the program also benefits from funding from the territorial government, as discussed below.[30] A key partner in this program is Northview Apartment REIT, the large for-profit landlord.

Housing First for Families, administered by the YWCA, serves approximately twenty households. The YWCA leases apartment units from Northview and then places families in these units – in all cases, families that have been barred from the private market for a number of reasons, including for being recipients of IA.[31] This initiative also receives HPS funding.[32]

SideDoor operates a Housing First program for youth and young adults ages fourteen to twenty-four, funded in part through HPS. This program also benefits from territorial funding, as discussed below.

---

30 Randi Beers, "Yellowknife's Housing First eyes expansion and graduating 1st clients out of program," *CBC News*, 25 June 2018, https://www.cbc.ca/news/canada/north/yellowknife-housing-first-update-1.4717121.

31 Northview Apartment REIT will not rent to those who need to pay more than 30 per cent of their income on rent (unless they have a guarantor).

32 Beers, "Yellowknife's Housing First eyes expansion."

There is currently no city-wide, client-level data system for persons experiencing homelessness. There is growing interest, however, in moving towards such a system and in better triage for homelessness services in Yellowknife. It is not clear which order of government might lead this process. The City of Yellowknife has provided training to local agencies on how to use the Homeless Individuals and Families Information System, a database containing information on homeless individuals and families and funded by HPS.

The Trudeau government has been increasing funding for the HPS across Canada. Annual HPS funding by fiscal year 2021/22 was projected to be double (in nominal terms) what it was when the Trudeau government took office in 2015 (figure 2.1). Budget 2021 earmarked $2.2 billion for HPS funding across Canada, though this increase does not necessarily translate into increased funding for Yellowknife.

In June 2018, the HPS was rebranded by the Trudeau government as *Reaching Home: Canada's Homelessness Strategy*, and was formally launched on April 1, 2019. At present, HPS funds in the NWT are used only for Yellowknife-specific initiatives; however, the federal government has indicated that more communities across Canada will be eligible for Reaching Home funds than are currently eligible for HPS funds. Under the program, all communities receiving HPS funding are required to have a formal triage system for determining which specific individuals will be prioritized for funding support. Communities are also required to have good data-collection systems.

It is also worth noting that, in May 2018, the federal government's Advisory Committee on Homelessness recommended a greater focus on Indigenous homelessness and increased homelessness funding for all three territories.[33]

In November 2017, the Trudeau government unveiled a National Housing Strategy. Although much of its content and funding levels had already been broadly outlined in the previous budget, the Strategy provided further detail on the content of a renewed federal role in affordable housing. One of the Strategy's stated objectives is to reduce chronic homelessness across Canada by 50 per cent over ten years. And one of the Strategy's key features was the announcement of the federal government's intent to create a Canada Housing Benefit – that is,

---

33 Advisory Committee on Homelessness, *Final Report of the Advisory Committee on Homelessness* (Ottawa: Employment and Social Development Canada, 2018).

Figure 2.1. Annual Federal Funding for the Homelessness Partnering Strategy, fiscal years 2015/16–2021/22

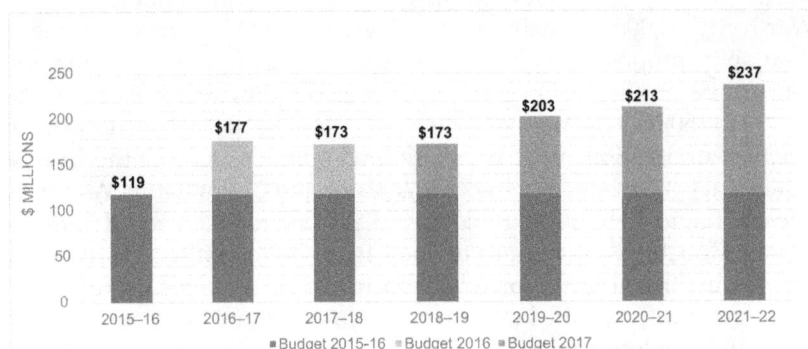

Source: Janice Chan, "Calgary Homeless Foundation" [blog], 30 March 2017.

a portable housing allowance that provides financial assistance to low-income tenants struggling to pay rent.

Territorial Funding Initiatives

Although HPS funding for homelessness is important, a much larger share of funding for homelessness initiatives in Yellowknife comes from the NWT government.

The Transitional Rent Supplement Program (TRSP) provides subsidies of up to $500 per month for low-income tenants who rent from for-profit landlords. People currently in arrears with a public housing provider in the NWT are ineligible for this program. A tenant must make less than $70,000 annually to be eligible, but persons receiving IA are not allowed to access this. This benefit is for the so-called working poor. The subsidy is paid directly to the landlord. At one time, eligible tenants could receive assistance through the program for a maximum of two years, but this has since been extended.[34]

---

34 Jackie McKay, "Rent subsidy program 'critical' to preventing homelessness in N.W.T. gets revamp," *CBC News*, 26 June 2017, https://www.cbc.ca/news/canada/north/critical-program-homelessness-nwt-revamp-1.4178919.

The Anti-Poverty Fund, run by the Department of Health and Social Services, is earmarked for poverty-related initiatives throughout the territory, many of which help prevent and respond to homelessness. Worth $1,000,000 annually, in fiscal year 2018/18, it received more than sixty proposals requesting $4.4 million in funding. Ultimately, forty-three applications were approved, with awards ranging from $5,000 to $50,000. Examples of such projects are $50,000 for SideDoor's eviction prevention program in Yellowknife, $50,000 for the Inuvik Emergency Warming Shelter, $40,000 for the Yellowknife Women's Society Rapid Rehousing Project, and $10,000 for the City of Yellowknife's Housing First initiative. The City of Yellowknife also received $50,000 in 2018/19 for Housing First for youth – a subsidy for those renting from for-profit landlords and professional staff support for recently homeless youth.[35]

The Shelter Enhancement Fund, administered by the NWTHC, provides single-year funding to homeless shelters and homeless-serving agencies for capital upgrades and the purchase of equipment. Over the years, this funding has been used to improve both energy efficiency and accessibility for persons with physical disabilities.[36] The annual cost of this program is $100,000.

Homelessness Assistance Funding, worth $125,000 annually, is for individuals who are referred by a community agency. The referral is then received by an intake worker and evaluated by the Homelessness Assistance Fund Committee. It is one-time funding worth up to $3,000. Every year, approximately sixty applications are approved. Funds can be used for first month's rent, rental arrears, utility arrears, and a damage deposit; most of the approved funds are for rental arrears to prevent eviction. Funds can also be used for a one-way flight to a supportive environment – for example, a person's home community.[37]

Rapid Rehousing focuses on persons experiencing transitional or episodic homelessness – that is, not chronic homelessness. It provides funding for damage deposits, rent supplements, bridge funding (to cover gap periods), and rental arrears. The YWCA operates rapid

---

35 Northwest Territories, "GNWT announces anti-poverty funding recipients" 2 May 2018, https://www.gov.nt.ca/newsroom/news/gnwt-announces-anti-poverty-funding-recipients.
36 Northwest Territories Housing Corporation, "Shelter Enhancement Fund," https://www.nwthc.gov.nt.ca/en/services/shelter-enhancement-funding.
37 Northwest Territories Housing Corporation, "Homelessness Assistance," https://www.nwthc.gov.nt.ca/en/services/homelessness-assistance.

rehousing for families in Yellowknife, while the Yellowknife Women's Society operates it for single adults without dependants in Yellowknife. The NWTHC provides $300,000 annually for this initiative, with half going to the YWCA and half to the Yellowknife Women's Society. In fiscal year 2018/19, assistance was provided to thirty 30 households, both families and individuals.

Territorial Funding Initiatives Specific to Yellowknife

Single Room Occupancy. A multiyear agreement provided a total of $600,000 for the Yellowknife Women's Society to convert its basement into eight single-room-occupancy units. Renovations were completed in December 2017. Spaces were offered first to people living at the shelter. Tenants pay to rent these units, and there is no time limit on how long people can stay.[38]

Housing First for Singles receives, in addition to the HPS funding discussed above, $150,000 annually from the NWTHC for rental subsidies.

Housing First for Youth, also discussed above, benefits from funding from both HPS and the NWT government. In fiscal year 2018/19, the territory's Anti-Poverty Fund provided $50,000 for the program.

Rapid Rehousing, a Yellowknife initiative is funded by the NWTHC. Focusing on persons experiencing transitional or episodic homelessness (not chronic homelessness), it provides funding for damage deposits, rent supplements, bridge funding (to cover gap periods), and rental arrears. Funding flows directly from the territory to a qualifying non-profit agency. The Yellowknife Women's Society received $112,000 annually over fiscal years 2018/19 and 2019/20.

The Yellowknife Women's Society provides emergency spaces for thirty women without a partner or dependants who are homeless. Funding is provided by the Department of Education, Culture and Employment, and funding levels are based on a daily rate per bed along with an administration fee.

Yellowknife's Emergency Shelter for Men, which has capacity for about fifty per night, is operated by the Salvation Army. Most men sleep on bunk beds; there are also some mats, which tend to be used by

---

38 Northwest Territories Housing Corporation, *Homelessness in Yellowknife: Community Partnership Forum April 26–27* (Yellowknife: Government of the Northwest Territories, 2016).

men who are very intoxicated. One room has five single beds intended for men who are typically sober and often gainfully employed. The Department of Education, Culture and Employment provides $515,000 annually to the shelter, based on a daily rate per bed along with an administration fee.

Supported Independent Living Homes, operated by the Yellow-knife Association for Community Living and funded exclusively by the Department of Health and Social Services, targets people whose main challenges are intellectual/developmental disabilities. Association staff help tenants find housing on the private market and provide case management once tenants are housed. Tenants pay market rent, their only financial assistance for rent coming from IA and employment income. All of the approximately twenty tenants in the program make some income from employment. The program receives between $1.5 million and $1.9 million per year, depending on the number of people supported.

Transitional Housing for Families. Until an October 2018 fire destroyed its building, Rockhill Transitional Housing was operated by the YWCA, supporting mothers, fathers, and children. Transitional housing units and some staff support were funded by rent paid by tenants. Monthly rent for a one-bedroom unit was $1,350, and $1,550 for a two-bedroom unit, and a total of twenty-seven units. Most tenants were receiving IA, while the others worked at low-paying jobs. Households in the units typically stayed for several years before moving into either public housing (often having paid off their public housing arrears while staying in Rockhill) or market housing. They were not protected by landlord-tenant legislation. After the fire, the YWCA leased twenty-three units from Northview Apartment REIT, and each tenant immediately faced an average increase in rent of $600 per month. Any unpaid portion of this rent was paid by the YWCA, which held the leases on the units. As well, the twenty-three new units were in scattered sites – in buildings whose focus is not on these types of tenants and, consequently, there is no on-site staff support.[39]

Emergency Shelter for Families. Until the recent fire, the NWT government supported six emergency units (with eleven beds) for families in the same building as the Rockhill transitional units discussed above.

39 Gabriela Panza-Beltrandi, "YWCA NWT concerned for tenants' safety following Rockhill apartment fire," *CBC News,* 24 October 2018, https://www.cbc.ca/news/canada/north/ywca-family-safety-after-rockhill-fire-1.4875680.

Those staying in emergency units did not pay rent and could stay for a maximum of three months. The NWT Department of Education, Culture and Employment provided $221,000 annually for these emergency units; this funding was based on a daily rate per bed along with an administration fee. Emergency units are now located in scattered site buildings near the YWCA's housing office, but at rents that are much greater than when they were located at Rockhill – meanwhile, territorial funding levels for these emergency units have not changed. There are no security staff on site at the emergency units, which limits their safety.

Bailey House is transitional housing operated by the Salvation Army for single men without dependants. It has thirty-two rooms, half of them bachelor units with kitchens and the other half single rooms whose occupants share a common kitchen with three other residents. Residents are not covered by tenant-protection legislation and are subject to random drug testing. Residents pay "program fees," as opposed to rent. Staff are on-site twenty-four hours a day, seven days a week. Residents typically stay for up to three years. All residents have a case worker with whom they make an "individual goal plan." Case workers typically refer residents to other services, such as budgeting, résumé writing, substance use counselling, and so on. Guest speakers are occasionally brought in. The Salvation Army receives approximately $200,000 annually from the Department of Health and Social Services to operate Bailey House.

Lynn's Place, operated by the YWCA, is transitional housing for women and women with children fleeing violence (unlike Rockhill, it does not assist fathers). The only direct government funding received for this is $160,000 annually from Northwest Territories Health and Social Services, Yellowknife Region. There are two three-bedroom units as well as six bachelor units for single women that do not have full kitchens; instead, the building has a common area for cooking. Tenants at Lynn's Place typically stay for a few years before moving on. They might pay off public housing arrears while there and then move into either public housing or market housing. Households residing there are not protected by landlord-tenant legislation. Single women who stay at Lynn's Place are typically over age forty-five and have lived in violent relationships for most of their lives. There is staffing support on-site for roughly eighteen hours per day.

Day Centre and Sobering Centre. In September 2018, a newly renovated space opened as a day centre and "sobering centre." Co-ed services at this facility are funded by the Department of Health and

Social Services and operated by the NWT Disabilities Council. The facility includes showering and laundry facilities. Services offered at the day centre include case management, peer support programming, group therapy, and sewing circles. Staff also assist clients to return to their home communities in some cases. The sobering centre assesses if a person needs medical attention in hospital. Staff embrace a harm-reduction philosophy, meaning that they work with clients who are not necessarily striving towards complete abstinence from substance use. The facility is open twenty-four hours a day.[40]

Integrated Case Management Program, led by the Department of Justice, is a partnership with other territorial departments, including Education, Culture and Employment, Health and Social Services, the Northwest Territories Health and Social Services Authority – YK Region, and the NWTHC. This program assists individuals with complex needs in accessing and navigating services in Yellowknife. The program's *pathfinders,* or case managers, work with participants referred to them from other territorial departments to help them access housing, income assistance, mental health services, legal aid, physical health services, substance use treatment, and cultural supports. Key to the program's success is that pathfinders have considerable political leverage. The program also works at the policy level to support systems change by working with other territorial departments to identify systems gaps and barriers.

Employment Support. The Department of Education, Culture and Employment provides the Yellowknife Women's Society $72,600 annually to help women to attain and keep employment. It also helps to troubleshoot if the person is struggling to maintain work. Part of this work involves helping participants get First Aid training, licensing, and other qualifications, and includes "coaching" –for example to deal with conflict in the workplace.

Youth Shelter. SideDoor operates a twenty-four-hour shelter for up to twelve youths at a time ages fourteen to twenty-five, and receives $110,000 annually from the Department of Health and Social Services. In fiscal years 2018/19 and 2019/20, SideDoor also

---

40 Gabriela Panza-Beltrandi, "New Sobering, Day Centre a huge improvement, say Yellowknife's homeless," *CBC News,* 24 September 2018, https://www.cbc.ca/news/canada/north/yellowknife-homeless-new-day-sobering-centre-improvement-1.4836833.

received $25,000 per year from the Department of Justice to continue with daytime shelter hours. It should also be noted that the NWTHC provides flexible funding annually for internship positions – youths who work at the shelter, in transitional housing, and at the resource centre.[41]

Transitional Housing for Youth. SideDoor provides eleven transitional (temporary) housing spaces for youth ages fourteen to twenty-five, with funding received from the Department of Health and Social Services. This transitional housing is offered in the same building as the youth shelter.

Youth Resource Centre. In fiscal year 2018/19, the Department of Education, Culture and Employment provided SideDoor $57,000 for youth employment services, including help with résumé writing, job search, literacy training, and addictions counselling.

City of Yellowknife Funding Initiatives

The City of Yellowknife provides its own funding for homelessness initiatives.

Employment Support for Women. A women's employment program operated by the Yellowknife Women's Society is funded entirely by the City of Yellowknife, which provided $100,000 in 2018. This is a garbage pick-up program, paying both a full-time coordinator and casual staff. Essentially, the City of Yellowknife outsourced some of its garbage collection to this program.[42]

Employment Support for Youth. In 2017, the City of Yellowknife provided SideDoor with one-time funding of $50,000 for youth employment initiatives. The program had participants work three hours a day. The work placements included minor repairs, prepping and painting interiors and exteriors, yard care, and collecting and disposing garbage.

Street Outreach. The Yellowknife Women's Society administers a street outreach program that responds to people in distress, mostly due to intoxication. It then helps get them somewhere safe (typically

---

41 Northwest Territories Housing Corporation, *Homelessness in Yellowknife.*
42 City of Yellowknife, "An Update"; Gabriela Panza-Beltrandi, "'I feel really happy': Yellowknife's homeless take pride in new employment program," *CBC News,* 25 May 2018, http://www.cbc.ca/news/canada/north/yellowknife-homeless-new -employment-program-1.4677362?cmp=rss.

by driving them). This program is offered from 12 noon until midnight. One of the program's major goals is to reduce calls to first responders that are related to public intoxication. The City of Yellowknife provided this program with $160,000 for 2017 and $360,000 for 2018.[43]

Youth Shelter. SideDoor received $99,000 (over two years) from the City of Yellowknife to operate its youth shelter during the daytime. This funding spanned fiscal years 2017/18 and 2018/19.

AIWF Healing Camp. The City of Yellowknife has supported the development of a healing camp operated by the Arctic Indigenous Wellness Foundation (AIWF). This initiative targets Indigenous men (including youth) who are both homeless and at risk of suicide. Culturally specific mental wellness supports are provided by traditional counsellors and healers.

Yellowknife's 10-Year Plan

In June 2017, Yellowknife City Council endorsed a "10-Year Plan to End Homelessness" in the city. The plan was drafted after extensive community consultation, and contained recommendations pertaining to governance, spending, local coordination of resources, culturally appropriate programming responses, and Housing First. The costed-out plan proposed approximately $11 million annually in new funding over a ten-year period (see figure 2.2).

As discussed earlier, the City of Yellowknife's establishment of a Homelessness Commission to champion the 10-Year Plan came in direct response to one of the plan's recommendations. Likewise, the Interagency Council, which coordinates homelessness services, is also as a result of an explicit recommendation made in the plan.

That said, the plan was a City of Yellowknife initiative, and its recommendations focus on what could be done at the local level in Yellowknife. Although the plan discusses socio-economic issues in the NWT more broadly, it made no policy recommendations aimed at addressing persistent territory-wide challenges relating to high unemployment, poverty, education, and violence.

---

43 City of Yellowknife, "An Update."

Figure 2.2. Operations and Capital Costs of the 10-Year Plan to End Homelessness, by Intervention

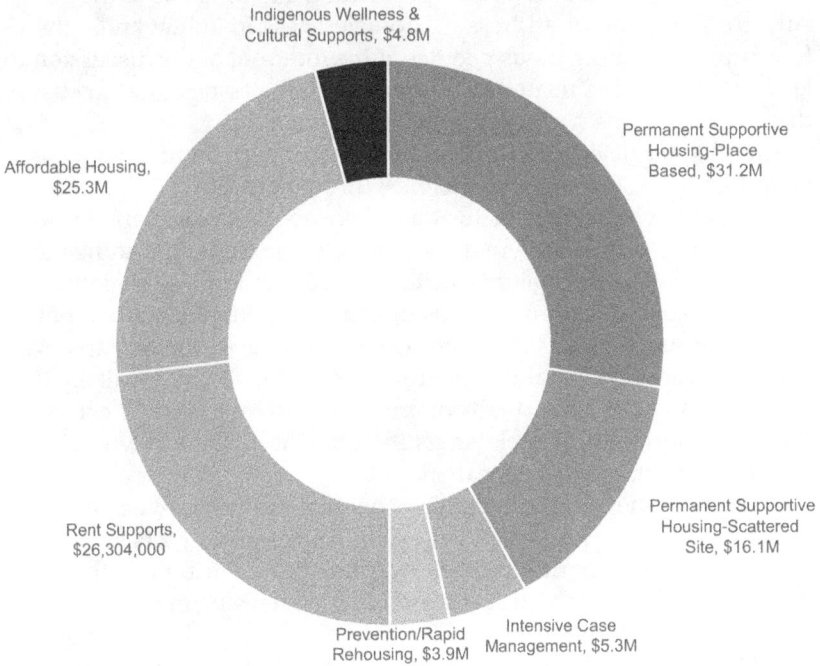

Indigenous Wellness &
Cultural Supports, $4.8M

Permanent Supportive
Housing-Place
Based, $31.2M

Affordable Housing,
$25.3M

Permanent Supportive
Housing-Scattered
Site, $16.1M

Rent Supports,
$26,304,000

Prevention/Rapid
Rehousing, $3.9M

Intensive Case
Management, $5.3M

Discussion

The themes illustrated in this chapter can help us understand the complexities of homelessness in Yellowknife. They can also help us understand a broader theme discussed in this book's Introduction – namely, the movement of persons from rural to urban settings, creating "new forms of ... social service provision, as well as social inclusion for people experiencing homelessness."

Indigenous peoples, who account for 50.7 per cent of the NWT's total population, are coming to terms with more than one hundred years of settler activity in the territory that has included residential schooling, the loss of culture and language, family break-up, violence, and trauma.

These deep-seated challenges help explain both the flow of people from small communities into Yellowknife and the fact that more than 90 per cent of Yellowknife's homeless population identifies as Indigenous. Any consideration of addressing homelessness in Yellowknife, therefore, must have Indigenous peoples at the forefront of the discussion to lead in all decisions related to addressing homelessness and to ensure that policy responses are culturally appropriate.

This chapter discussed troubling indicators pertaining to education, unemployment, income, and violence throughout the NWT, especially outside Yellowknife. One factor that likely accounts for many of these disparities between other regions and Yellowknife is that Indigenous peoples make up the majority of the population in these regions, and they are recovering from decades of settler activity and public policy largely detrimental to their well-being. As long as major gaps exist between other regions of the territory and Yellowknife, it is likely that the flow of people from small communities into the city will continue. Properly addressing homelessness in Yellowknife therefore requires a territorial effort, not just a local one.

Housing in the NWT is expensive to build and expensive to operate, and it deteriorates quickly. Outside Yellowknife, these costs exacerbate socio-economic disparities. In Yellowknife, they contribute to the city's having one of Canada's most expensive rental housing markets – a phenomenon made worse by the holding of a near monopoly by a large, for-profit landlord. It is important to be mindful that climate makes housing affordability challenges greater in the NWT than in southern regions of Canada. The role of the federal government therefore remains crucial in the debate on homelessness in Yellowknife. Housing support for communities outside of Yellowknife should focus on repair and renovation; within Yellowknife, it should focus on affordability. Further, territorial officials should consider better regulation of the rental market, possibly with enhanced tenant-protection legislation.[44]

The precise migration patterns of people from NWT communities into Yellowknife is not fully understood. However, recent survey results suggest that most people experiencing absolute homelessness in Yellowknife once lived in other NWT communities. Considering the many socio-economic disparities in other regions of the territory, it is reasonable to suggest that in-migration is a major contributor to homelessness

44 For a consideration of rent regulation regimes across Canada, see Hugh Grant, *An Analysis of Manitoba's Rent Regulation Program and the Impact on the Rental Housing Market* (Winnipeg: Government of Manitoba, 2011).

in Yellowknife. This reinforces the argument that, to address homelessness in Yellowknife properly, it is important to address socio-economic challenges across the NWT.

The Integrated Case Management program is quite innovative – it might be the only program of its kind in Canada, and the NWT government deserves praise for it. A program evaluation was carried out on this program during fiscal year 2019/20. The report, which was made public in 2020,[45] merits further review, as such a program evaluation could help officials demonstrate the program's effectiveness, increase its long-term viability, and be a lesson for other jurisdictions.

Most public housing in Yellowknife is inaccessible to various subgroups of persons experiencing homelessness. Admittedly, those who are prioritized for public housing, such as persons with disabilities and seniors, are in great need of affordable housing. Having said that, it might be time to reconsider who should be prioritized for such units.

Public officials in Yellowknife are beginning to "up their game" when it comes to data collection and triage in the delivery of services for people experiencing absolute homelessness, likely mirroring similar triage processes in other parts of Canada, which tend to prioritize high-need households. Good data collection and thoughtful triage processes can improve public policy responses to homelessness and demonstrate to funders that good practices are being used to manage scarce resources.

Over the past two decades, IA benefit levels for single adults without dependants in the NWT have seen substantial growth, even after accounting for inflation. More recently, the maximum allowable amount an IA recipient can receive each month for rent has been relaxed, making it easier for IA recipients to access rental housing from for-profit landlords. The NWT government deserves praise for these measures.

There is something unsettling about the Productive Choice system for IA recipients discussed earlier in this chapter. If a person has to be forced to attend programs or counselling, it is reasonable to suggest that such activities might not be well designed for the individual in question. What is more, there is the cost to the public treasury of paying public officials to monitor these activities. It would be more sensible to design supportive housing and related programming that an IA recipient actually would *want* to attend, rather than be *forced* to attend. The

---

45 Northwest Territories, "Release of the Integrated Case Management Program Evaluation and Social Return on Investment Report" (Yellowknife, 10 June 2020), https://www.gov.nt.ca/en/newsroom/release-integrated-case-management -program-evaluation-and-social-return-investment-report.

Productive Choice aspect of IA needs an evaluation, and it would be helpful if led by a third party.

In the immediate aftermath of the October 2018 Rockhill fire, no formal commitment was made by any order of government to finance a new building. The initial response was to house tenants temporarily in private market units, but this option proved unsustainable for the YWCA and likely for the tenants as well. In late 2022, the organization received $12.5 million from Canada Mortgage and Housing Corporation's Co-investment Fund to build a new 21-unit family housing facility.[46] The City of Yellowknife also provided $5 million from its federally sourced Rapid Housing Initiative money and also granted a five-year tax abatement for the property that will equal just under $450,000 in support. The YWCA was also able to source funds from its own account and obtain contributions from the Yellowknife Community Foundation and other local donors.

Conclusion

This book's concluding chapter notes that "northern homelessness emerges through a complex network of rural and urban experiences and mobilities." Yellowknife's homelessness picture is no exception. Per capita levels of absolute homelessness in Yellowknife are very high relative to other Canadian cities – an entirely logical phenomenon when one considers various contextual factors. Slightly more than half of the NWT's total population is Indigenous, and many communities outside Yellowknife have poor education outcomes, high unemployment, low income levels, and high rates of violence. These factors likely contribute to people with low socio-economic status moving to Yellowknife, which has one of Canada's most expensive rental housing markets. Indeed, all of this creates the perfect storm in which many NWT residents not originally from Yellowknife become homeless once in the city.

In response, public officials have designed a large assortment of initiatives to deal with absolute homelessness in Yellowknife. Governance arrangements are becoming more elaborate and there is growing awareness that providing immediate, subsidized housing with professional staff support is an effective way to respond to a household's homelessness. There have been funding initiatives pertaining to

---

46 Simon Whitehouse, "YWCA transitional housing construction to be completed in July," *NNSL Media*, 10 April 2023, https://www.nnsl.com/news/ywca-transitional-housing-project-on-track-to-open-in-july/.

financial assistance for low-income households in Yellowknife, as well as capital upgrades to emergency homeless shelters throughout the territory. Funding initiatives are also in place for transitional (temporary) housing, a day shelter, a "sobering centre," and employment supports for persons experiencing absolute homelessness. An innovative program, the Integrated Case Management initiative, is attempting to break down silos within the territorial government and help homeless and marginally housed people with complex needs. Further, Yellowknife's 10-Year Plan to End Homelessness is a further step forward.

However, as long as communities outside Yellowknife experience poor socio-economic outcomes, further in-migration to Yellowknife is inevitable. This makes local funding initiatives (even with better coordination) akin to pushing the ocean back with a spoon. Funding and policy responses in Yellowknife remain crucial, but so is a territorial effort to improve education outcomes, reduce unemployment, raise income levels, and reduce levels of violence – especially in communities outside Yellowknife. Put differently, a combination of Indigenous-led prevention and emergency responses is needed. Indeed, effectively addressing homelessness in Yellowknife requires substantial social investment throughout the territory by all orders of government.

3 An "Urban" Issue, and the Issue with "Urban": Contextualizing Homelessness in Whitehorse

ALEX NELSON

My roots grow in jackpine roots ... I grow here. I branch here.
— Tlingit Elder Kitty Smith[1]

Roots, unyielding interconnections, and bonds that span spatial and temporal chasms: in the quote above, Elder Kitty Smith's words stand resolute in claiming her ties to her homeland, her history, her future, and her community. The image Smith evokes is powerful, weaving her identity together intimately with a sense of place that is both physical and emotional. She and the jackpine, together, have both laid down strong and sturdy ties to Yukon, and these roots scaffold her ways of knowing and being in the world; to break those bonds would be to sever ties that exist beyond one point of connection or one individual life. For many Yukoners experiencing homelessness, these life-affirming roots have been grievously disrupted: in fact, scholars have suggested that Indigenous experiences of homelessness are perhaps more accurately reflected by the term "rootlessness."[2] Dominant urban-settler conceptions and definitions of homelessness fall far short of grasping these realities; more generally, notions of "urban-ness" are unable to encompass the full social,

---

1 Julie Cruikshank et al., *Life Lived like a Story: Life Stories of Three Yukon Native Elders* (Vancouver: UBC Press, 1990), 163.
2 See Jesse Thistle, *Definition of Indigenous Homelessness in Canada* (Toronto: Canadian Observatory on Homelessness Press, 2017); and Julia Christensen, *No Home in a Homeland: Indigenous Peoples and Homelessness in the Canadian North* (Vancouver: UBC Press, 2017).

historical, economic, and political context of "rootlessness" in northern Canadian cities, where homelessness exists as a crystallization of larger, longstanding frameworks of power and colonial relations. In this chapter, I am interested in unpacking the geographical imagining of "the Urban" and its limitations as both a spatial marker in northern Canada and a tool through which to understand northern homelessness. By examining the geographies of homelessness in Whitehorse, and the promising approaches to policymaking taking shape there, I take Kitty Smith's sentiment to heart as I explore homelessness in Yukon not just as a matter of housing, but also as a matter of home – and of *restoring one's roots*. In other words, to attribute any and all experiences of homelessness to a "lack of housing" would be a mistake, as such a linkage obscures and ignores the political, social, and historical context of individual and community experiences. This is particularly true in the northern Canadian context, where over 80 per cent of those experiencing homelessness are Indigenous.[3] Homelessness, as it is experienced by Indigenous peoples across Canada, is intimately tied to ongoing colonial systems of power. In the 2017 Definition of Indigenous Homelessness in Canada, Métis scholar Jesse Thistle argues that, as a concept, Indigenous homelessness:

> is not defined as lacking a structure of habitation; rather, it is more fully described and understood through a composite lens of Indigenous worldviews. These include: individuals, families and communities isolated from their relationships to land, water, place, family, kin, each other, animals, cultures, languages and identities. Importantly, Indigenous people experiencing these kinds of homelessness cannot culturally, spiritually, emotionally or physically reconnect with their Indigeneity or lost relationships.[4]

Although not all people experiencing homelessness in Yukon are Indigenous, the dispossession and dislocation Thistle describes undergird the overwhelming majority of experiences of homelessness across northern Canada. In northern contexts, programs of uprooting, displacement, and imposed settlement of Indigenous communities served as a longstanding tool to entrench settler-colonial supremacy – the

---

3 Kate Mechan, *Whitehorse PiT Count 2018: Point-in-Time Count Findings* (Whitehorse: Council of Yukon First Nations, Yukon Planning Group on Homelessness, 2018).
4 Thistle, *Definition of Indigenous Homelessness in Canada*.

ramifications of which can be seen in the experiences of Indigenous peoples today. Carol Kauppi, Michael Hankard, and Henri Pallard (Chapter 4), as well as Joshua Moses (Chapter 5) offer a more in-depth discussion of these recurring and ongoing patterns, although this theme is woven throughout much of the work in this volume. Approaches to understanding and confronting homelessness in Whitehorse, Yukon, must address this reality directly and, most importantly, *holistically*. To that end, I mobilize the concept of "ecology" to render these complex interconnections visible. As in an ecological system, an emphasis on interrelatedness and holism runs through the chapter. If homelessness arises as a result of fracture and dispossession, redress can be achieved only through healing the ties that continue to be loosened and damaged by colonialism. This includes approaches to homelessness that enable the reconnection of people to land, language, and Indigenous ways of knowing, alongside efforts that explicitly confront structural forms of oppression and exclusion. Although traditional "victim-blaming" discourse is reviled across the literature on homelessness, it is often reproduced unconsciously in contemporary technical writing, policy, and practice.[5] Providing housing, support, or resources to a single individual does not fix the longstanding power dynamics that paved that person's pathway to homelessness. This is not to suggest that housing, support, and resources are not vital for those experiencing homelessness; rather, service-based approaches cannot come at the expense of critical self, institutional, and structural examination. The only way homelessness can be addressed effectively is through shifting conversations *away from* shaping "flawed" individuals in the image of hegemonic values, and *towards* changing the structures that produced these normative values in the first place. Through examining two Yukon community-based

---

5 For excellent examples of scholars who have critiqued reductive or "victim-blaming" homelessness and poverty discourse over the decades, see Edwin Eames and Judith Goode, "On Lewis' Culture of Poverty Concept," *Current Anthropology* 11, no. 4/5 (1970): 479–82; Lived Experience Advisory Council, *Nothing about Us without Us: Seven Principles for Leadership and Inclusion of People with Lived Experience of Homelessness* (Toronto: Homeless Hub Press, 2016); Peter Somerville, "Homelessness and the Meaning of Home: Rooflessness or Rootlessness?" *International Journal of Urban and Regional Research* 16, no. 4 (1992): 529–39, https://doi.org/10.1111/j.1468-2427.1992.tb00194.x; and Thistle, *Definition of Indigenous Homelessness in Canada*.

policy plans – *Safe at Home*[6] and *Ours to Build On*[7] – I identify the ways in which activists, advocates, policymakers, community members, local governments (at the territorial, First Nations, and municipal levels), and workers in non-governmental organizations (NGOs) have come together in Whitehorse to address homelessness in a manner that takes what I call this "ecology of needs" and interwoven realities seriously, doing work that is both contextually – and culturally – relevant.

Understanding the Texture of Homelessness in Whitehorse

I came to reflect on these promising approaches to northern urban home-lessness while living in Whitehorse over the course of three months during the autumn of 2017 conducting research for a Master of Arts in Anthropology. Having survived over a decade of homelessness (as a settler-Canadian) in two southern Canadian cities – one large and one mid-sized urban centre – I was interested in understanding the ways in which women's narratives, lived experiences, and story sharing could be mobilized to inform the creation and revision of housing-related pol-icy. What spurred my interest in rethinking "the Urban" as it applies to the Whitehorse context was the following conundrum: homelessness is often associated closely with urban environments because of the nature of its visibility in city landscapes. Urban visibility has a harmful corol-lary – rural *in*visibility – which might serve to mask telling dynamics of rural settings. For example, Waegemakers Schiff and colleagues suggest that rates of homelessness in rural areas might *actually surpass* those of urban populations, when factoring in people "living in substandard or unfit housing."[8] Due to the overrepresentation of urban experiences in the literature, however, homelessness is often framed as a quintessen-tially *urban* issue.[9] I certainly experienced it that way; my aptitude for staying invisible among the tailored suits of the downtown after-work crowd and bunking down in big-city shelters can corroborate this.

---

6 Yukon, Health and Social Services, *Safe at Home: A Community-Based Action Plan to End and Prevent Homelessness in Whitehorse, Yukon* (Whitehorse: September 2017), http://www.hss.gov.yk.ca/pdf/Safe_at_Home-Report.pdf.
7 Canada and Yukon Housing Corporation, *Ours to Build On: Housing Action Plan for Yukon: 2015–2025* (Whitehorse, 2015), https://yukon.ca/en/housing-action-plan-yukon.
8 Jeannette Waegemakers Schiff et al., "Rural Homelessness in Canada: Directions for Planning and Research," *Journal of Rural and Community Development* 10, no. 4 (2015): 86.
9 Ibid.

As a result of this urban bias, homelessness occurring outside of conventionally urban spaces has garnered attention only recently. Most volumes on "urban theory" or "urban anthropology" inevitably devote at least one chapter to homelessness.[10] University of Calgary researchers Jeannette Waegemakers Schiff and Alina Turner posit that this is because "[understandings of, and approaches to homelessness] evolved in an urban context."[11] This sentiment is also echoed in the introduction to this volume. The rendering invisible of rural homelessness is compounded when urban southern frameworks are applied uncritically to the North. Ideas about homelessness are transported to the North from fundamentally disparate contexts; when applied to northern experiences, these conceptualizations simultaneously obscure northern lived realities and reproduce southern settler ideas and biases about homelessness.

Whitehorse provides an interesting case through which to approach, rethink, and reframe urban homelessness. It is the capital of Yukon Territory, as well as its administrative, economic, service, and transportation centre. Importantly, it is also the last Canadian city one reaches en route by road to Alaska. Through my time in the city, I came to recognize the innovative approaches that engaged Whitehorsians are taking to address homelessness "in context" – as a phenomenon symptomatic of larger social, historical, political, and economic connections and clefts. In Whitehorse, and across the circumpolar North, rural and urban spaces are linked in a symbiotic relationship: what happens in an urbanized northern centre directly and immediately affects the rural areas that are interdependent with it. This is one important trait that distinguishes northern rural-urban flows from southern counterparts: "ecology" as a metaphor serves a particularly apt descriptor when considering northern rural-urban synergy. Within Yukon, landmark land agreements have resulted in eleven of fourteen First Nations achieving self-governance.[12] These governments – alongside the federal gov-

---

10 For example, see Mark Gottdiener and Leslie Budd, *Key Concepts in Urban Studies* (Thousand Oaks, CA: SAGE Publications, 2005); George Gmelch, Robert Kemper, and Walter Zenner, *Urban Life: Readings in the Anthropology of the City* (Long Grove, IL: Waveland Press, 2010); Gülçin Erdi and Yıldırım Şentürk, eds., *Identity, Justice and Resistance in the Neoliberal City* (London: Palgrave Macmillan, 2017).

11 Jeannette Waegemakers Schiff, Rebecca Schiff, and Alina Turner, *Housing First in Rural Canada: Rural Homelessness & Housing First Feasibility across 22 Canadian Communities* (Calgary: University of Calgary, Faculty of Social Work, 2014), 7.

12 These are Vuntut Gwitchin First Nation (14 February 1995); Champagne and Aishihik First Nations (14 February 1995); First Nation of Na-Cho Nyäk Dun (14 February 1995); Teslin Tlingit Council (14 February 1995); Selkirk First Nation (1

ernment, the territorial government, and the municipal government of Whitehorse – form a complex ecosystem in which the interests, policies, and bureaucracies of fourteen separate governing bodies, not to mention an incredibly robust non-profit sector, influence and make decisions about everyday life in the territory. Whitehorse itself is nestled within the traditional territory of (and thus exists under the purview of) two of the eleven self-governing First Nations: Kwanlin Dün First Nation and Ta'an Kwäch'än Council. Approximately one-quarter of the population of Yukon identifies as First Nations, Métis, or Inuit.[13] Whitehorse is a large urban centre – the largest Canadian city north of the 60th parallel – but it also often overlooked or lumped into the homogenizing and totalizing category of "northern." This flattens out and obscures the realities of life in Whitehorse: realities that are categorically distinct, both from those in other northern hubs and from smaller Yukon population centres.

By drawing on statistical data, telling trends begin to emerge: as of late 2019, Yukon Territory was home to over 41,000 people, with around 33,000 in Whitehorse alone.[14] Relevant to discussions of housing, the population of Yukon has experienced significant growth in recent decades; in fact, the population has almost doubled since the 1970s. The 2016 census indicates that 84 per cent of the population growth from 2006 to 2016 was centralized in Whitehorse.[15] Dawson City – Yukon's second-largest city and the territory's capital prior to Whitehorse – with a population of 1,375, grew a mere 4 per cent over the same period, while Watson Lake, the third-largest centre, with 790 residents, *declined* by 7 per cent over the period.[16] It is thus a highly urbanized population and the most of the three northern territories. Whitehorse's rapid growth

October 1997); Little Salmon/Carmacks First Nation (1 October 1997); Tr'ondëk Hwëch'in (15 September 1998), Ta'an Kwäch'än Council (1 April 2002); Kluane First Nation (2 February 2004); Kwanlin Dün First Nation (1 April 2005); Carcross/ Tagish First Nation (9 January 2006). See Yukon First Nation Self-Government, "Our Agreements," *Mapping the Way*, 2 June 2016, https://mappingtheway.ca/our -agreements.

13 Yukon, Bureau of Statistics, *Aboriginal Peoples: Census 2016* (Whitehorse: Government of Yukon, 2016).
14 Yukon, Bureau of Statistics, *Population Report Fourth Quarter, 2019* (Whitehorse: Government of Yukon, 2019).
15 Anil Arora, "Yukon: Beautiful, Complex, and Changing," *Talking Stats: A Discussion Series with Statistics Canada*, 2 October 2018, https://www150.statcan.gc.ca/n1/pub /11-631-x/11-631-x2018006-eng.htm.
16 Ibid.

came immediately after a period of territorial out-migration.[17] Indeed, the history of the territory has involved similar wide fluctuations in population – largely of non-Yukoners and largely to the detriment of local First Nations. In a Yukon Status of Women Council investigation into women's homelessness, researchers Charlotte Hrenchuk and Judie Bopp explain:

> The history of the Yukon is one of boom and bust. The gold rush of 1896 brought the first white settlers. Cities were built and Dawson City boasted that it was the largest city north of Seattle. By the early 1900s, the rush was over leaving disease and a devastated landscape on what had been First Nation lands and beginning the process of colonization. Mineral and metal exploration continued on a reduced scale. The next rush of outsiders came with the building of the Alaska Highway. This changed the landscape and lives of Yukon First Nation forever. More "outsiders" came North bringing more exploration, trade, medicine and missionaries.[18]

The majority of Canada's existing housing stock was constructed during the ten-year period between 1971 and 1980; in Yukon, one-quarter of lived-in dwellings were constructed during this period.[19] As much of the territory's housing stock is aging, over 40 per cent of all Yukon dwellings require either minor or major repairs. This is compounded by the fact that one-quarter of renters in Yukon are deemed to be in "core housing need," meaning that their housing falls below standards of either "adequacy, affordability or suitability."[20]

Meanwhile, rural residents experience the simultaneous "push" of the erosion of local rural economies and infrastructure, and the "pull" of a rapidly gentrifying Whitehorse. This dynamic stems from federal increases in funding for resources, services, and development in urbanizing centres, while defunding rural hubs – a process described in the introduction to this volume, and elsewhere by Julia Christensen as "spatialized exclusion."[21] For many in rural communities, Whitehorse signifies access to vital services, connections, or resources: health care

---

17 Yukon, "Yukon Community Profiles" (Whitehorse: Government of Yukon, 2014), http://yukoncommunities.yk.ca/.
18 Charlotte Hrenchuk and Judie Bopp, *A Little Kindness Would Go a Long Way: A Study of Women's Homelessness in the Yukon* (Whitehorse: Yukon Status of Women Council, 2007), 20–1.
19 Yukon, Bureau of Statistics, *Aboriginal Peoples*.
20 Ibid.
21 Christensen, *No Home in a Homeland*, 143.

facilities, employment, housing, educational resources and other skills training, and often even the opportunity to be closer to social networks that have already relocated to the bigger urban hub. This reality is made more complex when factoring in the emotional layers that frame rural-urban (im)mobility. I think often of my family's relocation, even though the social and historical context for our leaving the city where I grew up was different than for many Yukoners. I still have a close affinity for my home city, and ties in the form of friends, family, and memories. I feel this connection strongly – enough to pull me back to a place my mom and I narrowly escaped. We had discussed leaving long before we actually did, but our choices were heavily constrained due to our lack of resources: movement is destabilizing, costly, and comes with a set of often unforeseeable risks. We would also have been leaving behind my aging grandmother and a city that we knew well enough to gingerly navigate its rough and jagged edges. The significance of these emotional factors *cannot* be overstated, especially in the complex con-nections to place felt in northern contexts. It was getting released from foster care for the second time, coupled with my grandma's death, that prompted our move – as well as the promise of a province with a more robust social safety net. The intersection of love, hope, fear, and pain that comes with home seeking and (im)mobility defies easy or straight-forward explanation. The roots one has to the place one is from extend beyond easily discernable economic and political pushes and pulls.

To borrow a term from Julia Christensen in *No Home in a Homeland*,[22] these data combine to reflect "uneven" rural and urban geographies in which leaving one's rural home community becomes the most viable – though certainly not the easiest – solution. Despite these demographic trends, not reflected at the census level are the individual cases and experiences of back-and-forth movement between territories, or urban-to-rural population shifts. As of 2017, 62.9 per cent of Yukon's popu-lation was born *outside* the territory in another province, territory, or country.[23] Interestingly, this figure is the highest in all of Canada: Yukon – more specifically, Whitehorse – has represented a place of "opportu-nity" for non-northerners since the territory's founding during the Gold Rush in the late 1800s.

Like the other territories, a significant portion of Yukon's revenue comes from federal transfers (over $1 billion annually). The pub-lic administration sector, comprised of all four levels of government,

---

22 Ibid., 41.
23 Arora, "Yukon."

employs approximately one-third of Yukoners, and the territory has the lowest unemployment rate in Canada. Yukon's economy is largely driven by the mining and tourism sectors, both of which are at the whim of seasonal and market-based fluctuations. Seasonal economic fluctuation generally has a significant impact on homelessness, but many of the people I interviewed for this research expressed specific concerns about the direct contribution of tourism to housing insecurity; since housing is scarce in the city, hotels and motels in Whitehorse that provide affordable housing during the winter kick tenants out during tourist season to accommodate the influx of higher-paying visitors.

For those seeking emergency shelter in Whitehorse, options are limited (see Chapters 1 and 2 in this volume for similar discussions in the context of Yellowknife). In early 2019, the Yukon government took control of the largest shelter in Whitehorse from the Salvation Army. The construction of the building was completed during my stay in Whitehorse in late 2017. The shelter, constantly in the news, had received myriad complaints about substandard care and programming under the Salvation Army, and is now operated as "low barrier" under principles of harm reduction. Simply put, this means that expectations placed on people seeking shelter are being removed or reduced.[24] For example, sobriety is no longer a requirement for accessing the facility; it is no longer possible to bar clients indefinitely from the shelter; the building is open 24/7; and there are no security guards in the building. The shelter also sought staff specially trained in de-escalation, as well as a social worker and an outreach worker.[25] In a backgrounder, the Yukon government announced plans to station a paramedic, a psychiatric nurse, and a mental health counsellor at the building, as well as implement culturally specific programming – importantly, client involvement was listed as a key priority, and a Guest Advisory Committee was implemented to advise and review future decisions and planning.[26]

Although the Whitehorse shelter is open to anyone seeking shelter, organizations exist in order to meet more specific needs of populations. For example, for women leaving violent domestic situations, the Women's Transition Home runs both an emergency shelter (Kaushee's Place)

---

24 Julien Gignac, "A new committee may keep tabs on the Whitehorse shelter," *Yukon News*, 8 February 2019, https://www.yukon-news.com/news/a-new-committee -may-keep-tabs-on-the-whitehorse-shelter/.
25 Ibid.
26 Yukon, "Changes at Whitehorse Emergency Shelter to Ensure Better Service," 28 October 2019, https://yukon.ca/en/news/changes-whitehorse-emergency-shelter -ensure-better-service.

and a "second stage" housing complex for longer-term stays (Betty's Haven).[27] Skookum Jim Friendship Centre runs a shelter open to young people between the ages of seventeen and twenty-three.[28] For a period in early 2017, Kwanlin Dün First Nation, the Yukon government, and the Yukon Anti-Poverty Coalition collaborated to create a temporary, low-barrier, ten-bed warming shelter. Although it has since closed, several interviewees indicated that this shelter offered the safest and most welcoming programming among the shelters they had either lived or worked in. The *Safe at Home* plan also describes this warming shelter as a vision for what is possible in responding efficiently and rapidly to community needs.[29]

The Research Approach

While conducting fieldwork, I was able to meet and interview individuals representing a diverse cross-section of "stakeholder" groups from all over Whitehorse. All of the interviews I conducted were with individuals who, in some way, worked in fields that intersect with housing policy or homelessness – such as gender equity, social assistance, social services, drug and alcohol services, or broader anti-poverty initiatives. Some of the participants were engaged in frontline work or service delivery, some worked for NGOs, others worked for First Nations governments. Roughly half the participants worked for the territorial government across a wide array of policy or service areas.

Throughout my work, I refer to the individuals who participated in this research broadly as "policymakers," although only a handful of them were engaged directly in the process of writing policy or had official policy-related positions. Most participants were involved primarily in advisory or advocacy work, which also often includes researching or revising policy and supporting its evaluation. I spent hours sitting around social service centres, chatting and drinking coffee with these individuals, engaging in conversations about the role of personal narratives in policy work. I was even able to take part in the beginning stages of both policy creation and revision while conducting my research. This work involved attending multiple community "town hall" policy consultations and brainstorming with the Yukon Anti-Poverty Coalition to

---

27 See the website of Women's Transition Home, https://www.womenstransitionhome
.ca, accessed October 2019.

28 Skookum Jim Friendship Centre, "Youth Emergency Shelter," https://skookumjim
.com/programs/youth-emergency-shelter/, accessed October 2019.

29 Yukon, Health and Social Services, *Safe at Home*, 5.

address social assistance policies in a letter to the Yukon Department of Health and Social Services. This process of "Deep Hanging-Out"[30] was instrumental in understanding how policy *works*, through observing and participating in peoples' quotidian lives and interactions.[31]

My experiences informed the way I approached my research and the way I frame these findings. Homelessness, to me, has always felt like being part of an ecology: a sticky web that ties together the movements and fluxes of people, policies, natural environments, histories, and socio-economic realities in an infinitely nuanced concert. Nothing in this ecology is inert, as every aspect has the capacity to influence every other aspect in manners both direct and indirect. Persistent and assiduous interconnectedness is, in fact, the most salient feature of the "ecology" metaphor. I came to visualize the complex reality of homelessness this way after my mother and I revolved through "visible" and "hidden"[32] forms of homelessness: couch surfing, motel hopping, living in shelters, sleeping on the floor of our unfurnished apartment, and even camping stiffly in the front seat of our cramped sedan.[33] An ecology of housing, homelessness, and intersecting social realities is wrought by the historical, environmental, economic, and political networks that enable and constrain life.

---

30 The term "Deep Hanging-Out" was established by James Clifford in 1988, and launched into somewhat more mainstream anthropological vocabulary in 1998 by Clifford Geertz. It refers to a specifically in-depth form of anthropological "Participant Observation" in which spending time building meaningful relationships with participants is, in itself, a core research method. See James Clifford, *The Predicament of Culture: Twentieth-Century Ethnography, Literature, and Art* (Cambridge: Harvard University Press, 1988).

31 Clifford Geertz, "Deep Hanging Out," *New York Review* 45, no. 16 (1998): 69.

32 Homelessness takes many forms, and is often described as existing on a "continuum": "visible" and "hidden" homelessness both fall along this continuum. "Visible" homelessness refers to people living in shelters, sleeping rough outdoors, or camping in other spaces deemed "unfit" for people to inhabit. "Hidden" homelessness refers to living situations that exist outside circumstances traditionally associated with homelessness; this could include staying in overcrowded conditions, temporarily living with friends and family, or couch surfing. Homelessness in northern Canada is often "hidden" due to a variety of factors (such as climate, camping by-laws, fear or a sense of risk felt accessing shelter space). Although these living situations can be experienced by anybody, "hidden" homelessness tends to fall along gendered dimensions; see Hrenchuk and Bopp, *Little Kindness Would Go a Long Way*.

33 It is important to note that hidden homelessness is *always* drastically undercounted by virtue of its invisibility. For a comprehensive study of gendered forms of homelessness (and hidden homelessness), see Kaitlin Schwan et al., *The State of Women's Housing Need & Homelessness in Canada: Literature Review*, ed. Arlene Hache et al. (Toronto: Canadian Observatory on Homelessness Press, 2020).

Through hours of chatting over cups of coffee, volunteering for initiatives and events across Whitehorse, and interacting with the many friends, colleagues, and community networks with which I connected during my research, I came to see the relevance of the "ecology" metaphor of homelessness to the Whitehorse context. Often, a narrative of homelessness is articulated in terms of one's "pathway" into or out of homelessness. In descriptions of "pathways into homelessness," broader forces and power dynamics are described insofar as they act on *individual* lives. Conceptualizing experiences of (and responses to) homelessness as part of a broader network of interwoven trends and events allows for a more robust understanding of how systems of power and oppression act on an individual, community, and societal scale. Moreover, embedded within the "ecology" metaphor is an implicit recognition of the connection between peoples, histories, and *place*; not only does it make space to understand "roots," as described by Kitty Smith at the start of this chapter, but so, too, does it allow for damaged or unsettled roots to be re-established.

Made in Yukon: Safe at Home and the Housing Action Plan

In the autumn of 2017, two documents were released that Yukon's housing advocates had long awaited. The first was Canada's new *National Housing Strategy* (NHS); the second was *Safe at Home: A Community-Based Action Plan to End and Prevent Homelessness in Whitehorse, Yukon*. The *Safe at Home* plan was an extension of the 2015 *Ours to Build On: Housing Action Plan for Yukon*, and both plans relied on funding and support stemming from the NHS. Although I do not expand significantly on the NHS in this chapter, it is important to highlight the strategy's explicit acknowledgement that homelessness and housing insecurity are reaching crisis levels, and can be addressed only through innovative and community-driven solutions. The NHS is also grounded in an extensive process of consultation, which is an ethic similarly upheld in *Safe at Home* and *Ours to Build On*. In Whitehorse, the *Safe at Home* stakeholders – including people with lived experience of homelessness – met regularly throughout the process of drafting the report, with each section deliberated on until consensus was achieved. The intensely collaborative process ensured that each person involved could "see themselves" throughout the plan's pages. Impetus for *Safe at Home* stemmed from the need both to address the city's growing population of people experiencing homelessness and for Whitehorse-specific housing solutions.

Safe at Home and *Ours to Build On* both centre the importance of "strengthening partnerships" between stakeholders. For *Safe at Home*, "strengthening partnerships" is highlighted by both the co-creation of the plan between Kwanlin Dün First Nation, the City of Whitehorse, Ta'an Kwäch'än Council, and the Yukon government, as well as the pride-of-place held by lived experts of homelessness. *Safe at Home* and *Ours to Build On* rely on "shared stakes," as emphasized by Clare Dannenberg (Chapter 9). Many lived experts who served as core members of the *Safe at Home* working group were graduates of the Voices Influencing Change (ViC) program. Started by the Yukon Anti-Poverty Coalition in 2017, ViC is a primary example of how lived experts in Whitehorse are supported to share their stories of surviving homelessness in order to have a positive effect on reducing poverty and homelessness in their community.[34] Meaningful collaboration with such lived experts is vital at all stages of policy and research creation, as lived experience offers a crucial lens for understanding and evaluating the causes and consequences of homelessness. In this volume, Sally Carraher and Travis Hedwig (Chapter 7) likewise articulate the importance of lived expertise in public discourse. In both *Safe at Home* and *Ours to Build On*, emphasis is also placed on knowledge sharing and extensive collaboration between the Yukon government and First Nations governments. The collaborative process employed here represents an important step towards community-wide involvement in addressing homelessness – a response called for throughout this volume.

Towards the beginning of my field research, I was fortunate enough to attend a *Ours to Build On* Implementation Committee meeting with representatives from NGOs, territorial, First Nations, and municipal governments, as well as local industry leaders. Interestingly, however, this was not exclusively a *housing* meeting – in other words, the web of what was to be considered a housing issue was exceptionally broad. At this meeting and in subsequent meetings with the same individuals, some of the key housing issues afflicting Whitehorse were considered: we discussed the fact that money directed from health into housing would benefit not only housing, but also health; we considered the impact of marijuana legalization on housing legislation; addictions and wraparound Housing First services; how housing professional employees in Yukon communities outside of Whitehorse was perceived by community members living in housing need; the profound need for in-community long-term care beds; sending permanent mental health care workers to communities; zoning and building restrictions; and future projects to meet Whitehorse's skyrocketing housing demands.

---

34 Yukon Anti-Poverty Coalition, "Voices Influencing Change," https://yapc.ca/actions /detail/voice-influencing-change, accessed June 2019.

Over the span of the relatively short meeting, I was fascinated by the fact that every person at the table was able to contribute something meaningful to the dynamic conversation. Issues were covered that appeared, at least on the surface, to relate only tangentially to housing, which spoke to the deliberate attention Whitehorse policymakers were paying to the densely interconnected web of experiences and networks that intersect with homelessness. Whitehorse, I was told, is investing considerable time and effort in addressing an "ecology of needs" for those living in housing insecurity or interacting in some way with the main territorial housing body – the Yukon Housing Corporation. This "ecology" lies in opposition to models traditionally used in providing care and services to those experiencing homelessness, which address peoples' needs in isolation from one another. *Safe at Home* also explicitly locates efforts to address homelessness within the *Truth and Reconciliation Commission*'s (TRC's) Calls to Action.[35] The *Safe at Home* report recognizes that the "work called for by the TRC is part of our shared future" – and efforts to end and prevent homelessness must meaningfully centre reconciliation, explicitly including redress for harms inflicted through brushing up against the engines of colonization.[36]

The main approach to ending homelessness that has gained popularity in recent years is known as "Housing First." In its most basic form, Housing First is the belief in and practice of providing immediate access housing to those experiencing homelessness who are most "at risk" of death, illness, or injury without access to shelter. At first glance, the key tenet of Housing First does appear to be progressive: housing *is* a human right, and being denied access to it is a violation of that right. Housing First as a discrete approach, however, has several drawbacks. It has, for example, been linked to higher rates of depression and suicide among those housed, as well as higher rates of overdose in those who inject drugs intravenously; isolation from communities, friends, and families also has a serious impact on overall health and well-being.[37] Further, evidence suggests that intake methods used to assess the vulnerability of people trying to access housing are not sufficiently sensitive to gendered and racialized forms of

35 Truth and Reconciliation Commission of Canada, *Calls to Action* (Winnipeg: 2015), http://nctr.ca/assets/reports/Calls_to_Action_English2.pdf.
36 Yukon, Health and Social Services, *Safe at Home*, 9.
37 Philippe Bourgois and Jeffrey Schonberg, *Righteous Dopefiend* (Berkeley: University of California Press, 2009).

vulnerability. This is incredibly significant, as Housing First programs that use tools which inaccurately assess structural forms of marginalization *reproduce and uphold* colonial, cis-heteropatriarchal oppression. This crude model of Housing First has been criticized by service providers, advocacy groups, survivors of homelessness, and academics for the way it approaches homelessness as existing in a vacuum, separate from other intersecting realities, a narrow focus that Travis Hedwig (Chapter 8) and Lisa Freeman and Julia Christensen (Chapter 1) also touch on in this volume. In Whitehorse, Housing First proponents met these very real criticisms with the "Housing First with Supports" model,[38] and deployed assessment tools that take layers of social oppression into account. In this way, services and support – as requested by the individual being housed – are provided in tandem with housing.[39]

The majority of the conversations I found myself a part of during my fieldwork revolved around Yukoners experiencing housing insecurity or homelessness. In Whitehorse, I heard this "ecology of needs" as faced by housing-insecure individuals variously called "Housing First with Supports," "Housing with Wraparound Services," and "Every Door Is the Right Door." All of these terms represent an effort to meet a Housing First mandate, while simultaneously meeting the complex and often multiple needs of individuals who need access to housing.

Similar to the approaches illustrated by Hedwig and Freeman and Christensen in this volume, the Housing First model used by Whitehorse has five key components: "immediate access to permanent housing with no housing readiness requirements, consumer choice and self-determination, recovery orientation, individualized and client-driven

---

38 Many critics of Housing First practices neglect to mention the gendered realities of support through its programs: "The 100,000 Homes Campaign in the United States, based on a Housing First model, serves as a cautionary tale. The program housed 105,000 people. It was deemed a resounding success but here's the problem: of the people housed, 80 per cent were men. No new affordable housing was built." See Tracy Heffernan, Mary Todorow, and Helen Luu, "Why Housing First Won't End Homelessness," *Rabble*, 7 July 2015, https://rabble.ca/blogs/bloggers/views -expressed/2015/07/why-housing-first-wont-end-homelessness.

39 Carey Doberstein and Alison Smith, "Housing First, but Affordable Housing Last: The Harper Government and Homelessness," in *The Harper Record: 2008–2015*, ed. Teresa Healy and Stuart Trew (Canadian Centre for Policy Alternatives, 2015), 265–78.

supports, and social and community integration."[40] Not only does this progressive Housing First model address individual agency and autonomy – something that has long gone ignored – but it also sees social and community ties as integral to the framework of tackling chronic homelessness.

During the same *Ours to Build On* implementation meeting mentioned above, a question was posed that I heard on several occasions throughout my time in Whitehorse: is Yukon a totally unique case, requiring totally unique political and social approaches, or are those in charge of making policy decisions "reinventing the wheel" by touting Yukon exceptionalism? As in any other province or territory, local political, historical, social, and economic realities make everyday life and politics look slightly different (while still operating under federal guiding legislations). Frank Tester (Chapter 6) similarly questions the ways in which contextually – and culturally embedded realities frame an understanding of what homelessness means in Inuit Nunangat. The NHS, recognizing the delicate balance that must be struck between federal templates and regionally appropriate and specific policymaking, dedicated $300 million out of the total $40 billion budget specifically to housing in northern Canada.[41] In Yukon, as *Ours to Build On* rolls out, an unprecedented number of housing projects are moving forward in communities across the territory – critically, within *and beyond* Whitehorse's urban expanse.

When I conducted my research in 2017, Yukoners were calling for housing solutions tailored to the territory's needs, a sentiment echoed in many of the chapters in this volume calling for approaches that address the unique conditions of northern life. Now, two years later, several governments (both territorial and First Nations) are in the process of constructing tiny homes and designing barrier-free supportive housing projects. Tiny homes represent a type of housing that is constructed quickly, at relatively low cost, and is easy to transport. As many of the policymakers I interviewed suggested, the most in-demand form of accommodation in Whitehorse is the ubiquitous one-bedroom unit. Tiny homes and other prefabricated, modular dwellings offer a northern-based solution to a specifically northern problem. Low-barrier or barrier-free housing is crucial

---

40 Housing Hub, "Housing First," http://homelesshub.ca/solutions/housing
-accommodation-and-supports/housing-first, accessed June 2018.
41 Randi Beers, "Federal housing strategy won't lead to more public housing units in
N.W.T," *CBC News*, 12 December 2018, https://www.cbc.ca/news/canada/north
/federal-housing-strategy-nwt-update-1.4941924.

to ensuring accessible accommodation exists for all Yukoners and that sobriety, income source, history of incarceration, lack of government-issued identification – often marks of interaction with a violent and colonial state apparatus – are not obstacles to obtaining shelter. Supportive housing offers resources and services as needed and requested by the person accessing housing. Such projects reflect both the particular historical, geographical, environmental, and social Yukon context, and the innovative approaches necessary to overcome housing-related obstacles. Importantly, the array of programs and opportunities being implemented across the territory's communities – with housing solutions that meet the needs of people accessing supportive housing, rental housing, *and* home ownership – mean that the pressure imposed by uneven rural-urban resource allocation is lessened.

Urban Landscapes: Problematizing the "Wilderness City"

"Not immediately appealing, Whitehorse rewards the curious," states the *Lonely Planet* guide to Whitehorse.[42] Contained in this description are some of the defining tropes informing desires for "Canada's North": it hints that travellers have to be tough, seasoned "explorers" to approach "the North," and those who do venture there are rewarded with some abstract notion of riches, treasure, or adventure virtually unknown to others. As feminist cultural geographers Annette Pritchard and Nigel Morgan explain, travel guides describe "Canada's North" as a "blank space" on the map – a space upon which a (largely white-settler and male) audience can write their own adventures.[43] Motifs of "wildness" and "adventure" harken back to Klondike times and the untold riches of the gold rush – à la Jack London. This imagined masculine, rugged, colonial landscape renders invisible the imagined social, private, and therefore feminine-coded realities of people living in the North – itself a constructed category.[44] Northern Canada is not constructed as a place

---

42 Lonely Planet, "Whitehorse in Detail: Planning," https://www.lonelyplanet.com /canada/whitehorse/planning/a/nar/dbe5adf8-faf5-4b4e-824b-911dc9dc39ca /361467.

43 Annette Pritchard and Nigel J. Morgan., "Privileging the Male Gaze: Gendered Tourism Landscapes," *Annals of Tourism Research* 27, no. 4 (2000): 884–905, https:// doi.org/10.1016/S0160-7383(99)00113-9.

44 The gendering of landscape is a useful and exceptionally relevant conceptual framework for discussing Whitehorse's popular appeal (and the North more broadly). For further reading, see Pritchard and Morgan, "Privileging the Male Gaze"; Jo Little, *Gender and Rural Geography: Identity, Sexuality, and Power in the*

in which people *live*; rather, "the North" as a conceptual category has become a landscape where a nebulous and somewhat abstract collective Canadian identity from elsewhere is written into existence – something in which I, as a researcher from southern Canada, am also complicit. Whitehorse's informal moniker is "The Wilderness City" – a deceptively simple title that demonstrates the two key aspects of the city's identity between which it must constantly oscillate: Whitehorse is at once an "urban centre" and a city that hawks itself to tourists with its stunningly "wild" vistas – neither facet being factually incorrect or unrealistic. The city centre butts up against the Yukon River on one side, and is cleaved on the other by scraggly, green cliffs. Driving into town at sunrise from the Alaska Highway, a rush of cars descends into the misty basin at the foot of the surrounding mountain range, illuminated in equal parts by the pinky-oranges of the cresting sun and the brake lights of the vehicles ahead. This juxtaposition of two tropes that could not be more at odds results in an interesting tension: "the wild" is everything "the city" is not, but somehow both exist together in Whitehorse as a harmonious crossing, or as if "the wild" has swallowed "the city" whole – even though, as *Whitehorse News* reporter Keith Halliday articulates:

> If you look at Google Earth's nifty time-lapse satellite imagery from 1984 to today, you see the city steadily expanding, eating away at the green on the screen. It's like a strangely unstoppable alien blob, relentlessly blotting out the hapless spruce trees in its path ... Areas such as Marwell, McCrae and the airport business zone all show steady infill and expansion. New access roads creep into the forest like tendrils. Zooming in on downtown reveals lots of new construction, particularly at the north end around Shipyards Park and the condos behind Boston Pizza. The dump oozes outwards as forest disappears. Even the residents of the cemetery needed more space.[45]

Many Whitehorsians describe the urbanization, development, and expansion of Whitehorse – in a reality voiced by Halliday and echoed by folks who participated in my research – referencing new developments, housing projects, and infrastructure. The romantic southern

---

Countryside (Upper Saddle River, NJ: Prentice Hall, 2002); and Doreen Massey, *Space, Place, and Gender* (Minneapolis, University of Minnesota Press, 1994).

45 Keith Halliday, "Whitehorse time machine: Yukon's capital added 10,000 people over the last three decades, no YESAB application needed," *Yukon News*, 18 January 2018, https://www.yukon-news.com/opinion/whitehorse-time-machine/.

ideal of "the North" leaves no room for the runoff, the dust, or the detritus of cities, the unavoidable consequences of the presence of human bodies and complexities. The romantic images of northern Canada originate "from somewhere" – existing in a spatial and temporal state that is "radically historically specific."[46] In this context, the notion of "northern" as a bounded and discrete conceptual category must do a great deal of work to retain its structure, while "urban" and "rural" do not face the same pressures. Nature – and, by extension, "the wild" – exists only at the firmly restricted edge of "the urban."

Heightened pressures to fit contradictory southern expectations do not end at the *concept* of "the North" – these ruptures and intensities have implications (policy and otherwise) across the territorial and provincial "Norths." For example, researcher Michel Beaulieu explains that "[s]tate policies towards the northwest [of Ontario] have not only reinforced a hinterland-metropolis relationship ... and a sense of alienation; they have also been adversarial, and steeped in attitudes of colonialism that regional concerns are secondary."[47] One interviewee chuckled as he related to me the almost allegorical history of Dawson City architecture. sharing his bitter amusement about the impact of melting permafrost on the foundations of Dawson's buildings – many of which are now slanted due to the newly malleable ground on which they sit. The interviewee likened this to other instances of southern practices and approaches downloaded onto northern locales – with disastrous results. Beaulieu outlines similar instances in regard to northern Ontario policymaking: "When policy [moved] beyond resource extraction ... systems were imposed ... that might have worked for southern Ontario but [were] wholly unsuited for the north."[48] Kenneth Coates, geographer, northern historian, and himself a Yukoner, suggests the following in regard to southern Canadians' awareness of northern spaces and peoples: "A few hardy promoter-adventurers like Vilhjalmur Stefansson and Farley Mowat have been drawn to the northern environment, and, upon returning south, have popularized their visions of the region. Such visionaries, more romantics than pragmatists, remain propagators

---

46 Donna Haraway, "The Biopolitics of Postmodern Bodies: Constitutions of Self in Immune System Discourse," in *Simians, Cyborgs, and Women: The Reinvention of Nature* (London: Free Association Books, 1991), 208.
47 Michel S. Beaulieu, "A Historic Overview of Policies Affecting Non-Aboriginal Development in Northwestern Ontario, 1900–1990," in *Governance in Northern Ontario: Economic Development and Policy Making*, ed. Charles Conteh and Bob Segsworth (Toronto: University of Toronto Press, 2013), 94.
48 Ibid., 96.

of an ideal that Canadians pay homage to, then consciously reject."[49] Beaulieu and Coates both describe instances where the power dynamics present in the very real categories of North-South, and urban-rural come crashing together – although these realities are often defined by a southern-centred audience. Coates, quoting the late British Columbia premier Edward Prior, notes that "'Victoria is 3,000 miles from Ottawa whereas Ottawa is 30,000 miles from Victoria.' This attitude applies equally today in the Canadian North."[50]

After returning from fieldwork, I engaged in some online research on a database that collects and makes available resources, research, and information regarding homelessness in Canada. In one recent post, a researcher was giving his responses to questions submitted on the database's question form. I immediately recognized someone whose question was being answered as one of the people who participated in this research. The question he had posed, however, surprised me: he asked, "Is there any qualitative research available on homelessness in Yukon?" The reason I was taken aback by this question was that he, alongside his hardworking colleagues, had produced a great deal of excellent qualitative research (*and* quantitative research) on homelessness in the territory. Although I can never be certain of the motivation behind this question, it seems to me that reflected in this query was the internalization of the narrative that has been sold regarding "the North" – where validation comes from southern Canadian recognition or contributions. This tension was reflected in many conversations I was a part of in Whitehorse. Although there are many progressive and thoughtful approaches not just to homelessness, but also to policymaking in general taking shape in Whitehorse today, these approaches go almost completely unacknowledged in southern discourse.

There is something disquieting about the way the North is cast as something monolithic, foreign, and, most troubling of all, "remote." In a 2016 article entitled "The Trouble with Remoteness," Roger Epp explores this phenomenon in the context of reporting on school shootings in La Loche (northern Saskatchewan) and youth suicides in Attawapiskat (northern Ontario). Epp argues that casting a locale as "remote" – to describe *physical* distance between *places* – becomes a way to describe social distance between people. Epp goes on to argue that alongside the label of "remote" comes "dangerous" and "uninhabitable," and these

---

49 Kenneth Coates, *Canada's Colonies: A History of the Yukon and Northwest Territories* (Toronto: James Lorimer, 1985), 12.
50 Ibid., 237.

places become zones where it is unthinkable to raise a child or where residents are seen as victims – worse yet, victims who deserve what happens to them in times of crisis or need.[51] In the article, Epp describes the treatment of two towns by urban, southern Canadian reporters: "In each case, the spotlight was brief, and the solutions seemingly as elusive as the situations were urgent. Communities with complex histories and power structures were introduced by single adjectives: 'isolated' or, more often, 'remote.' As if those words explained almost everything. The pathological treatments of remoteness quickly followed."[52] Epp follows this by explaining, "remoteness can be experienced as isolation, even as a trap; but it can also be a preference – a home."[53] Spaces thought of as being remote or "blank" are certainly not so for people who live there – one's home is the centre of the world, though not every person has the power to define it as such. I realize that Whitehorse (and Yukon Territory, more broadly) is not a place that everybody "knows." I am regularly met with quizzical or puzzled responses when I say that my research is on homelessness, housing policy, and gender in *Whitehorse*. On several occasions, since returning to southern Ontario from fieldwork, I have been asked to explain how someone could be homeless in the North: "it's so cold there," people remark with incredulity, "why don't they [the homeless] leave?" or "how does homelessness *work* up there"? Underlying these questions is an implicit accusation, and the same argument posed by Roger Epp. People who know what urban, southern Canadian homelessness looks like have a hard time reconciling that image with their notions of the North.

Addressing Homelessness through Reconnection

The ways in which "urban" and "rural" spaces and identities are constructed takes on a particular significance in the context of northern Canada. An aspect inherent to "the urban" is that it is seen as the de facto space in which policy and key governing decisions are made. In Canada and beyond, this favouring of urban space is the result of longstanding "pro-urban mythologies" that privilege cities as "the seat of culture, learning, government and civil order."[54] These mythologies

---

51 Roger Epp, "The Trouble with Remoteness," *Northern Public Affairs*, 29 June 2016, http://www.northernpublicaffairs.ca/index/the-trouble-with-remoteness/.
52 Ibid.
53 Ibid.
54 Lewis Holloway and Phil Hubbard, *People and Place: The Extraordinary Geographies of Everyday Life* (London: Routledge, 2001).

are spurred by hegemonic social, economic, colonial, and political phi-
losophies, and lie at the heart of the movement towards urban densi-
fication. In *No Home in a Homeland*, Christensen discusses the complex
realities of Indigenous peoples who are experiencing homelessness
in the Northwest Territories.[55] Although the effect of decades of rural
exodus is present across the North American landscape, nowhere is it
felt more intensely than in northern Canada, where "rural settlements
[have been rendered] spaces of inopportunity."[56] Unlike rural spaces
elsewhere, however, urbanization in northern Canada has dovetailed
with the uprooting, displacement, and dispossession of Indigenous
communities from traditional homelands. Issues of "uneven" opportunity and a rural-urban divide intersect sharply with legacies of settler-
colonial oppression.

Considering these factors, the following question still remains: how
does one presume to make a study, based in a northern urban centre, generalizable to other regions and communities? I argue that the
ways in which images and notions of the North are constructed keep
a southern Canadian audience largely unaware of the applicability of
a case study that takes place in a northern urban centre – especially
one deemed "remote." Roger Epp elaborates on this notion: "[The
word remote is sometimes] invoked either in place of, or together with,
other words like reserve or First Nations or Indigenous. As a substitute,
remote sometimes serves as polite, non-racialized code for ideas too
raw for public discourse. Better to talk about *remote* communities. *We
know what that means.*"[57]

Further, migration from "remote" places is often framed as an escape
from rural spaces to "the city." Much like cities in the South, northern
cities experience population inflows *and* outflows: people from small
communities outside Whitehorse move back and forth from their home
communities regularly. Epp tersely describes this framing by southern
audiences: "[F]rom this perspective, living in a remote community is
not only proof of an unwillingness to confront root problems; it is the
root problem. Short of out-migration, there can be no brighter future."[58]
On urban migration, Christensen notes, "remoteness, ... although
manifest in the distance between communities, is also a social construct given that physical distances are reinforced by social policy that

---

55 Christensen, *No Home in a Homeland*.
56 Ibid., 161.
57 Epp, *Trouble with Remoteness*.
58 Ibid., par. 6.

emphasizes urban life and locale."[59] In regard to Indigenous homelessness, Christensen mobilizes the concept of 'uneven geographies' to lay bare the "layers of social, economic, and infrastructural unevenness that shape northern geographies of homelessness."[60] Although the ethnographic context Christensen describes is that of the Northwest Territories, the primary driving forces and structural tensions undergirding experiences of homelessness that she outlines are paralleled in Yukon: "Although rural-urban migration is an experience across Canada, in the Northwest Territories it is intensified by the recent history of government-created programs of centralization and northern settlement, making northern rural settlements places of inopportunity ... Rural northern settlement communities emerged through the colonial process as places of inadequate housing and economic disadvantage, detached from mainstream socio-economic opportunities."[61]

This political, social, and economic "unevenness" is faced by Indigenous peoples across Canada. I was fortunate to meet Jesse Thistle in October 2017, and to hear him speak about the new Definition of Indigenous Homelessness in Canada.[62] As mentioned in the introduction to this chapter, Thistle's definition fills in some of the context neglected by other studies on Canadian homelessness. In the definition, he discusses the profound and ongoing impact that colonization and the subsequent displacement from land, community, and culture have had on Indigenous peoples. Directly confronting systems, structures, and institutions that interact to create homelessness is not as common an approach as it ought to be. Although common understandings of homelessness have shifted significantly since the 1980s and 1990s neoliberal victim-blaming pattern – which locates the cause of homelessness squarely in individual pathology – I still find subtle shades of these judgments in contemporary policy literature or technical writing on homelessness. For instance, profiles or portraits of people experiencing homelessness that often appear in reports or documents are framed as though pure tragedy is inseparable from those experiences or identities: being a struggling single mother, a veteran, a child coming out of foster care, experiencing mental health issues, or surviving childhood sexual assault appear as explanatory devices for one's homelessness – all of these descriptors are intended to provide metonymic evidence of one's "pathway" to homelessness. An array of "isms" escapes unobserved:

---

59 Christensen, *No Home in a Homeland*, 42.
60 Ibid., 42.
61 Ibid., 161.
62 Thistle, *Definition of Indigenous Homelessness in Canada*.

colonialism, racism, cis-heterosexism, ableism, ageism, neoliberalism, paternalism. These institutions appear less often as paving stones on the "pathway" than corresponding individual identity markers. It is much "simpler," for example, to provide trauma therapy to a former foster child than to fix a flawed system that results in millions of apprehended children in the nebulous space of child welfare and the fractured families it leaves in its wake.

As a final illustrative example, in Whitehorse, a program (loosely) working in tandem with policy has seen initial success. Landlords Working to End Homelessness (LWEH) provides information and support to private market landlords who house clients relying on income assistance for payment of rent. LWEH brings together housing navigators and support from a wide array of community organizations serving populations at risk of homelessness or experiencing homelessness. LWEH works as an assurance for both renters and landlords, acting as a third-party mediator subletting rooms, apartments, or houses to social assistance clients. Homelessness, as it is universally understood, exists as a result of multiple systems breaking down in chorus: LWEH is a stopgap measure that arose in response to some of these failures. Where affordable and supportive housing for "vulnerable" and "at-risk" individuals does not currently exist, Whitehorse advocates have found a solution that meets the needs of their community – relying on the participation of private market property owners. Sometimes, as one policymaker explained to me, the role of the LWEH housing navigator is to act as a sort of translator, speaking across the gulf posed by the power imbalance between landlords and those experiencing housing insecurity.

All of the policymakers I interviewed during my research cited to some degree the complexity of ending homelessness in Whitehorse. What I did not anticipate was the overwhelming emphasis (and hope) interviewees placed on *collaborative* efforts to address homelessness. Poignantly, one young policymaker told me, "it's kind of like 'it takes a village to raise a child.' It's going to take our whole entire community to heal these broken ties." This same sentiment was expressed time and again in Freeman and Christensen's research with support providers and advocates in Yellowknife (see Chapter 1). There, too, collaboration and interagency coordination are seen as key to addressing homelessness, but they require significant support and additional funding to ensure sustainability. Together, our chapters illustrate that the route to integrating and injecting living, breathing narratives of lived experience – both of homelessness and support provision – into the domain of policy might lie in having policies align more closely with programs or organizations that can bring people together in a collaborative manner.

Conclusion

The specific texture of homelessness depends partially on a given local context and the corresponding social landscape. It is difficult to frame these complex historical, political, and economic dynamics effectively in brief policy documents, but both *Safe at Home* and *Ours to Build On* refer to and make room for the specific housing realities northerners face. Both plans represent two pieces of a continuum, taking steps to address the flow of people between Yukon communities that arises from geographies of "unevenness." The push of rural northern economic inopportunity and the pull of Whitehorse's economic, infrastructural, and social resources shape the landscape of Yukoners' in-territory movement. The taxonomy of Whitehorse as a "Wilderness City" – as a veritable playground for the southern Canadian adventurous imaginary – serves both to both mask and reinforce the social, economic, and political innovation taking place there. Homelessness-reduction plans and methods in Whitehorse approach homelessness in a manner that sufficiently recognizes and responds to this complexity. *Safe at Home*, *Ours to Build On*, Landlords Working to End Homelessness, and *Voices Influencing Change* are some of the primary instances that mark Whitehorse as an exemplar for promising practices in reducing and preventing homelessness. The reasons these approaches are particularly progressive are threefold: first, these efforts centre the voices of those who have experienced homelessness and who understand first-hand the complex ways that systems and structures operate on those who are most marginal; second, they centre reconciliation and government-to-government relationships with self-governing First Nations; and third, they reflect the long and storied history of Whitehorse, the dynamic lived realities of its residents, and the fluid, flexible, and locally contingent approaches to policymaking that can be fostered there.

To revisit the words of Elder Kitty Smith from the beginning of this chapter – in the context of homelessness – the "roots" integral to many Yukoners' sense of self and connection to place have been damaged and must be restored. Indigenous homelessness, in particular, is exacerbated by intentionally fractured ties – to homelands, to natural environments, to familial bonds, and to language – which must be rehabilitated in the process of addressing homelessness. Homelessness across northern social landscapes exists as the direct result of long and jagged histories of settler colonization: the two are intimately linked. In Whitehorse – and across the urban North, as evidenced by the other chapters in this volume – efforts to tackle homelessness begin from the premise that the issue is the result of interconnected phenomena that are difficult to parse out. Throughout this chapter, I have referred to homelessness through the metaphor of "ecology" –in terms of both experiences of homelessness and approaches to addressing it. Even now, as an adult living thousands of kilometres away from the locus of my memories of homelessness, I am still caught off guard by the way this past echoes in my more stable present. The web I was tangled in has left its traces; histories, especially violent ones, endure. In this meshwork, even time ceases to be linear. This is why I found the particular metaphor of ecology to resonate throughout my fieldwork in Whitehorse. The interwoven and interdependent nature of ecologies offers a foundation on which to begin unpacking and contextualizing homelessness in that city.

Whitehorse offers an ideal locus for a case study on engaged responses to homelessness within the broader framework of northern urban policymaking. The method applied by Whitehorse advocates, activists, and policymakers in confronting homelessness is not only innovative, but lends itself to conversations surrounding homelessness at the national and international levels. This nuanced approach highlights the ways in which homelessness is rooted simultaneously in local and systems-level factors; it also teases out the often-obscured links and pathways between homelessness and myriad other interconnected phenomena – colonization, cis-heterosexism, ableism, child welfare, incarceration, environmental degradation, and mental and physical illness, to offer just a handful of examples. The particular case posed by the "Wilderness City" is highly applicable to efforts to reduce and understand homelessness across and beyond the circumpolar North.

4 Homelessness, Mobility, and Migration from the James Bay Region

CAROL KAUPPI, MICHAEL HANKARD, AND HENRI PALLARD

Shelter is a basic human need. Housing shortages and homelessness affect northern communities in Canada, and research shown a strong link between homelessness or poor housing and health outcomes.[1] The Ontario Medical Association has made a compelling statement recognizing housing as a key social determinant of health.[2] Researchers from St. Michael's Hospital in Toronto have reported that health problems experienced by vulnerably housed individuals and homeless individuals are the same: "the division between these two groups is false ... Instead of two distinct groups, this is one large, severely disadvantaged group that transitions between the two housing states [vulnerable housing and homelessness]."[3]

Respiratory illness, sleep deprivation, and depression are some of the health problems linked to overcrowding in homes. The experiences of housing hardship and homelessness are not benign. Yet housing circumstances are precarious for many people in subarctic regions, notably those who are Indigenous. Indeed, according to James Anaya, UN Special Rapporteur on the Rights of Indigenous Peoples,[4] the housing circumstances of Inuit and First Nations communities in Canada

1 James Krieger and Donna Higgins, "Housing and Health: Time Again for Public Health Action," *American Journal of Public Health* 92, no. 5 (2002): 758–68, https://doi/org/ 10.2105/ajph.92.5.758.

2 Kathryn MacKay and John Wellner, "Housing and health: OMA calls for urgent government action, housing-supportive policies to improve health outcomes of vulnerable populations," *Ontario Medical Review* (July/August 2013).

3 Emily Holton, Evie Gogosis, and Stephen Hwang, *Housing Vulnerability and Health: Canada's Hidden Emergency* (Toronto: Research Alliance for Canadian Homelessness, Housing, and Health, 2013), 2.

4 James Anaya, "Statement upon Conclusion of the Visit to Canada" (United Nations Special Rapporteur on the Rights of Indigenous People, October 2013).

constitute a crisis, noting that their housing situation contributes to a wide range of physical and mental health challenges. The overrepresentation of Indigenous people in homeless populations reflects the failure of government policies to address the underlying causes of problems such as core housing need, homelessness, limited employment opportunities, and poor access to services.

This chapter explores subarctic living conditions, migration, housing hardship, and homelessness. It is based on research from our six-year study dealing with poverty, homelessness, and migration in northern communities in Canada, including remote, fly-in coastal communities of the James Bay region.[5] Somewhat surprising was our finding that, too often, Indigenous people who migrated from their communities to towns and cities of the near North, when seeking solutions to social, health, and housing issues, found themselves living in similar circumstances to those they had left behind. A project combining photographs of housing conditions with interviews documents a phenomenon in which Indigenous people encountered racism, marginalization, social exclusion, and poor housing in urban centres – conditions replicating histories of colonialism in the North.[6] Based on this prior research and the published literature on housing shortages, homelessness, and migration, consideration of migration in relation to subarctic living conditions can inform practice and lead to a better understanding of the housing and infrastructure needs in the North.

Migrants are often the most disadvantaged people in the homeless population, and Indigenous people are greatly overrepresented among homeless migrants.[7] Confronting and dealing with homelessness and migration in northern Indigenous communities requires an understanding of interconnected social, economic, political, environmental, and historical processes.

---

5 Henri Pallard, Carol Kauppi, and Jessica Hein, "Photovoice and Homelessness in Subarctic and Urban Communities," *International Journal of Social, Political and Community Agendas in the Arts* 10, no. 1 (2015): 25–41, https://doi.org/10.18848/2326-9960/CGP/v10i01/36408.

6 Jessica Hein and Carol Kauppi, "Living on the Outside: A Photo Exhibit Using Art in the Struggle for Social Justice," *International Journal of Social, Political and Community Agendas in the Arts* 8, no. 304 (2014): 31–41, https://doi.org/10.18848/2326-9960/CGP/v08i3-4/36404.

7 Carol Kauppi and Henri Pallard, "Migratory and Transient Homelessness in Northern Ontario, Canada Pathways to Homelessness in Sudbury and Its Related Impacts," *OIDA International Journal of Sustainable Development* 8, no. 4 (2015): 67–98, https://ssrn.com/abstract=2612100.

Indigenous leaders have emphasized the need to address the pressing social and economic issues of First Nations communities in the western James Bay region, warning that failure to do so might increase the risk that significant numbers of Indigenous people will face unemployment poverty and homelessness.[8] The severe problem of substandard housing in First Nations communities has been identified through research[9] and media reports. Media coverage has described flood-related incidents that have exacerbated already poor conditions in the James Bay communities of Kashechewan and Attawapiskat.[10] Similar problems of substandard housing and overcrowding exist in other James Bay communities, but they receive less attention from the media.[11]

Northern Communities

Definitions of the North have shifted over time, but central concepts involve wilderness, hinterland, and relative isolation[12] as well as lifestyles and values.[13] James Bay is the southern extension of Hudson Bay, the inland sea that is part of the Arctic Ocean, and the lowlands are influenced by weather patterns and prevailing winds that bring Arctic temperatures to this region (see figure 4.1).

---

8 Josh Brandon and Evelyn Peters, "Moving to the City: Housing and Aboriginal Migration to Winnipeg," in *Poor Housing: A Silent Crisis*, ed. Josh Brandon and Jim Silver (Winnipeg: Fernwood Publishing and Canadian Centre for Policy Alternatives, 2015), 81–92.

9 Dennis Patterson and Lillian Dyck, *Housing on First Nation Reserves: Challenges and Successes* (Ottawa: Standing Senate Committee on Aboriginal Peoples, February 2015).

10 Brian Beaton, "Family of 11 homeless after fire destroys house: Community unable to house them," *Kuhkenah Network*, 18 October 2008, http://media.knet .ca/node/5521; "Kashechewan evacuees heading home," *CBC News*, 17 May 2018, https://www.cbc.ca/news/canada/sudbury/kash-residents-returning -home-1.4666924; J. Hunter, "Kashechewan mourns its own," *Wawatay News Online*, 6 January 2006; Josh Wingrove, "Poor weather hampers James Bay flood rescue," *Toronto Star*, 26 April 2008, https://www.thestar.com/news/ontario/2008/04/26 /poor_weather_hampers_james_bay_flood_rescue.html.

11 James Thom, "Massive sewage backup damages 8 Attawapiskat homes," *Wawatay News Online*, 30 July 2009, https://nationtalk.ca/story/massive-sewage-backup -damages-8-attawapiskat-homes-wawatay-news.

12 Glen G. Schmidt, "Remote, Northern Communities: Implications for Social Work Practice," *International Social Work* 43, no. 3 (2000): 337–49, https://doi.org/10.1177 /002087280004300306.

13 Roger Pitblado, "So, What Do We Mean by 'Rural,' 'Remote,' and 'Northern'?" *Canadian Journal of Nursing Research* 37, no. 1 (2005): 163–8.

Figure 4.1. Map of the Hudson Bay and James Bay Lowlands

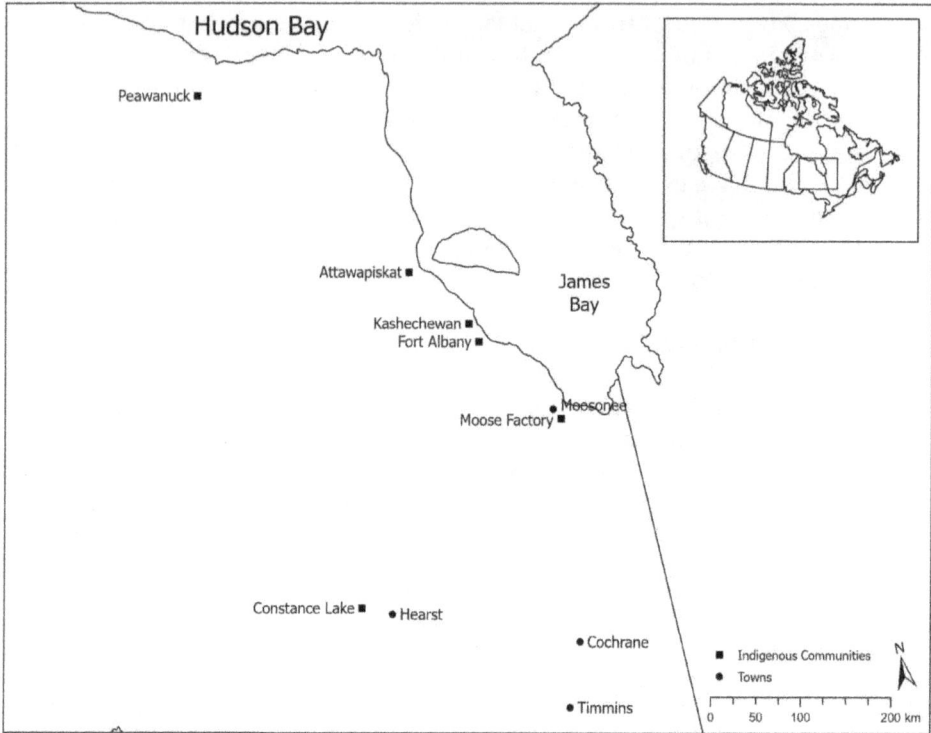

Our project studying migration, homelessness, and northern housing need looked at four northeastern Ontario towns: Timmins, Cochrane, Hearst, and Moosonee. It also included Indigenous people from several communities in the western James Bay region: Peawanuck, Attawapiskat, Kashechewan, Fort Albany, Constance Lake, and Moose Factory. Falling within the boreal forest region, they are considered northern communities as defined by Bone. The study also included the near-northern cities of Sudbury and North Bay in order to understand issues surrounding poverty and migratory homelessness for people who leave northern communities and migrate to cities in the near-North. The communities to the north and northeast of Timmins are single-industry towns, with economies based on natural resources. Mining and forestry are the primary sources of employment.

Approximately 90 per cent of the residents of Moosonee, on the southern tip of James Bay, are Indigenous. The northern Cree and Oji-Cree First Nation of Constance Lake is situated within the traditional territories of the Omushkegowak Cree peoples of the James Bay lowlands and is connected to James Bay by major river systems that are used for hunting and fishing activities. The western James Bay First Nations of Attawapiskat, Kashechewan, and Fort Albany are fly-in communities, while Moosonee and Moose Cree are accessible only via rail or air, except for short periods from January to March when winter roads are open. With no year-round road access, these communities are remote and isolated. They are classified by the Canada Revenue Agency as being within the Northern Tax Zone A,[14] a designation determined on the basis of four indicators of hardship and isolation: population, distance from an urban centre, climate, and vegetation.[15] The cost of living in these isolated northern communities is higher than in communities farther south: western James Bay communities have a cost-of-living index of 115 or more, which reflects the high price of food, clothing, and household operations due to their relative inaccessibility and high transportation costs associated with shipping goods from major urban centres through ice roads, rail, or air.[16] Employment in Northern Tax Zone A is concentrated in mining, forestry, energy development projects, administrative units, military installations, and tourism. The economy in these sectors tends to be seasonal or cyclical in nature.[17]

Research can help to understand how the conditions of life in northern communities are related to core housing need, homelessness, and the decision to move away. Several challenges for people in these communities are evident, including the limited availability of housing,

---

14 Canada Revenue Agency, "Line 255 – Do you qualify for the northern residents deductions?" (Ottawa, 2009), http://www.cra-arc.gc.ca/tx/ndvdls/tpcs/ncm-tx /rtrn/cmpltng/ddctns/lns248-260/255/qlfy-eng.html, accessed 11 August 2009; Canada Revenue Agency, "Line 255 Zone A – Prescribed northern zones" (Ottawa, 2009), http://www.cra-arc.gc.ca/tx/ndvdls/tpcs/ncm-tx/rtrn/cmpltng/ddctns /lns248-260/255/zn-eng.html#onA, accessed 11 August 2009.

15 Chuck McNiven and Henry Puderer, "Delineation of Canada's North: An Examination of the North-South Relationship in Canada," Geography Working Paper Series (Ottawa: Statistics Canada, 2000), https://www150.statcan.gc.ca/n1 /en/catalogue/92F0138M2000003.

16 Treasury Board of Canada Secretariat, *Isolated Posts and Government Housing Directive: Appendix H Criteria for Determining Levels 2* (Ottawa: National Joint Council, 2009), https://www.njc-cnm.gc.ca/directive/d4/v237/s631/en#s631-tc-tm.

17 Marc-André Pigeon, *Federal Northern Residents Deductions* (Ottawa: Parliamentary Information and Research Service, Economics Division, 2004).

transportation, and services, as well as cultural differences between rural and remote communities and urban centres of the near-North and South.

Colonization in James Bay Communities

In Canada, Indigenous peoples have been subject to a century and a half of concerted state effort of civilization and assimilation – a period in Indigenous history marked, in 1857, by the passage of the Act for the Gradual Civilization of Indians. Its stated goal was to transform Indigenous peoples into Europeans, to replace Indigenous languages with English, to replace Indigenous family structures with European family structures, to change the nature of Indigenous economic life, to replace Indigenous knowledges with European knowledges, and to replace Indigenous spiritualities with Christian ones. The damaging effects of this long assault upon economic lives, education, families, culture, language, and spirituality have been thoroughly documented over the past half-century.[18] First Nations people of the James Bay region have been greatly affected by adverse experiences linked to colonialism and residential schools.

Europeans began to explore Hudson Bay and James Bay early in the seventeenth century, leading to extensive trading relationships with the Omushkegowak Cree by the late 1700s.[19] The effects of colonization, religious conversion by Christian missionaries, residential schooling, the legacy of broken treaties, and the establishment of reserves are well known.[20] The First Nations on the western coast of James Bay were created early in the 1900s with the signing of Treaty 9. Attawapiskat, Fort Albany, and Moose Cree were established on the coast, despite the concerns of the Cree people that the locations were unsuitable for permanent villages. These sites had been summer meeting places, and Cree people had always moved inland during the winter and spring to access traditional hunting grounds.

---

18 David Newhouse and Yale Belanger, "The Canada Problem in Aboriginal Politics," in *Visions of the Heart: Canadian Aboriginal Issues*, ed. David Long and Olive Patricia Dickason (Toronto: Oxford University Press, 2011), 352–80.

19 Louis Bird, *Omushkego Legends and Histories from Hudson Bay* (Toronto: University of Toronto Press, 2005).

20 Barbara Waterfall, "Native People and the Social Work Profession: A Critical Analysis of Colonizing Problematics and the Development of Decolonized Thought," in *Canadian Social Policy*, ed. Anne Westhues (Waterloo, ON: Wilfrid Laurier Press, 2003): 50–66.

The encroachment of Catholic and Protestant religious orders into Cree communities created divisions that persist into the present. In Fort Albany First Nation, the conversion of people to Catholicism and Protestantism split the community, resulted in the movement of a substantial number of people from Fort Albany to the opposite side of the Albany River, and led to the creation of Kashechewan First Nation on part of the lands set aside in Treaty 9 for Fort Albany. The notorious residential school in Fort Albany, St. Anne's, had a powerful impact on the experiences of children and families in the area, and contributed to cultural genocide perpetrated through assimilationist policies.

Kashechewan: From Bad to Worse

The federal government established Kashechewan First Nation on the flood plain of the Albany River, despite protests that this decision was problematic,[21] as the location results in seasonal flooding of the community. The Albany River is one of Canada's largest rivers, producing ice jams that frequently lead to extreme flood events. Residents of Kashechewan and Fort Albany report that spring breakup is often a terrifying event characterized by thundering, booming sounds and huge chunks of ice being ejected onto the river banks. The government's response to the flood problem was to build a ring dike that completely surrounds Kashechewan in 1997. The dike is 5.3 kilometres long and three metres high.[22] The community remains susceptible to flooding, however, and its location in a "bowl" prevents viewing of the area's scenic landscape.

Construction on flood plains is problematic in many locations where it has been undertaken in Canada. It also consumes a disproportionate segment of total federal disaster relief funding. Construction on flood-prone sites is widespread in Canada – roughly 75 per cent of federal funding allocated for total disaster relief (which includes natural and artificial disasters) is spent on rebuilding after floods.[23] Flooding is

---

21 Lauren La Rose, "Kashechewan a 'community in crisis,'" *Toronto Star*, 7 February 2007, https://www.thestar.com/news/2007/02/07/kashechewan_a_community_in_crisis.html.

22 "Kashechewan First Nation Community Profile," *Wakenagun Community Futures Development Corporation*, 1999, http://www.wakenagun.ca/ PDF/Kashechewan%20 Profile.pdf.

23 Julie Ireton, "Experts urge caution before rebuilding on floodplain," *CBC News*, 14 May 2017, https://www.cbc.ca/news/canada/ottawa/floodplain-engineers-rebuilding-1.4113386.

expected to continue to play a significant role during the current period of climate change.

Acknowledging problems in the community, the federal government commissioned a study over two decades ago to determine how to deal with the ongoing issues.[24] The resulting Pope Report noted the deteriorating dike surrounding the community, the housing situation, water treatment plant and water services, waste treatment and disposal, health, policing, fire protection, schools, and economic development. The report also stated that the federal government had underestimated the population of the community by a substantial amount: 40 per cent. This error had negative effects on Kashechewan's finances, as the Band had to spend more on housing and services than the amount allocated to it. The Pope Report recognized that housing was inappropriate in terms of both design and accommodation. Based on family size and traditional living arrangements of the Cree people, the houses were too small. In addition, the report stated that many homes did not meet current standards with respect to building, fire, electrical, or environmental codes. The report recommended that the First Nation be moved to a site near Timmins, Ontario, 414 kilometres south of Kashechewan and far from the community's traditional territory on James Bay.

Following the release of the Pope Report, the First Nation commissioned Dr. Emily Faries, a Cree professor of Indigenous Studies, to conduct a survey of community members. The results, based on the participation of 863 people, showed that the people of Kashechewan disagreed with the recommendation to move south. Nearly two-thirds (63 per cent) wished to move upriver to higher ground, potentially to a site approximately 30 kilometres away. Only 5 per cent wanted to move south to an urban centre.[25] Given the community's decision not to move south, the government in turn refused to move the community to a location upstream. The annual need remains to evacuate the community during the spring breakup and to deal with flooding, sewage contamination, and damage to housing.[26] The recommendation to

---

24 Alan Pope, *Report on the Kashechewan First Nation and Its People*, Report submitted to Aboriginal Affairs and Northern Development Canada (Ottawa, October 2006), 40.
25 Emily Faries, "Voice of the People on the Re-Location Issue: Kashechewan First Nation, Ontario, Canada," *OIDA International Journal of Sustainable Development* 8, no. 4 (2015): 99–110, https://ssrn.com/abstract=2612102.
26 Arshi Shaikh, Carol Kauppi, and Robert Case, "Flooding in Kashechewan First Nation: Is It an Environmental Justice Issue?" *Canadian Journal of Native Studies* 37, no. 2 (2017): 105–30, https://www.researchgate.net/publication/328676214 _Flooding_in_Kashechewan_First_Nation_Is_it_an_environmental_justice_issue.

move the community to Timmins is reminiscent of the folly of moving Indigenous people against their will and better judgment, such as the catastrophic relocation of the Sayisi Dene to the outskirts of Churchill, Manitoba, in 1956. That relocation resulted in the deaths of about a third of the people who were moved[27] and the social disintegration of a previously thriving community.

Poverty, Housing Hardship, and Migration

Given the extremely cold climate and the challenges of surviving outdoors, most people experiencing forms of homelessness in this subarctic region must find temporary accommodation with friends, family, or through the few emergency shelter beds that exist. The forms of homelessness most prevalent in James Bay communities involve hidden homelessness (e.g., "couch surfing," "double bunking," overcrowding or housing hardship in substandard living conditions). Hence, poverty, core housing need, homelessness, and health are among the most pressing social problems affecting northern communities. Even though these issues have a strong impact on many northern communities, insufficient research has been conducted to gain a solid understanding of the nature and effects of poor housing to provide a sound basis for problem resolution.

Relatively little information is available about the underlying dynamics of homelessness among Indigenous people in subarctic communities. Yet there is evidence that the extent of homelessness in Moosonee, the "Gateway to the Arctic," is extremely high, at 20 per cent of the Indigenous population.[28] The problems of insufficient, substandard housing and health impacts in the communities in the western James Bay region are further magnified by Cree people's attempts to cope with challenging conditions, often through migration into and out of their home communities in search of better living conditions. Due to insufficient funding from the federal government, the quality of existing housing in Indigenous communities has deteriorated. Chie Sakakibara[29] has

---

27 Ila Bussidor and Üstün Bilgen-Reinart, *Night Spirits: The Story of the Relocation of the Sayisi Dene* (Winnipeg: University of Manitoba Press, 1997).

28 Carol Kauppi and Emily Faries, "Housing and Homelessness in Moosonee, Ontario: Experiences of Indigenous and Non-Indigenous People" (paper presented at the National Conference on Ending Homelessness, London, ON, November 2016).

29 Chie Sakakibara, "'Our home is drowning': Iñupiat Storytelling and Climate Change in Point Hope, Alaska," *Geographical Review* 98, no. 4 (2008): 456–75, https://doi.org /10.1111/j.1931-0846.2008.tb00312.x.

documented how flooding and erosion have destroyed ancient villages in the Arctic, contributing to the loss of housing and to struggles in maintaining connections to disappearing places. These findings are similar to our research in the James Bay region, where the flooding of coastal communities displaces Indigenous people and damages homes each year.[30]

Most housing on First Nations territories, and more particularly in northern Indigenous communities, is substandard due largely to the imposition of southern housing designs that are inappropriate for northern conditions. Yet research is required to understand how housing conditions in northern towns and cities are linked to forms of homelessness and patterns of migration. Naomi Adelson[31] has described how higher rates of disease, disability, and premature death among Indigenous people might be traced to inequities and colonial histories in which discriminatory practices led to changes in living patterns. For example, forced relocation of communities, removal of children and their placement in residential schools or child welfare systems, as well as inadequate housing and services on-reserve are central components of the history of colonialism in Canada. The available findings about specific health issues among homeless people in the North show similar patterns indicating that mental health issues – including substance use, depression, and physical disabilities – are common.[32] Understanding the intersection between the establishment of the reserve system and the loss of homelands, and housing hardship, homelessness, and health impacts from the perspective of Indigenous people is vital to developing strategies for positive change. For example, sharing housing is a core aspect of Indigenous culture; public policy must change to reflect such traditions and current patterns of living.

Equally pressing is the need to understand how limited opportunities for school or work, lack of suitable housing, and health issues lead to the decision to move away from a northern community.

30 Shaikh, Kauppi, and Case, "Flooding in Kashechewan First Nation."
31 Naomi Adelson, "The Embodiment of Inequity: Health Disparities in Aboriginal Canada," *Canadian Journal of Public Health* 96, Supp. 2 (2005): S45–S61, https://doi.org/10.1007/BF03403702.
32 Meghan Wilson and Marie Lowe, *The Extent of Homelessness in the Kenai Peninsula Borough* (Anchorage: Institute of Social and Economic Research University of Alaska, 2007); Michael Young and Joshua Moses, "Neoliberalism and Homelessness in the Western Canadian Arctic," *Canadian Journal of Nonprofit and Social Economy Research* 4, no. 2 (2013): 7–22, https://doi.org/10.22230/cjnser.2013v4n2a147.

Migration is a strategy to overcome difficult living circumstances, but it can lead to further housing problems or homelessness in destination communities.[33] There is a gap in the published literature about the migration patterns and associated adverse effects on homeless Indigenous people who move away from their communities in the Canadian North.

Structural Bases of Homelessness and Social Exclusion

Various theories have been put forward to account for the interconnected problems of homelessness, migration, and health among Indigenous people. Both Indigenous and non-Indigenous writers identify forced displacement from homelands,[34] racist and genocidal policies and practices,[35] and a general failure on the part of governments to act on existing well-developed legal frameworks and their constitutional responsibilities in the face of general prosperity in mainstream society.[36] Further, the general nature of the Indian Act and its ongoing historical effects contribute to homelessness on- and off-reserve. For example, the Indian status system denoting a person's classification as 6–1, 6–2, or 6–3 depends on whether or not the person's parents or grandparents intermarried with non-indigenous people; this classification determines access to on-reserve housing and even the ability to live on-reserve with family members. In addition, there are often tensions between those living on-reserve and off-reserve that affect access to services such as medical transportation funding.[37]

33 Arshi Shaikh, Henri Pallard, and Carol Kauppi, "Migration and Homelessness: Exploring Attachment to Place amongst Francophone, Anglophone and Indigenous People in Northeastern Ontario," *Spaces and Flows: An International Journal of Urban and Extra Urban Studies* 3, no. 1 (2013): 97–108, https://doi.org/10.18848/2154-8676 /CGP/v03i01/53682.

34 Bussidor and Bilgen-Reinart, *Night Spirits;* Minnie Grey, "From the Tundra to the Boardroom and Everywhere in Between: Politics and the Changing Roles of Inuit Women in the Arctic," in *Indigenous Women and Feminism: Politics, Activism, Culture,* ed. Cheryl Suzack, Shari Huhndorf, Jeanne Perreault, and Jean Barman (Vancouver: UBC Press, 2010): 21–8; Faries, "Voice of the People."

35 Joshua Price, *Structural Violence: Hidden Brutality in the Lives of Women* (Albany: State University of New York Press, 2012); Sheila Wilmot, *Taking Responsibility, Taking Direction: White Anti-Racism in Canada* (Winnipeg: Arbeiter Ring Publishing, 2005).

36 Anaya, "Statement."

37 Michael Hankard, *Access, Clocks, Blocks and Stocks: Resisting Health Canada's Management of Traditional Medicine* (Vernon, BC: J. Charlton Publishing, 2015).

According to Joshua Price,[38] social structures associated with colonial histories create and perpetuate forms of "violence" against marginalized groups. Further, social exclusion, which is connected to the systemic and structural conditions of homelessness, has been defined as a complex process often involving numerous domains; it affects the quality of life of individuals, equity, and cohesion within society as a whole.

The challenges that people face in subarctic communities are varied. They include the limited availability of housing, transportation, and health services, as well as cultural differences between subarctic, rural, and remote communities and urban centres in the South and near-North. As well, cultural differences between Indigenous and non-Indigenous people often lead to a sense of culture shock for migrants who leave First Nation communities.

An Indigenous Definition of Homelessness

Researchers and policymakers use definitions of homelessness to classify individuals into categories of homelessness. Jesse Thistle has developed an Indigenous definition of homelessness that is holistic and does not focus on housing. Thistle defines Indigenous homelessness as

> a human condition that describes First Nations, Métis and Inuit individuals, families or communities lacking stable, permanent, appropriate housing, or the immediate prospect, means or ability to acquire such housing. Unlike the common colonialist definition of homelessness, Indigenous homelessness is not defined as lacking a structure of habitation; rather, it is more fully described and understood through a composite lens of Indigenous worldviews. These include: individuals, families and communities isolated from their relationships to land, water, place, family, kin, each other, animals, cultures, languages and identities. Importantly, Indigenous people experiencing these kinds of homelessness cannot culturally, spiritually, emotionally or physically reconnect with their Indigeneity.[39]

Thistle's definition is based on 12 dimensions: 1. historic displacement homelessness; 2. contemporary geographic separation homelessness; 3. spiritual disconnection homelessness; 4. mental disruption and

38 Price, *Structural Violence*.
39 Jesse Thistle, *Definition of Indigenous Homelessness in Canada* (Toronto: Canadian Observatory on Homelessness, 2017), 6.

imbalance homelessness; 5. cultural disintegration and loss homelessness; 6. overcrowding homelessness; 7. relocation and mobility homelessness; 8. going home homelessness; 9. nowhere to go homelessness;
10. escaping or evading harm homelessness; 11. emergency crisis homelessness; and 12. climatic refugee homelessness. These dimensions are
helpful in understanding the forces that have led to the high rates of
homelessness among Indigenous people. This chapter draws upon
Thistle's dimensions to explore the experiences of people who have
migrated from First Nations on James Bay. This definition also informs
the two major themes and subthemes that we identify.

Housing Exclusion

The approach to the definition adopted by the European Union (EU)
and the European Observatory on Homelessness considers three
domains of homelessness and housing exclusion: the physical (habit-
ability of the dwelling or space), the legal (security of occupation or
legal title), and the social (provision of privacy and enjoyment of social
relations).[40] Homelessness results from a deficiency in these domains.
This definition, termed the European Typology on Homelessness and
Housing Exclusion,[41] has been applied in research and policy for more
than a decade.

Migration

Afsaneh Rahimian and colleagues[42] have identified three categories
to describe the length of stay of migrants in a destination community:
short stays (0–12 months), intermediate stays (13–60 months), and long-
term stays (5 or more years). Building on that study, this chapter also
defines migration in terms of three groups: individuals who have been
in the community less than one year are recent migrants, those who
have been in the community between one to five years are intermedi-
ate-term migrants, and those who have been in the community more

---

40 Bill Edgar and Henk Meert, *Fourth Review of Statistics on Homelessness in Europe*:
    The ETHOS Definition of Homelessness (Brussels: European Federation of National
    Organisations Working with the Homeless, November 2005).
41 FEANTSA, *Ethos – Taking Stock* (Brussels: European Federation of National Organizations
    Working with the Homeless, September 2006).
42 Afsaneh Rahimian, Jennifer Wolch, and Paul Koegel, "A Model of Homeless Migration:
    Homeless Men in Skid Row, Los Angeles," *Environment and Planning* 24, no. 9 (1992):
    1317–36, https://doi.org/10.1068/a241317.

than five years are "stayers." Thus, we considered migrant stayers to be a separate subgroup of migrants that should be considered in research on migratory homelessness.

Our Approach

The Centre for Research in Social Justice and Policy received approval from the Research Ethics Board at Laurentian University to use a methodology known as "period prevalence counts" in various communities, as well as interviews and other methods. The procedures for data collection and all aspects of the study met the standards required by the Tri-Council Policy Statement on research ethics.

Two different methods were used to collect information from people living with homelessness in northeastern Ontario towns and cities, including Cree migrants who were experiencing homelessness. First, surveys were conducted between 2011 and 2015 in six towns and cities: Sudbury, North Bay, Timmins, Hearst, Cochrane, and Moosonee. The surveys were conducted over seven consecutive days in each community to allow for greater accuracy, as some people do not access services every day.[43] Next, data were collected from homeless persons through a structured questionnaire that gathered information regarding background, experiences, forms of homelessness, health issues, and migration. As the questionnaire collected specific information that allowed for the elimination of duplicate cases, extending the time frame of the study did not raise concerns about counting the same person more than once. We used the same questionnaire in all six communities. The surveys produced a database of 5,898 participants, among whom 49.8 per cent were women, 43.8 per cent were Indigenous, and 37.0 per cent were migrants. Of the Indigenous participants, 45.0 per cent were migrants.

Second, interviews with people who had lived with homelessness offered narratives about experiences of housing hardship and homelessness. Research using a qualitative, narrative method examined the

---

43 The extension to seven days is recommended by the US Department of Housing and Urban Development, "Point-in-Time Count Methodology Guide," *HUD Exchange*, March 2015, https://www.hudexchange.info/resource/4036/point-in-time-count-methodology-guide/.

complex issues related to pathways into and out of homelessness for a Cree woman and man from First Nations communities on western James Bay. Excerpts from these two Cree participants, who spoke about challenges linked to housing and homelessness, are used to illustrate themes discussed in this chapter.

Nuna (a pseudonym) was born near Moose Cree First Nation into a family that lived a traditional, migratory lifestyle on the land. Nuna was interviewed when she was in her early sixties, but she spoke about her childhood and adolescence when her family migrated from James Bay to a small town. Nuna's family was required to move to an urban centre so that the children could attend school; in the alternative, the children would have been sent to a residential school. Her family migrated from Moose Cree to Kapuskasing, 241 kilometres away but still within the traditional territory of the Cree people.

Keme (a pseudonym), was born and grew up in Moosonee and Kashechewan First Nation. He was forty-seven years of age when first interviewed, and in his early fifties when last interviewed. At the time of his first interview, he had recently exited homelessness after twenty years on the streets. He provided informed consent each time he was interviewed, as we conducted fourteen interviews to explore various issues. From his living homeless for so long, Keme had an extensive history of long-distance migratory homelessness after being expelled from his community of Kashechewan. Just prior to participating in the current study, he had obtained housing in an urban centre in northern Ontario.

Research Questions

Five key questions guided this exploration of migration from James Bay.

1. Who are Cree migrants? What are their characteristics?
2. Where do Cree migrants go? What are the communities of origin and destination?
3. What are their reasons for leaving their communities?
4. What are their experiences of homelessness and reasons for becoming homeless?
5. What forms of social exclusion do they experience in towns and cities?

Out-Migration from Cree Communities

A first important theme appearing from analysis of the data pertains to rural-urban migration and the interaction between urbanization and homelessness in the North.

Characteristics of Cree Migrants

The number of migrants in the sample, including children, was 288; however, the total number of people who had moved away from their Cree communities was larger than that, as more than half (61 per cent) reported that others – spouses, partners, parents, siblings, other family members, or friends – had migrated with them (table 4.1).

Close to two-thirds (63 per cent) of the migrants had been absolutely homeless in the past and about a quarter (24 per cent) had slept outdoors or on the streets in the year preceding the study. Most of the 149 migrants (61 per cent) were women, a finding which suggests that Indigenous women might be more likely than men to move away from their communities in search of housing, education, and employment, or to leave violent situations. Many women (39, or 53 per cent) stated that they had moved because of family issues, violence or abuse, or divorce. The average age of women who moved away (thirty-nine) was slightly less than that of men (forty-one), but the difference is not statistically significant. The women aged in range from sixteen to seventy-four and the men from twenty-one to seventy-two. Both men and women were mostly single, including those who were divorced, separated, or widowed, but 41 per cent of women and 28 per cent of men were married or in a common-law relationship. Most women (53 per cent) who migrated had children; collectively, they had 108 dependent children, while men had 31 dependent children.

People who had migrated to towns and cities in northeastern Ontario had come from the First Nations communities shown in table 4.2. Over two-thirds came from three communities on James Bay: Moose Cree First Nation or Moose Factory Island, Attawapiskat, and Moosonee. About 90 per cent of the population of Moosonee is Indigenous, mostly coming from other Cree communities, and the town is itself a destination community, but people who cannot find suitable housing there often move elsewhere.

Table 4.1. Share of Cree Migrants (%) Reporting an Accompanying Person, by Relationship

Relationship	Share Reporting an Accompanying Person
Family members (parents, siblings, other family members)	54
Children	25
Spouse or partner	16
Friends or acquaintances	5
Total	100

Table 4.2. Cree Migrants' Communities of Origin

Community of Origin	Share of Migrants
Moose Factory Island/Moose Cree First Nation	29
Attawapiskat First Nation	22
Moosonee	18
Kashechewan First Nation	13
Fort Albany First Nation	7
Peawanuck, Taykwa Tagamou, Constance Lake, Waskaganish First Nations	11
Total	100

Early Experiences

Nuna and Keme described their early lives on James Bay. Nuna was born on the land near Moose Cree First Nation. She explained her family's origins, living on the land in the 1950s: "I was born in Moose River, Ontario. That's along the tracks going to Moosonee. And my family were originally Moose Cree, [but] we lived in Moose River. And we moved [when] I was just a baby. I was born in a tent there. I was the last one in my family to be born in a tent."

Her family decided to move to the town of Kapuskasing, in northeastern Ontario, in response to the requirement that the children attend school. In moving to Kapuskasing, Nuna and her siblings avoided residential schooling because they were placed in "Indian Day Schools," a boarding school program. This system required that children stay in boarding homes during the week and then return to their families only on the weekends. A class action lawsuit has been initiated on behalf of Indigenous children who attended these schools and had adverse experiences similar to those of residential school survivors, including physical, emotional, and sexual abuse, as well as negative effects on their language and culture.[44]

Keme was born in the hospital in Moosonee and later lived with his family in Kashechewan, where he attended an "Indian Day School." In Fort Albany, however, where his parents had taken him to a clinic for a course of treatment for scabies when he was six, Keme was taken after his treatment by a religious "Brother" to the residential school. Keme stated: "That's where the abuse started – in that school. Yeah, he sexually abused me when I was there." After six months, members of Kashechewan brought him back to his parents' community, where he attended a day school. Keme was also sexually abused by a female teacher at his new school: "[Much] abuse was right there in front of the people, in front of kids, right? In that school I was abused differently, quietly, alone. That's where I was sexually abused by this lady. It was a born-again Christian that got lonely, I guess, I don't know. She had issues ... I was a young boy, I was scared."

In later years, in discussions with a friend, Keme compared experiences in Anglican and Catholic schools. He concluded that the experience was equally bad in both: "Everything, abuse and sexual abuse, beatings." In a Catholic-run residential school, his mother had experienced repeated beatings. Keme said: "She blamed herself for everything that happened there. She wasn't allowed to blame anyone else."

Migration

Most of the migrants were recent (in the study community for up to a year) or medium term (in the community for one to five years); over a third had been in the study community for more than five years (figure 4.2). As the participants were living with homelessness, intermediate and long-term (stayer) migrants in the study community likely have experienced ongoing difficulties. Keme (a migrant stayer) had

---

44 Kathleen Martens, "Ottawa set to start negotiations with Indian Day School survivors: Lawyer," *APTN National News*, 27 July 2018, https://www.aptnnews.ca/national -news/ottawa-set-to-start-negotiations-with-indian-day-school-survivors-lawyer/.

Figure 4.2. Length of Time of Migrants in an Urban Centre

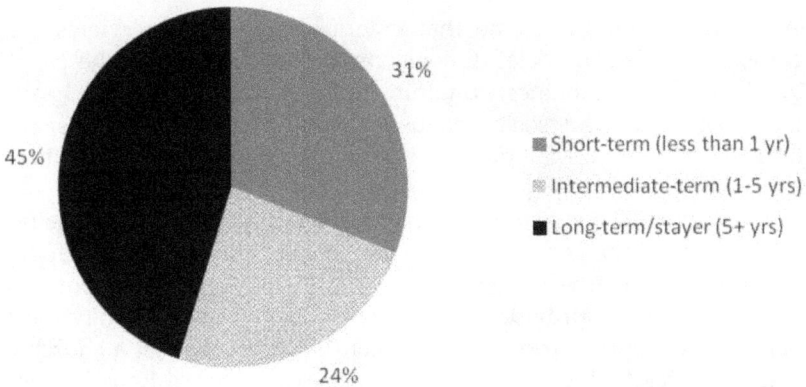

migrated many years prior to his participation in the study, but the additional time spent in the community did not resolve issues linked to homelessness, such as being banned from services, including detox programs.

Two-thirds (68 per cent) of the migrants had learned their Indigenous language (usually Cree) first, and about the same proportion (65 per cent) still spoke it. This finding is potentially important for the retention of Indigenous languages, as migration raises concerns about retention. When people move from their home communities, they become immersed in the dominant language of their destination communities. Migration to towns and cities might disrupt the active use of an Indigenous language as opportunities to converse with others decline. Children's use of their Indigenous language might become restricted to the home, losing broader exposure to it and ultimately their Indigenous language skills. The experience of francophones in northeastern Ontario has shown that language loss and assimilation have resulted when francophone communities are not supported by strong cultural institutions, such as schools that offer instruction in French.

Most migrants (71 per cent) had not completed high school, but nearly all (89 per cent) stated that they could read and write. Those without a secondary school diploma or equivalent, however, might experience difficulty finding employment in destination communities, while those who could not read or write likely encountered challenges in navigating through daily life in the dominant culture.

Supports and Plans following Migration

A second important theme that emerges from the interviews concerns the particular social dimensions of homelessness in the North. We identified subthemes pertaining to physical and mental health, marginalization and social exclusion, increasing homelessness, and housing insecurity. Material and structural inequalities traverse these subthemes.

A majority (62 per cent) of migrants stated that someone had helped them after they had arrived in the study community. Even though they had not been referred to services, close to half (45 per cent) obtained help from service providers; others were supported by family members (33 per cent) or friends (20 per cent). A few said that a church or a stranger had helped them. Despite the experience of homelessness, three-quarters stated that their circumstances had improved after they moved, and over three-quarters (83 per cent) planned on staying in the destination community. One-fifth (20 per cent) had returned to their home community following migration.

Mental and Physical Health

A quarter of the migrants reported that they had mental health challenges, and a third stated that they had physical health challenges; 12 per cent reported both mental and physical health problems. Taking into account the combination of reported mental and physical health challenges, over half (58 per cent) were suffering from one or both types of health problems. The most commonly reported mental health issues were depression or being suicidal (58 per cent) or anxiety and stress (21 per cent). Some reported serious mental illnesses such as bipolar disorder and schizophrenia (8 per cent). Regarding physical health, participants reported serious issues such as kidney problems, hepatitis C, liver problems, diabetes, and problems with blood pressure.

In his interviews, Keme spoke extensively about the mental and physical health challenges he had experienced since a baby and the effects on his mental and physical health stemming from a life of physical, mental, and sexual abuse. He was taken from his parents twice by religious clergy, once at birth and, as noted, a second time when he was six years old. He believes that he would have been part of the sixties scoop, as his mother was told that he was stillborn following his birth in Moosonee. Family members were monitoring the situation, however, and each time removed him from the institutional settings where he was being held. Keme shared this experience:

> Somebody told me – an Elder – you walk beside it [the abused child] and look at it once in a while, but don't leave it behind. Just walk beside it and pick at it. Eventually, it'll evaporate, so I'm doing that with all these programs. I'm not leaving anything behind me, just like that little boy I was, when I was tied up, that was in Moosonee. Now I don't remember why I was in that hospital ... [But] I saw my mom and my brothers and I was just crying, trying to get away [from the hospital], you know? I asked my Mom 'Why did I stay in Moosonee when I was a baby for a long time when I was strapped [to a gurney] ... I remember they came to visit me on Christmas and New Year's, I was put back to my bed that day.

Although Keme was later reunited with his family, the time spent in the hospital was terrifying and traumatic. He was physically abused and suffered fear, loneliness, and isolation, and had experienced mental health challenges throughout his life that were linked to these events. He stated that as a child he wanted to die, and made several attempts to kill himself during early adulthood. Keme also described the physical health challenges he was living with in the city: "Yeah, the health and Listerine, I [drank], wine, pretty much anything with alcohol and [look] what it did to me. Now I am suffering from cirrhosis of the liver. I have Hep C and with that I got cancer in September. I was battling that all winter, with Hep C. It killed my kidneys, my liver, my way of thinking, my memory, most of it. Pretty much killed every relationship I ever had. It's killing me now, I am fighting for my life. It does end the life, all that drinking."

The mental health challenges related to early trauma and the physical health problems that came from homelessness were serious ongoing issues in Keme's life, but his resilience and connection to Indigenous healing were powerful factors mitigating some of these effects.

Marginalization and Social Exclusion

Indicators of marginalization and social exclusion of survey participants arise from their responses regarding employment, referrals to services, and histories of homelessness. Eighty per cent of participants stated that they did not have employment, while 78 per cent had not been referred to any support services. Disconnection from systems of support and employment can have serious effects on outcomes for homeless migrants, as they often rely on services to fulfil basic needs for food, shelter, clothing, and transportation. In prior studies in Sudbury, we found that service providers focused on the resident homeless population rather than on migrants.[45] The mandates of many agencies specify priorities for services that can lead to the exclusion of recent migrants, restrictions on the provision of services to particular populations, such as francophones, or the redirection of Indigenous people to Indigenous-specific programs.

Keme suffered social exclusion in all the three domains and ten dimensions delineated by Ruth Levitas and colleagues.[46] Marginalization and exclusion affected the material resources available to him, and his access to services and social resources such as support from family and friends in his community of origin. As Keme was required, by a Band Council Resolution, to leave his community, he was separated from social networks, including his wife, children, extended family, and community members. As a migrant living with homelessness, he was marginalized and excluded from participation in the four main social structures (economic, social, cultural, political). His participation in social and cultural aspects of life was limited primarily to the street community. Keme's health and well-being were compromised by the harsh realities of living on the streets and the challenges of obtaining access to health services. His living circumstances were difficult, as he slept outdoors and accessed any form of shelter he could find while banned from nearly all services. Police targeted Keme, he was jailed for various offences, and he spent a considerable amount of time in prison. On at least one occasion, he was wrongly jailed for a crime he did not commit.

Nuna also lived with social exclusion in terms of the three dimensions of resources, participation, and quality of life. She did not have access to material resources; public services offered little, if any, help; and the move away from her community on James Bay limited her social resources. Nuna's separation from her parents to attend school disrupted her participation in economic, social, cultural, and civic domains of society. The quality of her living environment was challenging due to the constant movement between different places, the circumstances of homelessness, and the periodic separation from her parents.

45 Carol Kauppi, Henri Pallard, and Emily Faries, "Poverty, Homelessness and Migration in Northeastern Ontario, Canada," *OIDA International Journal of Sustainable Development* 8, no. 4 (2015): 11–22, https://ssrn.com/abstract=2612092.
46 Ruth Levitas et al., *The Multi-Dimensional Analysis of Social Exclusion* (Bristol, UK: Townsend Centre for the International Study of Poverty and Bristol Institute for Public Affairs, January 2007), https://dera.ioe.ac.uk/6853/1/multidimensional.pdf.

Reasons for Migration and Homelessness

The primary reasons migrants gave for leaving their communities were unemployment and the need to access varied services, including health, social services, and education. Over a quarter of the participants were also encouraged or assisted to migrate. Housing challenges were cited by less than a tenth of the participants as a reason for moving (table 4.3). More than a quarter of the participants reported that they were homeless because they were unemployed or seeking work. Social assistance was another factor linked to homelessness due to problems such as being cut off from benefits, payments that were late, people deemed ineligible, or benefits that were simply inadequate to pay for living expenses. All these reasons provide information about the forms of social exclusion migrants experience in urban centres.

Nuna spoke about her family's experience of migrating to Kapuskasing:

[We] moved to Kapuskasing area for trapping. And there were a lot of trapping lines opening up there, so [Dad] moved to [the] Kap area with his family. We had no home. We sort of landed in Kapuskasing in January on a really cold winter's day. My Mom and Dad set a tent up right in the snow. Slapped up one of, like, those little tin stoves and that was our temporary home for a good three months. So we lived that lifestyle for a while. It was cold. But my parents – my Dad was very [traditional] – he lived off the land. We moved to Mile 62, which is another area of Kapuskasing. So there they set up shop to go trapping, and trapping was the way of life back then.

Nuna's family moved to Kapuskasing because of a change in government regulations regarding trapping that affected Indigenous people: the Registered Trapline System, implemented in Ontario in 1946. According to David Finch, the system was developed in southern Ontario with little understanding of the conditions in northern Ontario: "[Changes occurred with] the imposition of southern land tenure systems upon northern communities, specifically the creation of registered trapline territories in the mid-20th century. This followed decades of increased wildlife conservation practices, also imposed by southern agencies, and changing economic conditions that promoted a wage economy at the expense of a traditional one" (Finch 2013, 1).

Finch interviewed seventeen Cree Elders to explore the effects of policy changes relating to traplines, about which the Elders consistently expressed negative views. Following the imposition of the new trapline system, the Ministry of Natural Resources placed quotas on animals

Table 4.3. Reasons for Migration and Homelessness, by Share of Participants

Reasons for Migration	Per cent
Unemployment or seeking work	32
To access health, social services or education	32
Encouraged and assisted to migrate	27
Housing issues (inability to pay rent or eviction)	9
Total	100
Reasons for Homelessness	
Unemployment or seeking work	28
Problems with social assistance	18
Inability to pay rent or mortgage/low income	13
Family issues/violence or abuse	11
Mental or physical illness	10
Addictions	8
Housing issues/eviction/problematic living conditions	7
Incarceration	5
Total	100

Note: Percentages are based on multiple responses.

and, in particular, limits on the number of beavers a family could harvest in a year – the upper limit was ten. Finch reported that a beaver die-off occurred in the 1950s due to an outbreak of tularemia, an insect-borne infectious disease that can attack both beaver and muskrat. Indigenous families in the Hudson and James Bay lowlands had relied heavily on beavers as a food source. As Finch reports,[47] "people began to starve after [the Ministry of Natural Resources] established the boundaries for the registered trapline system in 1947." The ministry required Indigenous people to stay in the area demarcated by the traplines, whereas traditionally they had followed the movements of animals on the land. Staying within trapline boundaries limited their access to game, and restrictions on trapping beaver further limited food sources. The hardships resulting from regulations imposed by the Ontario government were severe and led to forced migration and even to starvation.

---

47 David Finch, "It Is Only the Beginning: An Ethnohistory of Mid-Twentieth Century Land Tenure in Fort Severn, Ontario" (Master's thesis, Lakehead University, 2013), 108.

As Nuna noted, her family moved from the James Bay region to Kapuskasing because traplines were opening up. Another reason for the migration was the requirement that the children attend school: "So it [the move to Kapuskasing] allowed us to be able to move closer to the railroad tracks where you can get to Smoky Falls and Smoky Line [85 km northeast of Kapuskasing], where there's [rail] transportation going back and forth. We had to do that to be able to have access to schools. Because we had to go to school, I think I was five. We didn't have residential school but we had boarding homes. Meaning, we had to leave home in order to go to school."

Income

Our studies in 2011 to 2013 revealed that migrants moved due to a combination of push and pull factors such as the desire for connection and involvement in employment and services. The results for sources of income for migrants were consistent with the high rate of unemployment, since for most Cree migrants the source was government income support, primarily from social assistance (Ontario Works, 38 per cent) or the Ontario Disability Support Program (19 per cent), but also employment insurance, the Child Tax Credit, Workplace Safety and Insurance Board benefits, and the Canada Pension Plan/Old Age Security. Employment was a source of income for a small proportion (15 per cent). A further source of income support for three individuals was family members, while 7 per cent stated that they had no income. Figure 4.3 shows the distribution of income sources.

The economic implications of treaties signed in the past reverberate into the present. The creation of the reserve system served the interests of the colonial governments, as the treaties specified that Indigenous people were ceding and surrendering all rights to the land. The "reserves" were often located on territories that, in rural or remote locations, offered few prospects for economic prosperity. Even though mining, forestry, and electric power generation projects now take place on the traditional lands of the Cree people, most people in Indigenous communities live in deep poverty.[48] Keme's narrative

---

48 Barbara Waterfall, "Native People and the Social Work Profession: A Critical Analysis of Colonizing Problematics and the Development of Decolonized Thought," in Westhues, *Canadian Social Policy*, 50–66.

Figure 4.3. Migrants' Sources of Income

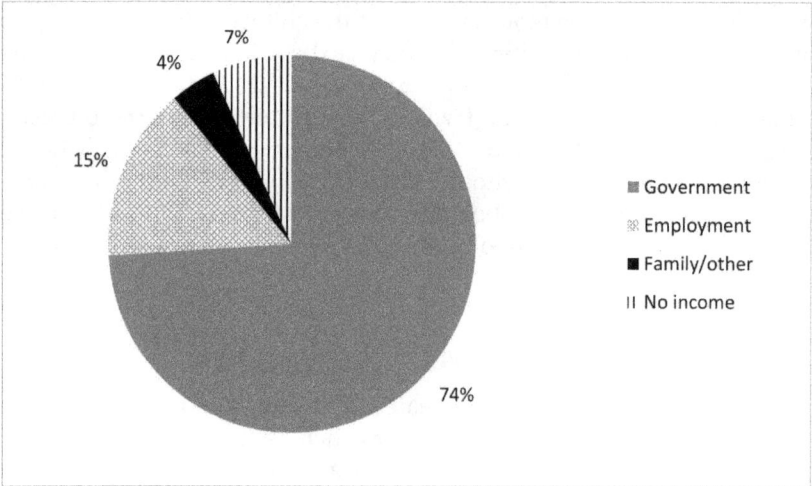

reveals his childhood experiences of poverty: "Ever since I came out of my Mom's womb, I was homeless. Sad but it's true. Thirteen people crammed in there [small house]. Think of it this way. I never had a bed let alone a bedroom in my parents' house, ever in my life. I was always that kid who was sleeping on the floor, or on a couch, if I was lucky. That's it, one room [for] everybody. It was a tiny house, eh? But yeah, we were poor but we managed." Keme stated that the poverty his family experienced "was normal, there was nothing wrong with it." However, he also described the experience of near starvation in Kashechewan, which he and his friends combatted by going to the local dump in search of food.

For families living on the land, there was some support from government programs, such as social assistance after 1946.[49] However, Nuna explained how her family struggled to survive living in Kapuskasing: "Living in town, during the summer, my Dad had temporary work. And when there was none and trapping wasn't available, we'd move to Hearst but that wasn't [good], we would move to Kapuskasing but that wasn't very good because there was a lot of alcohol involved. And we never really had a home as well

---

49 Finch, "It Is Only the Beginning."

in Kap. We lived here and there with friends. And sometimes my parents would get an apartment but that wasn't a very good setup. Sometimes we slept in the park because we didn't have a place to stay."

The narratives of Nuna and Keme bear similarities in terms of the struggle to survive despite the differences in their living circumstances. Nuna's family lived in or near the town of Kapuskasing, while Keme's family lived on Kashechewan First Nation. Migration to Kapuskasing did not improve conditions for Nuna's family. For Keme, migration from Kashechewan led to years of homelessness and negative effects on his health and well-being.

The Need for Supports

Most participants (77 per cent) reported on their need for supports (table 4.4). Frequently, people needed help with housing or furniture or with education or employment. Immediate needs were for food, clothing, and transportation, and many frontline services for people living with homelessness provide these items. Research on homelessness and food insecurity shows, however, that the food available in soup kitchens or food banks might not meet needs because it might be rationed (e.g., available only once a month) or of poor nutritional quality. In addition, problems with access to food cause worries and anxiety.[50]

Nuna alluded to the hardship that she and her family endured because of the requirement to move to Kapuskasing: "And I remember, that really had an impact on me – seeing young people and knowing that they had no place to sleep, because we did that, as well, my sisters and I – sometimes by choice, sometimes by not having a choice – because we didn't have a place to stay. Because my parents were living in the bush and we were in town and we had nowhere to go." Living homeless in the town while her parents were on their trapline meant that Nuna and her sisters found ways to survive without a home. Nuna escaped homelessness when she moved to a northern First Nation in the 1970s in her late teens through a relationship with her future husband.

---

50 Areej Al Hamad et al., "Food Insecurity and Women's Health in Canada: Does Northern and Southern Ontario Residency Matter?" *International Journal of Health, Wellness, and Society* 9, no. 1 (2018): 1–18, https://doi.org/10.18848/2156-8960/CGP /v09i01/1-18.

Table 4.4. Migrants' Need for Supports

Type of Support Needed	Percentage of Migrants Needing
Housing or furniture	33
Education or employment	20
Financial supports	18
Basic needs (food, clothing, transportation)	18
Health services	5
Other/general (e.g., need help)	6
Total	100

Note: Percentages are based on multiple responses.

Keme experienced greater hardship following his migration from Kashechewan. His life story illustrates the interconnections among the historical, cultural, economic, geographic, social, and legal aspects of life for Indigenous people. He was adversely affected by the colonial past and its discriminatory child welfare policies, including practices within government-funded, Christian-run educational institutions. The assimilationist strategies embodied in policies, practices, and institutions undermined traditional Indigenous cultures and ways of life, disrupted family relationships, and damaged self-esteem and sense of identity. Living through extreme poverty in a remote region governed by the Indian Act and the federal Department of Indian Affairs and Northern Development (first changed to Aboriginal Affairs and Northern Development Canada and recently to Indigenous and Northern Affairs Canada) meant that his family life was controlled by external agents. He also mentioned that the effects were intergenerational: his mother had attended residential school: "My Mom grew up in residential school. She did her best, which was awesome. And my Dad was a very abusive man. He wasn't sent to residential school. It was just chaos from family."

Keme associated the destructive experiences in his formative years with the trajectory into homelessness: "[I'm coping] through counsellors and [dealing with] post-traumatic stress ... The terrible experience as a kid – it's in me. It sticks with me and, yes, it did fuck up my way of thinking for a long time, as a kid. But as I learned what they taught me and what I went though, what I thought was right, is terribly wrong. You know?"

A recent analysis of Keme's life history concludes that he is a survivor, much like those who have experienced traumatic events such as residential school:

> In his early years, he learned to survive at all costs, or die. For example, he learned to eat from the dump or starve. He demonstrated the will to survive throughout his life on the street; it is how he was able to survive prison, racism, violence, assault, poverty, the elements, abandonment and loneliness. He survived by numbing his pain with alcohol and drugs, by running away, by creating street families. He survived by learning how to fight, so he could protect himself from being beaten up or murdered. [Keme] was a true survivor his whole life ... The results clearly show that the more colonial violence [e.g., racism and assimilationist policies and practices] [Keme] experienced, the more abuse, suicidal ideation, and trauma he faced.[51]

Consideration of the circumstances of the 149 Cree migrants who were living with homelessness when they participated in these surveys of homeless people in urban centres indicates that interviews, rather than enumeration surveys, are required to provide the in-depth contextual information needed to assess the significance of Thistle's twelve dimensions of homelessness. Nevertheless, survey data have provided information about several dimensions, including some types of homelessness that must be inferred while other types were evident and overt.

Table 4.5 summarizes the dimensions that can be applied to the survey data on the survey participants and to the information available for Keme and Nuna. Due to his participation in numerous interviews over several years, more information is available about Keme's experiences than those of Nuna. From these results, several dimensions are relevant – five for the survey participants and five for Nuna, while Keme's narrative reveals that, for him, all twelve dimensions are applicable to understanding the pathways leading to homelessness.

---

51 Brian Slegers, "A Case Study of Homelessness in Sudbury, Ontario Understood through the Anishnaabe Seven Life Stages" (Master's thesis, Laurentian University, 2018), 86.

Table 4.5. Application of Thistle's Twelve Dimensions of Homelessness

Dimension	Surveys of Migrants	Nuna	Keme
1. Historic displacement	✓	✓	✓
2. Contemporary geographic separation	✓	✓	✓
3. Spiritual disconnection			✓
4. Mental disruption and imbalance	✓	✓	✓
5. Cultural disintegration and loss			✓
6. Overcrowding			✓
7. Relocation and mobility	✓	✓	✓
8. Going home homelessness			✓
9. Nowhere to go		✓	✓
10. Escaping or evading harm	✓		✓
11. Emergency crisis			✓
12. Climate refugee			✓

Source: Jesse Thistle, *Definition of Indigenous Homelessness in Canada* (Toronto: Canadian Observatory on Homelessness, 2017).

Conclusions

Migration from northern First Nations communities is marked by a number of considerations. Of the participants in our survey, the majority of migrants were women, approximately forty years old, and had migrated with an average of 2.8 dependent children. Most left their community with a family member but not with a spouse or partner. Cree migrants were from all communities on James Bay, as well as other Cree communities of the North. Most migrants still spoke their Cree language when they moved away. A majority had not completed high school but reported that they could read and write. Over half were suffering from mental or physical illness. More than three-quarters were unemployed and the same proportion had not been referred to any support services. Despite the lack of referrals, participants reported that they needed supports for housing or furniture, education or employment, financial supports, and help with basic needs for food, clothing, and transportation. The main reasons for migrating were unemployment and a desire to access health, social services, or education. Over a quarter were encouraged to move and assisted to migrate. More than half the participants were receiving financial support from Ontario Works or the Ontario Disabilities Support Program. In light of these findings, social policies and practices should be modified to become more sensitive and responsive to the needs of Indigenous people, including women and children, who move to towns and cities.

The Indigenous definition of homelessness[52] helped to explore the experiences of participants in this study. Although the results are tentative because data collection was completed before the development of the definition, the analysis shows the relevance of Thistle's twelve dimensions to Keme's narrative. Thistle's definition is also helpful in examining survey data, as five dimensions were identified as significant to Indigenous migrants living with homelessness and five were relevant to Nuna's narrative. In future research, the twelve dimensions could be incorporated into survey questions to provide for more complete data on homelessness.

Thistle[53] has asserted that homelessness is "negative, stressful and traumatic." The Cree participants in this study had encountered challenges following their migration from northern First Nations, even though most stated that their circumstances had improved after migrating to a town or city. Our interviews consistently showed that migration can heighten struggles associated with homelessness, as both Nuna's and Keme's narratives indicate. Among migrants to urban centres, social exclusion is a common experience. This occurs especially when people who are homeless do not have identification documents, when they are excluded from services, when communication issues or culture shock impede connections to others, or when legislation, such as the Ontario Safe Streets Act, is used to criminalize homelessness through targeting, ticketing, or expelling people from a town or city.

Further, migration is often associated with loss. From his earliest years, Keme experienced the results of multigenerational trauma from colonization and the residential school or boarding school systems. He grew up in a community affected by poverty, assimilation, oppression, and cultural genocide. In discussing experiences of mobility, however, Keme asserted that his people were traditionally migratory and that movement is a component of his culture. Noting that foraging lifestyles have emerged due to colonial dislocation, Peter Jordan[54] has used the terms *modern* or *urban forager*, noting that people have developed varied

---

52 Thistle, *Indigenous Definition of Homelessness.*
53 Ibid., 8.
54 Peter Jordan, "The Ethnohistory and Anthropology of 'Modern' Hunter-Gatherers," in *The Oxford Handbook of the Archaeology and Anthropology of Hunter Gatherers*, ed. Vicki Cummings, Peter Jordan, and Marek Zvelebil (Oxford: Oxford University Press, 2014), 903–17.

strategies of subsistence that might be discerned at the local level. This concept could be relevant for understanding experiences of Indigenous homelessness, as migration in the current context is associated with the establishment of the reserve system and forced displacement of Indigenous people from traditional territories. Exploring strategies of survival in urban settings can help identify patterns of subsistence, as people engage in active searches and use knowledge about ways to obtain food, clothing, and shelter in urban settings.

Place attachments and connections to traditional territories are strong. They grow from meanings, memories, and identities associated with lands, natural spaces, or built environments containing physical, social, and structural elements. Forced displacement leads to additional challenges – even trauma – and its role in inequality and exclusion needs to be recognized. Within the context of colonization, exclusionary practices erode the sense of self, connection to land and traditional territory, culture and language, and social cohesion among people living with homelessness. People experiencing migration and homelessness have often left behind social networks, and typically do not have security of tenure in private dwellings. They are also often excluded from public places, or adversely affected by laws on loitering, surveillance, regulations regarding access to certain public places (e.g., parks, malls, street locations), and the closure of shelters or other services during the day, weekends, and holidays.

Josh Brandon and Evelyn Peters[55] have argued that the primary strategy for addressing Indigenous homelessness and migration to cities must be the development of more affordable, safe housing that incorporates Indigenous beliefs and principles. They note that Indigenous people's urban relocation is complicated by "barriers caused by poverty, colonialism and discrimination coupled with cultural differences and a lack of ... experience needed for urban living."[56] Settlement services for Indigenous people could assist with the adjustment process when people move to urban centres. Also needed are more social housing units to provide affordable accommodation in increasingly expensive towns and cities. As Tyler Craig and Blair Hamilton have observed,[57] there are few urban Indigenous housing cooperatives in Canada. Yet this model is consistent with Indigenous values of shared

---

55 Brandon and Peters, "Moving to the City."
56 Ibid., 92.
57 Tyler Craig, and Blair Hamilton, "In Search of Mino Bimaadiziwin: A Study of Urban Aboriginal Housing Cooperatives in Canada," in Brandon and Silver, *Poor Housing*, 81–92.

ownership of the property and self-governance that is not simply a colonial extension of the settler state. As an appropriate model exists, investment is required to establish more Indigenous housing cooperatives; more generally, Indigenous social housing is needed. Perhaps most important, the structural aspects of society leading to Indigenous homelessness – poverty, unemployment, discrimination, and racism – must be addressed to avoid detrimental effects perpetuating some of the worst features of colonial society.

Acknowledgment

This research was supported by the Social Sciences and Humanities Research Council of Canada and several First Nation communities in northeastern Ontario.

5 A Different Kind of "Ecological Refugee": Land Claims, Migration, and Inequalities in Northern Labrador

JOSHUA MOSES

In February 2011, I boarded a plane at Newark International Airport headed for Labrador. I was starting work on a project funded by the National Science Foundation (NSF) on social networks and the impact of land claim settlements on Inuit communities of the north coast of Nunatsiavut, the autonomous area claimed by the Inuit of Newfoundland and Labrador. After a succession of planes, each one smaller and smaller, first to St. John's, the provincial capital of Newfoundland and Labrador for an overnight stay, then Happy Valley-Goose Bay, where due to high winds I had to spend the night, then a short stop at Deer Lake, and finally landing at Nain, where the Twin Otter plane deposited me beside a small shack. My luggage was left outside, rapidly disappearing into the swiftly falling snow.

I watched as the few other people on the plane were picked up by family and friends on snowmobiles dragging wooden sleds used for hauling wood and game, and frequently carrying giggling children in thick parkas. Eventually, I was the only one left waiting. I stood in the swirl of wind and snow for some time, not having a phone or phone number to call, not knowing where to find the house I was to stay in.

After a while, my host showed up – a white man from Australia who had been living in Nain for thirty years. He excavated my luggage from the snow and drove me on ski-doo to the small house typical of northern communities that I was to stay in for nearly six months. Nain is where I had my first research experience in the North, when I began my ongoing education in circumpolar regions. The following year, for the second half of my fieldwork in Labrador, I spent several months in Happy Valley-Goose Bay, the regional hub, following the lives of people who had left North Coast villages like Nain.

In this chapter I contend that the liberal valorization of Canadian Inuit land claim settlements elides the experiences of those on the margins, who are pushed still farther, sometimes forced to leave the land claim settlements themselves.[1] I illuminate the ways intertwining ecological destruction and intensified inequality along pre-existing internal fissures contributes to an environmentally embedded violence that, for many, forecloses the possibility of village life. As Rob Nixon reminds us, "environmental violence needs to be seen – and deeply considered – as a contest not only over space, or bodies, or labour, or resources, but also over time."[2] In this sense, ecological fragmentation and colonial dispossession produce homelessness in ways not immediately obvious, where effects of polices are dispersed over time. The shapes of policies made generations ago can be discerned in the present. Ecology as a set of relationships includes time as a variable on multiple scales: geological, generational, the time it takes an eighteen-year-old young man with holes in his boots to walk across Happy Valley-Goose Bay.

What is at stake here is a re-engineering of governance that shifts responsibility for Inuit communities from federal hands to Inuit self-governance, while at the same time creating, with remarkable sleight of hand, new engines for large-scale resource extraction.[3] This is done frequently under the cloak of celebrating "traditional culture,"[4] while making increasingly precarious the futures of the very people whose culture is being celebrated.[5] In other words, those whose lives most depend on the land, who are closest to the economic margins, are held up as symbols of Inuit culture while disappearing from the land, which was meant to improve their lives, or hanging on in an increasingly fracturing landscape dominated by a global search for raw materials.

---

1 Kirk Dombrowski et al., "Relocation Redux: Labrador Inuit Population Movements and Inequalities in the Land Claims Era," *Current Anthropology* 57, 6 (2016): 785–805.
2 Rob Nixon, *Slow Violence and the Environmentalism of the Poor* (Cambridge, MA: Harvard University, 2011).
3 Kirk Dombrowski, "The White Hand of Capitalism and the End of Indigenism as We Know It," *Australian Journal of Anthropology* 21, no. 1 (2010): 129–40, https://doi .org/10.1111/j.1757-6547.2010.00071.x.
4 Joshua Moses et al., "Confounding Culture: Drinking, Country Food Sharing, and Traditional Knowledge Networks in a Labrador Inuit Community," *Human Organization* 76, no. 2 (2017): 171–83, https://www.jstor.org/stable/26536860.
5 Dombrowski et al., "Relocation Redux."

Many have benefited from historic land transfers to Indigenous communities. Undoubtedly this is a critical step in redressing ongoing colonial violence. Not everyone has benefited, however, and the distribution of benefits has not been distributed equally. Nunatsiavut is embedded in the structural dynamics of capitalism, which nearly guarantees stark inequalities that reflect the global order in which it is embedded. Land claim settlements are negotiated in the context of settler laws and regulations not chosen by Indigenous communities, but that they are forced to navigate. The young people I describe here are individuals who are particularly vulnerable, as they lack the financial resources and status that can buoy one up during difficulty and times of rapid social and economic change. The NSF-funded study that brought me to Nain and Happy Valley-Goose Bay focused on the impact of land claim settlements, and how they did – or did not – improve village life. Surely, it is very costly to build new houses in the Canadian North, and intergovernmental shifts in power and attendant policy changes can take a long time to affect day-to-day life. But the young people without money and nowhere to go described here do not have much time, and often they are asking only for the minimum conditions for life: a warm and safe place to go – something that does not seem too much to demand from one of the wealthiest countries on the planet.

This chapter aims to reveal the environmentally embedded violence that structures day-to-day relationships for some in Labrador. First, I provide a historical context of the land claim settlement in Labrador; then I describe the lives of several of the young people I spent time with in Happy Valley-Goose Bay – the first stop for most Inuit leaving Nain.

Many of the people I worked with in Happy Valley-Goose Bay were disappeared in a double sense: from the villages they call home and from the ethnographic record. Culture, in this way, acts simultaneously as a tool for organizing politics and mobilizing the resources essential for regaining rights to land and, unwittingly, as a force for the elision of particular people from the very gains that were meant to improve their lives. Culture has both violence and liberation attached to it, making it one of the most complicated and volatile terms in the English language – a word that has had a particular impact on the daily lives of Indigenous people in the North. In this sense, anthropologists (and other academics) have played a significant role in how life in the North is imagined and structured.

Background

Nain, with a population of about 1,200, roughly 90 per cent of whom identify as Inuit,[6] was established as a Moravian mission in 1771. Nain has one main road, and during the time I was there, a grocery store and several smaller "convenience stores" where one could purchase staples, as well as rent movies. The beautiful old wooden Moravian Church, built in the early twentieth century, sits towards the northern end of town, where many of the older weathered homes – many at the time of my visit did not have plumbing – dot the gently sloped landscape.

During the time I spent in Nain and Happy Valley-Goose Bay, I heard the former referred to as "*Viet*nain," and the "rough" side of town was known as the Bronx. As someone who was born in the Bronx and grew up in the New York City area during the seventies and eighties, its invocation had a particular resonance. The Bronx became a national symbol of urban decay, racialized violence, and the failure of social policy – at the very least "the Bronx" suggested the perception that Nain was a dangerous or violent place. The reference to Vietnam signalled a sense of chaos, unravelled social order, and perhaps even struggles against colonial occupation. It is true that I heard a great deal about day-to-day violence in Nain. But, of course, this was not the whole story. People were also kind, generous, and welcoming, and took nearly every chance to go off on the land and have a "boil up" – where we would light a fire, boil up some black tea, and eat hot dogs roasted over the fire. They exhibited the strength of community that continued to struggle against ongoing colonial occupation and inequality with a deeply admirable sense of magnanimity and fortitude.

It did not become a population centre, at least by Arctic standards, until the forced relocation of Inuit from Hebron, roughly 190 kilometres to the north, during the mid- to late 1950s. The relocations of Inuit communities are considered one of the great tragedies of Canadian treatment of Indigenous peoples.[7] As part of the post–Second World War bureaucratic consolidation of Arctic populations, Inuit communities were forced to move to villages for the purposes of state sovereignty and control. Relocations continue to haunt many communities,

---

6 Statistics Canada, "2011 National Household Survey Aboriginal Population Profile – Indian Bands/Métis Settlements/Inuit Regions" (Ottawa), accessed 12 November 2018.
7 Frank James Tester and Paule McNicoll, "Isumagijaksaq: Mindful of the State: Social Constructions of Inuit Suicide," *Social Science & Medicine* 58, no. 12 (2004): 2625–36, https://doi.org/10.1016/j.socscimed.2003.09.021.

providing major social and economic fault lines.[8] Relocatees continue to be among the most marginalized community members in Nain. They also frequently remain marginalized in the communities to which they migrate – in this case, Happy Valley-Goose Bay.

In 2005, after a long political struggle, the Village of Nain became the administrative capital of Nunatsiavut, which in English means "Our Beautiful Land." Since the 1970s, Canada has seen the settlement of numerous disputed and massive Indigenous land claims. Following years of courtroom negotiations, research – frequently by anthropologists – has focused on traditional cultural use of lands, environmental impact statements, and mapping.[9] A vast array of documents was amassed, including the nearly 400-page *Our Footprints Are Everywhere*,[10] under the editorship of anthropologist Carol Brice Bennett, who was instrumental her use of the anthropologist's professional tools in creating the legal and cultural arguments that played a critical role in settling the claims in Labrador. The result has been, at least in part, the transference of tremendous land, wealth, and autonomy to Labrador Inuit communities.

As is widely documented, Labrador Inuit have high rates of suicide, among other social challenges. Suicide rates are frequently more than ten times the national average.[11] Housing shortages, unemployment rates reaching nearly 50 per cent,[12] and the rapid influx of capital through payments from the Impact Benefits Agreement have resulted in increasing inequality (for some), which continues to fragment relationships and make village life a struggle for many. As Dombrowski and colleagues write, "economic conditions in communities at the

---

8 Kirk Dombrowski et al., "Kinship, Family, and Exchange in a Labrador Inuit Community," *Arctic Anthropology* 50, no. 1 (2013): 89–104, https://doi.org/10.3368/aa.50.1.89.

9 Pamela R. Stern and Lisa Stevenson, eds., *Critical Inuit Studies: An Anthology of Contemporary Arctic Ethnography* (Lincoln: University of Nebraska Press, 2006).

10 Carol Brice-Bennett and Labrador Inuit Association, *Our Footprints Are Everywhere: Inuit Land Use and Occupancy in Labrador* (Nain: Labrador Inuit Association, 1977).

11 Nathaniel J. Pollock et al., "Suicide Rates in Aboriginal Communities in Labrador, Canada," *American Journal of Public Health* 106, no. 7 (2016): 1309–15, https://doi.org/10.2105%2FAJPH.2016.303151; Carmela Alcántara and Joseph P. Gone, "Reviewing Suicide in Native American Communities: Situating Risk and Protective Factors within a Transactional-Ecological Framework," *Death Studies* 31, no. 5 (2007): 457–77, https://doi.org/10.1080/07481180701244587; Laurence Kirmayer, Lucy Boothroyd, and Stephen Hodgins, "Attempted Suicide among Inuit Youth: Psychological Correlates and Implications for Prevention," *Canadian Journal of Psychiatry* 43, no. 8 (1998): 816–2, https://doi.org/10.1177/070674379804300806.

12 Statistics Canada, "2011 National Household Survey Aboriginal Population Profile."

centre of successful land claims can change significantly and for the worse for those on the community's social margins despite the new opportunities."[13]

For those who have no experience with the North, it is difficult to imagine the immensity of Arctic territories and the size of the land claims. The territory of Nunavut, for instance, established in 1999, is the fifth-largest subdivision in the world and the largest in North America. These are some of the largest land transfers in recent history.

The logic of land claim settlements requires meticulous legal documentation of land use. Their success rests on the extent it can be proven that claimants rely on land-based activities for their household reproduction, as well as archaeological evidence of long-term habitation, or use of land from "time immemorial." The legal structure itself requires a documentation and particular performance of *nativeness*.[14]

Thousands and thousands of hours of recorded material exist on the specificities of who hunts what with whom. How many partridges did you catch with so and so? How many caribou? How many salmon, char, or cod? How many seals? How many polar bears? Where exactly were these harvested? How long has your family used the piece of land? This kind of work has formed much of the core of Arctic anthropology, playing a determining role in how the Arctic is imagined both inside and outside the scholarly world.

The point here is that the legal process of the claim requires a certain kind of nativeness, one predicated on a particular kind of difference[15] –not simply an abstract otherness, but one that can be counted, quantified, and measured – where, to be Inuit, to *have* Inuit *culture*, is to be tied to land, to engage in practices of hunting, fishing, and gathering.[16] To cease to live in this way is, in the view of the state and many white people, is to cease to be Inuit. Land claim processes create an intensely pressurized dynamic where identity, *Inuitness* (and Indigenousness), has tied to it very real political-economic

13 Dombrowski et al., "Relocation Redux," 794.
14 Elizabeth Povinelli, *The Cunning of Recognition* (Durham, NC: Duke University Press, 2022).
15 Gerald Sider, *Living Indian Histories: The Lumbee and Tuscarora People in North Carolina* (Chapel Hill: University of North Carolina Press, 2003).
16 Pamela Stern, "From Area Studies to Cultural Studies to Critical Inuit Studies," in *Critical Inuit Studies*, ed. Pam Stern and Stevenson (Lincoln: University of Nebraska Press, 2006), 253–67.

consequences, as well as less decipherable psychic, relational, and psychological importance.

Like many other Indigenous political organizations, the Labrador Inuit Association was formed in the early 1970s. For over thirty years, the organization advocated for Labrador Inuit self-governance, which was granted in 2005. After more than two hundred years of colonial dispossession, missionaries, false promises, and welfare colonialism, in other words, Canada, so the narrative goes, had finally gotten nice (or nicer) and given land back to the Inuit.

As an example of the affective logic of the state's shifting largesse, the *inukshuk*, a symbol of Inuit culture, appeared in the 2010 Vancouver Winter Olympics,[17] announcing that Canada had embraced Inuit identity fully into the national imagination – along with profits from the Olympics. The coming together of settlers and Inuit, the "healing" of Canada's ongoing shame for this blemish in its liberal progressive narrative, heralded a new era – one in which Inuit could maintain their cultural difference, their communities, while having the possibility of economic autonomy and, simultaneously, be truly welcomed as Canadians. Inuit culture would now be preserved, protected by self-determination and emancipation from colonial governments. Subsistence ways of life, celebrated by the land claim process, would be secure. The land, which was taken and enclosed by the Crown, would now be Inuit land, developed in ways to perpetuate the flourishing of new generations.

The story, however, is not so simple. Large-scale resource extraction projects are intertwined with most recent large land claim settlements in the Canadian North.[18] Voisey's Bay, one of the largest nickel deposits in the world, was discovered in 1993 just outside Nunatsiavut and not directly subject to the land claim settlement; the mine was sold to Vale Inco for $4.3 billion. The mine was said by some Inuit, industry, and government officials to hold the key to the future of Labrador Inuit.[19] To give an idea of the financial scale and the rush towards development, following the discovery of Voisey's Bay there was an exploration rush not seen before in Labrador.

---

17 Christine M. O'Bonsawin, "'No Olympics on stolen native land': Contesting Olympic Narratives and Asserting Indigenous Rights within the Discourse of the 2010 Vancouver Games," *Sport in Society* 13, no. 1 (2010): 143–56, https://doi.org/10.1080/17430430903377987.
18 Dombrowski et al., "Relocation Redux."
19 Christopher Alcantara, *Negotiating the Deal: Comprehensive Land Claims Agreements in Canada* (Toronto: University of Toronto Press, 2013).

Annual expenditure on exploration in Labrador between 1990 and 1994 increased from $75,000 to $3.7 million, rising to $61.5 million in 1995, and to $81.4 million in 1996. Following 2005, another wave of exploration occurred – primarily for uranium and iron ore – with a price tag during that year of over $30 million.[20] A three-year moratorium on mining was lifted in 2011, and exploration in the region appears to be ramping up.[21]

Similar dynamics can be found in other Inuit contexts of Nunavut, the Inuvialuit Settlement Region, and Nunavik. Mineral exploration seems to hasten the settlement of Indigenous land claims – in Alaska as well as in Canada.[22] But, as David Harvey observes, "providing legal title for land and property ownership in the hope that this will bring economic and social stability to the lives of the marginalized will almost certainly lead in the long run to their dispossession and eviction."[23] Although life improves for many after land claims are settled, for others the benefits are not as clear. Through an alchemical process of corporate-governmental transmutation, independence, for some, begins to look a great deal like another form of dispossession. As Dombrowski and colleagues write:

> Even as traditional subsistence and land-based practices lay the groundwork for the justification and delimitation of claims, mineral, energy, and other natural resource extraction degrades the sustainability of those lifestyles and livelihoods via a process of environmental damage, population concentration, competing housing needs from the influx of new (development and self-government) workers, and a general process of inflation that goes with a more thorough immersion in a global cash economy.[24]

20 Keith Storey, Larry Felt, and David Vardy, "Action Canada Papers on Labrador Mining, Aboriginal Governance and Muskrat Falls" (St. John's: Memorial University of Newfoundland, Harris Centre), https://www.mun.ca/harriscentre/media/production/memorial/administrative/the-harris-centre/media-library/reports/research/2011/ActionCanadaReportOct2011Web.pdf, accessed 10 May 2022.
21 Evan Careen, "Labrador Uranium Inc. looking for a big deposit in the Big Land," *Saltwire*, 25 October 2021, https://www.saltwire.com/atlantic-canada/business/labrador-uranium-inc-looking-for-a-big-deposit-in-the-big-land-100649853/.
22 Kirk Dombrowski, *Against Culture: Development, Politics, and Religion in Indian Alaska* (Lincoln: University of Nebraska Press, 2001).
23 David Harvey, *Seventeen Contradictions and the End of Capitalism* (New York: Oxford University Press, 2014).
24 Dombrowski et al., "Relocation Redux," 786.

The legal mechanism for this process is Impact Benefit Agreements (IBAs), which provide for closed-door direct negotiations between Indigenous governments and corporations.[25] It is also a mechanism whereby the federal government removes itself from the negotiation process, allowing newly formed Indigenous governments to negotiate deals with some of the wealthiest and most powerful multinational corporations in the world. Such deals are confidential, so the details are unknown. But we do know that land is exploited in ways that would not easily be accepted if it had remained Crown land.[26] The land, then, said to be liberated in ways congruent with a particular narrative of Inuit culture, is exploited in new ways that benefit some Labrador Inuit while excluding others, and benefiting corporations and provincial and federal governments.

Those who are left out are frequently those who were closer to what had been presented as the ideal of Inuit culture, closer to subsistence lives, and less reliant on the cash economy. Many are younger people, who are pushed out of small communities like Nain and make their way to Happy Valley-Goose Bay, roughly 370 kilometres away by plane. Happy Valley-Goose Bay is the regional hub city where – although outside the land claim settlement – a hospital, nursing homes, and a jail can be found, as well as an escape from increasingly difficult village life. It is the young people who end up there who concern me in this chapter.

Arctic anthropology as a subfield has maintained an overwhelming focus on village life. In particular, anthropologists have focused on traditional knowledge – hunting, fishing, food sharing, navigation, and crafts. Although very important, this focus on village life typically ignores those who *leave* villages, disappearing them from the ethnographic record.[27] What I describe here little resembles the villages depicted in many northern ethnographies. Instead, it bears a greater resemblance to rural and urban poor throughout North America, where young people negotiate lives in the interstices of bureaucracies and roadways more frequently than in pristine Arctic landscapes. Northern cities are not frequently the subject of Arctic anthropological imagination, providing little in the way of "traditional knowledge" and other

---

25 Ken J. Caine and Naomi Krogman, "Powerful or Just Plain Power-Full? A Power Analysis of Impact and Benefit Agreements in Canada's North," *Organization & Environment* 23, no. 1 (2010): 76–98, https://doi.org/10.1177/1086026609358969.
26 Dombrowski, "Against Culture."
27 Dombrowski et al., "Relocation Redux."

subjects of classic Arctic ethnography. I now turn to Happy Valley-Goose Bay, where I did the second part of my fieldwork[28] a year after working in Nain.

The Urban in the North

Northern cities have their own urban form. With the feeling of a transient crossroads, sprung out of flat, circumpolar landscape, Happy Valley-Goose Bay was founded as a military base during the Second World War. The old section of town is filled with rusting corrugated steel buildings, old airstrips, and decaying military machinery. Several people told me about the hidden toxic dumps behind the base. Flat and sprawling, the town has no centre, few sidewalks, and few public spaces. In the winter, wind whips through the boreal forest, bending dwarf conifers. Snowbanks of 3 metres or higher are not uncommon. Spring is a season of boot-sucking mud, giving way in summer to cracked earth and dust that swirls in the air, getting into clothing, homes, and eyes.

To the "southern" eye, Goose Bay provides no succour in the form of familiar building styles, a downtown, or welcoming restaurants and cafes. Instead, an unnerving sense of vulnerability, of being small against the backdrop of vast space, pervades. The streets are laid out in such a way as to make a walker feel small against the wide roads and the landscape just outside of town – and if you are without money or a home, smaller still. The centre of activity is the Tim Hortons coffee shop; it always has a long line of trucks outside. Newer suburban-style houses typify residential streets, in surprising contrast to older, smaller homes and the stark subarctic landscape just beyond the settlement's sprawl. The Churchill Falls hydroelectric project brings big dollars and large numbers of labourers from the South, but you can still find trappers running trap lines living in tents outside of town through the winter, not far from large new houses under construction. Many I spoke with looked to the horizon for a world of hunting and fishing that seemed to be rapidly diminishing.

---

28 Research was carried out with the oversight and approval of the Nunatsiavut Research Committee. All participants gave informed consent to be interviewed. Participants were compensated monetarily for their time.

No Place to Go

Rona

In Goose Bay, I met several relocatees from Nain whom I had spent time with the previous year. Through our conversations, I began to see how they embodied the ways in which village life had become untenable for them. When I met Rona, I immediately remembered her from our first meeting in Nain a year earlier.

"I saw a wolf out on the ice the other day," Rona told me when I first met her in Nain.

"What'd you do?" I asked.

"I ran it over with my ski-doo," she replied. I didn't know what to say.

"Wow," I said, trying not to sound judgmental or surprised, "and then what happened?" I asked.

"I kept running it over and over. It wouldn't die, so I kept running it over and over. It wouldn't die."

I thought about telling her there was no need to run down a solitary wolf on the winter ice and repeatedly maul it with a snowmobile. But I didn't. Being the good lay student of natural history, I had read that wolves rarely attacked people. This particular conversation continues to haunt me – the phrase *it wouldn't die*. I pictured a young girl on the ice on her snowmobile, alone, and a wolf, trotting along, and the bloody encounter that ensued. I could not imagine why she would do such thing.

When I met Rona again in Happy Valley-Goose Bay, I asked, "Rona, you left Nain?"

"Yes, couldn't take it anymore. Too much drinking, too much problems, too much suicide, violence."

Rona, like many of the others I interviewed, articulated this sense of miasmic, pervasive violence. "Too much drinking, too much problems, too much suicide, violence." I had heard nearly the same sentence dozens of times. It got to the point that I heard the words in my head before they were even said. Playing back my interviews, I was struck by how accustomed I became to hearing stories of suicide and violence. No longer did I stop interviews but instead would go on, politely acknowledging that something tragic had been shared, but no longer taken aback. There was a year in Nain that people spoke of where there were eleven suicides in a nine-month period. Suicide is one way to get out of an impossible situation, where inhabitable futures are in short

77

supply. Another way is to get on a boat in the night and leave behind your family, your community, and your land. Still another way is to end up in jail or in a treatment centre. In all of these cases, people disappear from village life.

While Inuit youth become data in ever-growing heaps of data on suicide and other well-documented struggles with daily life, one of the main sources of the ongoing and sometimes intensified dislocation is left largely unstated.[29] Self-governance in northern Canada *is* resource extraction, and resource extraction is big dollars and big politics. De Beers, Vale, and BHP, to name a few of the multinationals involved, drive a great deal of the politics. The complex ways that such dispossession works on the life chances of young rural Inuit appear to be of little interest to governments. This form of governance is yet another way of disavowing responsibility for the lives of young Inuit, in effect disappearing them,[30] rendering them disposable while at the same time proclaiming that their culture has been safeguarded by land claim settlements.

Walkers in the Snow

If you stood on the corner near the Friendship Centre for any length of time during my stay I was in Happy Valley-Goose Bay, you would likely see Boas, Larry, or Lee silently walking either a threesome or alone. All three were from Nain and had arrived in Goose Bay for different reasons. But they all had experiences with housing scarcity and a daily life seemingly bent on grinding them down, on making a tenable future in Nain unlikely.

Boas told me that he left Nain because he was being teased too much and ultimately could not find anywhere to stay. A soft-spoken young man with a speech disorder, he told me, "People kept picking on me, picking on me. And then finally I had to leave."

Lee also spoke little. He had a twitch in one eye. When I asked him why he left Nain, he replied, "I got kicked out."

"Of where," I asked, "of the whole town?"

"I had nowhere to stay," he replied. "Nowhere to go."

---

29 Lisa Stevenson, *Life Beside Itself: Imagining Care in the Canadian Arctic* (Berkeley: University of California Press, 2014).
30 Audra Simpson, "The State Is a Man: Theresa Spence, Loretta Saunders and the Gender of Settler Sovereignty," *Theory & Event* 19, no. 4 (2016), https://doi.org/10.3138/9781487532048-004.

His sister later told me that he had had a glue-sniffing problem, which explained his mental lurches, his twitches, and the sporadically rolling eyes. Lee began paying daily visits to the office where we work. He would sit outside, seemingly wanting to talk. Throughout the time I spent in Goose Bay, I ran into young men like Lee numerous times. Sometimes we would sit together quietly, or I would question them about their lives.

"What have you guys been doing?"

"Walking, we've been walking," they would inevitably report.

"Where do you go?" I asked.

"We go to the Friendship Centre. Then, if the library is open, we go there for the computer, and then we walk to Northmart [the grocery store], and then we just walk."

Sometimes I would run into them late at night. Once, at two in the morning, when coming back from a late-night walk in the subzero weather, I ran into Boas, walking alone. "What are you doing out so late, Boas?" I asked, surprised and pleased to see him.

"Just walking," he said, disappearing quietly into the freezing night.

For me, these three young men came to signify the displacement and homelessness experienced by many of the young people who leave Nain and other parts of the North Coast. After interviewing nearly 250 people in Goose Bay, it was the eerie sense of displacement and their predictable reply to my queries – we are walking, just walking – that continue to echo. Despite freezing Arctic winds, they would walk – not so much because they liked to walk, it seemed, but because they had nowhere else to go, nothing else to do. The land claim settlement – you could see a large sign for the Impact Benefit Agreements Office near where I often saw them –seemingly had done little to make their lives better.

Once, we went to visit Boas at Newman's Boarding House. I had heard about the place, read articles, and even listened to people talk about it on the radio. The place had become a source of local frustration and anger, the kind you might find in any suburban community that was trying to "clean up" and deal with the "problems of homelessness." Newman's was a privately owned boarding house that took contracts from the province, frequently for people re-entering from prison or being released from hospital. A de facto shelter, it had the reputation for maintaining a harsh regime, forcing guests to be up and out in the morning, regardless of weather.

We visited Newman's on a slushy, rainy March day. Smoke-filled, battered, dark halls made it difficult to locate Boas. We found him watching TV in his room. He agreed to come down to Burger King for an interview, where we bought him a burger. During the interview, we learned that he was twenty-one years old. His speech was difficult to understand. Boas spent four years in Ontario for treatment, though when I asked him what it was for, he said he couldn't remember. He was in three foster homes. He said that he had wanted to move back to Nain to see what it was like, but when he returned it did not take him long to realize that he could not live there.

"Why did you want to leave Nain?" I asked.

"I didn't like the drinking," he replied. "People spent all their money on booze and drugs. No money to buy food. Hard life. No food. It's hard life up there. People were picking on me and stealing my money. Too much suicide, drinking, and smoking. People were always picking on me. There was a couple months where I only ate bread and water and some soup."

"Boas," I asked, "would you move back there?"

"No," he says, "I couldn't live there again."

"Do you like living in Goose Bay?" I asked, "Do you like it better than Nain?"

"Yes, I like it a lot better," he said without pause.

I thought about Newman's, the smoky halls and holes in the wall, and the late-night walking in the cold. I thought about his boots with the holes in them, and how cold his feet must be walking around in the night. To find this life much better, it seemed, meant that what he was leaving behind was indeed a painful and desperate life, a life made to make life unlikely, unliveable. That Boas considered his life in Goose Bay better was an indictment of the forces that structured his possibilities for a decent life, one with dignified housing, safety, and the community of care he required.

I had experience of what Boas was talking about. I had met some of his family when I spent time in Nain. What struck me about Boas's words, and those of his constantly walking friends, was the sense of utter abandonment. Boas found himself in the interstices of space, of capital, rendering him and others like him disposable, leaving them on the trash heaps of the global search for resources. He was an inheritor of colonial time's accumulation of violence, which marked his body and created the conditions for his homelessness – and here in the Canadian liberal state, in an era of land claim settlements, of self-governance, and when the state finally had "gotten nicer." In 2014, after thirty years, Newman's closed. The thirty-three residents were given twenty-four hours to move out. "I almost feel like an animal," one of the former residents was reported by the CBC as saying.[31] New trucks and growing subdivisions continue to populate Goose Bay.

Melanie

Melanie, a young woman, had planned to leave Nain for several years. Finally, at the age of seventeen, she and her cousin boarded a boat bound for Goose Bay.

"What was it that told you needed to get out?" I asked.

She responded: "At that time before I moved, I was seeing a counsellor and not having enough food for myself and no jobs around and the peers at that time weren't peers. They were more I guess enemies just trying to pick on other people. I don't trust a lot of people, because everyone I grew up with stole. My sister and brother stayed with me and stole. Don't really let people into my house."

I asked, "Do you mostly spend time with other folks from the Nain, other Inuit?"

"Well, I'm home twenty-four-seven with my girls ... but I don't let them into my house because they steal from me," she replied.

She told me that she didn't currently work because there was no one to trust with her three girls, particularly her family. "I don't have any adults to talk to," she said. "Mostly I'm at home. Can't trust people."

Melanie's vigilant protection of her children required isolation from the very networks that are frequently seen as a source of support. This sense of social isolation, "the strength of no ties," points to deep fragmentation, where isolation becomes one of the few tools left for survival and for protection of children. It is a strength born of deep sadness and a near-unspeakable psychic homelessness. It is part of an ongoing dispossession: of land, of livelihood, of care, of home.[32]

Conclusion

In this chapter, I have sought to articulate how land claim settlements – underwritten by large-scale resource extraction – produce new forms of marginality while proclaiming improvement of the Canadian state's

---

31 Johnny Hodder, "Homeless in Happy Valley-Goose Bay remain plagued by lack of housing and programs," *CBC News*, 29 September 2018, https://www.cbc.ca/news/canada/newfoundland-labrador/labrador-homeless-transient-housing-1.4841125.
32 Julia Christensen, *No Home in a Homeland: Indigenous Peoples and Homelessness in the Canadian North* (Vancouver: UBC Press, 2017).

treatment of Inuit. I have also suggested the ethical responsibility of contemporary ethnography to engage with current Arctic social life. We need to jettison our beloved fantasies, to recognize that the ongoing political-economic production of marginality and the processes of dispossession in the Arctic are intertwined with the production of knowledge – in particular, *anthropological knowledge* – and the political life of culture, which have very real continuing implications for how people live and die.

Researchers – particularly anthropologists – have a bad name in the North. Anyone who has conducted a few interviews in northern Indigenous communities is familiar with phrases such as "I don't trust researchers. They just want to take and don't give anything back." Many researchers have contributed thoughtfully to conversations on how to make their work more ethical. Some have embraced Indigenous methods, abandoning anything that looks like traditional ethnography or what they consider to be extractive forms of research. Others continue to believe that "objective" ethnography has yet a role to play. I don't know what is right. I have not found a way to conduct research with northern Indigenous communities that seems commensurate with their needs. I continue to question whether or not the needs of the academy can be reconciled with the needs of Indigenous communities. Does the world need more ethnography on northern communities, published on academic presses – with price tags upwards of $40? I am not so sure. Might there be better ways to structure and share the kinds of knowledge produced in the academy? The discipline of anthropology still fetishizes the monograph, frequently published years after the original research was conducted, and read by few. It seems to me that there are many other ways one could imagine contributing meaningfully to communities in the North (and elsewhere). Many people are already doing this vital and creative work, despite the limitations of the academy. But perhaps the very idea of the academy that we have become accustomed to is unravelling in ways that we are only beginning to truly take in (particularly in the United States), as part of both a process of "decolonization" and a process of dissolution of so many of the institutions that we have come to take for granted.

This piece was composed with a sense of sadness and hesitation. In September 2018, *CBC News* published an article with the headline, "Homeless in Happy Valley-Goose Bay remain plagued by lack of housing and programs."[33] Once, we took Lee to see his grandfather at a nurs-

---

33 Hodder, "Homeless in Happy Valley-Goose Bay."

ing home at the edge of town. In remote Labrador communities, older people are usually faced with hard end-of life choices: to die at home with limited medical care or to fly to Happy Valley-Goose Bay to die in a hospital far from home. Separated by fifty years, both Lee and his grandfather had experienced dislocation, both had witnessed incarnations of governmental malfeasance, both were refugees in their own land, experiencing the long loneliness and remarkably malleable state policies bent on rendering them disposable people. For me, this was a metaphor of sedimented relocation, how Canadian Inuit have been dislocated for a hundred years, and this the latest incarnation. Age facing youth, both pushing against a structure bent on rendering them disposable. And a testament to survival.

6 Making Place Home: The Contradictions of Inuit Housing in a Liberal Democracy

FRANK TESTER

In considering housing, homelessness, social policies, and programs affecting the Inuit challenge of "making home," we might start by asking what it is we don't know. The history of contemporary Inuit housing has been documented and analysed in the context of a northern crisis in the history of modernism: the provision of housing by a state wrapped in welfare liberalism that emerged following the Depression and Second World War.[1] This history is understood in relation to processes of political-economic constraints, often inadequately appreciated by both policy analysts and community activists. National social housing policies, since 1945, involve a contest between housing as a market commodity and housing as social need, with the state reluctantly acting to address a failure of the market to provide housing for all.[2] The provision of Inuit housing has been, and continues to be, an exercise in planned cultural change.[3]

---

1 Elizabeth Debicka and Avi Friedman, "From Policies to Building: Public Housing in Canada's Eastern Arctic 1950s to 1980s," *Canadian Journal of Urban Research* 18, no. 2 (2009): 25–39, https://www.jstor.org/stable/26193259; Frank Tester, *Iglutaq (In My Room): The Implications of Homelessness for Inuit – A Case Study of Housing and Homelessness in Kinngait, Nunavut Territory* (Kinngait, NU: Harvest Society, 2006); Peter Collings, "Housing Policy, Aging, and Life Course Construction in a Canadian Inuit Community," *Arctic Anthropology* 42, no. 2 (2005): 50–65, https://www.jstor.org /stable/40316646; Frank Tester and Peter Kulchyski, *Tammarniit (Mistakes)* (Vancouver: UBC Press, 1994).
2 Greg Sutor, *Still Renovating: A History of Canadian Social Housing Policy* (Montreal; Kingston, ON: McGill-Queen's University Press, 2016).
3 Frank Tester, "Iglutaasaavut (Our New Homes): Neither 'New' nor 'Ours': Housing Challenges of the Nunavut Territorial Government," *Journal of Canadian Studies* 43, no. 2 (2009): 137–58, https://doi.org/10.3138/jcs.43.2.137; Peter Dawson, "Seeing Like an Inuit Family: The Relationship between House Form and Culture in Northern Canada," *Inuit Studies* 30, no. 2 (2006): 113–35, https://doi.org/10.7202/017568ar;

What we know does not stop there. Anthropologists and aspiring architects, planners and designers from southerly climes have detailed change and adaptations to settlement living, the shift from forms of shelter associated with Inuit culture before relocation to settlements, and considerations of cost, climate, and technical constraints in providing modern accommodations in Inuit settlements.[4] Attempts to bend form and structure to accommodate Inuit culture, and the failure to do so in the presence of socio-economic realities and cultural biases embedded in "the idea of progress," have received further attention.[5] Empirical techniques have tracked movement and the use of space in Inuit homes. The results are revealing of resistance to design as an exercise in planned cultural change.[6]

The condition of Inuit housing in Canada has been extensively documented since the early 1990s. Since 1993, concern over social housing has increased with the planned, gradual exit of Canada Mortgage and Housing Corporation (CMHC) from fiscal responsibility for its maintenance.[7] An audit of the Nunavut Housing Corporation (NHC) has

---

David Thomas and Charles Thompson, *Eskimo Housing as Planned Culture Change* (Ottawa: Department of Indian Affairs and Northern Development, Northern Science Research Group, 1972).

4 Lola Sheppard and Mason White, *Many Norths, Spatial Practice in a Polar Territory* (New York; Barcelona: Actar Publishers, 2017); Peter C. Dawson, "'Unsympathetic users': An Ethnoarchaeological Examination of Inuit Responses to the Changing Nature of the Built Environment," *Arctic* 48, no. 1 (1995): 71–80, https://doi.org/10.14430/arctic1226; Robert Robson, "Housing in the Northwest Territories: The Post-war Vision," *Urban History Review* 24, no. 1 (1995): 3–20, https://doi.org/10.7202/1019226ar; Harold Strub, *Bare Poles: Building Design for High Latitudes* (Ottawa: Carleton University Press, 1996); John Honigmann and Irma Honigmann, *Eskimo Townsmen* (Ottawa: University of Ottawa, Canadian Research Centre for Anthropology, 1965).

5 Sheppard and White, *Many Norths*; Jason Warren Borg, "[Re]interpreting Iqaluit's Social Housing Archetypes" (Master's thesis, Carleton University, 2014); Allen Marcus, "Place with No Dawn: A Town's Evolution and Erskine's Arctic Utopia," in *Architecture and the Canadian Fabric*, ed. R. Windsor Liscombe (Vancouver: UBC Press, 2011); Tester and Kulchyski, *Tammarniit*; J. Fried, "Settlement Types and Community Organization in Northern Canada," *Arctic* 16, no. 2 (1963): 93–100, https://www.jstor.org/stable/40507146.

6 Peter C. Dawson, "Unfriendly Architecture: Using Observations of Inuit Spatial Behaviour to Design Culturally Sustaining Houses in Arctic Canada," *Housing Studies* 23, no. 1 (2008): 111–28, https://doi.org/10.1080/02673030701731258.

7 In 1993 CMHC decided to end all subsidies for the maintenance and operation of social housing in Canada. In the 1996 March budget, the federal government withdrew from responsibility for social housing in Canada. The federal debt at the time was $607.3 billion and the deficit was $38.5 billion (Jason Clemens, Charles Lammam, and Niels Veldhuis, "What Canada needed was a Chrétien budget

addressed problems with local housing organizations, reporting, and management,[8] while surveys have identified the extent and nature of homelessness in Inuit communities, with temporary residents found to make up 4 per cent of the population.[9] Temporary residents are primarily Inuit who would be homeless if not accommodated by relatives or others. Thirty-five to 54 per cent of homes in Nunavut are overcrowded, depending on the standard used.[10] Homelessness is made hidden, made invisible in the concept of overcrowding, as no one can live on the streets of an Arctic suburb for long, given the climate. The concept of overcrowding and the application of standards used in Euro-Canadian households have been critically examined, but are seldom tied to the concept of homelessness.[11] In Inuit communities with strong extended family ties and obligations that include accommodating those who might otherwise have nowhere to stay, the concept of homelessness means problems finding a home.

Housing conditions and their relationship to physical and mental health – particularly of women – have been studied in Canada and Greenland. The Standing Senate Committee on Aboriginal Peoples and academic researchers have focused on implications of the housing shortage for social functioning (education, employment, and interpersonal relations).[12] Strategies for dealing with the housing crisis are

2.0," *Globe and Mail*, 27 March 2017). In 2016, the NHC estimated operation and maintenance costs of one social housing unit at $20,000 per year. By 2037, all federal subsidies under the Social Housing Agreement with CMHC will have disappeared, with serious implications for the budget of the NHC. The impact on the housing situation in Nunavut will be considerable.

8 Auditor General of Canada, *Audit of the Nunavut Housing Corporation*, Report to the Legislative Assembly of Nunavut (Ottawa: Office of the Auditor General of Canada, May 2008).

9 Nunavut Housing Corporation, *An Analysis of the Housing Needs in Nunavut: Nunavut Housing Needs Survey 2009/2010* (Statistics Canada, Income Statistics Division, for the Nunavut Housing Corporation, October 2010).

10 "Nunavut government continues homelessness survey in Iqaluit, Rankin Inlet," *Nunatsiaq News*, 17 April 2018, https://nunatsiaq.com/stories/article/65674nunavut _government_continues_its_homelessness_survey_in_iqaluit_and_ra/.

11 Nathanael Lauster and Frank Tester, "Culture as a Problem in Linking Material Inequality to Health: On Residential Crowding in the Arctic," *Health & Place* 16, no. 3 (2010): 523–30, https://doi.org/10.1016/j.healthplace.2009.12.010.

12 Canada, Parliament, Senate, Standing Senate Committee on Aboriginal Peoples [hereafter cited as Standing Senate Committee on Aboriginal Peoples], *We Can Do Better: Housing in Inuit Nunangat* (Ottawa: Senate of Canada, March 2017); Fran Klodawsky et al., "Indigenous and Non-Indigenous Respondents to the Health and Housing in Transition (HHiTT) Study: An Intersectional Approach," in *Indigenous Homelessness in Canada*, ed. Evelyn J. Peters and Julia Christensen (Winnipeg:

characterized by a tension between housing as public provision and housing as a market commodity.[13] Social housing accommodates approximately 50 per cent of Nunavummiut – Inuit of the territory of Nunavut – a figure skewed by Iqaluit, the capital, where privately owned homes account for a larger portion of dwellings than in other communities. If government housing is included, the NHC is responsible for a majority of housing units in the territory. Since at least 1965, housing in most communities has been and remains social housing.

Annual reports of the NHC are thorough, laying out in considerable detail the challenges facing the corporation in dealing with issues of rent, maintenance, and the provision of new units in communities where they are most needed. The corporation is aware of changing demographics and limited capacity in some communities to address the need for housing and maintenance. The NHC has taken notable steps towards streamlining, regulating, and systematizing construction processes for which it is responsible, and it has taken initiatives to encourage training of Inuit in building trades.[14]

Macro-economic considerations relevant to explaining the struggle with public housing and meeting housing needs in the North have been sadly neglected. Liberal democracies in the Western world have encountered fiscal crises, parallel to the growing financial inequalities documented by renowned French economist Thomas Piketty.[15] Not unlike that of other Western countries, Canada's debt has grown since 1975, with the exception of some decline between 1995 and the fiscal crisis of 2008. Growing social costs associated with inequality, environmental challenges, and social needs – including health, education, and social housing – account for this trend. The fiscal crisis was also a revenue crisis, complicated by a globalized economy where industry can relocate to countries with lower wages and tax rates. The re-entry of the federal

---

University of Manitoba Press, 2016): 91–115; Mylene Riva, Christina Viskum Lytken Larsen, and Peter Bjerregaard, "Household Crowding and Psychosocial Health among Inuit in Greenland," *International Journal of Public Health* 59 (2014): 739–48; Tester, *Iglutaq*.

13 This tension, and the impossibility of meeting the housing needs of the vast majority of Inuit households through any private sector initiative, is evident from a read of *Nunavut Housing Requirements, Needs and Demand to 2016*, prepared in 2004 by Bayswater Consulting Group as a background report for a ten-year Nunavut housing strategy being developed at the time.

14 Nunavut Housing Corporation, *Annual Report 2016–17* (Iqaluit, NU: September 2017).

15 Thomas Piketty, *Capital in the Twenty-First Century*, trans. Arthur Goldhammer (Cambridge. MA: Harvard University Press, 2014).

government into the provision of affordable housing, announced in November 2017 as a *National Housing Strategy*, in part subsidizes the private sector for the provision of affordable housing – a classic liberal attempt to deal with an ongoing crisis by subsidizing private interests to meet public needs.

The Inuit housing crisis has been extensively documented. Problems remain, however – notably the desperate need for more housing stock and the socio-economic and personal problems that intersect with problems of tenancy and management. This chapter focuses on two considerations relevant to the current crisis in Inuit housing, where homelessness and overcrowding are intertwined: the meaning of protest and the meaning of home. Protest, seen internationally as an important dimension of social change – especially visual presence intended to attract public and political attention – has no history among Inuit, who, with rare exceptions, historically dealt with conflict through mediation, negotiation, and compromise.[16] Appreciating struggles with the meaning of home requires an examination of housing as an element of a colonial history bent on making Inuit "ordinary Canadians."

The Meaning of Protest

It is often the case that only public protest and outrage – to the extent that they threaten the legitimacy of the party in power – ensures that any degree of adequate funding is directed to social problems. Social change requires public protest (among other things), given the workings of liberal democracy. Knowledge of colonial histories, evidenced by the Truth and Reconciliation Commission of Canada, can be an important source of motivation for public protest and change.

In Nunavut, important problems related to tenancy cannot be solved simply by addressing the need for more units, though more units would help. The construction of housing units required to address the

---

16 Joe Karetak, Frank Tester, and Shirley Taglik. *Inuit Qaujimajatuqangit: What Inuit Have Always Known to Be True* (Halifax, NS: Fernwood Publishing, 2017). However, Inuit did have forms of protest directed at colonial officials in the period when Inuit were relocating, or being relocated, from land-based camps to settlements. This was particularly true of resistance to game laws affecting Inuit hunting. These forms of resistance were personal and clever initiatives designed to trap RCMP officers and others in follies of their own making. See Peter Kulchyski and Frank Tester, *Kiumajut (Talking Back)* (Vancouver: UBC Press, 2007). The effectiveness of uncoordinated and individual protest in relation to social or collective needs is, however, limited.

Figure 6.1. Declining Social Housing Agreement Funding in Nunavut, fiscal
years 1998/99–2037/38

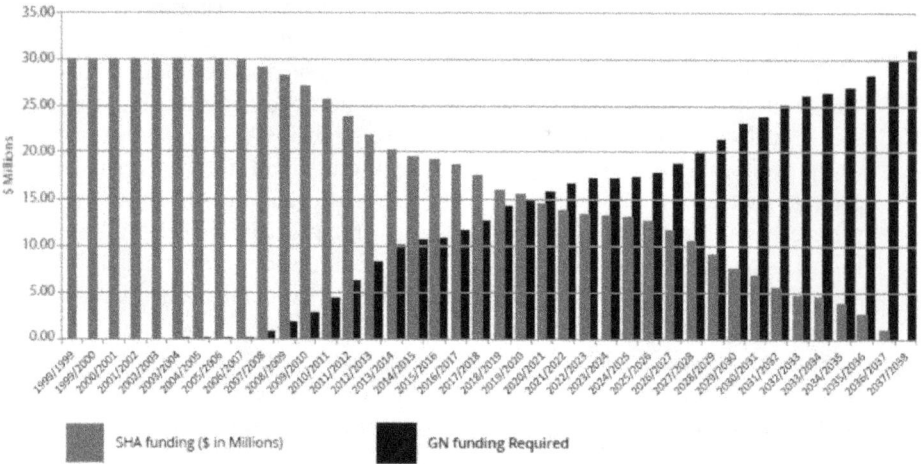

Source: Nunavut Housing Corporation, Brief submitted to the Committee, 23 March 2016.

extensive waiting lists and the critical shortage is a problem with far-reaching consequences. Writing in *i*POLITICS, Kyle Duggen noted in 2018 that $2 billion was needed to provide enough units to make occupancy levels and levels of overcrowding comparable with those experienced by the average Canadian.[17] The Senate report, *We Can Do Better: Housing in Inuit Nunangat*, cites Terry Audla, at the time president of theNHC, as stating that "3,000 housing units were needed to close the housing gap between Nunavut and the rest of Canada."[18] Unless social housing in Nunavut becomes a public issue generating the concern and public attention that makes it a federal priority, there is little reason to believe, based on what has happened to date, that needed changes will happen.

Public concern and support are difficult to achieve in a remote territory of 39,000 people living in widely dispersed communities. Effective protest often involves the occupation of space. Bringing people together from scattered communities, only accessible by air, is

---

17 Kyle Duggen, "Senators to address worsening Northern housing crisis," *iPOLITICS*, 1 May 2018, https://ipolitics.ca/2016/08/18/senators-to-address-worseningnorthern-housing-crisis/.
18 Standing Senate Committee on Aboriginal Peoples, *We Can Do Better*, 14.

challenging and prohibitively expensive. Effective public concern and protest require an appreciation of what one is up against – where the power to make changes lies, who is responsible, and what agencies and individuals can affect change. Canadians are known for letter writing and media campaigns, petitions, lobbying decision makers, and taking to the streets. In Nunavut, cultural, historical, geographic, and social realities compromise these methods of drawing attention to the need for social housing.

Inuit are challenged by socio-economic realities that all Canadians face. Yet, understanding and addressing limits to social change are not well understood by most Canadians, despite a long history with liberal democracy. Inuit, who signed the agreement in 1993 that established Nunavut Territory in 1999 and who suffer from limited educational opportunities, low high school completion rates, and a colonial history, are even more challenged by structural realities affecting the making of social housing policy. What insights are important to better appreciate the challenges of meeting an essential need in this social, political, and geographic climate?

There are many theories that help explain the relationship between fiscal crisis and the making of social policy. Some are arguably better than others. In 1973, James O'Connor published a book titled *The Fiscal Crisis of the State*.[19] His work is perhaps more relevant to explaining and understanding the economics, politics, and crises of the Canadian state in the 2000s than it was to the fiscal crisis of the 1970s. O'Connor's thesis is useful in critically examining state support for forms of capital development that meet Inuit needs for employment and government needs for revenues to meet the social and environmental costs of development, and of social costs in general. This is a legitimation function. It includes ensuring that people have health care and shelter, that the homeless are housed, that children have accessible and quality education, and that people have enough to eat, rights that are respected, and, consequently, are satisfied with those in power. Legitimation functions cost money.

Another state function O'Connor identifies is that of assisting vested interests in the accumulation of capital, particularly the monopoly sector of the economy from which the state derives substantial revenues. This sector is dominated by large, highly advanced and concentrated industries, including, especially in Nunavut, mining. Taxes from this

---

19 James O'Connor, *The Fiscal Crisis of the State* (New York: Routledge, 1973).

sector are an important source of revenue for meeting social needs, including social housing.

O'Connor suggests that the costs of encouraging, subsidizing, and meeting the social and environmental costs of many forms of development are likely, over time, to outstrip tax and other revenues generated by the developments in question. The relationship between Arctic mining, seen as central to the economic future of Nunavut, and the social costs it engenders, have received some, but inadequate, attention.[20] The long-term social and environmental costs could be substantial. The tensions between meeting legitimation functions and aiding the accumulation of capital are many.

The monopoly sector enhances its profitability and grows by taking advantage of automation – replacing, wherever possible, people with machines. Labour relocates from higher-paying skilled jobs to the lower-paid services sector. This places more demand on the legitimation function of the state, as irregular and low-paid employment creates a demand for services.

Addressing the social housing needs of Inuit is a legitimation function – the provision of an essential and costly social good. The result is that needs have always been partially, but never completely, met. Addressing the starvations in the Kivalliq region of Nunavut in the winter of 1957–58 was a clear example of a legitimation function that included the reluctant provision to Inuit of the first rigid frame and matchbox houses and the relocation of Inuit to settlements.[21] At the same time, meeting social need in the most parsimonious way and keeping costs to an absolute minimum are how legitimation functions are typically exercised. Taking additional or exceptional revenues in the form of taxes from the monopoly sector of the economy threatens the accumulation function of the state. In a globalized economy, capital has other places to go. There are, consequently, limits to exercising a legitimation function such as providing $2 billion to give Inuit a housing standard comparable to that of other Canadians.

In some cases, accumulation functions and legitimation functions coincide. The creation of the Thelon Game Sanctuary in 1927, in which only Indigenous peoples could hunt, is an example of a legitimation function: making sure that Indigenous people had exclusive access to fur-bearing species in the territory to keep welfare payments minimal by

20 Karina Czyzewski et al., *The Impact of Resource Extraction on Inuit Women and Families in Qamani'tuaq, Nunavut Territory: A Qualitative Assessment* (Ottawa: Pauktuutit, Inuit Women of Canada, 2014).
21 Tester and Kulchyski, *Tammarniit.*

preventing white trappers from depleting the resource. Especially during the early years of the Depression, this policy initiative also ensured that the Hudson's Bay Company (HBC) was the sole recipient of furs trapped by Indigenous peoples and that its near monopoly was protected. State policy was designed simultaneously to meet Inuit needs for income (a legitimation function) and the HBC's needs for profit (an accumulation function). The social costs of the activities of the HBC, the near singular dependence of Inuit on the fur trade for cash income, and the collapse of that trade in the late 1940s and early 1950s, initiated the move to settlements – Inuit urbanization – and the need to provide Inuit with some minimal form of social housing.[22]

The state has never been willing to pay the considerable social costs associated with the operations of monopoly capital, characteristic of economic development in the northern territories. Alternatively, it has faced residual social and environmental costs that can quickly deplete revenues derived from resource exploitation.[23] The only way to meet Inuit social housing needs, given that no end of research, reports, and surveys have failed to produce results of notable significance, is to make social housing a national social issue. Inuit have to play an increasingly important role in raising these issues and making their social housing needs a national concern.

The housing affordability crisis in Canada increasingly has made headlines and generated public concern. One response was the introduction in the November 2017 federal budget of the Liberal government's *National Housing Strategy*, an initiative that, in effect, aided the accumulation of capital by private sector developers by subsidizing their provision of more affordable housing, a move that spawned public protests across the country.[24] This was a classic liberal initiative,

---

22 Ibid.
23 The costs of dealing with the arsenic left behind in the shafts of the former Giant Yellowknife Gold Mine have been estimated at well over $2 billion; see Indian and Northern Affairs Canada and Government of the Northwest Territories, *Giant Mine Remediation Project: Developer's Assessment Report* (October 2010). This is not a "historical accident," unlikely in an age of tighter regulations and monitoring. The 2014 collapse of a tailings dam at the Mount Polley copper and gold mine in British Columbia will cost the provincial government about $40 million to clean up, with ongoing debate about what the long-term environmental and social costs might be.
24 The strategy was to spend $40 billion over ten years to address the housing crisis, including the transfer to private sector developers of $15.9 billion in exchange for producing 30 per cent of units in their redevelopment or refurbishing of multiple dwelling units that rent for 80 per cent of, or below, the median market rate for twenty years. This has been called a subsidy for gentrification likely to displace as

attempting to address accumulation and legitimation functions at the same time. It included $240 million for Inuit housing; $24 million a year over the ten-year period covered by the strategy, enough to build about forty-eight houses a year in Nunavut. The only protest came from Terry Audla, who noted that, at that rate, it would take sixty years to address the crisis.[25]

The housing crisis in Nunavut owes its strength and persistence, at least in part, to the lack of a culture of activism and protest among Inuit. This is hardly a criticism; rather, it is a recognition that avoidance of conflict and confrontation is integral to Inuit culture and cultural practices. In another study, an Inuk was quoted as saying "I really believe in the Inuit law never to retaliate and to be patient and long-suffering. But this was used to the advantage of these new-comers ... The laws and our belief that you should ... be submissive, was turned against us at a time when we also had no other authority to appeal to. Every newcomer had power over us at that time."[26]

The only notable protests in Nunavut started in 2012, with attention to food prices and food security. The initiator of the protest, which was called "Feeding My Family," clearly understood what she was up against. Organized by Lessee Papatsie, who was reported to spend $600 a week on groceries with only one child at home, this protest was what the *Globe and Mail* correctly identified as "an unprecedented sight in the territory." Inuit paraded in front of Iqaluit's Northern Store carrying placards protesting food prices. "It's against our culture," Ms. Papatsie said. "The Inuit never protested. Traditionally, for the Inuit to survive, everybody had to get along and we didn't create friction. But if we don't start saying something about high costs, then people will think it's okay."[27] In the revised introduction to the 2017 edition of *The Fiscal Crisis of the State*, O'Connor states that his intellectual pursuits were capped by his own commitment to struggle – as he puts it, "within and

<hr>

many poorly housed people as it helps; see Peter Zimonjic, "Liberals detail $40B for 10-year national housing strategy, introduce Canada Housing Benefit," *CBC News*, 22 November 2017, http://www.cbc.ca/news/politics/housing-national-benefit-1.4413615.

25 "$240M for Nunavut housing 'nowhere near' what territory needs, says housing corp," *CBC News*, 6 December 2017, https://www.cbc.ca/news/canada/north/240-million-national-housing-strategy-nunavut-housing-corporation-1.4435911.

26 Karetak, Tester, and Taglik, *Inuit Qaujimajatuqangit*, 184.

27 Ingrid Peritz, "Speaking out against $600-a-week grocery bills," *Globe and Mail*, 17 January 2014, https://www.theglobeandmail.com/news/national/the-north/why-is-food-so-expensive-in-nunavutshop-for-yourself-and-find-out/article15915054/.

against the state" and the importance of democratizing *all* institutions in society.[28]

Inuit participation and opposition to governmental decision making, and government policies and programs, for the reasons outlined by Lessee Papatsie, are in early and fragile stages of development. On northern Baffin Island, the Nunavut Planning Commission held hearings in 2018 on a proposal by Baffinland Iron Mines Corporation to introduce a railway into the transportation corridor between its Mary River mine and a port at Milne Inlet. This produced voices of opposition only when a young member of the Pond Inlet Council took it upon himself to seek help in organizing such a voice. A few residents of Pond Inlet were alone in their efforts. The federal government, territorial government, and even the Qikiqtani Inuit Association – with a mandate to defend Inuit rights and culture – gave the proposal a largely uncritical and passive nod of approval. Inuit protest and initiative has stopped seismic testing offshore from Clyde River and a proposal for an open-pit uranium mine at Qamani'tuaq. Historical and culturally important problems confront Inuit in affecting public policy. A culturally based orientation to non-confrontational means for resolving differences and reaching decisions fits poorly with a liberal democratic tradition characterized by opposition, protest, and contestation in the making of public policy. With respect to action on social housing, this is deserving of attention.

The most significant attempt to incorporate Inuit cultural sensibilities and processes into the making of public policy has been the Nunavut Roundtable for Poverty Reduction, a one-year process conducted between October 2010 and October 2011 that resulted in the Collaboration for Poverty Reduction Act and *The Makimaniq Plan: A Shared Approach to Poverty Reduction*. The purpose of the Act was to establish a participatory process via a roundtable, including participation from non-governmental organizations, with the objective of implementing and monitoring *The Makimaniq Plan* in a manner consistent with Article 32 of the Nunavut Land Claims Agreement. One of the thematic areas contained in *The Makimaniq Plan* is "Housing and Income Support."[29]

Healing from the past and collaboration between Inuit and their government are central to the plan. What is unique about the eastern Arctic

---

28 O'Connor, *Fiscal Crisis of the State*.
29 *Memorandum of Understanding on the Nunavut Roundtable for Poverty Reduction*, signed 24 October 2012, https://www.tunngavik.com/files/2012/10/MOU.pdf.

is that, unlike the rest of the country, the colonial history does not, in any significant way – and contrary to claims made by Maggie Crump, involve settlement or settler relations.[30] Few non-Inuit have chosen to "settle" in Nunavut Territory. What dominates the legacy of Nunavut is a history of administrative presence – principally exercised from Ottawa and Yellowknife – with very different implications than settler-Indigenous relations in other parts of the country.

The legislation and *The Makimaniq Plan*, and the manner in which they were developed, was "intended to serve as a model for the development of social that ensures that Inuit have the right to participate in the development of the territory's social and cultural policy."[31] The process and outcome illustrate what O'Connor describes as a need to address the shortcomings of the capitalist state – for an emphasis on "individual initiatives, horizontal sharing of information and decision making, and the porosity of the state from the standpoint of social movements."[32]

At the same time, while pointing in a constructive direction, there are limits to the roundtable as a way of achieving this emphasis. Social movements are practically unheard of in Nunavut, and the composition of the roundtable includes business interests and representatives of other governments. This raises familiar questions about power and influence in the making of policy.[33]

The Meaning of Home

I now approach the second consideration relevant to making a difference in the attention given to the dire state of Inuit housing. I caution that, in taking the approach below, I am not discounting the reality of overcrowding in Inuit homes or the problems to which it gives rise. Rather, my point is that overcrowding is not a simple problem of "something wrong." It can also be seen as a matter of "something right," where families accommodate youth who might be moving back and forth between jobs in urban centres such as Iqaluit and Rankin Inlet, as well as other family members dealing with unemployment or personal problems.

A focus on meaning is likely to do for the making of housing policy and the process of designing and providing housing, something akin to

---

30 Maggie Crump, "Public Engagement and the Nunavut Roundtable for Poverty Reduction: Attempting to Understand Nunavut's Poverty Reduction Strategy," *Northern Review* 42, no. 1 (2016): 69– 96, https://doi.org/10.22584/nr42.2016.005.
31 Crump, "Public Engagement," 88.
32 O'Connor, *Fiscal Crisis of the State*, xvii.
33 *Memorandum of Understanding*.

what the roundtable process is attempting to do in addressing poverty among Nunavummiut. The question of meaning is wide open to multiple interpretations. This is its decided strength.

Researching the meaning of home is an exercise beset with problems. French philosopher and activist Jean-Paul Sartre had much of importance to say of relevance to the making of meaning, locating it in a struggle for freedom in the face of systems, material circumstances, the behaviour of the Other, and contradictions that press upon us at every turn. Some of his most interesting work includes observations on, and a response to, the anticolonial struggles (1954–62) that freed Algeria from French rule.[34] For Inuit, making meaning includes struggles with a colonial history and a cultural logic not of their making. Making "home" is an exercise bigger than a focus on structure or dwelling.

Many scholars have tackled the problem of meaning and home. The topic has been approached only marginally in dealing with Inuit housing. Julia Christensen, for example, explores what she calls "spiritual homelessness": a trajectory that primarily examines the impact of colonial relations on the meaning of home.[35] What I suggest here takes this consideration in a forward-looking, rather than a historical, direction and focuses on a dimension of decolonization. What needs to happen to bring meaning back to the idea of home?

Shelley Mallett reviews ways the concept of home has been used. She asks if categories should consider home as "place(s), (a) space(s), feeling(s), practices, and/or an active state of being in the world?"[36] The literature describes home as conflated with or related to house, family, haven, self, gender, and journeying. As Mallett notes, many authors

---

34 This struggle, which takes many different forms and is aimed at many different aspects of "the human condition," is, for me, best captured in a collection of Sartre's essays: Ronald Aronson and Adrian Van Den Hoven, eds., *We Have Only This Life to Live: The Selected Essays of Jean-Paul Sartre, 1939–1975* (New York: New York Review of Books Classics, 2013). Sartre's writing suggests the importance of the arts – poetry, theatre, sculpture, and writing – to freedom and the making of meaning in the face of all forms of oppression. Returning design – especially of space – to Inuit minds and hands must be part of this liberation.

35 Julia Christensen, "'Our Home, Our Way of Life': Spiritual Homelessness and the Sociocultural Dimensions of Indigenous Homelessness in the Northwest Territories (NWT), Canada." *Social & Cultural Geography* 14, no. 7 (2013): 804–28, https://doi.org/10.1080/14649365.2013.822089.

36 Shelley Mallett, "Understanding Home: A Critical Review of the Literature," *Sociological Review* 52, no. 1 (2004): 64, https://doi.org/10.1111/j.1467-954X.2004.00442.x.

also consider notions of being-at-home, creating or making home, and the ideal home.

The history of Inuit housing is a history of colonial relations of ruling and attempts at assimilation. The policy that provided Inuit with minimal housing based on A-frames and matchbox designs, commencing in 1959, was a "rent-to-own" initiative intended to introduce the concept of ownership and to ensure that Inuit did not come to expect hand-outs from the state. Houses were provided based on "ability to pay," not need. This was an exercise in safeguarding the balance between accumulation and legitimation in the making of public policy. Attention was given to providing housing in relation to need, only reluctantly, after public health officers with the Indian and Northern Medical Services Branch of the Department of National Health and Welfare made a significant issue out of the health implications of the shack housing in which Inuit were, at the time, living – and dying.[37] The first social housing program was introduced in 1965. Based on need rather than ability to pay, its origins are found in more than one disastrous experience with the matchbox housing provided under the 1959 policy.[38]

Wood-frame houses have no historical place in Inuit culture. This introduces interesting considerations with regard to meaning. Meaning, while resting with the individual, is contained within cultural and historically created cultural practices. The dilemma this creates is not hard to understand when one compares functions accommodated by *iglus*, tents, and *qamaqs* (sod houses) and the well-documented problems encountered in attempts to accommodate these within wood-frame houses.[39] The picture is further complicated in light of the fact that approximately 50 per cent of Inuit households are currently accommodated in approximately five thousand units of public housing. Occupants are not involved in their design, marginally involved in their construction, and not able to make structural changes to accommodate their needs and interests. The normative question, "What should (could) the meaning of home be for Inuit?" is well placed. For a number of important reasons, asking Inuit what home means to them is problematic.

My experience with doing this produces an acquiescent response in the form of well-worn tropes: "Home is where the heart is – right?" or

---

37 Tester, "Iglutaasaavut."
38 Frank Tester, Paule McNicoll, and Quyen Tran, "Structural Violence and the 1962–1963 Tuberculosis Epidemic in Eskimo Point, N.W.T," *Inuit Studies* 36, no. 2 (2012): 165–85, https://www.jstor.org/stable/42870824.
39 Dawson, "Unfriendly Architecture."

"I guess it's where your family lives" or "It's the place where I live and where I keep my stuff." Concerned with the basics – food and a place to lay one's head – questions about meaning are remotely esoteric. There is little space (or time) for their consideration. Studies look at the use of space, with the idea that where Indigenous people spend their time and what they do in those spaces give some clue as to the meaning space has for them. Researchers are more likely listening in on the ongoing struggle Inuit face in dealing with overcrowding and the long list of personal and social problems that accompany it.[40]

More often, I have been confronted with the observation, in relation to Inuit communities, that "being in town feels like being in jail" and that many Inuit "feel free" once they are out of town and at their land-based cabins or camping "on the land." This comment on the community is likely, for many, a comment on the home, not unlike a jail cell, a place and space over which many Inuit have very little control. In one study, an Indigenous Elder related to researchers that he had once been homeless due to addiction issues. He said that being in the bush and being on the land was "being at home." For him, and for many others who have experienced a transient life, the bush, or the land, is a quiet, private place where one is in control of one's activities.[41]

My conviction in visiting questions of meaning in relation to Inuit homes is that the implications of severe restrictions on the making of meaning have been inadequately considered and researched. Donald Appleyard makes observations about the relationships between the making of space and the making of self, consistent with Sartre's notions of Being, or Becoming.[42] The ultimate form of self-expression in relation to space is the construction of one's home – what the construction of an iglu, qamaq, or sealskin tent was all about. In fact, accounts of the annual and collective sewing of the sealskin cover for qamaqs by Inuit women and girls make it clear how important this event was to the relationships and building of solidarity among Inuit women and to the education of young girls. And although most Qallunaat (non-Inuit) no longer

40 Frank Tester, "Iglu to Iglurjuaq," in Critical Inuit Studies: An Anthology of Contemporary Arctic Ethnography, ed. Pamela Stern and Lisa Stevenson (Lincoln: University of Nebraska Press, 2006), 230–52.

41 Marleny Bonnycastle, Maureen Simpkins, and Annette Siddle, "The Inclusion of Indigenous Voices in Co-constructing 'Home': Indigenous Homelessness in a Northern, Semi-urban Community in Manitoba," in Indigenous Homelessness, Perspectives from Canada, Australia, and New Zealand, ed. Evelyn J. Peters and Julia Christensen (Winnipeg: University of Manitoba Press, 2016).

42 Donald Appleyard, "The Environmental as a Social Symbol," Journal of the American Planning Association 45, no. 2 (1979): 143–53, https://doi.org/10.1080/01944367908976952.

build their own homes – something not uncommon in Canada a hundred years ago – the ability to decorate, change, modify, and redefine space is still what making a house a "home" is all about, self-expression being an integral element of self-development. Given the amount of time spent in the home – especially in northern climates – the importance of space in the making of self has been largely overlooked.

The relationship between culture and meaning making raises important questions about who is to be involved in the making of policy and the design and construction of Inuit homes. In a culture experienced by Canadians at more southerly latitudes, there are multiple and competing means for the development of self. The acquisition and manipulation of space is perhaps of less importance to meaning making than in settings where self-expression in the face of unemployment, disability, age, poverty, and climate are more likely to restrict one's presence to the home. I am reminded of one of the more interesting findings from a 2006 study of homelessness in the Nunavut community of Kinngait. Women sometimes feared being at home when poverty and unemployment made it difficult or impossible for their spouse to leave home and "get out on the land." They implied that these circumstances might give rise to moods and behaviours they found threatening.[43]

Citing Appleyard, Nigel Rapport and Andrew Dawson locate ideas about the development of identity in a process – in particular, Peter Berger and Thomas Luckmann's concept of a dialectic between individuals and society, and R.D. Laing's notion of ontological security.[44] This includes notions that an impersonal environment over which someone can exert no control and that can harm a secure sense of identity threaten to engulf or "reify" the individual. The built environment has implications for the development of human identity, as well as for mental health.

Overcrowding is both a symptom and a contributor to a long list of problems confronting Inuit. Findings in Canada and Greenland have associated inequalities in psychosocial health and social well-being with household crowding.[45] A lack of privacy (and other things related

---

43 Tester, *Iglutaq*.
44 Nigel Rapport and Andrew Dawson, *Migrants of Identity: Perceptions of Home in a World of Movement* (Oxford: Berg, 1998).
45 Riva, Larsen, and Bjerregaard, "Household Crowding and Psychosocial Health; Julia Christensen, "Indigenous Housing and Health in the Canadian North: Revisiting Cultural Safety," *Health & Place* 40, no. 1 (2016): 83–90, https://doi.org/10.1016/j.healthplace.2016.05.003; Sarah Fraser, Valérie Parent, and Véronique Dupéré, "Communities Being Well for Family Well-being: Exploring

to the built environment) can contribute to feelings of anger and frustration. The home becomes a symbol of what is wrong in life – one's inability to provide the necessities of life. Acting out these feelings can result in different forms of homelessness: someone being asked to leave or being removed from the premises, forced to seek shelter at the home of a relative where their presence and the drugs and/ or alcohol used to manage these feelings cause problems in another space. With this dynamic, overcrowding is both a contributing factor and a product – at least in part – of the space in which people find themselves. The meanings made can be as negative as they are positive. Home can be jail, or a place where I have meaningful exchanges with friends and family.

Meaning is to be understood in relation to culture, colonial history, and material circumstances – the latter including the design and condition of the occupied dwelling. Culture is a significant consideration in taking on the case of overcrowding and its implications. Feelings of overcrowding can be mediated by culture as well as by the power, control, and command that some occupants might have over space. For this reason, the formula used to measure overcrowding as an absolute empirical standard, applied across cultures, should be reconsidered critically.[46] As Nathanael Lauster and Frank Tester note: "The failure to incorporate a theoretically informed consideration of culture as a consideration relevant to subjective feelings of crowdedness and their relationship to health is (a) problem in using comparative measurements of crowding. This results in clouded interpretations of the data linking crowding measures to health and well-being."[47]

This observation is relevant to considering the problem of homelessness (overcrowding) in the public housing of Nunavut. The claim that powerlessness – the inability of residents to "make a house a home" – is important to answering the question: "Is this home overcrowded?" It is more important than results obtained by applying the standard of number of persons per room or the Canadian National Occupancy

the Socio-ecological Determinants of Well-being in an Inuit Community of Northern Quebec," *Transcultural Psychiatry* 55, no. 1 (2018): 120–46, https://doi.org/10.1177/1363461517748814; Maria Ruiiz-Castell et al., "Household Crowding and Food Insecurity among Inuit Families with School-Aged Children in the Canadian Arctic," *American Journal of Public Health* 105, no. 3 (2015): e122-e32, https://doi.org/10.2105/AJPH.2014.302290.
46 Lauster and Tester, "Culture as a Problem."
47 Ibid., 525.

Standard, a measure considering the demographic of the household in relation to sex, age, familial relationships, and bedroom availability. Power, and the ability or inability to control what happens in the space one occupies – particularly in a setting characterized by social and personal problems requiring attention and a physical environment that does not support conventional notions of homelessness – also bear on questions of meaning.

Questions of meaning and identity draw attention to the importance of subjective experience, which in turn is linked to the capacity of occupants to make and derive meaning from the space they occupy. The number of women in Inuit homes who welcome a house full of children, who might crowd a space by playing and sleeping over on a regular basis, is illustrative. The most important theme in Inuit culture related to wellness, happiness, health, and healing is the central importance of family and kinship; including being with family, visiting, sharing food, and other activities.[48] All have implications for a very full and busy home. Space that enables family relations as a source of meaning has clear implications for design and how overcrowding is to be understood; hence, the importance of attention to subjective experience used in studying homelessness in Kinngait.[49] Rules affecting tenure in Nunavut social housing are sometimes minimal. In some jurisdictions, rules governing the length of time that guests can stay over, the impact of child welfare decisions on housing tenure in single-parent homes, and rules governing changes to space are all considerations that affect and thwart the exercise of power and the development of self-identity in social housing units. At the same time, these rules might address problems that tenants have with "guests" who exhibit problems that cause serious problems.[50]

If choices and actions make meaning, it is clear that Inuit have limited choice and capacity to act in making housing home. A "Community and Housing Design Charrette" sponsored by the NHC and CMHC and held in Arviat for two days in October 2005, illustrates what is implied by this observation.[51] The charrette is another example of what O'Connor

---

48 Michael Kral et al., "Unikkaartuit: Meanings of Well-Being, Unhappiness, Health, and Community Change among Inuit in Nunavut, Canada," *American Journal of Community Psychology* 48 (2011): 426–38, https://doi.org 10.1007/s10464-011-9431-4 /.
49 Tester, *Iglutaq*.
50 Christensen, "Indigenous Housing and Health."
51 Canada Mortgage and Housing Corporation, *Research Highlight: Arviat Community Housing and Design Charrette* (Ottawa, June 2006), http://publications.gc.ca/collections/collection_2014/schl-cmhc/NH18-22-106-112-eng.pdf.

advances as "democratizing the state bureaucracy (or administration) through struggles within and against the state."[52] The charrette, deliberately or unwittingly, by virtue of those participating, can be seen as part of a process with the potential for democratizing decision making.

The forty charrette participants included staff from NHC's maintenance, design, and delivery sections, climate change representatives from the Nunavut Department of Environment, and Arviat community Elders and other community members. It also involved facilitators from the Nunavut Department of Education, students and teachers from the local school, and representatives of the Arviat Housing Association and the Community Health Centre, as well as technical experts from Natural Resources Canada and the Yukon Housing Corporation. Active participation is important to the horizontal sharing of information and decision making and the porosity of the state from the standpoint of social movements (a cross-section of representative Inuit in this case).

Two figures included in a report on the charrette are worthy of note. Taken together, they hint at the possibility of being more creative – of addressing the colonial imposition of housing on Inuit by relating present-day form to concepts at the heart of Inuit culture.

A sketch by Donald Uluadluak is unremarked in the text of the Charrette, but its importance lies in the way it challenges the pictures of an *iglu* commonly produced by those outside of Inuit culture. The structure consists of a series of connected *iglus* of different size and shape, suggesting different functions for each of the elements. Multiple *iglus* with sleeping benches bring together extended family members by connecting snow tunnels. Another figure in the text suggests ways of configuring housing units to meet cultural needs and keeping extended families within close proximity to one another.

An appeal to the importance of meaning and recommendations coming out of two days of deliberation and discussion are documented in the text of the charrette. All of these speak to the importance of "meaning making and home," although it is not surprising that participants also looked longingly to the possibility of private sector interests playing a greater role in the provision of Nunavut housing. At the same time, they called for the creation of a cooperative building society and co-op and co-housing alternatives. Of particular interest is the list of six design problems identified. Four of these speak to meaning making

---

52 O'Connor, *Fiscal Crisis of the State*, xvii.

in particular ways: a lack of control over siting, design that meets cultural needs, the importance of kinship and extended family, and bylaws that inhibit innovation and the expression of housing innovations. The problems identified were that:

- the Arviat Housing Authority determines the location and the orientation of houses on new lots;
- there is no input by future residents, with the result that house designs do not meet cultural needs;
- there is no effort to keep extended families within close proximity to one another.
- there are few building regulations for private builders and no formal building-inspection process;
- existing zoning bylaws can inhibit housing innovations; and
- foundation issues, such as hard-to-adjust space post-construction.[53]

Nunavut Arctic College offers programs that train Inuit in building trades and mine-useful employment. The Nunavut government, through the Department of Economic Development and Transportation, has a Nunavut Mine Training Fund offering up to $200,000 to mining companies undertaking to train Inuit for their industry. The Qikiqtani Inuit Association offers training in cooperation with Baffinland, operating an iron ore mine near Pond Inlet on Baffin Island. Arctic College has operated special degree programs to educate lawyers and nurses. It offers a teacher education program and education for social service workers on an on-going basis. But housing (along with health) is arguably the responsibility that most seriously challenges the Nunavut government.

Here is what Inuit youth contributed to the charrette: "Young people need to be recognized as important contributors to their community. In-house training in home design, building, surveying and related skills would give them a sense of purpose and self-reliance."[54] Nothing could have spoken more clearly to the importance of "making housing home" and addressing identity formation and meaning in the process than this eloquently put observation: "recognized ... important contributors ... would give them a sense of purpose and self-reliance." Yet, in the years since this was clearly stated, neither Arctic College nor the Nunavut

53 Canada Mortgage and Housing Corporation, *Research Highlight*.
54 Ibid.

government has undertaken any initiative to train Inuit and Inuit youth in architecture, design, and the planning of Inuit homes – this, despite a generation of Inuit young people who live "online" and who have many talents in graphic arts, design, and the use of computer programs that remain largely unrecognized.

Conclusion

The training of Inuit planners and designers is critical to producing built forms that address meanings associated with Inuit conceptualization and use of space. The development of cooperatives and extended family-based housing clusters, including shared and common spaces for childcare, and building and repairing equipment, furniture, and appliances – giving Inuit control over their space and helping to develop environmental competency in successive generations – has yet to be realized. An emphasis on the importance of kinship that puts Elders in touch with family members, facilitates the provision of childcare, and assists extended family members in preventing the apprehension of children are important to the configuration and design of Inuit housing. Housing must meet the needs of elderly family members to better address family problems and issues while, at the same time, providing personal space that individuals can access when needed. This requires thinking outside the box, literally. What Inuit are currently occupying are, with some exceptions, units that pay increasing and necessary attention to energy conservation and technical considerations, but that have mostly left social and cultural considerations on the sidelines.

Addressing the housing crisis and hidden homelessness in Nunavut is far more than a matter of supply. The provision of social housing as a public good is located, as are all social policies and programs, in a contested field between the obligation of the state to meet the exigencies of capital accumulation and the necessity of addressing the legitimate needs of populations upon which, in a liberal democracy, the right to govern depends. Inuit history with liberal democracy and the shortcomings of capitalist and liberal democratic logic is not long. It is a colonial history, still being "unpacked."

Protest, conflict, and opposition are, in many ways, foreign to the consensus that is an integral element of *Inuit Qaujimajatuqangit* (traditional knowledge). Fledgling initiatives of Inuit and other actors in addressing food security, mining, and seismic testing in the territory make it clear that developing this capacity, and an appreciation of its importance in the making of policy, is an important – and admittedly long-term project – necessary to affecting housing policy and design.

"Making housing home" requires the presence of Inuit in creative and culturally informed design, planning, and construction. The active participation of Inuit in all aspects of making housing home is not only a matter of producing housing and developing communities that work. It is a matter of respecting and contributing to the making of Inuit identity and meaning.

SECTION TWO

Alaska

Regional Introduction: Alaska

SALLY CARRAHER AND TRAVIS HEDWIG

Homelessness has been increasing in Alaska these past three decades, and recently has become a major political, economic, and public media concern. The majority of funding and other resources allocated for addressing homelessness is handled through similar federal, state, tribal, and non-profit mechanisms as used in the contiguous United States. As we discuss below, this is problematic because it exacerbates, rather than alleviates, social inequities and health disparities between Alaska's urban and rural settlements; even more so for the most remote and isolated settlements. We have discussed elsewhere that, because Alaska's geography and settlement history are more similar to those of Canada's northern territories and Greenland than to the rest of the United States, patterns of homelessness experienced in Alaska are part of a broader northern geography of homelessness.[1] We believe that focusing on the social geography of the North is a useful way to frame the experiences of homelessness in Alaska, as well as the successes and failures of attempts to "end homelessness." Working to end or alleviate homelessness in Alaska requires public engagement, political will, and creative service provisioning that is a better fit for Alaska's northern politico-economic and socio-cultural geography. In this introduction to the section on Alaska, we describe what is known and what is unknown about homelessness within the context of Alaska's rural and urban geography; discuss and critique regional governance and major social policies affecting the patterns of homelessness we are seeing; and

---

1 Julia Christensen et al., "Homelessness across Alaska, the Canadian North, and Greenland: A Review of the Literature on a Developing Social Phenomenon in the Circumpolar North," *Arctic* 70, no. 4 (2017): 349–64, https://www.jstor.org/stable/26387309.

provide an overview of key issues and themes in research and knowledge of homelessness in Alaska.

The Urban and Rural Geographies of Homelessness in Alaska

Alaska is more densely urbanized than the northern Canadian provinces and territories and Greenland, but still significantly rural relative to the rest of the United States and southern Canada, with its villages, hamlets, towns, and cities spaced far apart from each other. Alaska is the largest state in the United States, but contains the fourth-smallest population, and has the smallest population density, at just over one person per square mile (1 person per 1.6 kilometres). In the 2010 federal census, only 26 of Alaska's 352 settlements had a population of more than 1,000 people.[2] Many people from rural Alaska are pulled towards the two largest urban areas – Fairbanks, population about 32,000, and the Anchorage Bowl/Mat-Su Valley area, population about 400,000 – to access health care, employment, education, meet family, relocate to a new place, or as a connection to further travel outside the state. It is within this vast but patchy network of small settlements, hub towns, and a few urban centres that we see the housing crisis manifest, and that determines where in Alaska we see (or do not see) different types of homelessness, including chronic, episodic, occasional, and "hidden homelessness," as well as "overcrowding" in limited housing stock.

Colonial contact with Indigenous peoples in Alaska occurred later than in the rest of southern Canada and the contiguous United States. The place that we call "Alaska" today was originally home to twenty distinct regional Indigenous cultures. Some of these cultural groups, such as the Gwich'in, Hän, Upper Tanana, Tlingit, and Tsimshian, traditionally live on lands that became internationally divided between Russian Alaska and Canada, while Siberian Yup'ik people living on what is now called St Lawrence Island (*Sivuqaq* in their language) traditionally travelled between mainland Alaska and mainland Siberia prior to and after the establishment of these Western colonial borders. Alaska was first colonized by Russia in the late 1700s and later by the United States with the transfer of Alaska in 1867 under the Treaty of Cession.[3] The US government declared all responsibility for making decisions

---

2 United States, Department of Commerce, Census Bureau, "Population and Housing Counts, CPH-2-3" (Washington, DC, 2012), https://www.census.gov/library/publications/2012/dec/cph-2.html.

3 Importantly, the language in this treaty distinguished between "residents" (people with full or partial Russian ancestry living as Russian subjects) and "uncivilized

about land, resources, and the "general welfare" of Indigenous peoples, who would not be granted US citizenship until 1924. In many areas of Alaska and Canada's western Arctic, Indigenous peoples were not contacted by outsiders until well into the 1800s, most often through the fur trade or commercial whaling, and always quickly followed by the appearance of Christian missions. Land claims that were not addressed in the 1867 Treaty of Cession would remain unsettled until the passage of the Alaska Native Claims Settlement Act (ANCSA) of 1971, another twelve years after the Alaska Territory was granted statehood in 1959. Although no research exists yet on how multigenerational trauma and the colonial roots of socio-economic inequities are linked to Indigenous experiences with homelessness today in Alaska, many of the themes identified in work from Canada are similar to peoples' experiences as described here.[4]

As in Canada's western Arctic, Alaska's socio-economic infrastructure was built out of the profits generated in economic boom times – gold rushes and, later, oil booms – followed inevitably by major busts and recessions. Also as in Canada's North, Alaska's development was rapid and uneven during and after the Second World War, resulting in a network that unevenly ties on- and off-road rural settlements to regional hub towns, and from hub towns to urban centres. The state-wide economy continues to be characterized by a large percentage of cyclical seasonal employment and unemployment among the working-age population. This influences in-state migration between rural settlements and hub towns and urban centres where work, medical care, and educational opportunities are more available,[5] and this is anecdotally linked to patterns of chronic and episodic homelessness, indicating an area for future research.

"Homelessness" means different things to different people, but often is tied in our imaginations directly to *house*lessness, and thus to a region's overall housing stock and housing policy. This can be particularly problematic for Indigenous peoples, as we see often that, in Indigenous ways of knowing, "home" evokes a deep sense of

---

tribes" (all other Indigenous peoples living in Alaska), granting US citizenship to the former and denying it to the latter.

4 Evelyn J. Peters and Julia Christensen, eds., *Indigenous Homelessness: Perspectives from Canada, Australia, and New Zealand* (Winnipeg: University of Manitoba Press, 2016); Julia Christensen, *No Home in a Homeland: Indigenous Peoples and Homelessness in the Canadian North* (Vancouver: UBC Press, 2017).

5 E. Lance Howe, "Patterns of Migration in Arctic Alaska," *Polar Geography* 32, no. 1 (2009): 69–89, https://doi.org/10.1080/10889370903000422.

connection to land, place, family, and culture, not material security per se. The fact that Indigenous peoples in Alaska continue to be over-represented within the homeless population in Anchorage and else-where in the state indicates that differences in cultural constructions of home and place continue to matter. If left unchecked, these differences can become part of a broader rationalization and justification for the persistence of disparities in housing outcomes. By extension, this can perpetuate and further entrench inequalities in even the most well-intentioned policies.

The cost of housing is the largest expenditure for most households in Alaska. At an average of 40.2 per cent of a household's total annual income in 2018, housing cost was well above the housing affordability income standard for the United States, set at 30 per cent of total income.[6] However, this is only part of the total picture of the cost of living. Alaska's urban centres have more job opportunities, and Anchorage particularly pays on average higher wages than surrounding towns, so average household income for people in many rural settlements is significantly lower, while costs for heating fuel and food are significantly higher than in urban centres.[7] Furthermore, there is significantly less housing stock in rural settlements, leading to "doubling up" and even "tripling up" of extended families in single-family homes or even smaller apartments. The US Senate has recognized that it is not unsheltered, or street, homelessness, but rather "overcrowding" in limited housing stock that is the most common problem in rural, often predominantly Indigenous settlements.[8] Unsheltered and street homelessness is more visible in Alaska's urban centres, but "hidden" forms of homelessness, including overcrowding in small housing spaces, represent a growing percentage of the overall population experiencing homelessness.

The Governance Landscape of Alaska

Like the physical geography, the social policy and governance landscape of Alaska connects rural and small settlements to regional hubs and urban centres, and then to Outside – but the flow of federal dollars from Washington, DC, becomes significantly bottlenecked after arriving in Anchorage. Specifically, federal funding for housing and homelessness-related

---

6 Neal Fried, "The Cost of Living: 2018 and early 2019" (Juneau, AK: Department of Labor Statistics, July 2019), 10, https://www.labor.alaska.gov/trends/jul19.pdf.
7 Ibid.
8 United States, Congress, Senate, "Field Hearing before the Committee on Indian Affairs," Hearing 115–404 (Washington, DC, 25 August 2018), https://www.govinfo.gov/content/pkg/CHRG-115shrg33406/html/CHRG-115shrg33406.htm.

resources and services is divided between Anchorage and the "Balance of State" – which literally includes every other settlement in all of Alaska. While this is true for all US states, it is particularly problematic for Alaska given its vast size and significant rural population. Because the majority of funding to address homelessness comes from the federal government, service providers have to follow US federal policies and definitions for homelessness to access even the most basic support resources. This is a problem because so many rural settlements are too small to host Housing and Urban Development (HUD) satellite offices, and there is little to no technical support for small communities to apply for increasingly limited resources. As such, no "community choice" (i.e., "section 8") vouchers or other housing subsidies are available in Alaska's smaller settlements, which are located anywhere from a hundred to over a thousand miles away from the nearest town large enough to offer support and services for housing, health care, education, veteran's benefits, and so on. Tribal Housing Authorities are beginning to partner with state and local housing and homeless coalitions to access HUD funds administered through the Alaska Office of Native American Programs, but developing local capacity to administer and manage grants requires targeted outreach, access to technical assistance, and ongoing support. This raises important questions of community engagement as service providers, academics, and activists try to find effective ways to translate the stories and lived experiences of rural and small settlements to appropriate federal authorities. Increased flexibility in how policy is designed and implemented in Alaska will allow opportunities for local settlements and regions to play a more prominent role in developing solutions that are responsive to their unique needs and circumstances. In Chapter 7, we discuss the lack of infrastructural supports to operationalize available federal funding for housing assistance and other related programs in rural Alaska, and speak to the general theme of governmental and organizational challenges that are becoming recognized across Alaska, Canada's North, and Greenland. As in Canada, much of the assistance for people experiencing housing insecurity or homelessness in both Alaska's urban and rural settlements falls upon the shoulders of non-profit and other private sources.

What We Know, and Do Not Know, about Homelessness in Alaska

The literature available on homelessness in Alaska is sparse, with no data available from many settlements. Part of this is the result of poor outreach to rural and small communities and a lack of technical assistance to conduct "Point in Time" (PIT) counts, which are part of a nationwide effort to estimate homelessness conducted each year in January. As imperfect as they are, these estimates are one of the few mechanisms we have to communicate Alaska's needs to the federal government. From a federal perspective, no PIT data for a settlement means homelessness does not exist there. Timing of the count, often in the middle of winter, has also been raised as a limitation, as seasonal changes in emergency shelter and other service use patterns make it difficult to achieve accurate estimates. Furthermore, PIT counts do not count people living in overcrowding housing stock as "homeless." These limitations are obviously a huge problem, and Alaska needs to find ways to communicate this to federal officials as we navigate increasingly limited federal resources.

Although homelessness has been recognized as a growing problem since the 1980s in Alaska, we also know we have only a partial picture of what is going on and who is affected. Prior to 2009, studies of how many people are living homeless are scant: two studies surveyed people in the Municipality of Anchorage, one in the 1970s and again using the same survey in the early 1990s.[9] In 1978, approximately 700 people were classified as homeless in Anchorage, with approximately double that number by the early 1990s, although both surveys were conducted only with people actively using the city's shelter system. Estimates from the annual PIT count for Alaska between 2009 and 2018 indicate that homelessness ranged between 1,784 people (in the lowest count in 2014) and 2,128 people (in the highest count in 2011). These totals include those using emergency shelter, living in transitional housing, and are unsheltered at the time of the PIT count.[10] It is widely understood, however, that the PIT count is an underestimate of the true number of people experiencing homelessness. PIT data for 2016, for example, represent just 8 settlements across the state, while in 2018, 14 out of Alaska's 352 settlements participated.

---

9 Dennis Kelso, Stevan E. Hobfoll, and W. Jack Peterson, *A Descriptive Analysis of the Downtown Anchorage Skid Row Populations* (Anchorage: University of Alaska Anchorage, Center for Alcohol and Addiction Studies, 1978); G. Reynolds et al., "A 14-Year Comparison of Alaska Homeless," *Arctic Medical Research* 53, suppl. 2 (1994): 209–12.

10 Alissa Parrish, "AK Statewide PIT 2009–2018" (Juneau: Alaska Coalition on Housing and Homelessness, April 2018), https://public.tableau.com/profile/alissa.parrish#!/vizhome/AKStatewide2009-2018PIT/Dashboard1?publish=yes, accessed 21 November 2018,

Despite the dearth of information, we can discern some geographic trends: Alaska's urban settlements, especially the largest cities, pull in people from more rural settlements – some of whom become homeless in the city and then cannot or choose not to return to their home community, for a variety of reasons. As well, however, in the cities the homeless population is also made of both people from that city originally and people from outside Alaska. So, there are three distinct migration flows from which urban Alaska's homeless are coming that each warrant further attention, research, and outreach.

We know very little about rural experiences with homelessness in Alaska, although it seems likely that people are facing challenges similar to those identified in rural Canada. In their examination of five case studies on rural homelessness across Canada, Rebecca Schiff and colleagues found "a fairly consistent picture of a lack of affordable housing, lack of subsidized housing, low income levels, and a lack of support services as main factors driving people into homelessness in these areas."[11] The authors also identified three interrelated factors at work in rural Indigenous homelessness across these five settlement regions: 1) both absolute and hidden homelessness is occurring in rural settlements; 2) homelessness is influenced by migration between rural and urban settlements; and 3) racism against Indigenous peoples drives homelessness through actions such as discrimination by landlords.[12] It should be noted, however, that the authors also found that, in some areas, Indigenous peoples are not overrepresented among the rural homeless population and that chronic housing stock shortages and inadequate resources are issues with which all rural residents live.

The homeless in Alaska face special vulnerabilities that need to be better understood and addressed through policy. Exposure, for example, is an ever-present danger in winter, and exposure-related deaths are an all-too-familiar occurrence in many cities and hub towns. In smaller settlements, existing housing stock is deteriorating, and extreme weather (such as high winds) threatens to destroy many structures in an already strained and limited housing stock.

There also appear to be particular gendered experiences with homelessness in Alaska. Women, especially, are more likely to out-migrate from smaller settlements to access education, employment, or health

---

11 Rebecca Schiff, Alina Turner, and Jeannette Waegemakers Schiff, "Rural Indigenous Homelessness in Canada," in *Indigenous Homelessness: Perspectives from Canada, Australia, and New Zealand*, ed. Evelyn J. Peters and Julia Christensen (Winnipeg: University of Manitoba Press, 2016), 185–209.
12 Ibid.

care in larger settlements.[13] Child and family homelessness is rising,[14] along with youth homelessness overall, as indicated by the number of youth entering Covenant House Alaska in Anchorage who originally came from out of state or from rural settlements in "Bush" Alaska.[15] This chapter's authors also personally know that LGBTQA+ individuals in Alaska experience specific kinds of gendered, homophobic, and transphobic discrimination that sometimes results in their becoming or staying homeless, but there is no research to date on homelessness within this subpopulation in Alaska. There are, however, some grassroots programs, such as "Choosing Our Roots," that work to help LGBTQA+ youth find safe housing.[16] This raises questions about what kinds of resources are needed to best support people experiencing different types of discrimination, poverty, and homelessness, and who have different needs for accessing and being able to keep stable housing.

The realization that homelessness is growing and evolving in Alaska's urban geography in unique ways compared to the rest of the United States has not yet been translated, however, into how homelessness and housing policy and social services are provided. In Chapter 9, Clare Dannenberg discusses the challenges service providers in Anchorage face as they try to roll out "global best practices" without any modifications for local settings.

Overview of Key Themes in Literature on Housing and Homelessness

The three chapters presented in the Alaska section of this volume reflect the great chasm between urban and rural experiences (and our knowledge or lack of knowledge about) homelessness in urban and rural Alaska. In fact, the one overarching theme identified in this volume that the Alaska section particularly addresses is that of "an incomplete picture of homelessness." Especially missing is information about rural experiences of the housing crisis and resulting types

13 David Driscoll et al., "Assessing the Influence of Health on Rural Outmigration in Alaska," *International Journal of Circumpolar Health* 69, no. 5 (2010): 528, https://doi.org/10.3402/ijch.v69i5.17683.
14 Barbara Armstrong and Sharon Chamard, "The Homeless: Who and How Many?" *Alaska Justice Forum* 31, no. 1–2 (2014): 2–26, http://hdl.handle.net/11122/6581.
15 Stephanie Martin and Alejandra Villalobos Meléndez, "Youth in Crisis: Characteristics of Homeless Youth Served by Covenant House Alaska" (Anchorage: University of Alaska Anchorage, Institute of Social and Economic Research, March 2010), 18, http://hdl.handle.net/11122/4286.
16 "Choosing Our Roots" (website), http://www.choosingourroots.org/#about.

of homelessness in rural communities. For example, all three chapters in the Alaska section are by authors who work and live in Anchorage, and all are about how issues of homelessness are perceived in the Anchorage area. We nonetheless do get a glimpse of how rural Alaskans experience and understand what homelessness looks like for them in Chapter 7, particularly in Nome, the regional hub town for northeast Alaska on the Seward Peninsula. While each chapter contains important information that advances our collective understanding of this understudied issue – and points to several potential starting points for future investigation – we also acknowledge that many Alaskans' voices and community-level perspectives are missing from this discourse. We can only work with the information we have, as little as it is, but these three chapters do address several of the themes identified at the 2018 workshop in Yellowknife that indicate a pattern of "northern homelessness" that differs in important ways from the more urban, more southern areas of North America.

Importantly, these three chapters discuss perceptions of homelessness, housing challenges, social policy, governance, and community response from different points of view. In Chapter 7, we discuss the conversations that emerged from bringing houseless and housed people together to discuss homelessness in Alaska – while creating a space that centred the voices of people with actual experience living homeless. In Chapter 8, Travis Hedwig measures the fidelity of the Housing First program in Anchorage to Housing First principles from the perspectives of the tenants living there, and thus adds a critically important dimension to discourse on homelessness and Housing First. Finally, in Chapter 9, Clare Dannenberg's linguistic analysis of public and media discourse about homelessness and the people others label as "homeless" advocates for involving more local community members in the planning and implementation of policies and programs to address homelessness.

One common thread of these chapters is the recognition not only that more research is needed on the diversity of experiences with homelessness across the rural-urban geography of Alaska, but also that experiences, perspectives, and voices of people living homeless need to be brought to the attention of government, non-profit, and other community-based service providers.

Learning more about how people actually experience homelessness and housing insecurity in Alaska, as well as about their experiences on the receiving end of service provisioning and outreach, could go a long way to addressing the problems that arise when service providers in Anchorage try to fit global approaches to the urban North. Developing community-engaged and humanistic research that works in partnership with people experiencing homelessness and housing insecurity, as well as in partnership with service providers, should seek to address knowledge gaps, challenges, and faults, and build on the strengths and successes identified in this volume. We know this work will be especially difficult now, as Alaska is in the middle of a severe economic recession and the State budget has been deeply slashed for the past several years in a row, with every indication that this trend will continue for the next few years. But this work still must be done. We hope that the chapters in this section of the volume help to a call to action by scholars, activists, service providers, and others to investigate homelessness more critically and more humanely, placing the lived experiences and perspectives of homeless people in Alaska first and foremost in efforts to identify meaningful and effective social policies and community practices that are uniquely fitted to our northern geography and cultures.

7 Northern Voices on Homelessness: Engaging the Public and Promoting Inclusivity for Homeless Alaskans in Public Discourse

SALLY CARRAHER AND TRAVIS HEDWIG

What does it even mean to be "homeless" in Alaska? Too often, public discourse around "homelessness" – what it is, to whom it happens and why, and what should be done about it – is dominated by the voices of people who have never experienced it. Stereotypes proliferate, unchecked and unchallenged. Policy decisions are often based more on personal tastes or political persuasions of a current administration than on an accurate picture of homelessness or evidence of best practices, and almost always without direct input from the very people targeted by such policies. To better understand homelessness as it is commonly experienced in Alaska, we must address both these problems: the lack of accurate information on which people and how many experience different types of houselessness or homelessness in Alaska, and the lack of inclusion of those who have lived experience with homelessness in the design and implementation of solutions.

On 7 March 2015, a team of University of Alaska Anchorage faculty and students who had worked in allyship with homeless advocacy groups and providers locally, organized a public forum called "Northern Voices on Homelessness" to discuss what "homelessness" looks like in Alaska. The plural use of "voices" was intentional, as it represented the diverse population of the state overall, as well as the diverse experiences of being homeless in Alaska. "Northern" is an equally important word, implying a shared geographic context and promoting a sense of solidarity among all peoples and systems involved in this effort. At this forum, we purposefully set out to engage the public in destabilizing common stereotypes about homelessness and the "type" of people who are homeless; in identifying the diverse experiences with homelessness across Alaska; and in discussing ways in which the public can become more engaged in creating inclusive and welcoming spaces that bring housed and houseless Alaskans together. Communities across Alaska were invited to participate via the Online With Libraries (OWL) teleconferencing system through their local public libraries. In Anchorage, we invited people with experience of being homeless, as well as service providers and academics to be key speakers to lead discussion in the first part of the forum. Afterwards, participants broke up into small groups for follow-up discussion. In the final part of the forum, participants were asked to complete an anonymous "sticky note" questionnaire, and to hand in their sticky notes to us for later analysis. Participants in Anchorage placed their sticky notes in a box we provided; those in other Alaskan libraries were asked to email their responses, but we received responses only from Anchorage. The sticky note questionnaire was as follows:

1. Please tell us one new thing you learned today.
2. If money was no object, please tell us one thing you think should be a priority for addressing homelessness in Alaska.
3. Please name one thing that could be done to better engage the public on issues surrounding homelessness.

From this forum and the feedback we collected in the sticky notes, we learned both that people in Alaska experience several distinct types of homelessness, and that people who have lived homeless for long periods have great insights into how things have changed – and not changed – in urban Alaska since the 1980s. Overwhelmingly, the key message participants articulated was the need to humanize public discourse about homelessness and the people who experience it. Our analysis of the forum's discourse draws upon a growing body of research and practice that aims to understand how the public uses social and physical spaces to either include or exclude persons through displacement and "othering,"[1] and to work to dismantle systemic racism, discrimination, and exclusionary discourses while creating new, inclusive discourses about homelessness as a social issue.[2]

---

1 Lisa M. Vandermark, "Promoting the Sense of Self, Place, and the Belonging in Displaced Persons: The Example of Homelessness," *Archives of Psychiatric Nursing* 21, no. 5 (2007): 241, https://doi.org/10.1016/j.apnu.2007.06.003.
2 Meaghan Bell and Christine A. Walsh, "Finding a Place to Belong: The Role of Social Inclusion in the Lives of Homeless Men," *Qualitative Report* 20, no. 12 (2015): 1974, https://nsuworks.nova.edu/tqr/vol20/iss12/4; Eoin Devereux, "Thinking Outside the Charity Box: Media Coverage of Homelessness," *European Journal of Homelessness* 9, no. 2 (2015): 261–73, https://www.feantsaresearch.org/download/devereuxejh2-2015article11259989678303316558.pdf.

Building an Inclusive Space: From Experiment to Lessons Learned

"Northern Voices on Homelessness" was designed to bring people together from across hundreds of miles of rural and urban Alaska and to create a space that centred the perspectives and voices of people with direct experiences with homelessness. We used the state library's OWL system because it was available in several settlements across Alaska and provided a way for people in rural and remote locales to participate without needing to own a home computer, Internet plan, or smart phone. Although this worked well in Alaska, any approach to multi-sited discourse needs to be built carefully around what technologies, facilities, and schedules people can access in their social and geographic networks.

We wanted to build a sense of social inclusion that – at least for the duration of the event – worked to dismantle or reverse the uneven balance of power that is commonly levied upon unhoused people in daily life (table 7.1). "Ground rules" for the event, which were written on large paper signs in Anchorage and verbally explained by the moderator at the beginning of the event for those elsewhere, asked participants to "respect all people" and "please keep an open mind," and reminded them that "topics may be sensitive" and that "anyone is free to leave or ask an organizer for help at any time." The turnout for the forum was good, with fifty people attending in Anchorage, four in Nome, one in Fairbanks, three in Kodiak, one in Mat-Su, and one in Juneau.

We learned a number of crucial lessons from this event, which we categorized into two types: lessons learned about public perceptions of homelessness in Alaska, and, lessons learned about how to engage the public and to build spaces where homeless individuals feel welcome and can participate meaningfully in public discourse.

Regarding public perceptions, key speakers described the diversity of types of homelessness in Alaska. This included discussion of the structural inequities known to lead to homelessness in Alaska, including the uneven distribution of funding, housing support, and services for homeless people between urban and rural Alaska. Key speakers who were residents at one Housing First location, Karluk Manor, as well as a couple of self-identified individuals in the audience with previous histories of homelessness, discussed common stereotypes from their own perspectives and helped to dispel some stereotypes held by non-homeless participants.

Analysing the responses to the first sticky note question – "Please tell us one new thing you learned today" – we found that several public

Table 7.1. Dismantling Exclusionary Practices and Promoting Inclusion: Lessons from the "Northern Voices on Homelessness" Forum

Common exclusionary practices	What we did to promote inclusion
Community council meetings about what to do about homelessness in Anchorage (and other Alaskan towns) often do not include people experiencing homelessness.	We invited tenants of a Housing First program to come to the event and to participate as much as they liked. Other people who were homeless saw our flyers in Anchorage and joined the forum.
Public perceptions of homelessness are influenced by the media, sometimes combined with personal observations of visible homelessness, such as street homelessness, public intoxication, and homeless camps in public parks. This leads to public perceptions that overestimate the extent of chronic, visible street homelessness while underestimating or completely missing other experiences of homelessness.	Key speakers with experience of being homeless spoke about their knowledge of homelessness in Alaska and changes they had seen, sometimes spanning several decades. They also led the brought up issues that were important to them, and answered other participants' questions. Key speakers and small group discussions emphasized the plurality of experiences, including less publicly visible types of homelessness and hidden homelessness; key speakers were encouraged to share their knowledge about diverse types of homelessness (rural versus urban), hidden, youth homelessness, elder homelessness, etc.
The media do not always report the perspectives or personal experiences of homeless people with the same frequency or depth as that provided by politicians, police and first responders, local business owners, and service providers.	We encouraged people who have experienced homelessness to share their perspectives on what it was like for them and to prioritize for other participants what they felt were the most important things for the public to know about homelessness in Alaska.

perceptions about homelessness did not match the available evidence of who and how many people were experiencing homelessness in Alaska, or even what sorts of social policy and services were currently in place in the state. For example, a few participants stated they were surprised to learn from the key speakers that only about 20 per cent of Alaska's unhoused population in 2015 was defined as "chronically homeless" – or, put another way, that a majority of people experiencing homelessness in Alaska were experiencing *acute* or *episodic*, rather than chronic, homelessness.

Many participants reported that they were previously unaware of the diversity of experiences with homelessness or the diversity of pathways into homelessness expressed by key speakers. For example, youth might become homeless when they flee a family or foster home, and in these cases simply "going home" is usually not an option. They might also be part of a family that is experiencing homelessness and cycle back and forth between staying in cars, hotels, or couch surfing with friends or extended family. Older residents might become homeless because they are no longer able to afford living in their own homes, and affordable housing alternatives simply do not exist. Thus, although many youth had problems finding stable housing in which they can live independently, many older Alaskans were at risk of losing the only housing they had. Homelessness was also experienced differently in urban and rural settlements due to the uneven and piecemeal landscape of available housing stock, employment, and health care access across the state. The limited evidence then available suggested that a significant number of people were getting caught in the flow of out-migration from Alaskan villages and ending up homeless in hub towns and larger cities, often with no means for returning home if they wanted to.[3]

Although scholarly literature is lacking for Alaska, Christensen's work in the Northwest Territories paints an eerily similar picture to what key speakers from rural Alaskan communities discussed regarding chronic housing need, rural settlements' lack of access to urban institutional flows for funding, extremely high building costs, limited material and human resources, and the attraction of opportunities to access employment, education, and health care in urban settlements.[4] A key speaker from the Nome Emergency Shelter Team spoke about the need for the public to understand the unique challenges faced outside urban Alaska:

> I appreciate what Anchorage said, but believe me, Nome has no availability of housing. Part of that is due to the fact of the tremendous high cost of construction in rural Alaska ... I do want to add that the other challenge in

---

3 Robert Travis, "Homelessness, Alcoholism, and Ethnic Discrimination among Alaska Natives," *Arctic* 44, no. 3 (1991): 247–53, https://www.jstor.org/stable/40511246; Stephanie Martin and Alejandra Villalobos Meléndez, *Youth in Crisis: Characteristics of Homeless Youth Served by Covenant House Alaska* (Anchorage: University of Alaska, Institute of Social and Economic Research, 2010), 18, http://hdl.handle .net/11122/4286.

4 Julia Christensen, "'They Want a Different Life': Rural Northern Settlement Dynamics and Pathways to Homelessness in Yellowknife and Inuvik, Northwest Territories," *Canadian Geographer* 56, no. 4 (2012): 419–38, https://doi.org/10.1111/j.1541 -0064.2012.00439.x.

rural Alaska [is that] we are completely ineligible for all of those voucher programs that AHFC [Alaska Housing Finance Corporation] offers. That ... there isn't a large enough caseload in any small community to justify having an office to manage those vouchers. Therefore, we get none. No VASH [Veterans Affairs Supportive Housing] vouchers. None of them ... and then there's also the perception [that] all the Native corporations are taking care of things or the regional housing authorities are taking care of things. And I can assure you there are many people falling through the cracks ... so ... while the state may be different than the Lower 48,[5] there's a lot of differences *within* the state as well (emphasis in original).

Several participants in Anchorage responded in their sticky note questionnaires that they were previously unaware of the non-existence of transitional and emergency housing in the majority of rural settlements in Alaska. Some were also surprised to learn about disparities in access to housing assistance for rural Alaskans who were otherwise legally eligible for these forms of support, such as VASH housing vouchers for US veterans and other assistance through the AHFC and other federal Housing and Urban Development (HUD) satellite offices. Tribal Housing Authorities, including Cook Inlet Housing Authority, were playing an increasingly important role, but lack of federal investment and limited capacity in smaller communities remained challenging. Complicating things further, people discussed cultural differences in defining what "counts" as homelessness, and varying cultural values around caregiving and community support. This meant that some people who fitted researchers' or providers' definitions of "homeless" might not identify themselves as such or be recognized by their surrounding community as such. For example, multigenerational households of people sharing limited space are common in Alaska,[6] as well as in Canada's northern regions,[7] and although many Alaskans recog-

5 The "Lower 48" is a common saying in Alaska for the forty-eight contiguous US states.
6 Steven C. Dinero, "Analysis of a Mixed Economy in an Alaskan Native Settlement: The Case of Arctic Village," *Canadian Journal of Native Studies* 23, no. 1 (2003): 135–64, https://arctichealth.org/en/permalink/ahliterature297103; Amy Craver, "Domestic Function and Iñupiaq Households," *International Journal of Circumpolar Health* 63, Suppl. 1 (2004): 49–52, https://doi.org/10.3402/ijch.v63i0.17775.
7 Peter Collings, "Economic Strategies, Community, and Food Networks in Ulukhaktok, Northwest Territories, Canada," *Arctic* 64, no. 2 (2011): 207–19, https://www.jstor.org/stable/23025694; Peter Usher, Gérard Duhaime, and Edmund Searles, "The Household as an Economic Unit in Arctic Aboriginal Communities, and Its Measurement by Means of a Comprehensive Survey," *Social Indicators Research* 61 (2003): 175–202, https://doi.org/10.1023/A:1021344707027.

nized that the housing stock available in their settlements was rapidly deteriorating, many people living "doubled up" in urban as well as rural settlements did not consider themselves to be "homeless."

Discussions during the forum illuminated the differing perspectives of people who had lived in Anchorage for decades about whether visible street homelessness was better or worse than during the economic recessions of the late 1970s and early 1980s that occurred after completion of the Trans-Alaska Pipeline for oil. For example, one Karluk Manor resident said the patterns of homeless camping, street sleeping, and shelter use had changed in downtown Anchorage due to changes in the geography of service provision there: "In the eighties there [were] men and women sleeping in the corners [in downtown Anchorage]. It was bad. But you really don't see it that ... as much as it was in the eighties and seventies, when this was a really filthy city. You couldn't even walk down the street without knocking over ... half-gallons of stuff. It's getting better because back in the eighties all they had was the Anchorage Rescue Mission downtown. They didn't have Bean's Cafe. They didn't have [Brother Francis Shelter]." Another resident from Karluk Manor added: "It has changed a lot ... I mean ... it took [many] years. But you don't really actually see that many homeless people as much as you did in the eighties and seventies. So it is getting better. It's just taking its own little [while]."

Most of the self-identified homeless participants seemed to agree that visible street homelessness was actually a bigger problem for downtown Anchorage in the 1980s, which was news to some non-homeless participants who had not lived in Anchorage as long as these key speakers. However, not every long-time resident agreed about the history of homelessness downtown. One non-homeless participant who had owned property near Bean's Cafe and Brother Francis Shelter for decades saw the location of social and health services in downtown as a factor that had made homelessness worse, not better, over time:

Congressman Young made kind of a strange statement about wolves.[8] But actually there are wolves out there preying on the homeless. And I objected to Karluk Manor. [Housing] First is doomed to be a failure. Let

---

8 The speaker was referring to a comment made by Alaska Congressional Representative Don Young just two days earlier, on 5 March 2015, when stating his desire to have the gray wolf taken off the endangered species list. Young stated that, if gray wolves were introduced in Nome, "you wouldn't have a homeless problem anymore." The statement triggered a public backlash. See Colby Itkowitz. "Rep. Don Young: Wolves would solve homelessness," *Washington Post*, 5 March 2015, https://www.washingtonpost

me tell you the wolf issue ... The first wolf that exists [that] makes it very dangerous here in Anchorage is the drug war ... That's the number one wolf. The number two wolf [is] the social service agencies. And he hit it on the head [gesturing to a Karluk Manor resident who was speaking earlier]. The statistics. That, hey, we gotta go out, we gotta have outreach. We gotta do it in a low-income neighbourhood where an alleged problem is. Karluk Manor, I wasn't against so much the concept as much as the location ... And by association, by location, these guys' friends are right over the hill. The temptation to go back to their lifestyle, in fact in either direction, continues that destructive lifestyle. But worse are the social service agencies who didn't listen to the neighbourhood and say we have too many[9] ... And anyone who opposes anything you do [points to service providers in the room] to that holy word of "homelessness" is nothing but a lowdown dirty skunk. And the real skunks here are the social service agencies.

When new strategies are introduced to address housing access and homelessness, such negative public perception is not uncommon. For example, when Karluk Manor, a converted hotel formerly known as the Red Roof Inn which became a project-based Housing First facility, was first opened in 2012, protesters hung bottles of vodka and whisky along the fence line across the street from the property, and made signs that read "Red Nose Inn." Some people, notably some downtown and Fairview business owners, complained that the location of the facility would impinge upon the quality of life in the neighbourhood. Nearly ten years later, attitudes had changed somewhat, but the "not in my backyard" mentality still existed for many. Consciously building inclusive spaces for public discourse, as we aimed to do with "Northern Voices on Homelessness," can address these and other prejudicial viewpoints by helping to create spaces where people with experience living homeless can speak for themselves without being dismissed by others.

The second set of lessons we learned from organizing "Northern Voices on Homelessness" concerned building positive and inclusive public spaces in which participants could learn from diverse experiences and perspectives regarding homelessness in Alaska. We realized as the event unfolded that the choice of the library was very conducive

---

.com/blogs/in-the-loop/wp/2015/03/05/rep-don-young-wolves-would-solve-home lessness/.

9 Here the speaker was referring to the Fairview Community Council in Anchorage as well as some downtown business owners who were publicly outspoken in 2011 in their disapproval of the location for constructing the Housing First facility called Karluk Manor.

to making a space where homeless people felt welcome to participate in the day's discussion and activities. Libraries are often frequented by people with unstable housing circumstances because of their long open hours, access to warm, dry, quiet spaces, and access to other services, including free use of library computers and the Internet. The Z.J. Loussac Library, in particular, is a stop for several Anchorage bus lines, provides free parking year-round, and is adjoined by Cuddy Park, with grass, benches, and a winding trail that provide visitors with ample space to walk, sit, or sometimes to sleep. Some of the library staff and homeless patrons were familiar and friendly with one another. In addition to the five tenants of Karluk Manor who were key speakers, some participants in the audience in Anchorage identified themselves as homeless or formerly homeless during the breakout sessions in the afternoon. This was illustrated well by one man who entered at the beginning and said that, while hanging out at the library, he saw our event flyer. He then identified himself as homeless and asked if he could participate.

Darrin Hodgetts and colleagues have discussed how "libraries can be spaces of care where homeless people can be included. This particular public space has advantages over semi-private sites, such as traditional day centres and shelters, because ... [i]n a day centre or hostel, these [individuals] are located specifically as homeless people. Conversely, when in the library, homeless people can be present as regular library patrons ... Homeless and housed people can and do cohabitate in the library."[10] This is not to suggest that one's identity as "homeless" is temporarily lifted upon entering a library, nor that tensions between housed and homeless patrons never arise, but rather that libraries are often places in which people's right *to be in public* is recognized and accepted. As we learned, not only was use of the library convenient for us as organizers; it actually helped immensely in our goal to create inclusive dialogue since the library was already a more inclusive public space than some other venues.

That five residents of Karluk Manor agreed to come and be key speakers at the forum was definitely a large part of the event's success. Meaghan Bell and Christine Walsh found "identity talk"[11] among homeless street persons to be a primary means through which homeless individuals – lacking access to many economic and social material markers of status – use to

---

10 Darrin Hodgetts et al., "A Trip to the Library: Homelessness and Social Inclusion," *Social and Cultural Geography* 9, no. 8 (2008): 950, https://doi.org/10.1080/14649360802441432.
11 Bell and Walsh, "Finding a Place to Belong."

construct a sense of self.[12] Speaking about oneself in one's own way can be used to "talk back"[13] against the dehumanization and stigmatization that commonly occurs in media, political, and other public discourses. In public discourses, homeless people are either regularly denied the ability to narrate their own stories, or their stories are tightly controlled. For example, a reporter, constrained by deadlines and editorial expectations, might ask a narrow set of supposedly important questions, then cherry-pick quotes that best fit the framework for developing the story. In the media, police, paramedics, service providers, and frustrated neighbourhood business- or home-owners are often given more space to speak about homelessness, which ultimately frames and further amplifies the discourse that homelessness is a "public crisis,"[14] while at the same time reducing people to their perceived "deviance" or "dependence."[15] This can lead to misrepresentation and underrepresentation of homeless people in the media, which, regardless of intent, can further stigmatize them. Researchers working with and writing about homeless people can fall into the same trap, appropriating instead of pushing back against frames of homelessness constructed largely by non-homeless people. In contrast, during "Northern Voices on Homelessness," the residents of Karluk Manor were offered, and accepted, much more control over the discourse. They spoke up when they wanted to, talked back directly against what some other key speakers (service providers and academics) were saying, and candidly answered questions raised by participants while also keeping the discussion moving in the directions they wanted it to take.

In Our Own Words: The Many Faces and Meanings of "Homelessness" in Alaska

A total of thirty-one people in Anchorage handed in their sticky note questionnaires, although not everyone answered every question. The sticky notes were collected anonymously, with no names or identifying

12 David A. Snow and Leon Anderson, "Identity Work among the Homeless: The Verbal Construction and Avowal of Personal Identities," *American Journal of Sociology* 92, no. 6 (1987): 1336–1371, https://www.jstor.org/stable/2779840.
13 Kirsi Juhila, "Talking Back to Stigmatized Identities: Negotiation of Culturally Dominant Categorizations in Interviews with Shelter Residents," *Qualitative Social Work* 3, no. 3 (2004): 259–75, https://doi.org/10.1177/1473325004045665.
14 Katrien Cokeley, "Framing Homelessness as Crisis: A Comparative Content Analysis of Local Media Reports on Portland's Tent Cities" (Master's thesis, Portland State University, 2017), https://doi.org/10.15760/etd.5827.
15 Mao Yuping et al., "Framing Homelessness for the Canadian Public: The News Media and Homelessness," *Canadian Journal of Urban Research* 20, no. 2 (2011): 1–19.

information written on them. Overall, we identified four themes from the information participants shared about what it means to be homeless in Alaska: 1) personal connections to homelessness; 2) the "many faces of homelessness" in Alaska; 3) understanding homelessness in a northern context; and 4) the recognized need to "humanize the problem" (and the solutions).

Personal Connections to Homelessness

Many people participated in the forum because they were interested in homelessness and had personal experience of it. People with lived experience were invited to be key speakers, and additional participants who had experienced homelessness came because they saw the flyers at the library and were interested. However, "personal experiences with homelessness" was also a commonly stated reason non-home-less and never-homeless participants offered for why they came to the forum. Although the nature of these experiences varied, the common thread was that homelessness becomes important to people through *personal connection*. This was expressed by several attendees from multiple vantage points.

Key speaker, Anchorage academic:

> My research interest in the past ten years or so has been homeless encampments ... when I moved to Anchorage [several] years ago I moved into Fairview. And this was a neighbourhood that has a lot of conflict over public space in certain places. Fairview didn't seem like such a strange neighbourhood because I realized looking back on my childhood that I lived in a neighbourhood that was a lot like Fairview. I assumed it was just normal to have lots of different types of people on the street. But I guess some folks have issues with that. So, something I've been looking at in my research is ... how ... we deal with the fact that ... everyone is a citizen and everyone has access to public space – but yet there's a perception that some people have the more legitimate right to be in that space than others. How do we deal with that as a community?

Key speaker, Anchorage academic:

> In the past couple of years, I have come to become involved in home-less issues here in Anchorage. I've been working with the youth ... how our homeless youth ... navigate their environment and how it affects their social service utilization and likelihood of being a victim of crime.

Anchorage participant, social worker:

> I just happened to see the flyer upstairs. I've been concerned since I arrived in Anchorage a couple of years ago about the homeless population in general, but it's been more magnified to me about the elderly people that are homeless. Currently I'm working in in-home care for seniors. And I see the struggle of the healthy elderly population in their homes. Fighting to stay in their own comfort zone. And then I look at what that problem looks like out on the street with the elderly. They don't have a voice, I don't think, right now.

Key speaker, Juneau resident:

> I'm just a concerned citizen, basically. But I'm something of a media advocate for the cause of homelessness. And I made a two-minute promotion for this event. I interviewed a homeless man who told me about his experience as a chronic homeless man here in Juneau. And the problem of homelessness is very visible in Juneau. And it's been something that I've cared about for a long time because I recognize the fact that if it weren't for certain things that happened – just chance of fate – I could have become homeless myself, really. I think it's true that anybody could become homeless. And so I definitely have kind of a humanitarian view of it.

The fact that many participants were drawn to "Northern Voices on Homelessness" due to personal encounters – whether they had seen or known people who had been homeless or had been homeless themselves – indicated that personalizing issues of homelessness is an effective way to engage individuals in public discourse and policy discussions on homelessness.

Different Faces of Homelessness

Homeless and non-homeless participants alike expressed a desire for the public to see the "many faces of homelessness," particularly more "hidden" kinds of homelessness that occur in Alaska:

Key speaker, Anchorage service provider:

> One of the things we stress is the many faces of homelessness. A lot of times people pick up just on the chronically homelessness, especially with substance abuse issues. There [are] a lot … usually 20 per cent or less of the people experiencing homelessness in our community are the chronically homelessness … So, if only 20 per cent are chronically homeless, that means 80 per cent only

experience homelessness either for a brief period of time, only once, and they regain stable housing and will keep it for the rest of their life.

Key speaker, Anchorage service provider:

They're all different. I've seen people in cars, in camps, sleeping in an alleyway, couch surfing. All different ages. All different ethnicities. All families, children. People who are elderly or disabled. It really varies.

Several participants reported in their sticky note responses what they had learned about different types of homelessness and the different demographic groups that experience particular types of homelessness in Alaska:

"I didn't know 80 per cent of homelessness isn't chronic."
"Homelessness is varied and unique. Involves different types of individuals: alcoholics, youths, families, and recidivists."[16]
"I didn't know kids were getting out of the foster care system and becoming homeless."
"[I learned the] housing shortage pushes low-income people into shelters, limiting room for people with drug or mental issues."
"I learned about struggling in rural communities statewide."
"Even a town without a tree to sleep under has homeless problems."

Homelessness in a Northern Context

Although several key speakers emphasized the diversity of experiences of homelessness, a recurring theme was that Alaska, as the most northern US state, faces unique challenges that make it comparable to other subarctic and arctic regions. Patterns of northern homelessness and services use are tied directly to physical geography and climate, and shaped by the particular settlement history and economic development of the North.

Key speaker, Anchorage service provider:

I think one of the things that we see, particularly at our shelters, is how the weather impacts the youth coming in the shelter and leaving the shelter. Particularly on colder days, we'll have a higher number of youth in-taking.

---

16 Recidivism, as well as incarceration, is not something that was specifically mentioned or discussed during the forum, yet it did show up in this individual's sticky note response, indicating that the person was perceiving links between homelessness and recidivism.

Key speaker, Karluk Manor resident:

> I can remember back in the eighties, summertime, everybody was split [not staying in the shelters] … And in the winter, they come back … You know, people would go to detox. "Well, it's getting cold now, so I've gotta get a program."

Key Speaker, Nome volunteer service provider:

> [The Nome Emergency Shelter Team] began as an entirely volunteer effort in the spring of 2009 after the second person in Nome froze to death due to cold weather exposure and alcohol consumption. And as a community of approximately thirty-five hundred, you take our numbers, multiply by ten to get equivalent to Juneau. So, two people freezing to death in Nome would be twenty in Juneau.

In addition to the immediate threat of cold exposure from living or sleeping outside in the winter, even housed residents in rural settlements struggle to heat their buildings adequately. High heating costs, inadequately insulated housing, especially in rural and remote areas, and winter fuel shortages all continue to be a problem in Alaska, especially during extremely cold winters. Living in inadequate housing with inadequate access to heating resources is a key factor affecting housing insecurity in Alaska. Furthermore, the high cost and length of time to transport building materials and fuel out to widely dispersed settlements make up a unique northern geography of inaccessibility that exacerbates housing insecurity in northern settlements.

Key speakers also identified unique factors affecting homelessness that developed out of Alaska's settlement history and geography.

Key speaker, Anchorage academic:

> What sets Alaska apart [is that] … the Municipality of Anchorage and the North Star Borough[17] are the only two entities in the state that have taken health powers. And so the rest of the state doesn't have any sort of way to funnel money through to services or taxation. I mean, when you look at other states, they have this little tax for that and this little tax for that, and they put that money directly into services. And while some money, tax

---

17 Alaska is organized into boroughs, rather than counties or parishes as in much of the rest of the United States. North Star Borough contains Alaska's second-largest city, Fairbanks.

money, does flow back into services in Alaska to some extent, it's not the same as what you might see in other states.

In fact, over one hundred of Alaska's settlements have a local sales tax and over thirty have local property taxes.[18] The speaker's comment perhaps indicates that the general public can be uninformed about how economic resources and funding for services actually flow throughout the state's large and small settlements. However, this speaker's comment also echoed a commonly held public view that resources are not adequately dispersed between urban and rural Alaska. Furthermore, throughout the forum, people discussed the very real frustrations of rural Alaskans who were unable to access services they were entitled under the law to receive, such as housing assistance. HUD and Continuum of Care funding for federally funded homelessness and housing assistance programs is indeed divided between the Municipality of Anchorage and the "Balance of State" – meaning literally all the rest of Alaska. So, while several settlements large and small do generate local revenues through sales and property taxes, it is also true that many resources and services specifically intended to address housing and homelessness are simply non-existent in parts of Alaska.

These physical and social geographic factors affect not only who is most at risk of becoming (and staying) homeless, but also who has best access to supports and a way out of homelessness. Unfortunately, there is no comprehensive study yet of the pathways to homelessness experienced by people across Alaska, although some work on Arctic migration,[19] rural out-migration,[20] and the geographic origins of homeless youth who use services at Covenant House in Anchorage[21] suggests a pattern of pathways to homelessness similar to those examined in Inuvik and Yellowknife.[22] It should be noted, however, that many people experiencing homelessness in Anchorage also came from out of state. Thus, although rural-to-urban migration from within the state is a significant pattern shaping the demographics of homelessness in Alaska, there are other pathways to

---

18 Alaska, Office of the State Assessor, *Alaska Taxable 2017* (Anchorage, 2017), https://www.arcgis.com/apps/MapJournal/index.html?appid=bb631449256346db81bc026339f0e60c.
19 E. Lance Howe, "Patterns of Migration in Arctic Alaska," *Polar Geography* 32, no. 1–2 (2009): 69–89, https://doi.org/10.1080/10889370903000422.
20 David Driscoll et al., "Assessing the Influence of Health on Rural Outmigration in Alaska," *International Journal of Circumpolar Health* 69, no. 5 (2010): 528–44, https://doi.org/10.3402/ijch.v69i5.17683.
21 Martin and Meléndez, *Youth in Crisis.*
22 Christensen, "They Want a Different Life."

homelessness and other experiences and stories that should also be told to draw a more complete picture of homelessness in Alaska.

Humanizing the Problem (and the Solutions)

Overwhelmingly, the key message from the "Northern Voices on Homelessness" forum was that Alaskans need to work together to humanize public discourse on homelessness. We explicitly built the forum so that people experiencing homelessness could occupy the centre rather than the periphery of the discussion. Discussion revolved around calls for "humanizing homelessness" and "putting a face to homelessness" because "we are not just faceless numbers." Key speakers who had been homeless for a long time – sometimes decades – exercised agency in leading parts of the discussion and "talking back" against aspects of public discourses that they perceived as dehumanizing. Specifically, they talked back against the depersonalized, statistics-driven way that service providers and academics among the key speakers described homelessness in Alaska. A few homeless participants explained in after-speaker discussions and later in small-group discussions how this way of speaking contributed to the social isolation and discrimination they often experienced.

Key speaker, Karluk Manor resident:

> This problem is not gonna go away just because you guys put numbers on [us]. We're not numbers. Once you guys put numbers on us, just like [another participant] said, might as well bury us now. Get it over with. We're not no statistics. We're not no numbers. We're human.

The same speaker continued talking about the link between treating homeless people as "faceless numbers" and the violence they often experienced when interacting with other members of the public, sometimes at the hands of service providers whose job it is to help people. He recounted a story about his brother and the Community Service Patrol (CSP),[23] which picks up intoxicated persons from the streets and other public places to bring them to "sleep it off" at the Anchorage

---

23 The Community Safety Patrol officially changed its name to the Anchorage Safety Patrol (ASP) on 3 June 2013. Many Anchorage residents, however, still refer to it as the "CSP" in everyday language. ASP is managed by the Anchorage Department of Health and Human Services, with calls dispatched through the Anchorage Fire Department.

Safety Center, located next to the Anchorage Correctional Complex. He told us:

> You know, when my brother, he passed away, he got CSP beat the shit out of him. Beat him up. Broke his neck. And cops came over. And they looked at him. "He's not one of our regulars." 'Cause he just came from the village. And in the village we don't have no washer and dryer. We have a creek or river to go wash your clothes and stuff. And he came and he was dirty. And they looked at him. "He's not one of our regulars." They put him as a number. They gave him a number. He lasted three weeks with his neck broken. And I had to unplug him. And you guys want to put numbers on us. You guys got all numbers. Statistics.

This story seemed to carry a lot of weight for participants, as the small group discussions and sticky note responses revealed. One participant, who identified as a non-homeless woman, shared with us during the small group discussion that

> I think as a group we focused on celebrating the humanity of our homeless citizens. I think a lot of people are out of touch with the fact that we're all basically the same. We are all people that are deserving of the same equal rights. But we forget because some of us are bundled up sleeping on streets and some of us are driving around in nice cars.

In Nome, the hub town for the surrounding villages of the Seward Peninsula and Sivuqaq (St Lawrence Island), some see homelessness and public intoxication as a public problem – one that is very personal for most residents precisely because the problem is highly visible in daily life.

Key speaker, Nome volunteer service provider:

> I will say, for us in Nome, our homelessness and a lot of our problems are driven by alcohol ... Alcohol is in everybody's face in Nome. Because it's very public ... And I hate to put ourselves down, but we struggle. And there's also the problem that so many of the people we're trying to serve, once you're down, man, there's just no way up again ... And we just keep exacerbating the problem. So I don't have any kind of conclusions. Just that – I don't know. The deeper I get the more overwhelmed it feels as to how we're gonna find our way out of this ... I have to say I've lived here a long, long time, and the future looks bleaker than I've seen it look before.

She continued, detailing the laundry list of structural barriers that exist and the resources and funding that do not in Nome and north-

Figure 7.1. Sticky Notes from Participants

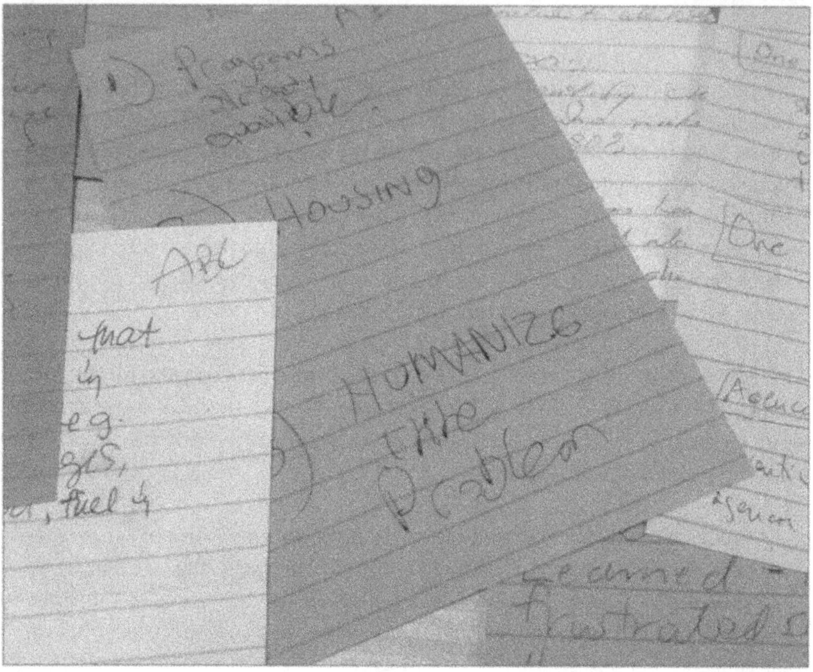

west Alaska. She concluded by identifying Nome's tight-knit social network – people who see homelessness as a very personal issue – as a good thing:

> You know, we get tremendous volunteerism and a lot of donations. There is still a sense of cohesion and a sense that homelessness and alcoholism – all of this is pretty personal here for us. It isn't just numbers.

Creating and facilitating public spaces where homeless people feel welcome, included, and comfortable participating in public discourse help to build more nuanced understandings of the gravity of the issues homeless people face. For example, although a Karluk Manor staff member corrected a common misperception that Housing First recipients did not pay rent, Karluk Manor residents jumped in to explain the consequence of this stereotype for them.

Karluk Manor staff member:

The other thing in terms of public misperceptions is the idea that the individuals who live at Karluk are actually rent-paying tenants. They're on a lease, like anybody else who enjoys an apartment. And I think that's commonly misunderstood. And I've seen it represented in the media that way. The notion of free housing, which –

Karluk Manor resident (interjecting):

"Yeah, we're freeloaders. They all say we're freeloaders."

This one moment is a particularly good example of the kind of "talking back" that is nearly impossible to achieve in typical news media, for example, where homeless individuals are not usually physically present to insert themselves into, and thereby claim space in, public discourse. Part of the ongoing challenge of community-engaged work on homelessness is to bring into a shared conversation disparate notions of what it means to be homeless, what key pathways lead to it, and what strategies can be put into practice to alleviate or end it.

Final Thoughts: What Did We Get Out of This?

The success of "Northern Voices on Homelessness" was measured differently by different participants. For some, simply showing up, listening, and learning something new made the entire event worthwhile. Several participants, both housed and houseless, were eager to follow up and discuss strategies to facilitate more dialogue in the future. For several participants from the service provider and academic worlds, the event was valuable in identifying some of what "we don't know that we don't know" about homelessness and the constellation of related social, economic, political, and cultural issues being experienced in different parts of Alaska. In particular, urban Alaskan residents who had never lived in rural settlements commented on how they were surprised to learn about the lack of offices, services, and capacity to provide funding and support for otherwise eligible people, such as housing vouchers for veterans and low-income residents living in remote settlements. Participants from rural and remote settlements such as Nome gained an engaged and sympathetic audience of urban Alaskans – which helped to address their frustrations regarding the (perceived and real) lack of awareness of many urban Alaskans about life in rural Alaska. Finally, we learned that too little research exists on homelessness in Alaska – especially about the role of shifting demographics, rural-to-urban migration, and the disproportionate provisioning of resources, services, and housing development statewide. As well, because of its similar physical and socio-political geography, homelessness in Canada's Northwest Territories parallels experiences in rural Alaska in key ways. Thus, collaborative research and strategic networking across stakeholder groups working on homelessness in the North across Alaska, Canada, and Greenland could help inform future programming, research, and everyday practice to address the socio-cultural, structural, and physical geographies in which northern homelessness is occurring, and that aims to engage, include, and prioritize the voices of people with experience of being homeless in the North.

Acknowledgments

The authors would like to thank Rebecca Barker, Madeline Hall, and Erica Mitchell, who served as Community Engaged Student Assistants (CESAs) and worked directly with us to organize "Northern Voices on Homelessness." We would also like to thank all the residents of Karluk Manor Housing First Program for serving as key speakers at the public forum, and all the service providers who also served as key speakers. We would like to thank Stacia McGourty, the Adult Services Coordinator for the Z.J. Loussac Library in Anchorage, for overseeing our use of Online With Libraries teleconferencing, and all the library staff who assisted with holding the public forum. This project was funded by the Alaska Humanities Forum, with matching cash and in-kind donations from the University of Alaska Anchorage Center for Community Engagement and Learning and the Z.J. Loussac Library.

8 Differing Meanings of Housing First: Lessons Learned from a Single-Site Program Evaluation in Anchorage, Alaska

TRAVIS HEDWIG

Housing First (HF) is an internationally recognized best practice developed in the early 1990s to provide stable housing, without preconditions of sobriety, treatment compliance, or program participation, for people with co-occurring psychiatric disabilities and substance use disorders. HF was not developed as a universal solution to address homelessness. Rather, initial applications of the approach prioritized individuals experiencing long periods of chronic homelessness along with co-occurring severe mental illness and substance use disorders. Early proponents of HF noticed that, by stabilizing the physical environment first and foremost, people might be in a better position to consider the range of service options available to them and participate if appropriate. What makes this model work is that it is built around autonomy and choice and offers the best possible starting point for dealing with homelessness – an offer of housing. In practice, however, implementation of HF values and philosophy in new housing programs is constrained by lack of resources, lack of education and training about HF principles, and lack of political will to address homelessness head on. Perhaps foreshadowing this problem, a HF fidelity scale was developed by leading researchers in the field to assess whether and to what extent programs that call themselves "Housing First" actually are.[1] As more programs continue to position themselves as HF and Alaska expands the range of permanent supportive housing options available to individuals and families in need, developing a shared understanding of what exactly HF means has become increasingly important. The scale offers a start-

---

1 Ana Stefancic et al., "The Pathways Housing First Fidelity Scale for Individuals with Psychiatric Disabilities," *American Journal of Psychiatric Rehabilitation* 16, no. 4 (2013): 240–261, https://doi.org/10.1080/15487768.2013.847741.

ing point for programs to reflect on current practices, identify areas for improvement, and better serve their tenants in community settings.

This chapter examines questions of HF fidelity in the context of a program evaluation in Anchorage, Alaska. The HF fidelity scale includes thirty-eight items divided across the five central HF tenets: housing choice, separation of housing and services, service philosophy, service array, and program structure.[2] It is intended to be used as a working tool to help programs track success, make improvements where possible, and measure adherence to the HF model. However, the implementation of HF in Alaska[3] has been challenging. Community perceptions, while increasingly more receptive, continue to push the narrative that HF enables substance abuse, despite voluminous evidence that it is an effective harm-reduction approach.[4] Although HF fidelity was not included as part of the evaluation specifically, for the purposes of this chapter tenant experiences are situated within a broader discussion of what counts as HF. Differences in how HF is understood and implemented in Alaska can affect both housing retention and tenants' overall quality of life.

Background

Tenants of Sitka Place, operated by the Rural Alaska Community Action Program, were recruited for in-depth interviews as part of this evaluation. Sitka Place is a fifty-four-unit project-based HF site located in Anchorage that serves individuals with long histories of chronic homelessness and co-occurring mental health and substance use disorders. "Project-based" differs from "scattered-site" models, where units are more integrated across the community within existing rental markets and generally serve people with longer histories of homelessness, complicated by more intensive mental and behavioural health challenges. Tenants in project-based HF units at Sitka Place also receive Intensive Case Management (ICM) services, which are offered on-site but kept

---

2 Sam Tsemberis, *Housing First: The Pathways Model to End Homelessness for People with Mental Illness and Addiction* (Center City, MI: Hazelden Publishing, 2010).
3 David Driscoll et al., "Changes in the Health Status of Newly Housed Chronically Homeless: The Alaska Housing First Program Evaluation," *Journal of Social Distress and the Homeless* 27, no. 1 (2018): 34–43, https://doi.org/10.1080/10530789.2018.1441678.
4 Susan Collins et al., "Where Harm Reduction Meets Housing First: Exploring Alcohol's Role in a Project-Based Housing First Setting," *International Journal of Drug Policy* 23, no. 2 (2012): 111–19, https://doi.org/10.1016/j.drugpo.2011.07.010.

separate from housing, whereas individuals living in "scattered-site" units are served through mobile Assertive Community Treatment teams. The importance of on-site case management for tenants at Sitka Place is described in detail in the results section below.

Sitka Place was named after the Tlingit cultural region of southeast Alaska and reflects the nearly 90 per cent of tenants who identify as Alaska Native. Overrepresentation of Alaska Native peoples in the facility is an alarming pattern that also exists among the homeless population in Anchorage broadly. Approximately 20 per cent of the total population of Anchorage identifies as Alaska Native, yet nearly 45 per cent of people experiencing homelessness identify as Alaska Native.[5] This disparity highlights the need to consider urban Indigenous peoples' perspectives and experiences in developing culturally responsive and meaningful programming, activities, and opportunities for social integration. The evaluation was conducted to measure the effect of HF from the perspective of tenants who had been living in Sitka Place for at least one year. The research team visited the facility, introduced the project, and worked closely with staff to identify people who might be interested in sharing their experiences since moving into their apartment. In all, thirteen tenants were interviewed. Each interview lasted approximately sixty to ninety minutes, and participants were compensated with a $15 gift card. Research protocols were approved by the Institutional Review Board at the University of Alaska Anchorage (UAA), and each participant reviewed and signed an informed-consent document prior to each interview. The form was also read aloud and copies were available to keep, which included information about the research and contact information for the researchers and UAA's office of research compliance.

Interviews included questions about how access to housing changed life circumstances in areas of social connection and integration, quality of life, and physical health/substance abuse. We asked about relationships with family and friends, and listened as participants explained their everyday activities, which included employment, transportation to medical and other appointments, meeting up with friends and family, or simply enjoying the safety and solitude of time spent alone in their apartment. Participants were also given an opportunity to share their overall impressions of Sitka Place, make recommendations for change, and discuss whether they would recommend it to friends or family. The

---

5 Alaska Coalition on Housing and Homelessness, "2018 Anchorage Point in Time Dashboard" (May 2018), https://www.alaskahousing-homeless.org/data.

evaluation provided critical context to compare tenant experiences with the core values of HF. It also provided an opportunity to consider program effectiveness and identify areas for improvement. Interviews were conducted in a private office or, if participants preferred, in their own private apartment. Each interview was audio recorded, transcribed, and later coded to identify key themes and structure analysis. In addition to semi-structured interviews, researchers engaged in unstructured observations in order to better understand the inner workings of the facilities and to establish relationships with tenants and staff. These observations were recorded in the researchers' notes to assist with interpreting the results.

During the analysis of qualitative data, questions related to HF fidelity began to emerge. Specifically, the core values of *housing choice and structure, service philosophy, and service array*, when viewed in light of tenants' perspectives and concerns, raised challenging questions about the meaning of HF and its implications for housing retention, stability, and autonomy. Within the domain of *housing choice and structure*, the issues most commonly expressed by tenants included lack of choice, especially when it involved co-housing with a romantic partner or significant other, lack of housing that is integrated in the community, and questions related to privacy and surveillance. With respect to *service philosophy*, tenants expressed concern related to harm reduction, substance use, and coercion. As for *service array*, tenants expressed a desire for more opportunities for social integration. In the analysis below, tenants' voices are situated within these fidelity measures, with the goal of understanding the implications for HF program implementation and everyday practice in Alaska.

Data Analysis

Interviews were transcribed verbatim from recordings. Researchers then independently reviewed interview transcripts and identified commonly cited themes, or codes, which were used to develop a draft codebook. This created consistency and uniformity in how interview transcripts were analysed. Following the drafting of an initial codebook, the researchers met to discuss similarities and differences in identified codes and to establish agreement on which themes were most salient and useful in structuring and analysing participants' responses.[6]

---

6 Clara Hill et al., "Consensual Qualitative Research: An Update," *Journal of Counseling Psychology* 52, no. 2 (2005): 196–205, https://doi.org/10.1037/0022-0167.52.2.196.

The resulting final codebook was then applied consistently across all interviews. This process ensured intercoder reliability and minimized potential bias in the interpretation of results. Three primary codes and several subcodes based on the interview guide and participants' responses to interview questions were included in the codebook. Primary codes included social connection/activity, quality of life, and overall wellness, including substance use, since moving into housing.

Secondary-level codes related to social connection/activity included connecting with friends and family (such as talking on the phone, visiting, and/or helping out), activities inside or outside the program (such as hobbies, going for walks, going shopping, etc.) time spent alone (such as reading or watching TV), and feeling alone. Secondary-level codes related to quality of life included sense of safety and independence, having a place of one's own, sleep, cooking, and having company. The codes also included conversations related to program likes and dislikes, connection to services, relationships with and help from staff, and whether participants would recommend the program to friends or family.

Results

Social Connection/Activity

Having a place of one's own was highly valued by tenants, who commonly positioned their housing as an important step towards family reconnection and a visible symbol of improved life circumstances. Tenants expressed desire for contact with friends and family, but, in many cases, had not seen or connected with them in quite some time. In some instances, housing offered opportunities to reconnect with or maintain social networks by hosting guests or simply by taking a break from everyday social life by staying home alone. With respect to the HF value of *housing choice*, several tenants described the importance of housing for their overall health and social well-being, but also expressed a desire for more autonomy and control over how those relationships were maintained, when and where friends and family were allowed to visit, and the sense that staff perhaps unnecessarily policed those interactions. This raised questions of fidelity with respect to tenants' voices, and whether or not people were recognized as rent-paying tenants who had choice over how they used their space. One tenant captured this in stating, "I like my time alone but I still like people coming over and visiting ... I wish my SO [significant other] could stay here but they won't let her."

Several tenants expressed the desire for co-housing with a spouse or partner, but this was not an option at Sitka Place. Having choice and control over the type of housing arrangement is an important aspect of HF fidelity and a critical consideration for programs looking to better support people in its housing units.

Some tenants described circumstances under which they lost contact with family, and linked that to their experiences growing up, leaving home to try life in a new place, moving in search of employment or other opportunities, and becoming homeless. Descriptions of everyday social life, both before and after moving into housing, included the importance of kinship and social connection to family and friends, as well as others who were experiencing homelessness in the community. It also included discussion of what it meant to have access to a community. This got into the core value of *integrated housing,* an HF fidelity measure that also falls under *housing choice.* Although there are fundamental differences between project-based and "scattered- site" HF models, both seek out spaces for housing units that are fully integrated into the community, rather than segregated and clustered in certain, less desirable parts of town. Sometimes this is positioned as a matter of necessity (when, for example, housing and services need to be densely clustered together to facilitate access), but the goals of HF are to have these units exist within, not apart from, the community. This is beneficial to both tenants of HF and community members alike. By maintaining an active visible presence within the community, tenants have opportunities to participate in activities away from their apartment, cultivate a sense of neighbourliness, and engage in everyday practices of citizenship, including voting and protest. As one tenant described, "I have three sisters here, a couple aunts. I keep in touch with one sister, daily basis, but don't always have a chance to meet up with her."

Daily contact or attempted daily contact with social networks of family and friends were mentioned by all interviewees. For some, communication was limited to phone and Internet (e.g., Facebook). Others described physically going out to meet with or check up on family, helping with chores, or just visiting. Several tenants described taking on the care of friends or family who were still homeless by walking to camps, sharing food, clothing, and other items no longer needed since moving into housing, and checking on their welfare generally. As one tenant articulated, "Well, my aunt, sometimes she has some Native foods and things like that to share, or she wants me to help her mow her lawn or probably do some housecleaning or something for her house."

For others, relationships with family were more strained, and attempts to reach out often went unanswered. Having an apartment, however, provided a setting from which at least to attempt reconnection, which was important for many tenants. One tenant explained: "I left a couple messages with my aunt and a couple sisters. They never returned the call, so – oh well, I tried. I gave up on that this past week. I talk to my sister Donna, though. She's good support."

Maintaining social connection was highly valued by all tenants, but they also expressed a desire to have access to the community more broadly. This is referred to as *social integration* within the HF fidelity index, and represents an area that could be improved across the board. Although developing a sense of community within the HF facility was widely recognized as important by staff and tenants alike, the integration of that community within Anchorage more broadly has been given less attention, despite tenants' desires. As one tenant described,

> I don't like to go bothering people just because I'm lonely. I take up the time watching TV. I do a little reading, I do my crosswords. I keep busy with my mind and my heart. Seems like it. I wish I had more friends to go hang out with ... I very rarely go anywhere. I mean, I can take the bus when I have to go to the store. And I rarely go anywhere. I mean, the other day I was watching the news and they had a great little party thing going on downtown there. I wish I coulda went to that. But I don't go out no more.

Feelings of social isolation coupled with expressions of desire to engage in community were common. Tenants also linked social integration to physical health (specifically mobility), mental health (feelings of loneliness), and lack of access to transportation. As this tenant further explained, "I don't wanna get around on these crutches all the time. I gotta go out there and take a bus. That costs me money. I gotta go get me a bus pass, which I can't do with the money I got. I still gotta plan that up on the horizon there."

Housing stability brings with it opportunities for engaging in a range of new activities, including social and/or recovery support groups offered on-site at Sitka Place, employment opportunities either by bus or on foot following a night of rest, or having a safe place to return to after a day of visiting friends and family "out there." Most of these activities occurred on-site, but several tenants expressed a desire to participate in their community more broadly. For example, one tenant described how she attended an Elders group once in a while to eat lunch with friends, but expressed a desire to do more beadwork through a group at the Alaska Native Medical Center. As she described, "I'd like to do beadwork ... Right now I'm getting bored with crocheting [by myself] ... I'm making a baby blanket, but I haven't worked on it for so long."

Finding ways to better support social activities that are integrated into the community is a key consideration with respect to HF fidelity. Although some tenants participated in activities provided on-site, without more opportunities to leave Sitka Place, many chose to stay in their rooms alone. This was described in both positive and negative terms. For many, the privacy of an apartment offered peace and quiet and was a welcome change from life before moving in. As one tenant stated, "I don't do much anymore. Like I say, I'm happy with my place and my privacy. That's a big thing [for me]." Another participant stated succinctly, "I feel safe here." Having the freedom and flexibility to choose how and with whom to engage in social activity was important for many. It offered a locus of control that was also an important *harm-reduction* strategy. Overall, every tenant interviewed enjoyed both expanded opportunities for social activity and an increased sense of safety and privacy, which was lacking prior to moving into housing. This was explained in stark terms by one tenant, who explained,

> I'm around people that's always inebriated, and I try to get away from them here. I don't wanna be around that, so I just avoid it. Just walk away from a few drunks from yesterday and just today, too. 'Cause some people down there just – I don't blame them for who or what they've become or whether they're using or not, so – I just say, 'Whoa, I'm leaving.'

The value of being able to shut the door and remove oneself from others was clearly positioned as a benefit with respect to *harm reduction*. There is a tension here, however, between the value of privacy and personal space and the potentially self-isolating effects of spending too much time alone. In this regard, the HF values of *privacy* and *social integration* are sometimes in opposition.

Similarly, the concept of *privacy* is also sometimes in conflict with *harm reduction*, especially with respect to staff, who must balance the often-competing ethical principles of respecting autonomy and promoting the beneficence of HF residents overall. This includes setting and enforcing rules regarding the use of one's private space (i.e., limits on certain appliances or household chemicals for cleaning), and limiting alcohol use. As one tenant explained,

> One time after I first moved in here, I had some bleach and some other kinds of stuff here that was just sitting right there. And I was gone somewhere doing something, and when I came back, it was gone. Because they

had the key to come in here, do inspections, or whatever. But one of those people on the staff probably thought it was theirs. That I might have took it from their place. But I had bought and paid for it. Then I walked out and I saw it in the shelf, in the office. I didn't say nothing, because I didn't wanna offend them or anything ... accuse somebody. I said I didn't see it. But I know it was mine. And it was gone from my place. That's the only thing that I really got angry about. It's my soap and whatnot. But I gotta go out and buy some more anyway now.

The notion that staff had essentially unfettered access to tenant units was seen as problematic, as indicated above, but there was also an understanding that staff were "looking out" for tenants and had their best interests in mind in terms of overall health and safety. For example, several tenants expressed a desire to be able to cook in their unit, but there are no kitchens in the units and limits on the kinds of cooking appliances that are allowed (e.g., hotpots). Although there was recognition that this was due to fire-safety issues, there was desire for more independence and autonomy with respect to cooking. A shared kitchen was available for tenants, but supporting *housing choice* could mean expanding the types of units available, including modifying existing units to include kitchens. One tenant, recognizing this tension, saw her current housing as temporary: "I'd like a place of my own. My own place with a stove and everything. A bigger place ... And I'm looking forward to that." She was thankful for her housing situation, but she wanted more flexibility to have family visit and stay with her, and was actively working on her recovery since she quit drinking. Describing her current situation, she continued, "Oh, it's going okay. I like it here. A place of my own, finally ... But I'm looking forward to finding another place so I can have my family move in with me ... I just wanna live my life – help others in some way, somehow ... And I wanna share my happiness with others, too."

There was also recognition of the tension between *privacy* and *harm reduction* in the context of alcohol management. While practices varied widely based on individual circumstances, some residents had staff manage their alcohol intake for them. They kept bottles of hard liquor under lock and key and had a shot every hour or two, which sometimes became a source of debate and conflict for residents. Here again, supporting individual choice while encouraging harm reduction existed in conflict. This was an ongoing challenge for staff as well as for tenants, who understood why limits on alcohol and drug use were encouraged, but they did not always like it. One tenant was thankful to have staff available to help, and felt they needed the extra encouragement, explaining, "You know, I've been a drunk so damn long I don't even know anymore. I still think I got some problems, but I mean I drank quite a bit, you know? I drank a lotta hard stuff ... Now I'm down to just beer right now and staff are a big reason for that ... I need that."

Staff generally tried to limited alcohol use to a six-pack of beer a day, but this was a precarious balance for many tenants at Sitka Place. Tensions between measures on the HF fidelity scale are what make implementation challenging. Although the scale was designed to be a tool for providers, what that balance looks like will vary across programs, depending on the population served and related differences in support needs. Clearly, however, HF fidelity is linked to everyday social lives of tenants in important ways, as we explore next.

Quality of Life

A central theme across all the interviews was that housing stability led to improvements in many aspects of everyday life. This included a more positive outlook, a sense of gratitude, opportunity and/or possibility regarding the future, and consideration related to overall health and well-being. For many tenants, the offer of housing represented an opportunity to make life changes that simply were not possible before. Once one's physical environment is stabilized, it is possible to imagine temporal horizons beyond the immediate needs of the present. This is perhaps one of the greatest contributions of HF: that stable housing is the solution to homelessness and many other challenges, including case management, access to mental health, addiction, and recovery services, and overall health and wellness generally. One tenant, recalling everyday life prior to moving in, stated, "Oh, really good. I mean, comparatively to what it used to be, hell, this is a blessing. This is like a home. I got all kinds of stuff in here. Oh, yeah. I got a freezer to keep food in. I got my clothing. My life here is really good. I can sit and read. Do what I want. I don't make no noise. I don't cause any trouble." Another tenant was also thankful for her current living situation, but expressed concern for the many others who were still homeless: "When I go to Bean's [a café and shelter for street-involved people] and see those people, or when I ride the bus and pass by, my heart goes out to them. I was like that once. I'm so happy to be here."

The selfless attitude many tenants took towards others who did not have housing was particularly noteworthy. They saw their changed circumstances as a blessing and wanted to share it with others. Many also felt lucky to be housed, knowing that there were still a large number of unsheltered residents in Anchorage. Expressions of gratitude about how much life had changed for the better since moving into housing were also common. As one tenant communicated, "It gives me a chance to think about other things, be more positive about either work or staying straight and clean, and work on better things than just, 'Yeah, I'm gonna waste my time.'"

Having staff available also played a significant role in tenants' quality of life. For example, in response to the question of how staff were helpful, one tenant replied, "Honesty, friendship. And they give me courage ... to make myself better than I was outside. Because when I was outside, I had no one. Sure, I'd go see my family, but, you know, they drink and smoke a lot. I said, 'No, not for me.' I'm trying to make myself better." These sentiments were echoed by another tenant: "Oh, yeah. Totally. From A to Z. And if I need something, I can go right down there right now and ask them [staff] for anything. And they'll probably find a way to get it. Or do something so I could get that help. They're willing, and they're gonna find a way to get the help. Oh, I love them. I love them all."

Staff were nearly universally described in a positive light. In addition to helping with reminders for appointments, assistance in applying for and accessing services, or just being a supportive person to listen and offer encouraging words, staff were a regular and reliable presence in tenants' lives. Staff were always available, even when others might not be. As one tenant explained, "But that's important, too, you know? Sometimes you get lonely, and just ... that's why I'll come out here, and staff will come out here and talk with me." Another tenant indicated that staff were the best part of the current living environment. She elaborated, "The most I like about living here is the staff. They're very friendly. They're helpful. And my case manager, she helps me out a lot. They talk to me. And they worry about me."

Overall, housing greatly improved tenants' perceptions of their quality of life, and offered opportunities to consider longer-term goals and make substantial life changes in a supportive environment. Tenants expressed desires to pursue employment, live independently, and improve their health and well-being. Although staff played instrumental roles in facilitating tenants' goals, expanding *service array* to better support these goals is a key HF fidelity measure that could be improved. Staff end up taking on multiple, often conflicting roles, and the physical and professional separation of those roles in the context of housing and services should be prioritized. Clearly, however, housing made possible new opportunities for tenants to engage selectively in social activities or to stay away if those activities might lead to undesirable outcomes, such as drinking or getting into trouble. Several tenants described this tension. Although they might want to connect with old friends or participate in activities they were involved with prior to moving in, there was increased awareness that choosing to stay at home if they wished was also a viable option, and many welcomed this.

Overall Wellness and Substance Use

A central tenet of Housing First is that, by stabilizing the physical environment first and foremost, other aspects of health and well-being can be addressed more readily. Feelings of safety and security improve overall health and well-being by decreasing stress and time spent worrying about personal safety, threats of violence from others, cold weather exposure, wildlife encounters, and other essentials such as where to sleep and eat. This opens up opportunities to consider reducing or eliminating alcohol or other substances, engaging in treatment and recovery services, and accessing primary and preventive care services. *Service array* is a key HF fidelity measure that can be used to improve permanent supportive housing initiatives in Anchorage.

For tenants who had experienced chronic homelessness (in some cases, for several decades) in addition to substance use disorders and co-occurring severe mental illness, housing was a catalyst for reduced consumption of alcohol and connection to primary and preventive health care services. Although mental health and substance abuse detox, treatment, and recovery services are limited in Alaska generally, the shift in service use patterns from emergency and corrections to primary care centres has resulted in better physical health outcomes and reduced public expenditures. Access to intensive case management services proved to be instrumental in helping tenants feel supported and connecting them to additional services and supports as appropriate. Many tenants described living for years with chronic but treatable physical conditions, including hepatitis C, tuberculosis, diabetes, HIV, and a variety of mobility impairments due to accidents. Stabilizing housing was the first step in addressing immediate physical health needs and connecting with providers. It also offered opportunities to reflect on life and consider long-term goals and desired outcomes, including employment, independence, recovery, or moving on to a new apartment. As one tenant described, "That's one reason why I moved here, because I wanted to be near [my daughter]. And my health, too. I get pneumonia easy, and I was – well, I'm HIV-positive. I have to take my medications daily, and take care of myself. This place has really helped me."

Another tenant described how housing helped him think about his alcohol and substance use in a different way, especially when considered through the lens of his own history of homelessness. He explained, "I was sleeping on the streets, and drinking every day. When I got moved here, I sobered up and started looking for work."

Having a home also allowed tenants the opportunity to disengage from their social networks if they did not want to interact or participate in activities they were trying to avoid, such as drinking and drug use. Tenants expressed that being able to distance themselves from the outside world was very important to their sense of safety and independence. Several tenants articulated the value of being able to shut the door of one's own room, although some still found it difficult to remove themselves from their social circles due to friendship and loyalty, even if they knew they would end up drinking together or possibly getting into trouble with the law. While still recognizing the value in their social relationships, having a door to close increased their ability to control whether and how to engage with friends. This proved to be an adjustment for many. As one tenant explained, "I slept at the shelter, and I would drink in the winter, just to go to sleep ... When I was thirty days out, I would just get drunk and just to go to sleep off, so I wouldn't have to sleep outside. And when I went here, I slowly realized alcohol isn't the answer. I should improve my life, take care of myself, so I have a hard time being around them now."

Making the adjustment from life on the streets to having an apartment proved challenging for many, but was also a point of great pride that many leveraged to help sustain their recovery. As one tenant described, "I don't wanna get all emotional, but I have to. It's not about joining a program. It's about effort, to get off the streets. I was homeless for five years before I got in here. I did not join a program. I worked hard for it." Difficulties adjusting to life in housing were echoed by another tenant, who stated, "You know, I'm still trying to adjust, I mean, even after almost two years."

The importance of housing to reducing alcohol consumption was described by most in the context of their overall health and well-being. One tenant explained, "My privacy is the biggest thing. And being sober ... I've been an alcoholic, gee, the last twenty years. Actually thirty. But I'm happy with my life now."

In addition to substance use, tenants described a variety of physical and mental health challenges that constrained their everyday lives. For example, one tenant who experienced a mobility impairment explained, "Oh, yeah, with these crutches, I hate getting around other people. And then have to make arrangements. 'Okay. We got a disabled place for disabled over here.' That'd be like, 'Okay. You gotta go outta your way to do something for me, which I don't like.' I'd rather be seen as a regular person. But with these crutches, I feel like I'm so disabled in a way that I don't wanna cause problems. You know what I mean?"

That tenant's perspective on disability and community segregation is also relevant in light of the HF fidelity measure of *integrated housing*, where ideally any given program should occupy no more than 20 per cent of total units in a building and people with disabilities should be integrated fully within housing complexes. Adhering to this principle involves community work that is often beyond the scope of everyday program work, but the question of community integration requires a community that is ready, willing, and prepared to support the full inclusion of all its citizens.

Given the long histories of homelessness tenants described, many reported feeling sad both at the thought of other homeless people in their community not getting the same level of support and at the grief and loss associated with losing friends and family who were homeless. As one tenant described, "Right now? I've been grieving because six of my nieces died. And I try to be strong. But I do it." Experiences of grief and loss were nearly universal among the tenants at Sitka Place, and this aspect should be considered carefully within the existing *service array* of programs. Grief is often the context in which separation and rupture of family occurs, and is frequently associated with and compounded by mental health and substance abuse challenges. As one tenant recalled, "I was hardly with my children, 'cause they got taken away by the state, 'cause of alcohol and drugs. And my son needs me. He's in prison right now, but I'm in touch with him, writing letters for the first time in a long time."

Other tenants described deaths of friends and family members in their street networks as a regular occurrence and something that helped keep their current experience in HF in perspective. One tenant elaborated: "Just 'cause I got my own place, you know? That's how I see some people, they got their own place, and bang! They're like pretty loaded down, most every day. See, I'm not falling into that category. We all know where they will end up." The acceptance of death as a regular occurrence is a stark reminder of how precarious housing can be. Given the extent to which people grapple with these questions in the context of their everyday lives, it is important for programs to find ways to support tenants in managing grief and loss within the spectrum of service offerings. This is another area where access to intensive case management services could make a difference for tenants. Having a person available for regular check-ins, even if brief, and referral to additional support if a person wished to engage would improve overall housing stability and is an often-cited reason for housing success and satisfaction from tenants' perspectives.

Conclusion

Although the tenants' experiences described above are just one example of an HF project in Anchorage, questions related to fidelity have major implications for future work on permanent supportive housing solutions in Alaska and elsewhere in the North. At a time of political and economic uncertainty with respect to federal and state funding for housing solutions, integrating Housing First fidelity measures into existing housing initiatives is of critical importance.

Programs with better fidelity have better housing retention,[7] and long-term housing stability has been linked to reductions in public expenditures for high-cost emergency and correctional services.[8] As such, adherence to the principles of HF is also important for program improvement and policy advocacy efforts. More important, based on the experiences of the tenants interviewed for this research, HF has an overwhelmingly positive impact on overall quality of life and the sense of wellness. It has allowed both a physical place and the phenomenological space to serve as a catalyst for reconnection with family and friends, and an opportunity for critical self-reflection and exploration of the temporal horizons and possibilities that exist outside the immediacy of where a person will sleep on a given night.

Since Housing First was designed for a southern, urban context, it is important to think about its fidelity at all stages of program development and implementation in Alaska. It is also important to continue efforts to demonstrate the efficacy of HF and translate that knowledge to elected officials, policymakers, program administrators, and frontline workers. The model is designed to be flexible and, as described above, many of the central values of HF can exist in conflict with one another in application and practice. This is to be expected and welcomed, and is exactly the reason having a tool like

---

7 Clare Davidson et al., "Association of Housing First Implementation and Key Outcomes among Homeless Persons with Problematic Substance Use," *Psychiatric Services* 65, no. 11 (2014): 1318–24, https://doi.org/10.1176/appi.ps.201300195.

8 Mary Larimer et al., "Health Care and Public Service Use and Costs Before and After Provision of Housing for Chronically Homeless Persons with Severe Alcohol Problems," *Journal of the American Medical Association* 301, no. 13 (2009): 1349–57, https://doi.org/10.1001/jama.2009.414.

the fidelity index can be useful for programs. As we continue to see the expansion of the label "Housing First," it is important to keep in mind what it is and what it is not. For Alaska, there is an opportunity to learn from what has come before and to find new and creative ways to make it work for Anchorage and other communities across the circumpolar North.

9 Alaska Is a Very Small Town: Moving towards an Understanding of Homelessness in the Urban North

CLARE J. DANNENBERG

The perspectives on homelessness in the urban North found in this collection engage in rich discussion on the many policies, standards of care, and best practices of dealing with homelessness across an array of populations in northern spaces. In this chapter, I want to extend this discussion by introducing a modicum of caution with regard to broad implementation of such policy, standard of care, and best practices without regard to community composition or geographic or social context. I intend to do so through sharing insights gleaned from an applied anthropological and linguistic investigation of Anchorage, Alaska.

Language is symbolically linked to cultural norms and behaviours.[1] Although the relationship between language and culture is correlative and not causal, carefully examining language in conversational context can enlighten the scope in which those in conversation engage in agency for change.[2] Such examination leads to a better understanding of the relationship between individual social responsibility (e.g., *I do*), cooperative, shared responsibility (e.g., *we do*), and absence of personal responsibility (e.g., *I won't, but they will/should do*) in the affectation of positive change. Moreover, careful examination

---

1 Dell Hyme, "On Communicative Competence," in *Linguistic Anthropology: A Reader*, ed. Alessandro Duranti (Oxford: Blackwell, 2001), 53–73; Michel Foucault, "The Subject and Power," in *The Essential Foucault: Selections from the Essential Works of Foucault 1954–1984*, ed. Paul Rabinow and Nikolas Rose (New York: New Press, 2003); Susan Gal, "Linguistic Anthropology," in *Encyclopedia of Language and Linguistics*, ed. Keith Brown, 2nd ed., vol. 7 (Oxford: Elsevier, 2006), 171–85.
2 Norman Fairclough, "Political Correctness: The Politics of Culture and Language," *Discourse and Society* 14, no. 1 (2003), 17–28, https://www.jstor.org/stable/42888547; Pierre Bourdieu and Loïc Wacquant, *An Invitation to Reflexive Sociology* (Oxford: Polity Press, 1992); Anthony Giddens, *The Constitution of Society* (Berkeley: University of California Press, 1986).

of language use in context allows for better discernment of how individuals gather (or not) in a community. How a community gathers, then, can function as a schema to inform *local* best practices, the filter through which *global* best practices are often vetted.[3] Together, the symbolic identity and the schematic of how a community gathers directly inform the level of uptake regarding positive change: higher uptake leads to more sustainable programming for community issues such as homelessness.

The Socio-cultural and Linguistic Context of Anchorage

The vast majority of Alaska's population (around 300,000) lives in Anchorage, located in the south of the state on the Cook Inlet. The second-largest populations in Alaska are Fairbanks, in the interior, and Juneau, in the southeast, at around 100,000 and 30,000, respectively. Anchorage is a thriving seaport and a railway hub, but the oil industry, military, and tourism make up the bulk of the economy. The municipality of Anchorage includes the town of Girdwood, forty miles to the south, and Eagle River, ten miles to the northeast. Anchorage is an urban oasis in the middle of the wilderness: one can drive ten miles from Anchorage and be in the bush, but Anchorage itself is quite developed as an urban area, with all of the affordances associated with that designation, including acting as the hub for Alaska's social service agencies. Hospitals, shelters, and mental health services are well developed relative to the rest of Alaska, and rural Alaskans in need of those services are often sent to Anchorage, sometimes without travel money back to their homes (see the discussion by Carraher and Hedwig, in this volume).

Although Anchorage is a young city, having celebrated its centennial in 2014, the area has been occupied for millennia. The Dena'ina Athabascan were Anchorage's first continuous occupants, approximately 1,500 years ago, and records of the first non-Indigenous populations in the area date back to the late 1700s.[4] Anchorage has a history of attracting a broad spectrum of people since that time, and although the majority of Anchorage's population identifies as White, the area is quite diverse. In the national ranking of diverse schools in the United States, Anchorage

---

3 Arjun Appadurai, "Grassroots Globalization and the Research Imagination," *Public Culture: Special Issue on Globalization* 12, no 1 (2000), 1–19, https://doi.org/10.1215/08992363-12-1-1.
4 Steve Langdon, *The Native People of Alaska* (Anchorage: Greatland Graphics, 2002).

hosts the top three diverse high schools, six out of the top ten middle schools, and nineteen of the most diverse elementary schools.[5]

Anchorage's homeless population is representative of the wider diversity across the municipality. The largest percentage of that population identifies as Indigenous (approximately 40 per cent) in each subcategory of groups (e.g., family, single, youth), although those who identify as White have shown numbers not far behind (about 30 per cent). Pacific Islander, Black, and multi-ethnic groups round out the top percentages.[6]

Linguistic Community(ies)

As many as 104 languages have been identified in the Anchorage school system, including 19 Alaska Native Indigenous languages. Analysis of languages suggests that Anchorage has an affiliation of community that indicates its distinctiveness as compared to other urban areas *outside* the urban North, despite the fact that Anchorage does have similarities with those locales, especially related to overall infrastructure and amenities (i.e., chain restaurants and stores). Instead, Anchorage shows a mixed community alignment. That is, symbolically, Anchorage maintains its distinctiveness as a community that is not quite a part of the rest of the United States and not exactly like the Alaskan bush. Anchorage is both a closed community – a big space with a small-town feel, where each person shares similar experiences of living in the North – and a community that is highly individualistic, where, when it comes to an institution or agency urging action, there is a decisive lack of uptake due to the focus on individualism.

In other terms, northern communities such as Anchorage have faced an increasing need to absorb migrating people who are no longer able to manage in their home communities, while urban, community-ready resources are unable to keep pace. Thus, these urban communities have begun to search for best practices that are effective across a broad array of community contexts. Moreover, urban communities in the North, including Anchorage, are also seeking practitioners with experience implementing broadly effective best practices. What the study of homelessness in Anchorage suggests – and the study of symbolic language behaviour in Anchorage supports – is that direct transfer of global practices adopted by practitioners outside the North does not easily

---

5 National Center for Education Statistics, "Local Education Agency (School District) Universe Study, 2012–13" (Washington, DC: Department of Education, December 2014), https://nces.ed.gov/ccd/pubagency.asp.
6 Point in Time Count, 2018.

translate across these communities. The global might be effective, but it needs to be interpreted in the context of the local community.

Homelessness in Anchorage

The symbolic identity for the Anchorage community, as discussed above, provided the scaffolding for the five-month study on homelessness, which was initiated to better understand how to convey messaging to the public and policymakers about changing policies and solutions intended to end homelessness. The goal was to solicit community uptake of best practices, such that any programming that was developed and showing some success would continue to have forward momentum. The goal for the Anchorage community resource partners was to make homelessness as "brief, rare, and non-reoccurring as possible," and garnering broad and pervasive community support was a key factor. Without widespread community buy-in at all levels (economic, social, ideological), solutions to homelessness are unsustainable. To those who work every day to create, implement, and strategize solutions for homelessness, gathering even the most basic positive community response can be frustratingly rare.

Methodology Informing the Study

This chapter is partly adapted from a community report put together by an Applied Anthropology class in spring 2018 and presented to stakeholders in the Anchorage community.[7] My students were the co-researchers and co-authors of that report and should be recognized as such. Our study drew on the theory, method, and practice of applied cultural and linguistic anthropology, which values and relies upon community participation to move towards a better understanding of how to address social justice issues within communities.

The community report gathered qualitative data from three sources: (1) a survey distributed by United Way of Anchorage in fall 2017; (2) ethnographic data gathered through Community Conversations addressing United Way Anchorage's question, "What will Anchorage look like when homelessness is solved?"; and (3) informal, spontaneous interviews with Anchorage community members.

---

7 University of Alaska Anchorage, Applied Anthropology Class Spring 2018, *Formative Report on Envisioning Anchorage without Homelessness* (report submitted to United Way Anchorage).

Community and Homelessness

What constitutes community and what fosters images of homelessness in that community differ from one community member to another. In our study, the term community was referred to in a number of different forms. Community was related to an entity – that is, a group of individuals acting as a whole towards some shared end – by, for example, setting policy – and shared geographical space (the Anchorage community). Community also invoked feelings of belonging (e.g., homeless individuals are also community members), as well as of strength or solidarity (e.g., the community needed to act together, not as individuals).

Close examination of the data suggested that Anchorage residents living in circumstances considered "unusual," "unsafe," or "undesirable," were acknowledged by others as separate and apart from socially acceptable practices. These lines drawn between populations resulted in a felt and perceived boundary between community members who were housed and those who were homeless. Those affected by homelessness were commonly associated with living in tent camps, spending time on the streets (loitering), having poor hygiene, abusing substances, and being panhandlers on roadways. Although people experiencing homelessness lived throughout Anchorage, they were frequently seen as outsiders.

The visibility of those living outside of a home seemed to invoke feelings not only of danger to those who were currently housed, but also of uncleanliness. Community members living without a home were highly noticeable, whether they were panhandling, living in camps, or leaving sleeping materials on the sidewalks, and participants reported homelessness as unpleasant to view. As a result, the image of persons living outside or in well-known shelters was the focus of responses to the question of what Anchorage would look when homelessness is ended – for example, "campers/camps gone," "clean parks, no needles in sand," and "less panhandlers." In this sense, homelessness was framed as fundamentally damaging and unclean, and participants focused on the elimination of this image as well as on how Anchorage would be safer and healthier as a result.

Media portrayals of homelessness and how it manifests in Anchorage are apt illustrations of the overall sentiment among community members. Those often depicted as homeless in popular media images tend to show visual likenesses to Alaska Native people. At the same time, there are relatively few images of children or families that surface in relation to media coverage of homelessness. Images portray adults with dirt on their faces and hands, torn clothing, and holding signs that ask for money. These pictures further reinforce stereotypes of community members affected by homelessness as dirty, panhandling Alaska

Native people. As a result, Indigenous people in Anchorage are further stereotyped, distanced from other community members, and placed in separate social and cultural categories.

Public commentary across a variety of media suggested that "homelessness" was a danger to those in proximity to community members living without a home. For example, as an *Alaska Dispatch News* article on homelessness stated, "The excessive concentration of emotionally and mentally challenged individuals exceeds the carrying capacity of the downtown area. The heart of our city is struggling to keep itself healthy under the daily assault of ill-mannered people with little respect for themselves, for others, for property and particularly not for the public realm of our commons."[8] This danger was often presented as a cost or loss to others: loss of the use of public spaces (territory), loss of feeling safe (at home, at ease), loss of cleanliness (health). In these tropes, community members living without homes were cast as taking away from innocent/deserving community members.

However, when discussing how to address homelessness and the costs and losses incurred by others, the regaining of public spaces, safety, and cleanliness did not appear as sufficient compensation for housing and services to homeless individuals. The agencies providing housing and services were described as "enabling" homeless individuals to remain indigent, addicted, and lazy: "If we permanently house them, all we're doing is enabling them. We're saying, 'It's ok.' Smack them on the wrist and keep going."[9] The media emphasized the need for community members to merit housing and services in focused ways by leaving addiction, working, and volunteering. These media portrayals of community members affected by homelessness rarely accounted for the specificities of programs in Anchorage aimed at assisting such persons.

Emergent Themes

Several different themes emerged from each data source in the study, as table 9.1 illustrates, but there were also some differences in degree and frequency across the sources.

8 Allen Kemplen, "A different approach to homelessness," *Anchorage Dispatch News*, 11 July 2018, https://www.adn.com/opinions/2018/07/11/a-different-approach-to-homelessness/.
9 Anne Hillman, "How to end homelessness in Anchorage together," *Alaska Public Media*, 18 October 2017, https://www.alaskapublic.org/2017/10/18/plan-to-end-homelessness-anchorage-solutions-desk/.

Table 9.1. Emergent Themes across Data Sources

Theme	Survey Data	Community Conversation	Informal Interviews
Safety	✔	✔	✔
Availability of community resources to help curb homelessness	✔	✔	✔
Prevention of homelessness versus emergency response	✔	✔	✔
Dichotomy of helplessness and hope regarding homelessness	✔	✔	✔
Systemic problems	✔		✔
Training		✔	✔
Trauma	✔	✔	✔
Mental health and substance abuse	✔	✔	✔
Perceived barriers	✔		✔
Availability of educational resources to help lift the homeless	✔	✔	
Degree of government involvement	✔		✔
Choice versus circumstance	✔		✔

While some sources concentrated on issues such as *perceived barriers* that might impede the health and welfare of those affected by homelessness, others concentrated on the necessary *training* that those who were creating and maintaining programs to serve the homeless might need. The theme of *choice versus circumstance* also emerged from different data sources. In both the survey and the interviews, participants shared their questions about the agency of the homeless in their decision to be without a home. Participants indicated that those who were homeless might have wished to be free of the burden of civilization, including a mortgage, electricity, and so forth. They further noted that this need for freedom was particular to northern spaces – that is, participants indicated that those who gravitated to northern spaces had a increased desire to be free of a set of social norms and community obligations. From all three data sources, however, a few other themes bubbled up, as discussed below.

Safety

Safety was the most salient theme, both in degree and frequency, across all sources. Comments demonstrated concerns about safety not only for community members – including individuals, families, and youth – who were homeless, but also for community members with a home. These concerns included issues about crimes against community members, but often highlighted potential threats to the most vulnerable, such as community members without homes, children, and individuals who like to explore local parks alone. Although few participants raised every safety issue addressed below, a majority noted more than one perspective on safety. Safety was identified as a clear priority for Anchorage community members.

For example, when people were asked, in terms of safety, what Anchorage would look like when homelessness was solved, they answered "safe walking spaces" and a "more comfortable commute," implying safe walking spaces unobstructed by people spending time in open spaces. Safety was ascribed not only to certain places, however, but also to life experiences and circumstances in general. This could be seen in examples of persons noting "no exposure deaths," "a decrease in prison recidivism," and "lower crime rates."

Additionally, community members observed that first responders, such as police officers, firefighters, and paramedics, all had uniquely challenging roles when it came to providing safety for all members of the community while also maintaining their own personal safety. Participants viewed particular areas of Anchorage as unsafe because of those camping there. Those who were observed as not currently homed were thought to need a "*safe* place to sleep." Ongoing perceptions suggested that participants deemed current shelters as unsafe or insecure. Some community members raised the issue that offering aid to those without a home could make them a greater target for victimization. One community member, for example, described how others preyed on those who received housing by taking it over and forcing them back to living without a home. People feared for the safety of children playing in parks or public spaces when homeless community members were present. There was a noticeable lack of trust between groups of community members who felt others were unpredictable, unsympathetic, and uncooperative.

At the same time, however, the data showed that safety was intertwined with constructs of Eurocentric ways of being. Feeling safe had little to do with actual physical threat, but tended to be directly correlational to culturally acceptable norms of behaviour. A person who was closer in dress, demeanour, and presence was safer than a person who varied from the White middle-class norm. For example, in one community conversation, a self-identified young White female articulated her fear of walking by herself in downtown Anchorage through what appeared to be a group of homeless Alaska Native men. She identified "loitering" as a trigger for her feeling of a lack of safety. As she began sharing her experience and concern for safety, another participant who identified as an Alaska Native person suggested that what White community members might view as loitering, Alaska Native groups would interpret as a way of being. Gathering as a social group in public spaces was not uncommon in the lived experience of Alaska Native people. As the above example shows, concerns about safety connected to perspectives of *them versus us* and to discussions about how definitions of "threatening" or "unsafe" behaviour might indeed vary culturally.

Responsibility and Resources

There were a multitude of perspectives among community members regarding the allocation of responsibility, roles, and resources to end homelessness. To begin, resources were associated with a collection of major topics: housing, shelters, mental health facilities, substance abuse centres, emergency rooms, and police enforcement, and those resources were addressed in aspirational terms. Topics under resources also connected to community members' perspectives of responsibilities – that is, who should provide, administer, and evaluate the resources became a key concern.

When asked what Anchorage would look like when homelessness was solved, participants became aspirational, envisioning that there would be more affordable housing as well as a growing housing market. Shelters were imagined as being shut down, and beds in mental health facilities were envisioned as available. Mental health centres would be plentiful, and emergency rooms would be "more efficient" due to fewer homeless patients.

Police enforcement related to those without a home shifted when Anchorage was envisioned without homelessness. Participants stated that "APD [Anchorage Police Force] [would be] able to focus on real crime, not homelessness" that "[there would be a] decrease in APD calls related to homelessness," and that "crime rates would go down."

Regarding roles and responsibilities, some community members said that government involvement was necessary to address the problem adequately while others suggested that government involvement caused and/or prolonged homelessness. The most commonly expressed opinions on responsibility for addressing homes for all Anchorage community members were as follows: 1) individuals should be expected to solve their own problems; 2) friends and family should do more to prevent the need for programs; 3) organizations should address housing; 4) government agencies should provide more assistance; 5) community members should *personally* participate in community services and efforts; and 6) the entire community should band together as one big team to solve the problem.

Concerns about resources and responsibilities were linked to discussions of the causes and complications of homelessness. Community members who focused on the choices, mistakes, or misdeeds of individuals as the cause for living without a home consistently pointed to the responsibility of individuals to ameliorate their living situation and lives, and consistently problematized aid, services, and programs designed to assist those individuals. Community members who focused on systemic causes of individuals, families, and youth living without a home consistently argued that services and programs should be better resourced. Within this group of community members, responsibility for addressing housing needs in Anchorage was specifically attributed to governmental, community, faith-based, and independent organizations, not individual members of the community.

Causes and Complications

Both substance abuse and mental health were described as major contributing factors of homelessness and the lack of success in limiting it. Community members expressed the need for resources for substance abuse treatment, citing, for example, "mental health and substance abuse centres as one," and "increased [mental health] and [substance abuse] treatment." Traumas, defined as single events that pose immediate risk to individuals, as opposed to chronic issues, were also identified as contributing factors to homelessness. Community members noted that trauma can result from experiencing homelessness as well. Of special note is that, as community members considered the complications and causes of homelessness, they conflated those considerations with images of Alaska Natives in Anchorage. Numerous responses to survey questions indicated that individuals living homeless were Alaska Native people who were presumed to have come from villages elsewhere in the state. Alaska Natives, to our participants, were the archetype for homelessness in Anchorage.

At the same time, community members expressed concern about the role of government in providing services to community members with substance abuse and mental health issues. In fact, community members asserted that *social services and the state* helped to prolong homelessness. These ideas were found in statements such as "hold providers accountable ... it's [homelessness] an economic disaster." Community members asserted that "handouts" perpetuated homelessness and that welfare programs designed to offer resources to homeless community members created a "culture of dependency." With respect to the contributions of substance abuse, mental health, and trauma to homelessness, community members overall maintained a contradictory position: they wanted more mental health and substance abuse facilities, while they thought that those living without a home should manage their issues on their own.

Education was also occasionally cited as a contributing factor to homelessness, but frequently also named as only a rare and brief means of helping community members achieve stable housing and employment. As lack of education was a factor contributing to homelessness, community members often focused on the need for financial knowledge and life skills, with educational opportunities – such as career and technical programs, higher education, and job-training programs – seen as helpful resources for navigating out of homelessness. During conversations, education was associated with the inability to cultivate educational resources for community members. When envisioning Anchorage without homelessness, respondents wrote that they would see "increased education opportunities," "free classes offered – financial, hygiene, life skill," and "more access to free education." Respondents envisioned an Anchorage wherein access to education, whether formal or informal, would be a major component of the community.

Youth education in the Anchorage School District was also a topic of conversation. When there was no more homelessness, "no taxis [would be] delivering kids to school" (taxis in Anchorage voluntarily work with shelters to take children to school). School attendance, graduation rates, and grades were all envisioned as rising. Education was looked upon in terms not only of formal institutions, but also of learning social and cultural skills acceptable to Anchorage standards.

Recommendations from the Study

In light of the themes and findings that emerged from the data sources, the five-month study made a few general recommendations to the United Way and the Anchorage Coalition on Homelessness in order to foster community acceptance of and support for their programs.

Increase Public Awareness

Survey results and observational data from community engagement events indicated that the majority of the participants were unaware of the efforts of the multiple agencies, despite those agencies' successes, such as the implementation by the Anchorage Coalition to End Homelessness of a comprehensive Housing First model. Also put in place was a centralized Coordinated Entry System, which worked to eliminate redundancy within and between support agencies throughout the city, and ensured progressive care for individuals in need of assistance once they were in the system. Unfortunately, the coalition lacked a dedicated, centralized voice to get its message out to the community at large. To that end, the study recommended yielding to a one-voice, one-message approach.

Frame the Community Positively

Vocabulary and language usage are vital to clear and meaningful communication within the Anchorage community. Rather than separating persons into categories such as "the Anchorage community," "community partners," "United Way," and "persons experiencing homelessness," the study recommended cohesive terminology across the community as a whole. For example, "community member without a home" should be preferred to "homeless person," which would strengthen the sense of belonging across groups. Reorienting the language in this way would give people the opportunity to hear their voices in proposed policies and programs, and create space for developing a positive cultural identity as a whole.

Gather Representative Voices in Aspirational Conversation

Since community conversations involved a narrow demographic, the study recommended diversifying locations of advertisements and specifically inviting community members who did not have a home. The lack of information about the aspirations of those who living without a home in Anchorage meant that providing space for those who with lived experiences of homelessness to have a voice would build understanding of the community's vision for the future of an Anchorage where homelessness was rare and brief.

Making Sense of Symbolic Identity and Community in Northern Spaces

There are four possible logical relationships between language and community. The first is that language determines culture/society/community – that is, when we choose to use standard forms of a language, we are sharing strong cultural ties. Second, culture/society/community determines language – that is, your language extends only as far as your traditions, heritage, and community practices permit. Third, as scientists interested in language capacity as a universal trait of humanness would argue, there is no important relationship between language and culture. Finally, language and the culture/society/community that uses it is mutually co-constitutive – that is, language, as it changes, likewise adapts the culture; and as culture changes, language is changed as well to accommodate new communities of practice.

This last relationship, where language and culture shape each other, is the frame within which I connect the constructs of symbolic identity and community in Anchorage based on the ongoing language and identity project *Talking Anchorage* and the five-month study on homelessness in Anchorage summarized in this chapter. The study of symbolic language identity in Anchorage again suggests that Anchorage communities see themselves as both insulated and distinct from comparable urban areas outside the North, while at the same time connected to the outside's trends and norms. Anchorage community members reflected a mixed alignment of identity. The five-month study suggested a similar alignment: an expression of distinctiveness regarding the issue of homelessness in Anchorage (e.g., Alaska Native and "off-the-grid" independence) was coupled with a need to adopt global best practices and bring in those with first-hand outside experience in using those best practices effectively.

In short, the symbolic identity of this northern urban space, and perhaps other places in the urban North, lives in tension between the local and the global, perhaps a by-product of relative social and geographic insulation (and sometimes isolation) over time. Many northern urban areas, are now easier to access – Anchorage, for example, is a port access point and a prime travel destination – but still relatively isolated from the mainstream. Such areas also tend to construct a notion of locality – in other words, insulation seems to invoke a strengthened sense of local identity.[10] At the same time, being geographically insulated does not lead directly to social insulation: communities that are isolated or insulated may be either endocentric (closed to outside influences) or exocentric (open to outside influences).[11] In urban areas of the North, as exemplified by Anchorage, communities display a mixed or "fuzzy" boundary between the local and the global. Indeed, many scholars support the idea that the term locality is scalar, multidimensional, and fluid, related to, but not necessarily confined by, geographic space while always integrated into the milieu of the non-local.[12] Michael Silverstein[13] notes that "communities, relativistically speaking, are 'local' when they are perduringly bounded through cultural means in relation to sociopolitical processes on a global scale"; thus, the *local* is defined, at least in part, by the global. J.K. Gibson-Graham[14] agrees, arguing that "the local cannot be fully interior to the global, nor can its inventive potential be captured by a singular imagining … a less obvious, less predictable, less binary relation [between local and global] must be affirmed as a truth and reaffirmed as a truism the global is not merely a geographical scale that subsumes and subordinates the local."

The tension between and multifaceted relationship of the local and the global, therefore, give way to less resolutely defined, or fuzzy, boundaries. The concepts of *fuzzy geography* and *soft spaces* are often used in the fields of geography and urban planning.[15] Unlike hard spaces that

---

10 Paul Kerswill, *Dialects Converging: Rural Speech in Urban Norway* (Oxford: Clarendon Press, 1995).
11 Henning Andersen, "Center and Periphery: Adoption, Diffusion, and Spread," in *Historical Dialectology*, ed. Jacek Fisiak (Berlin: Mouton de Gruyter, 1988), 39–84, https://doi.org/10.1515/9783110848137.39.
12 Appadurai, "Grassroots Globalization"; Arjun Appadurai, *Globalization* (Durham, NC: Duke University Press, 2002); Kevin Cox, *Spaces of Globalization: Reasserting the Power of the Local* (New York: Guilford Press, 1997); Erik Swyngedouw, "The Heart of the Place: The Resurrection of Locality in an Age of Hyperspace," *Roots of Geographical Change* 71, no. 1 (1989): 31–42, https://doi.org/10.1080/04353684.1989.11879585; Erik Swyngedouw, *Globalizations* (Philadelphia: Temple University Press, 2004); Michael Silverstein, "Contemporary Transformations of Local Linguistic Communities," *Annual Review of Anthropology* 27, no. 40 (1998): 401–26, https://doi.org/10.1146/annurev.anthro.27.1.401;. J.K. Gibson-Graham, *The End of Capitalism (As We Knew It): A Feminist Critique of Political Economy* (Cambridge, MA: Blackwell, 1996); J.K. Gibson-Graham, "An Ethics of the Local," *Rethinking Marxism* 15, no.1 (2003): 49–74, https://doi.org/10.1080/0893569032000063583.
13 Silverstein, "Contemporary Transformations," 403.
14 Gibson-Graham, *The End of Capitalism*, 50–3.
15 Phil Allmendinge and Graham Houghton, "Soft Spaces, Fuzzy Boundaries, and Metagovernance: The New Spatial Planning in the Thames Gateway," *Environment and Planning* 41, no. 3 (2009): 617–33, https://doi.org/10.1068/a40208.

mark physical, set geographic boundaries, fuzzy or soft spaces denote relational and negotiated spaces that may be socially defined (e.g., a community of practice) or ideologically constrained (e.g., community norms of behaviour).

Urban North communities, then, navigate the tension between the local and the global existing in those *fuzzy* spaces. Moreover, the ways in which the community networks itself often reflect these spaces. As the *Talking Anchorage* investigation suggested and the five-month study on homelessness in Anchorage reflected, the Anchorage community is tightly networked – that is, there are very few degrees of separation between families and friends in the area. Although two community members might not know each other, they will likely know others in common. Additionally, and perhaps because of the unique climate in the North, community members are quick to help and support one another. Unlike other closely networked communities, such as those found in rural areas, however, the fluid local-global community of Anchorage is highly individualistic. The Anchorage community maintains clear boundaries of self and neighbour, to the point of being largely unconcerned about how neighbours live their day-to-day lives. They remain unconcerned, that is, until neighbours encroach on their ability to live individualistically.

Putting It All Together: Symbolic Community Identity and Homelessness in the Urban North

I began this chapter with the claim that being aware of the symbolic identity and the schematic for how a community gathers offers direct insight into the levels of uptake of programming related to positive community change, such as solutions for homelessness. I also made the claim that sustainability of such programming, policy, and practice was correlative to that awareness. As our five-month study of homelessness in Anchorage suggested, even when policies and programming were contributing to positive change, the community remained unconvinced, citing issues of lack of safety, resources, and education with which to assuage homelessness. Community members distanced themselves from those who were not homed and resorted to an expectation of a Eurocentric lived experience, which then worked to maintain that distance.

Meanwhile, practitioners both from inside and outside Anchorage struggled to elicit community acceptance of local programming based on global best practices in order to continue forward motion. How do we resolve these kinds of conflicts in Anchorage, and perhaps across the Urban North, where symbolic identity and the community schematic reveal a mixed alignment, where a tightly networked community holds close to its individualism?

The most direct path to community uptake of positive change is, ironically, an indirect one. Anchorage agencies working towards abating homelessness have been quick to adopt global best practices and invite non-local practitioners into the community without modification. The rationale rightly has been not to "reinvent the wheel." As this chapter has suggested, however, Anchorage, and by association the Urban North, is distinctly networked and oriented in the context of the global environment. To translate, broadly and directly, best practices into these distinctly oriented communities is simply a harder path to take. Time and energy are needed to engage the community in multiple-stage conversations in order to create viable partnerships. But when practitioners and policymakers allowed community members to become stakeholders in the planning and implementation of programming, the uptake of positive change increased.

Media portrayals of homelessness in Anchorage, coupled with the survey results and interviews, showed the urgent need to create partnerships with individuals and then follow with larger community networks. Participants in the five-month study consistently referred to the urgency to end homelessness. Issues of homelessness evoked a sense of emergency where the larger community was endangered. This reactive position to ending homelessness was in direct contrast to the proactive programming that practitioners had been working successfully to implement. Moreover, continuing to respond to homelessness as an "emergency" paved the way towards complete disengagement with the homelessness issue – that is, if homelessness constituted a crisis, then individuals were stripped of their stake in a positive contribution. Abating homelessness instead became a problem for the municipality and the state to handle.

Creating partnerships is likewise critical as we work to include individuals who have been working historically to activate positive change. These individuals are long-time community activists, who are apt to disengage when global, outside practices are implemented. In all of the datasets across the five-month study, local community activists expressed disdain towards non-local best practices because they felt they knew their community better. They became resisters to efforts towards positive change, despite the observable positive outcome to abate homelessness.

Practitioners and policymakers then became frustrated with that resistance and further disengaged from wanting to invite partnerships across individual community members. In conversations with practitioners, they revealed a desire simply to stop trying to gain community acceptance of local programming. They thought that because the best practices being implemented were almost universally successful outside the urban North, then the community should be fully on board.

The point, however, is that community uptake in the urban North does not rely on successful practices and programming per se; instead, successful practices and programming in the urban North rely on community partnership and shared stakes. In effect, the direct path is indirect. Although the indirect path to positive change might not be unique to the urban North, it is certainly a defining characteristic of the symbolic identity and community orientation of these northern spaces.

Conversations, education, and shared understanding of local and non-local practices are key ingredients in the acceptance of positive change. Practitioners in Anchorage have been working tirelessly to provide opportunities for individual community members to become stakeholders. The symbolic identity of the urban North, as exemplified by Anchorage, invites shared vision but longs for individual contribution. The longer path is the sustainable one.

SECTION THREE

Greenland

Regional Introduction: Greenland

STEVEN ARNFJORD AND JULIA CHRISTENSEN

Greenland, the world's largest island, covers over two million square kilometres and stretches from Cape Farewell in the south to Oodaq Island in the high North. Although still part of the Danish realm, Greenland has self-rule government, with autonomy over central government activities such as social policy, education, health, economy, and housing. The majority of Greenland's fifty-six thousand inhabitants live in communities along the country's west and east coasts. Approximately 90 per cent of Greenland's population is Greenlandic (Inuit), while the remainder are Danish, Faroese, Icelandic, Thai, and Filipino. The official language is Greenlandic, although Danish is widely spoken and government websites are available in both languages.

Greenland is considered a welfare society after the Scandinavian model. Taxpayers pay approximately 40 per cent of their income in taxes in exchange for a wide spectrum of publicly administered services.

Housing Insecurity and Homelessness in Greenland

In Greenland, the geography of settlement and colonial administration and patterns of rural-to-urban mobility have framed the landscape of housing insecurity and homelessness. While under Danish control, Danish-led political commissions pursued the concentration of the Greenlandic people in permanent towns and settlements, including the shutting down of smaller settlements.[1] Approximately 87 per cent of the

---

1 Jens Dahl, "Identity, Urbanization and Political Demography in Greenland," *Acta Borealia* 27, no. 2 (2010): 125–40, https://doi.org/10.1080/08003831.2010.527528 ; Frank Sejersen, "Urbanization, Landscape Appropriation and Climate Change in Greenland," *Acta Borealia* 27, no. 2 (2010): 167–88, https://doi.org/10.1080/0800383 1.2010.527533; Anthony J. Dzik, "Settlement Closure or Persistence: A Comparison

population lives in urban areas, and the rate of urbanization is approximately 0.4 per cent.[2]

The modernization of Greenland took place from approximately 1950 to 1980. With an emphasis on high-density housing, this period was characterized by the construction of modern apartment blocks that included sanitation, electricity, central heating, and larger indoor spaces.[3] These developments took place concurrently with the expansion of social welfare services, which included the implementation of public health and further implementation of social services.[4]

The goal of the modernization process was to ensure a self-sufficient Greenlandic economy and to strengthen the overall educational level. However, the process had profound social and spatial implications, including the enforcement of Danish as the dominant educational and administrative language and the development of a distinct rural-urban geography characterized by movement into urban centres such as Ilulissat, Sisimiut, Nuuk, and Qaqortoq.[5]

Rental housing in Greenland is primarily available through either public housing or public sector employment. Public housing is administered by Greenland's public housing authority Inatsisartut Inissiaatileqatigiifik (INI) and in the large municipality Kommuneqarfik Sermersooq through the public company ISERIT. Individuals can sign their names to the housing waitlist starting at age eighteen. These waitlists can be excessively long, however – as much as fifteen years in some communities. Within the public sector, certain positions (e.g., teachers, medical professionals, nurses, officials) include assigned rental housing, allowing the person to have an apartment for the duration of the position. In short, the alternatives to public housing include getting an education in the hope of finding a position with an assigned apartment or purchasing a private house or apartment, which are both expensive

of Kangeq and Kapisillit, Greenland," *Journal of Settlements and Spatial Planning* 7, no. 2 (2016): 99–112, https://doi.org 10.19188/01JSSP022016/.

2 Central Intelligence Agency, "The World Factbook: Greenland," https://www.cia .gov/the-world-factbook/countries/greenland/.

3 Martin Hilker et al., *Blok P* (Copenhagen: Nordatlantens Brygge, 2014).

4 Steven Arnfjord, "Challenges with Greenland's Social Policies – How We Meet the Call for Social, Political Awareness," in *The Inuit World*, ed. Pamela Stern (New York: Routledge, 2021).

5 See Rasmus Ole Rasmussen, *Mobilitet i Grønland: Sammenfatning af Hovedpunkter fra Analysen af Mobiliteten i Grønland* [Mobility in Greenland: Summary of main points from an analysis of mobility in Greenland] (Nuuk: Mobilitetsstyregruppen, 2010).

and limited in supply. As a result, the housing landscape in Greenland can be highly problematic for Greenlanders without adequate education or employment.

Homelessness in Greenland began to emerge in the 1970s, but did not receive real media coverage before the 1990s and was largely focused on the capital, Nuuk,[6] although coverage of the issue later widened to include homelessness in smaller communities. Some public figures have stated that round 870 people were homeless countrywide in 2017.[7] Greenland has yet to conduct a scientific-backed monitoring process such as Point-In-Time, which makes it difficult both to assess the issue and to draw comparisons between different communities. Additionally, homelessness is largely considered to be an urban issue, as opposed to a national one requiring social policy attention.

Literature – both academic and grey, mostly in the form of unpublished government reports – on the topic of homelessness in Greenland began to emerge in the early 2000s, but is limited. Additionally, emphasizing the rural-urban divide, research has focused on larger communities such as Sisimiut (population 5.500) and Nuuk (18.000).

"Hjemløs i Grønland" (Homeless in Greenland), a short study commissioned by the Greenlandic Ministry of Family and Health in 2008, provided the first overall look at the country's homeless situation.[8] The report outlines the broader definitions of homelessness, ranging from people without shelter, people living in hotels or hostels, or people living in psychiatric or residential care institutions. Data were collected via a questionnaire distributed to the seventeen municipalities that existed before a 2018 reform reduced the number to five. Unfortunately, the level of municipal reporting was inconsistent: some municipalities did not report at all, while others had limited details on household composition, gender, and so on.

The final report includes a statistical analysis of 514 people, the majority of whom were between ages twenty and sixty. Of this group, 20 per cent were employed and 40 per cent, according to the municipalities,

---

6 Steven Arnfjord, "Hjemløshed i Grønland – Og Socialpolitiske Perspektiver" [Homelessness in Greenland – And socio-political perspectives], *Tidsskriftet Grønland* 67, no. 2 (2019): 71–81, https://uk.uni.gl/media/5081118/tg-2-2019-arnfjord-71-81 -final.pdf.

7 Sorlannguaq Petersen, "Der Er 878 Hjemløse i Landet" [There are 878 homeless people in the country], *Sermitsiaq*, 27 November 2017, http://sermitsiaq.ag/node/201653.

8 Greenland, Ministry of Family and Health, *Hjemløs i Grønland: Et Skøn over Samtlige Kommuners Hjemløse* [Homelessness in Greenland: An estimate of homelessness by municipality] (Nuuk, 2008).

had problems with substance abuse. The report provides some qualitative feedback from the municipalities, several of which stated that household overcrowding was exacerbated when a family was obliged to take in a relative who had no alternative but to live with them because of the lack of sufficient housing. Ongoing initiatives such as night shelters, shipping-container housing, and women's shelters were all described as only short-term solutions. The report concludes that homelessness in Greenland is not only a matter of unemployment, material poverty, or housing insecurity, but also tightly intersects with trauma and other psychological issues, addiction, domestic violence, and other forms of abuse.[9] Interestingly, the capital of Nuuk was not included in the study.

In 2013, a more comprehensive study, entitled "Hjemløshed i Grønland" (Homelessness in Greenland), was published by the Institute for Danish Housing Research at Aalborg University.[10] The report categorizes homelessness in three primary categories: "homeless" – i.e., those without a fixed place to shelter for the night; b) "houseless" – i.e., living temporarily with relatives or friends but without a house of their own; and c) "rehoused" – i.e., living in a halfway house because of their being in debt to the public housing organization INI or to ISERIT, a public municipal housing organization located in Sermersooq, in the Nuuk capital region. The authors use a combination of methodologies including statistics, photography, and qualitative interviews conducted in Greenlandic by a social worker.

The 2013 report cites a conservative estimate of approximately 600 people living homeless in Greenland as a whole.[11] In the capital Nuuk, the conservative estimate of people living under a more permanent state of homelessness was between 100 and 200.[12] Other research, using estimates from three non-governmental organizations (NGOs) that provide services for the homeless in Nuuk, suggests that, at the time, the number of homeless individuals in Nuuk alone was close to 350.[13]

---

9 Ibid.
10 Knud E. Hansen and Hans T. Andersen, *Hjemløshed i Grønland* [Homelessness in Greenland] (Aalborg: University of Aalborg, Statens Byggeforskningsinstitut, 2013).
11 Ibid., 24.
12 Greenland, Ministry of Family and Health, *Hjemløs i Grønland*; Hansen and Andersen, *Hjemløshed i Grønland*.
13 Steven Arnfjord and Julia Christensen, "Understanding the Social Dynamics of Homelessness in Nuuk, Greenland," *Northern Notes* 45 (Spring/Summer 2016), http://iassa.org/images/newsletters/Northern-Notes-Issue-45-Spring-Summer-2016.pdf.

The final report includes biographies of homeless individuals based on interviews conducted in Greenlandic. The report also documents the range of social issues influencing homelessness in Greenland, including abuse, lack of resources, and unemployment. Finally, the report establishes the link between the overall housing situation in Greenland, characterized by limited stock and chronic housing need, and the emergence of homelessness.[14]

A 2016 study[15] identifies four primary groups of homeless people in Greenland: 1) men over age thirty-five with addictions and without a place to live; 2) youth with family, social, or economic problems who migrate from small settlements to larger centres in hope of new opportunities; 3) women who either are single or no longer have custody of their children, and who have often been victims of domestic violence; and 4) men and women over age fifty-five who have been evicted from their housing after failure to pay rent.

The 2016 study finds that homeless women are particularly neglected in terms of social policies and services.[16] Despite evidence to suggest that homelessness among women in Greenland is of particular concern, it has not been possible to locate a specific research focus on women living homeless. For example, Nuuk has only a limited strategy aimed at securing a safe shelter for women in marginalized situations, despite approximately about seven hundred reports of domestic disturbances in the city annually.[17] Although there is support for mothers with young children and elderly women, very little exists for single women or women living in or leaving violent relationships.[18]

---

14 Hansen and Andersen, *Hjemløshed i Grønland*.
15 Arnfjord and Christensen, "Understanding the Social Dynamics of Homelessness."
16 Steven Arnfjord and Julia Christensen, "'De søger trygheden': Kvinder Ramt af Hjemløshed i Nuuk" ["They seek safety": Women affected by homelessness in Nuuk], *Psyke & Logos* 38, no. 1 (2017): 51–71, https://doi.org/10.7146/pl.v38i1.100078.
17 Grønlands Politi, "Årsstatistik 2017 Grønlands Polit" [Annual statistics 2017 Greenland politics] (Nuuk, 2018), https://politi.gl/-/media/mediefiler/gl/dokumenter/aarsstatistik2017.pdf?la=da&hash=4BDFE709A32C3F3B3A6895D0 A22FB8F65D66A7BF.
18 Mariekathrine Poppel, "Citizenship of Indigenous Greenlanders in a European Nation State: The Inclusionary Practices of Iverneq," in *Reconfiguring Citizenship: "Social Exclusion and Diversity within Inclusive Citizenship Practices*, ed. Mehmoona Moose-Mitha and Lena Dominelli (London: Routledge, 2016), 127–36.

Key Themes in the Greenlandic Homelessness Literature

Key themes in the literature on homelessness in Greenland are directly related to critical social issues in Greenlandic society and include uneven rural-urban geographies, intergenerational impacts of colonialism, and social welfare dependency.[19] Despite these issues, homelessness is not a prioritized social political issue in Greenland, and there are gaps in the current body of research.

The focus on alcohol abuse and its relationship to neglect, violence, and evictions has received substantial attention in the literature.[20] As a result, the research reduces social problems to the individual level as opposed to being symptomatic of broader, socio-structural processes that ultimately contribute to homelessness. Additional exploration of the linkages between individual and socio-structural factors has been identified as a gap that requires closing.[21]

Although limited, the literature on Greenlandic homelessness does explore the dynamics of social marginalization. However, the lack of literature that explicitly conceptualizes homelessness in Greenland

19 Hansen and Andersen, *Hjemløshed i Grønland*; Jonas Fievé and Paarnaq Hansen, "Flere Kvinder Søger Hjælp" [More women are seeking help], *KNR*, 25 November 2016, https://knr.gl/en/node/181892; C.P Pedersen and P. Bjerregaard, *Det Svære Ungdomsliv – Unges Trivsel i Grønland 2011: En Undersøgelse om de ældste Folkeskoleelever* [The difficult life of youth – The well-being of youth in Greenland 2011: A survey of the oldest high school students] (Copenhagen: Statens Institut for Folkesundhed, 2012); Poppel, "Citizenship of Indigenous Greenlanders"; Rådet for Socialt Udsatte, *Udsatte Grønlandske Kvinder i Danmark – En Undersøgelse af Kvindernes Livssituation, Problemer, Ressourcer og Behov* [Vulnerable Greenlandic women in Denmark – A study of women's life situation, problems, resources, and needs] (2016); Torben M. Andersen et al., *Vores Velstand og Velfærd – Kræver Handling Nu* [Our prosperity and well-being – Action is needed now] (Nuuk: Tax and Welfare Commission, 2011).
20 Steven Arnfjord, "Hjemløshed og Alkoholmisbrug i et Grønlandsk Socialpolitisk Perspektiv" [Homelessness and alcohol abuse in a Greenlandic socio-political perspective], in *STOF* no. 33 (Summer 2019): 13–16; Udvalget for Samfundsforskning i Grønland [Committee for Social Research in Greenland], *Rapport til Grønlands Landsråd om Alkohol Situationen i Grønland* [Report to the Greenland National Council on the alcohol situation in Greenland] (1960); Bo Wagner Sørensen, "Alkohol i Grønland: Problemorienteret Forskning i Lokal Drikkekultur [Alcohol in Greenland: Problem-oriented research into local drinking culture]," *Antropologi* 39, no. 1 (1999): 137–54, https://tidsskrift.dk/tidsskriftetantropologi/article/view/115176.
21 Julia Christensen et al., "Homelessness across Alaska, the Canadian North and Greenland: A Review of the Literature on an Emerging Social Phenomenon in the Circumpolar North," *Arctic* 70, no. 4 (2017): 349–64, https://www.jstor.org/stable/26387309.

within its specific geographical, cultural, and social context is a significant gap. For example, although research suggests that rural-to-urban and Greenland-to-Denmark migration is a significant factor in Greenland homeless geographies,[22] the broader discussion of rural-to-urban mobility and its role in homelessness is lacking. One study identifies education and employment, living conditions, social network, leisure opportunities, and access to public services as key motivations of rural-to-urban migration.[23] Additionally, the majority of Greenlanders moving from rural to urban areas are young people between the ages of fifteen and twenty-five.[24]

Relocation within the Danish realm is another element of the rural-to-urban divide. Greenlanders hold Danish citizenship, and approximately fourteen thousand currently reside in Denmark.[25] This move, however, could also be associated with homelessness. The Danish Council of Social Marginalization has noted the many challenges Greenlandic women face in Denmark, including language issues, challenges accessing education and employment, and disempowered social networks.[26] Unfortunately, there has been little joint effort between Greenland and Denmark to offer public help to or safeguard homeless Greenlandic women in Denmark, leaving them in the care of local Danish NGOs.[27] As well, a Danish study finds there has been a rise in numbers of Greenlandic young migrating to Denmark, where, in many instances they come in contact with an environment that uses hard drugs, which is an unknown phenomenon in Greenland.[28]

22 Mille Schiermacher, *Fra Grønland til Gaden – En Undersøgelse om Migration Mellem Grønland og Danmark* [From Greenland to the street – A study on migration from Greenland to Denmark] (Nuuk: Kofoeds Skole, 2020), https://menneskermedmere .dk/wp-content/uploads/2020/11/FraGroenlandTilGaden.pdf.
23 Rasmus Ole Rasmussen, "Why the Other Half Leave: Gender Aspects of Northern Sparsely Populated Areas," in *Demography at the Edge: Remote Human Populations in Developed Nations*, ed. Dean Carson, Rasmus Ole Rasmussen, Prescott Ensign, Lee Huskey, and Andrew Taylor, (Farnham: Ashgate, 2011), 237–54.
24 Rasmussen, *Mobilitet i Grønland*, 2010. A similar observation has been made by Schiermacher, *Fra Grønland til Gaden*.
25 S. Baviskar, *Grønlændere i Danmark: En Registerbaseret Kortlægning* [Greenlanders in Denmark: A census-based mapping] (Copenhagen: SFI, 2015).
26 Rådet for Socialt Udsatte, *Udsatte Grønlandske Kvinder i Danmark*.
27 Steven Arnfjord, *Sociale Udfordringer Hos et Mindretal af Grønlandske Kvinder i DK Skal Håndteres i (Rigs)fælleskab* [Social challenges concerning a minority of Greenlandic women in Denmark need to be handled within the realm] (Copenhagen: Socialpolitisk Forening, 2016).
28 Det Grønlandske Hus, *Drømmen om et Bedre Liv i Danmark – En Undersøgelse Blandt Unge Grønlændere i Københavns Udsattemiljø* [The dream of a better life in Greenland

Following the model of the democratic welfare society, Greenlanders affected by political decisions are engaged through public forums. However, a shift towards the neoliberal structures present in Alaska and the Canadian North has resulted in a reduction in this level of engagement. Despite the fact that Greenland does have a small organization of homeless people,[29] homelessness received just one paragraph in the coalition agreement between the ruling parties of the Greenlandic government in 2018.[30] This has since resulted in little actual policy, but is viewed as a small win in the form of political visibility. People living under homelessness are, however, rarely included in development of policy, including the policy that governs the daily operations of the public shelter in Nuuk. In 2020, there where one public hearing in Nuuk in an open forum that connected the homeless community with the political community; the ministers of social affairs and housing took part in the hearing. Shortly after, a COVID-19 lockdown came into effect, with few results following.

Among the few positive trends noted in the research is an increase in the number of NGOs involved in addressing the dynamics of social marginalization in Nuuk. Local NGOs collaborate with one another and express a common agenda to empower people experiencing homelessness and to provide facilities for people in that environment to voice their concerns.

- A survey among young Greenlanders in Copenhagen's vulnerable environment] (2018).

29 B. Rørdam, "Mange Hjemløse i Grønland" [Many homeless in Greenland], *Hus Forbi* 20, no.1 (2016): 5–6.

30 Greenland, *Koalitionsaftale 2018 – Nunarput i Udvikling – Med Plads til Alle* [Coalition agreement 2018 – Nunarput in development – with room for all] (2018).

10 In Search of Security: Women's Homelessness in Nuuk, Greenland

STEVEN ARNFJORD AND JULIA CHRISTENSEN

The reform period has been marked by a significant shift in population. It is necessary to distinguish between those who have volunteered to leave their former home and those who were forced to do so. Voluntary relocations are by far the most frequent and have apparently not resulted in a greater sense of uncertainty and insecurity. The forced relocations, on the other hand, have in many cases caused a lot of human rootlessness.[1]

A high number of citizens, estimated to be around 350, experience homelessness in Greenland's capital, Nuuk, a city of 18,000 inhabitants. This is a problematic circumstance in Greenland. In local media and official governmental reports, the issue of homelessness has been presented with little consideration for the role that gender plays both in the factors contributing to homelessness and in the experience of homelessness itself. Greenland experiences a high level of reported abuse of women compared to other countries within the Danish realm (which includes the Faroe Islands, Greenland, and Denmark). This increases the need for a renewed social professional focus on marginalized women's positions in society. Elsewhere in the circumpolar Arctic, there has been a focus on women's experiences of homelessness for some time.[2]

---

1 Det Grønlandske Kvindeudvalg, *Kalâtdlit-Nunâne Arnat Inûerat Atugaitdlo = Kvinders Liv og Vilkår i Grønland* [Women's life and conditions in Greenland]. *1, Arnaq Ínugtaoqatigíngnilo Íneriartorneq = Kvinden Og Samfundsudviklingen* [Women and the development of society] (Copenhagen: Statens Trykningskontor, 1975).
2 Judie Bopp and YWCA Yellowknife, *You Just Blink and It Can Happen: A Study of Women's Homelessness North of 60* (Yellowknife: Yellowknife YWCA, 2007), https://assembly.nu.ca/library/Edocs/2007/001483-e.pdf; Julia Christensen, "'They Want a Different Life': Rural Northern Settlement Dynamics and Pathways to Homelessness in Yellowknife and Inuvik, Northwest Territories," *Canadian Geographer* 56, no. 4 (2012):

The empirical background for this chapter is a prolonged field study and literature research on Arctic homelessness in both Greenland and Canada. The literature from Greenland is principally categorized as grey, which implies that we are dealing with official or public reports. The Greenlandic grey literature is supported by media research. We begin the chapter with the history of Greenlandic women from the 1970s onwards, and later discuss the modern circumstances of socially marginalized women. We conclude with a set of suggestions for the future about enhancing the focus on feminist perspectives and gender theory on a societal level.

Background

In 1976, the first homeless shelter was established in Nuuk. It was intended primarily for women leaving situations of intimate partner violence, although it was also open to men in some cases.[3] The shelter was run by the Danish branch of the YWCA – Young Women's Christian Association – until 1987, when it was handed over to the then-municipality of Nuuk, today the municipality of Sermersooq. The initiative was taken by the head of the Danish YWCA, Fanny Truels Jensen, and the first vice-bishop of Greenland, Jens Christian Chemnitz, and the shelter housed twenty residents.[4] In a YWCA jubilee letter of 1980, women's rights advocate Gudrun Chemnitz wrote that a need existed for more women's shelters and more counselling for women.[5] Nuuk's former mayor Agnethe Davidsen stated that, when the municipality took over and ran the shelter in the 1980s, it never really worked

419–38, https://doi.org/10.1111/j.1541-0064.2012.00439.x; Judy Shepherd, "Where Do You Go When It's 40 Below? Domestic Violence among Rural Alaska Native Women," *Affilia* 16, no. 4 (2001), 488–510, https://doi.org/10.1177/08861090122094389.

3 Bodil Harild et al., *Det Gælder Mennesket : KFUKs Sociale Arbejde 1947–1987 : Udgives i Anledning af 40 Års Jubilæum i Danmark og 25 Års Jubilæum i Grønland* [This applies to man: The YMCA's social work 1947–1987: Published on the occasion of the 40th anniversary in Denmark and the 25th anniversary in Greenland] (Copenhagen: KFUK, 1987); Thomas Munk Veirum, "Nye Tal: 878 Borgere Lever Som Hjemløse" [New figures: 878 citizens live as homeless], *KNR*, 27 November 2017, https://knr.gl/en/node/204921.

4 Fanny Truels Jensen, *Græsrødder og Trækroner : Et Liv – Set i Bakspejlet* [Grassroots and tree crowns: A life – In retrospect] (Valby, Denmark: Unitas, 1993).

5 Gudrun Chemnitz, "De Grønlandske Kvinders Udvikling Gennem Tiderne" [The development of Greenlandic women through the ages], in *Det Gælder Mennesket: KFUKs Sociale Arbejde 1947–1987* [This applies to man: YMCA social work 1947–1987], ed. Fanny Truels Jensen (Copenhagen: KFUK, 1987).

properly.[6] In 1998, shelters were again in the media – this time the story was about the costly prices in the municipality of Nuuk's shelter, which at the time had ten residents.[7] Towards the late 1990s, the media focus increased in the form of case-oriented reports of people experiencing homelessness. At that time, media reports estimated that about one hundred people were categorized as homeless in the country. Figures from 2013 placed the number at about five hundred countrywide.[8] By 2017, that number had risen to between eight and nine hundred, according to the Greenlandic government,[9] although it has been somewhat difficult to confirm how this number was estimated. The amounts also covered short periods, down to weeks or a few days; the report does not say much about more permanent or prolonged homelessness or anything about the extension of hidden homelessness, which the literature also terms "concealed homelessness."[10] The cited Greenlandic official reports do not refer to a precise number of citizens without residence and eviction from public housing programs.

In connection with the field study in Nuuk, we stablished contact with people on the street and those who frequented different day shelters or day services. In this environment, it was estimated that between two hundred and fifty and three hundred people were experiencing homelessness. Homelessness as a growing social political problem was almost exclusively a Nuuk matter: it was in Nuuk that our research was conducted, although we received frequent anecdotal reports about growing numbers of people experiencing homelessness in the south of Greenland as well.[11] The research comprised a joint project between Ilisimatusarfik (University of Greenland) and Memorial University of Newfoundland in St. John's that sought to

---

6 Kurt Kristensen, "Gågaden Naapittarfik i Nuuk Skal Have Nyt Liv" [The pedestrian street Naapittarfik in Nuuk needs a new lease of life], *Atuagagdliutit*, 24 September 1996.
7 Pauline Møller, "Dyr Køjeseng i Nuup Kommuneas Nødherberg" [Expensive bunk bed in Nuup Municipality's Nødherberg], *Atuagagdliutit*, 22 December 1998.
8 Knud Erik Hansen and Hans Thor Andersen, *Hjemløshed i Grønland* [Homelessness in Greenland] (Copenhagen: Statens Byggeforskningsinstitut, 2013).
9 Veirum, "Nye Tal"; Sorlannguaq Petersen, "Der Er 878 Hjemløse i Landet" [There are 878 homeless people in the country], *Sermitsiaq.Ag*, 27 November 2017, http://sermitsiaq.ag/node/201653.
10 Sophie Watson and Helen Austerberry, *Housing and Homelessness: A Feminist Perspective* (London: Routledge & Kegan Paul, 1986).
11 Steven Arnfjord and Julia Christensen, "Understanding the Social Dynamics of Homelessness in Nuuk, Greenland," *Northern Notes* 45 (Spring/Summer 2016), http://iassa.org/images/newsletters/Northern-Notes-Issue-45-Spring-Summer-2016.pdf.

uncover the social dynamics of homelessness and social problems such as housing insecurity and poverty.[12] During a prolonged field study in collaboration with non-governmental organizations (NGOs) such as the homeless agency union NoINI and the Salvation Army, we gathered a different perspective on homelessness in Nuuk.[13]

Until we began our research, there had not been an exclusive focus on women experiencing homelessness in Greenland. This might have been the result of the somewhat dormant state of the Greenlandic women's movement, but also perhaps due to the quantitative way in which previous research on homelessness and social marginalization had been conducted. Earlier research was not too insightful as to how homelessness manifested itself from a gendered perspective. It also could have been related to a general tendency to combine and conflate the housing insecurity of men and women in social research without applying an understanding of how gender plays a part in how homelessness is experienced. Homelessness is a social political topic that to a large extent is associated with men because men's homelessness is often more noticeable – the visible homelessness on which the media and politicians focus.[14] Yet this focus neglects experiences of hidden homelessness, often associated with women, which may be understood as housing insecurity – for example, accepting a situation of domestic violence or a tenant who is unable to pay the rent.

In Greenland's social policy, the general position on women is weak. Sermersooq (formerly Nuuk) does not have an updated social policy – a child and family policy was in effect from 2010 to 2013.[15] In the municipality's strategy introduced in 2016, there was a focus on the welfare of children, and adults were mentioned concerning their obligation to contribute to society. Housing policy was presented, but priority went towards public housing for the elderly, youth housing,

---

12 Ibid.
13 Steven Arnfjord, "Hjemløshed i Nuuk – et Kritisk Sociologisk- og Planlægningsperspektiv" [Homelessness in Nuuk – a critical sociological and planning perspective], in *Grønlandsk Kultur – Og Samfundsforskning 2015/2016* [Greenlandic culture and social research 2015/2016], ed. Jette Rygaard and Flemming Nielsen Kenneth Petersen (Nuuk, Greenland: Atuagkat, 2017).
14 Paul Cloke, Paul Milbourne, and Rebekah Widdowfield, *Rural Homelessness: Issues, Experiences and Policy Responses* (Bristol: Bristol University Press, 2002), https://doi .org/10.2307/j.ctt1t89cd7.
15 Kommuneqarfik Sermersooq, *Børne og -Familiepolitik 2010–2013* [Children and families policy 2010–2013] (Nuuk, Greenland, 2010).

family housing, and private housing,[16] while visions of halfway housing, transitional housing, or other forms of social housing were not
mentioned.

As a social phenomenon, homelessness has received significant
attention since 2012. Growing concern led to a political initiative in
2016 to build one hundred new residences for the homeless around
the country. The political initiative was well received and went
through a first round in the Greenland parliament in October 2016.[17]
A change of government led to the coalition agreement of 2018, in
which homelessness received its own headline in relation to housing
issues.[18] This was a sign of burgeoning political awareness, although
there was still a challenge with differentiation, as Greenlanders experiencing homelessness were by and large understood as a single,
homogenous group. In countries such as Denmark and Canada, public housing or shelters by service providers are an extension of care
centres. In Greenland, there is little experience with such institutions,
and we are yet to see social service initiatives in this area of the welfare society.

From our research, we identified four groups of people who were
experiencing homelessness in Nuuk:

- young people under the age of thirty-five;
- the elderly above age sixty (a considerable age in an environment
  with a history of substance abuse);
- men over age thirty-five with histories of alcohol and hashish abuse;
  and
- women, the differentiated group we examined for research
  purposes.

Within each category, there was significant diversity in the factors
that contribute to housing insecurity as well as of experiences of
homelessness.

---

16 Kommuneqarfik Sermersooq, *Hovedstadsstrategi* [Capital strategy] (Greenland, 2016)
17 Mimi Karlsen, *Forslag til Opførelse af 100 Midlertidige Boliger til Hjemløse Fordelt i Hele
    Landet* [Proposals for the construction of 100 temporary homes for homeless people
    distributed throughout the country] (Nuuk, Greenland: Inatsisartut, 2016), http://
    www.inatsisartut.gl/samlinger/oversigt-over-samlinger/samling/dagsordener
    /dagsorden.aspx?day=26-10-2016&dagsorden=1713.
18 Naalakkersuisut, *Koalitionsaftale – 2018–2022* [Coalition agreement – 2018–2022]
    (Greenland, 2018).

Women's Hidden Homelessness

In earlier research reports about homelessness in Greenland, the subject is almost analogous with Karl Marx's division of class into "the haves and the have nots" – in other words, these reports delineate between those who have a residence and those who do not.[19] Researchers classified homelessness into three types: 1) individuals who do not have secure place to sleep at night; 2) the rehoused, who have been evicted by Greenland's public housing organizations and who have temporary shelter; and, 3) the houseless, who are couch surfing or staying with family or friends, but who do not have a home of their own.[20] These categories are important, but the definition of homelessness implied here is one that focuses on the material (to have or not to have). As a result, this conceptualization of homelessness neglects any consideration of human dimensions and the social context. Preben Brandt, Danish psychiatrist and head of Projekt Udenfor (Project Outside), might have a more inclusive definition: "Homeless people, understood in a social policy context, are people who, in addition to lacking a home, have a number of complicated and mutually reinforcing social and health problems that give them difficulty in entering into some, but far from all social contexts. Many of these relationships are deeply rooted in the individual's life and are difficult to fix."[21]

Common to both of these definitions is that homelessness is coupled with the material, and the absence of a residence means that home havers can look at home not havers (the homeless) as people on the street with nothing: the hobo, the tramp, the "go-about," the bum, the home guard, the vagrant, the bag lady, the street sleeper.[22] These categories of marginalization do not work well in an arctic environment

19 Greenland, Ministry of Family and Health, *Hjemløs i Grønland – et Skøn over Samtlige Kommuners Hjemløse* [Homeless people in Greenland – an estimate of all municipalities' homeless people] (Nuuk, 2008); Hansen and Anderson, *Hjemløshed*.
20 Hansen and Anderson, *Hjemløshed*.
21 Preben Brandt, *En Pamflet om Hjemløshed: Refleksioner over og Kritik af den Gennemførte Hjemløsestrategi og den Efterfølgende Evaluering* [A pamphlet on homelessness: Reflections on and criticism of the homelessness strategy implemented and the ex-post evaluation] (Copenhagen: Projekt Udenfor, 2013).
22 See Nels Anderson, *On Hobos and Homelessness*, ed. Raffaele Rauty (Chicago: University of Chicago Press, 1998); Douglas A. Harper, *Good Company: A Tramp Life* (Chicago: University of Chicago Press, 1982).

or take into account the difference between women's and men's home-lessness. A Canadian study worked with definitions of homelessness that better matched the circumstances in Greenland:[23] *visible or absolute homelessness*, which includes people sleeping on the street, in shelters, in stairwells, or similar acute situations; *relative homelessness*, where people are living in places where it is basically unhealthy or unsafe to stay, such as abandoned houses,[24] tents in the natural environment, and similar dwellings; *hidden homelessness*, which can be applied to temporary living situations with friends and family or acquaintances and is a stay with an expiration date – sometimes it is called couch surfing, or hidden prostitution when it is about women living with men and being pressured into offering sexual services in exchange for a place to stay; and, finally, *risk of becoming homeless*, where the next negative step due to economic or social factors would be eviction. These definitions are relevant for the situation in Greenland because they refer to the fragility that sometimes surrounds homelessness, and how women who experience homelessness can drift in and out of these circumstances.

In Canada, Indigenous women are overrepresented among those who experience homelessness: close to one thousand women across Canada's three Northern territories.[25] Trauma and violence in the family are significant factors that lead to personal crisis and onwards to homelessness,[26] especially in northern Canada, where the supply of public housing available for rent is very low. The conditions and quality of the housing are also an issue. The affordable housing that is available is generally inadequate and crowding is commonplace, with several generations living under the same roof. As well, social services tend to be blind to gender and the ways in which trauma, violence, and post-traumatic stress disorder affect women's experiences.[27] In northern Canada, the majority of homeless women are not living on the street, but rather are the hidden homeless. The same

---

23 Bopp and YWCA Yellowknife, *You Just Blink*, 2.
24 "Hjemløse Onsdag" [Homeless Wednesday], *Nuuk TV*, 2 November 2016, http://www.nuuktv.gl/nyhed/brandvaesnet-lot/.
25 Rose Schmidt et al., "Trajectories of Women's Homelessness in Canada's 3 Northern Territories," *International Journal of Circumpolar Health* 74, no. 1 (2015), https://doi.org/10.3402/ijch.v74.29778.
26 Bopp and YWCA Yellowknife, *You Just Blink*; Schmidt et al., "Trajectories."
27 Nancy Poole and Judie Bopp, "Using a Community of Practice Model to Create Change for Northern Homeless Women," *First Peoples Child & Family Review* 10, no. 2 (2015): 122–39, http://www.ncbi.nlm.nih.gov/pmc/articles/PMC4959877/.

reality is reflected in Greenland,[28] where women are moving away from smaller societies to urban places in search of better social services, economic benefits, and employment opportunities. When they arrive, however, they often find they lack the necessary economic, social, and cultural resources to thrive in the city.[29] Moreover, unlike in northern Canada, there is little or no policy focus on women's housing and homelessness in Greenland. In Nuuk, there is no exclusive service provider aimed at a female clientele. The closest is a fur workshop, where women can come during the daytime to work with sealskin and other materials, at Kofoed's School, which opened in 2016.

The field study in Nuuk concentrated on people using services from the local Salvation Army, which runs a day shelter and a local work program called Kofoed's School (Kofoeds Skole). The general story that runs through this environment is that people experiencing homelessness have gone through several social services – for instance, treatment for alcohol abuse, parents having their children placed in foster care, and most individuals experiencing a trying relationship with the public system. In the day shelter, they see up to a hundred visitors a day, of which one in five are women; Danish surveys and Point in Time counts clearly show an overrepresentation of men.[30] To experience homelessness as a man and as a woman is to be understood as two very different circumstances, especially in relation to the concept of hidden homelessness. One core area where researchers and professionals agree is in relation to security. As a group, women are understood as being in a different position when it comes to personal safety in relation to men. The aspect of women's personal safety runs though the observation by Canadian researcher Rusty Neal: "For women, a home is more than roof over one's head. It is also a place where they, as women, can be safe and secure and

28 Rasmus Ole Rasmussen, *Mobilitet i Grønland: Sammenfatning af Hovedpunkter fra Analysen af Mobiliteten i Grønland* [Mobility in Greenland: Summary of main points from an analysis of mobility in Greenland] (Nuuk, Greenland: Mobilitetsstyregruppen, 2010); Rasmus Ole Tasmussen, "Why the Other Half Leave: Gender Aspects of Northern Sparsely Populated Areas," in *Demography at the Edge: Remote Human Populations in Developed Nations*, ed. Dean Carson et al. (Farnham, UK: Ashgate, 2011), 237–54.
29 Christensen, "'They Want a Different Life.'"
30 Robert Olsen, "Hjemløshed i Udvikling" [Homelessness in development], in *Socialt Arbejde – Teorier Og Perspektiver* [Social work – Theories and perspectives], ed. Jens Guldager and Marianne Skytte (Copenhagen: Akademisk Forlag, 2013).

have a little privacy and control over their living spaces ... Home is a place that is safe and secure and you don't have anybody there who is going to hurt you ... Where men seek, shelter, women seek a secure and safe place to make a home."[31]

In Greenland, there are few specifically female-focused services such as shelters that guard and protect women's rights to security and privacy separate from men. The overlooked perspective on the situation of marginalized women could be explained by the fact that the formerly strong women's movement in Greenland has been forgotten of late. We explore this further below.

Revisiting Research on Greenlandic Women

In earlier days, Greenland saw efforts towards more critical and radical organizations of women's voices.[32] These organizations made a great impact on Greenlandic women's history. Today, the feminist debate in Greenland is characterized by upper-middle-class and somewhat more conservative values such as whether it should be a criminal offence to drink during pregnancy or whether breast feeding should be accepted in public.[33] Those perspectives are a long way away from problems concerning maternity leave, equal pay, violence prevention, and systemic struggle against women's homelessness.

From a historical perspective, Greenlandic society can be described as functionally gender divided.[34] Anthropologist and rector of Ilisi-

---

31 Rusty Neal, *Voices – Women, Poverty and Homelessness in Canada* (Ottawa: YWCA Canada, 2004), http://ywcacanada.ca/data/research_docs/00000275.pdf.

32 Kirsten Bransholm Pedersen and Najaaraq Paniula, "De Grønlandske Kvindeorganisationers Rolle i den Politiske Udviklingsproces: Set i et Postkolonialt Perspektiv" [The role of Greenlandic women's organizations in the political development process: Seen in a postcolonial perspective], *Dansk Sociologi* 25 no. 4 (2004): 94–118.

33 Søren Duran Duus and Nukappiaaluk Hansen, "HHE: Derfor Må der Ikke Ammes" [HHE: Why breastfeeding is not allowed], *Sermitsiaq*, 4 February 2013, http:// sermitsiaq.ag/node/146895; Anja Rosa, "Mor til 1-Årig: Gør Dog Druk Ulovligt for Gravide" [Mother of 1-year-old: However, make drinking illegal for pregnant women], *Sermitsiaq*, 1 December 2016, https://sermitsiaq.ag/node/192255; "Sygepleje Debat" [Nursing debate], Sermitsiaq, 2016, http://sermitsiaq.ag/emne /amning.

34 Signe Arnfred, "Kvinder, Mænd, Arbejde og Seksualitet i Den Grønlandske Moderniseringsproces" [Women, men, work and sexuality in the Greenlandic modernization process], in *Kvinder i Grønland: Sammen og Hver for Sig* [Women

matusarfik (Greenland's university), Gitte Adler Reimer, has called
the society patriarchal.[35] The characterization is grounded in men's
historically prominent position in society, a position that is today still
somewhat recognizable. It is still typically the male politician who
occupies the most senior positions in parliament, it is the male busi-
nessman and the male head of the board who are the influencers.[36]
Here, we limit the historical analysis to the time following the 1950s,
in many ways a time of upheaval when Greenland was either moving or being "pulled" away from more traditional ways of life and
towards a more industrial and capitalistic way of life. It was also a
time of radical changes in family structures – especially gender roles.[37]
    When Greenland became a Danish county, women's situations
became a focus in a reaction to criticism from the United Nations and
on the advice of the Greenlandic country counsel.[38] Early on, social
scientist Guldborg Chemnitz focused on feminist perspectives and
urbanization with experiences of alienation and migration from smaller
settlements and into the capital Nuuk in the 1960s.[39] In a public report
from the Greenlandic Women's Committee on women's lives and life
conditions, the focus was explicitly on the central role of the woman
and the development of modern housing policies, nicknamed concentration policy because of the high housing density in the main coastal
cities.[40] Although the report focused on homelessness, the report also

in Greenland: Together and separately], ed. Lise Lennert (Nuuk, Greenland:
Atuakkiorfik 1991).
35 Gitte Tróndheim, *Slægtskab og Køn i Grønlandske Bysamfund – Følelser af Forbundethed
[Kinship and gender in Greenlandic urban communities – feelings of connectedness]*
(Nuussuaq, Greenland: Ilisimatusarfik: Ilimmarfik-instituttet, 2010).
36 Julia Christiansen, Peter Munk, and Lise Togeby, "Grønlands Elite" [Greenland's
elite], in *Demokrati og Magt i Grønland* [Democracy and power in Greenland] (Århus,
Denmark: Aalborg Universitetsforlag, 2004); Pia Vedel Ankersen and Peter Munk
Christiansen, "Grønlandisering: Grønlands Elite 2000–2009 [Greenlandization:
Greenland's elite 2000–2009]," *Politica* 45, no. 2 (2013): 195–216, https://doi
.org/10.7146/politica.v45i2.69779.
37 Verner Goldschmidt, "Udviklingen i Sociologisk Belysning" [Developments in
sociological illumination], in *Grønland i Udvikling* [Greenland in development], ed.
Verner Goldschmidt and Guldborg Chemnitz (Copenhagen: Fremad,1964).
38 Jens Heinrich, *Eske Brun og det Moderne Grønlands Tilblivelse* [Eske Brun and
the genesis of modern Greenland] (Nuuk, Greenland: INUSSUK Arktisk
forskningsjourna, 2012).
39 Chemnitz, *Grønlandske Kvinders*.
40 Chemnitz Guldborg et al., *Kvinden og Samfundsudviklingen – Arnaq Inugtaoqatigîngnilo
Ineriartorneq* [Women and the development of society] (Copenhagen: Det
Grønlandske Kvindeudvalg, 1975).

included chapters on safety and security, aspects attached to education and the flexibility one would expect in a country undergoing rapid
transformation.

During the period from the 1970s to the 1990s, there was a vast
output of political writings and research reports around women's
unions and gatherings. The author Eva Rude wrote about how one
women's union was organized around empowerment, the mobilization of women and their visibility, and shedding a light on their
agenda on a countrywide basis. Rude cited women's unions for the
following quote: "Greenland needs that you – as a woman – will gain
influence, will take responsibility – in order to create a Greenlandic
society where men and women are citizens on equal terms."[41] The
critical social political angle on Greenlandic women's positions in
society was apparent in Mâliâraq Vebæk's interview with the wom-
en's rights advocate and anthropologist Lise Lennert.[42] As Lennert
explained, "Women very quickly became aware of how dissatisfying
the circumstances were, but they were unaccustomed to complaining
in public, so they hesitated for a long time from speaking out. They
needed money. A lot of them were single moms."[43] Mobilization might
be a long way coming: in an interview, Lennert talked about the challenges of organizing working women, who, basically, were not used
to making their demands heard.

Working conditions for Greenlandic women in the factories were
well documented in a study of Greenland's second-largest town, Sisimiut, in the 1970s.[44] As well, the process of women's entry into the
Greenlandic labour market and the chaos of an unprepared social system and the need for daycare that followed from employers with total
control over working conditions and salaries were equally well documented by Norwegian anthropologist Benedicte Sandberg.[45] These
studies discussed the situation of working women from a Marxian
perspective. The conditions of working Greenlandic women by the

41 Eva Rude, *Arnat – Den Grønlandske Kvinde* [Arnat – The Greenlandic woman]
(Copenhagen: Gyrithe, 1991).
42 Mâliâraq Vebæk, *Navaranaaq og Andre: De Grønlandske Kvinders Historie* [Navaranaaq
and others: The history of Greenlandic women] (Copenhagen: Gyldendal, 1990), 221.
43 Ibid., 222.
44 Lene Aidt and Merete Borker, *Arbejderkvinder i Grønland* [Working women in
Greenland] (Ebbe Preisler Film, 1975), http://filmcentralen.dk/alle/film
/arbejdkvinder-i-gronland.
45 Benedicte Ingstad Sandberg, *Kvinnelige Arbeidsmigranter ved en Fabrikk i Grønland*
[Female labour migrants at a factory in Greenland] (Oslo: Benedicte Ingstad Sandberg,
1975).

beginning of the country's industrialization was a problematic repetition of how women entered the labour market in Europe. The English author and women's rights activist Joan Smith pointed out the injustice that European working women went through by suddenly being double employed, having a paid job in the industry, while still taking care of the household chores, which for many was also a full-time job, albeit unpaid.[46] The authoritarian working conditions in the household were somehow transferred to the labour market as well.[47] Lennert talked about this in terms of women lacking the experience to organize themselves. She also referred to the issues as evidence that women were unaccustomed to problematizing their roles as housewife and working woman. There are signs that this ongoing lack of organization keeps working women in Greenland in a historically oppressed position.

In the 1990s, some work was done on socially marginalized woman as a category in Greenland. Among the research was that of anthropologist Bo Wagner Sørensen, who worked on the topics of violence and abuse towards women.[48] Later research by MarieKathrine Poppel shows that domestic violence is linked to women's integration into the labour market and that education caused many women to become economically less dependent on men. This is a new pattern of gender roles: Greenlandic women are becoming educated, and men, over time, are become less educated than women and are therefore at risk of being marginalized.[49]

In modern media, there is a clear focus on violence against women, and Danish Crown Princess Mary even held a conference on the subject in Nuuk, but this attention has yet to have a significant impact on the reported violence statistics, which as figure 10.1 shows, rose over the 2013–17 period. Not all of this violence was directed at women, but for the sake of our study we assumed that this was the case when speaking about sexual offences. As table 10.1 reveals, many domestic

---

46 Chemnitz, *Grønlandske Kvinders*.
47 Cited in Neil Smith, *Uneven Development: Nature, Capital, and the Production of Space* (Georgia: University of Georgia Press, 2008).
48 Bo Wagner Sørensen, *Magt Eller Afmagt? Køn, Følelser og Vold i Grønland* [Power or impotence? Gender, emotions and violence in Greenland] (Copenhagen: Akademisk Forlag, 1994).
49 MarieKathrine Poppel, "Mænds Vold Mod Kvinder i Grønland i Nordisk og Arktisk Perspektiv" [Men's violence against women in Greenland in a Nordic and Arctic perspective], in *Grønland i Verdenssamfundet: Udvikling og Forandring* [Greenland in the world community: Development and change], ed. Hanne Petersen (Nuuk, Greenland: Forlaget Atuagkat, 2006).

Figure 10.1. Reported Sexual Offences, Greenland, 2013–17

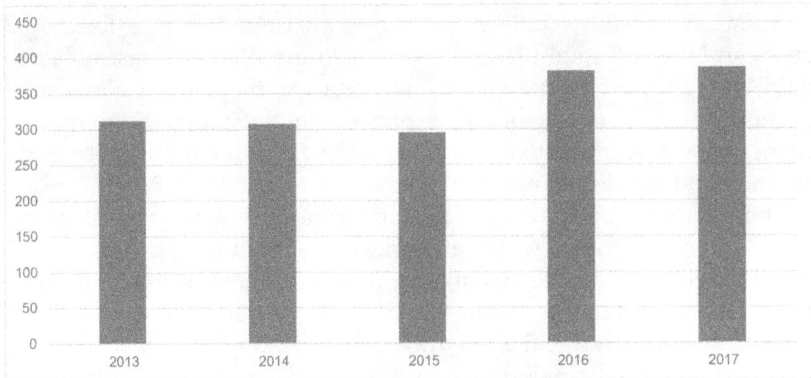

Source: Police Office of Greenland (2018).

Table 10.1. Domestic Disturbances, with or without Children Present, Greenland, 2013–17

Domestic disturbance with or without children present	2013	2014	2015	2016	2017
No children present	2,518	2,412	1,827	1,916	1,960
With children present	439	410	301	331	380

Source: Police Office of Greenland (2018).

disturbances occur with children present. Compared with the rest of the Danish realm, the level of reported violence in Greenland is four times higher and rape ten times higher.[50] The level of threats towards women remains essentially unchanged, and politically there are not many initiatives aimed at protecting women.

50 Grønlands Politi, "Årsstatistik 2017 Grønlands Politi" [Annual statistics 2017 Greenland Police] (Nuuk, Greenland: 2018), https://politi.gl/-/media/mediefiler/gl/dokumenter/aarsstatistik2017.pdf?la=da&hash=4BDFE709A32C3F3B3A6895D0A22FB8F65D66A7BF.

Methodological Approach

The empirical work – data gathering – consisted of a year-long field study in Nuuk. It might take days or even months for a researcher to gain enough trust for people to start sharing their experiences with homelessness. The collaborative project on the social dynamics of homelessness began with a broad approach to understanding the environment of homelessness in Nuuk as an Arctic capital.[51]

The quotes that follow come from interviews that have been anonymized. The interviews were categorized as based on services, everyday life, gender-specific statements, and a category we call "dreams for the future." From a social scientific ethical perspective, it is often a challenge to create real anonymity when dealing with a small environment such as homelessness in Nuuk – discussions of qualitative research have asked if interview-vulnerable is even an option that can be justified.[52] One factor that "helps" in this process is time – that is, the time between the interview and the publishing of research based on the interview. In the meantime, great changes might occur to individuals' life circumstances, making it that much more difficult to identify the people behind the interview quotes.

Qualitative knowledge is significantly contextual, meaning that overall reliability is founded in the situation in which we present and interpret homelessness. As we have stated, there has been a popular tendency to present social issues about Greenland in a quantitative form. It is a perspective that is not always meaningful, however, because it rarely leaves room for reflections about what exactly the object of the research would be. Reports on homelessness in 2008 and again in 2013, widely quoted in the media, were broad and vast, helped create an overview of the situation around homelessness, and are examples of how to put

---

51 Arnfjord and Christensen, "Understanding the Social Dynamics of Homelessness"; Julia Christensen et al., "Homelessness across Alaska, the Canadian North and Greenland: A Review of the Literature on an Emerging Social Phenomenon in the Circumpolar North," *Arctic* 70, no. 4 (2017): 349–64, https://www.jstor.org/stable/26387309.

52 Andrea Fontana and James H. Frey, "Interviewing – The Art of Science," in *Collecting and Interpreting Qualitative Materials*, ed. Norman K. Denzin and Yvonna S. Lincoln (London: Sage, 1998); Jacob Hilden Winsløw, *Videnskabelig Hverdag: En Sociologisk Undersøgelse af Forholdet Mellem Praksis og Selvforståelse i Empiriske Videnskaber* [Scientific everyday life: A sociological study of the relationship between practice and self-understanding in empirical sciences] (Holte, Denmark: SocPol, 1991).

numbers to a social political issue.[53] Here, we relate some insightful stories about the lives of people experiencing homelessness. The development of knowledge has come to a stop, however, with the report as an end product, either because the researchers have concluded the scientific work or because the government, which, in Greenland, has been behind the majority of the reports (the grey literature) has not issued a mandate to the researchers to come up with a list of recommendations. In one such report, paid for by the government, the researchers wrote: "This paragraph consists of some topics, which could be relevant for further focus should one wish to combat homelessness and the consequences that might follow. All the topics stem from the results of the study. It is not a recommendation for further action. That is not the assignment given to this study, and it does not provide a basis for pointing towards specific solutions" [authors' translation].[54] It might seem odd that researchers and experts hired through public funds would not offer recommendations, as their expertise suggests they should do so, leaving a void for action to be taken up by politicians and civil servants. This dilemma is common to the majority of quantitative reports on social issues in Greenland.

Women's Perspectives on Homelessness in Nuuk

During the field study, we asked a number of women about their experiences of homelessness in Nuuk. Even when promised anonymity, however, far from all wished to take part in a research interview – gaining their trust was a long process. Perhaps the interviews would have been easier to obtain if we had been dealing solely with women who were no longer homeless.

Below we present some observations during the field study and testimonies about women's situations by an NGO worker, a mother who was homeless in Nuuk with children for six months, and outtakes from secondary interviews.

An NGO Worker

We asked a woman who headed an NGO in the form of a women's café how many showed up for activities exclusively for women; the answer was just between two and eight. We also asked if, in her experience in

---

53 Greenland, Ministry of Family and Health, "Hjemløs i Grønland"; Hansen and Anders, *Hjemløshed i Grønland*.
54 Hansen and Anders, *Hjemløshed i Grønland*.

Denmark, she could see homelessness issues in Nuuk that differed from those in Denmark. She said:

> They [Greenlandic women] seem to need a close relationship with a man in order to feel safe. Some are in a hurry to find a new guy quite quickly after an ended relationship, so they can feel secure. In Denmark we see a lot more men than women at our places. Very few women came and when they came it was always with a man. Here [in Nuuk] we are seeing more women than in Denmark. Here we are also seeing very young women.

We also asked her what an exclusive service to women in Nuuk should look like. To this she suggested: "Maybe a place where they could get help and get on with their lives. Help to realize some of their dreams in life, i.e., education. Help to be able to get by without having to offer themselves to men in order to feel safe." When asked about the issue of safety in relation to her answer, she responded: "Safety. The answer lies in the second question actually. They are wishing for safety, and if they are in a good relationship they are happier."

A Mother Experiencing Homelessness

We interviewed a single mother with children who had travelled to Nuuk from another town. The family was on the run, the children were being harassed and felt unsafe in their hometown, and one had tried twice to commit suicide. They had come to Nuuk to seek therapeutic and social help. The mother herself was without a job and suffered from joint pains. At the time of the interview, she had just been approved for early retirement. While one child underwent treatment, the family was provided a temporary apartment. As she related,

> The municipality provided an empty apartment with mattresses on the floor. It was awful. We lived like that for four months. We lived helter-skelter. On top of one of my kids being in therapy we lost our place of residence, because the person who sublet the place did not pay rent. All of a sudden, I had a debt of eleven thousand kroner [CAD$2,000], it needed to be paid before we could move into a new place. I was sick from morphine for the pain on my crutches and could not get a job.

The family became homeless, and could not move back to its former town. The child being treated finished the sessions, but the home situation was still not safe. The psychologist who handled the child's therapy wrote the municipality stating that it needed to help the family, but the family received no immediate assistance. Instead, friends of the family helped economically. The mother continued:

> I was without any real place to live for six months. As a mother I ran back and forth between municipal offices. I wrote a lot of e-mails. For me it was about ensuring that the kids were treated right, while one was in therapy and the others were taken care of. The kids stayed with family in the city. But I myself could not always stay there. I was welcome, but as a guest but we were rubbing each other the wrong way. The kids needed a place to stay. They were living with different family members. I was in the mountains a lot at the time and had many dark thoughts.

Asked directly about what services she was offered by the municipality, she answered: "Not a damn thing, no economical help with electrical bills or rent. It was completely blank."

When asked what she wished for, she said: "Some compensation for my economic problems. For people in my situation with children to receive help. I thought a lot about some form of dispensation where the municipality would overlook rent as an issue. I needed some form of dispensation, or an apartment or something."

By the time of the interview, she was back in her hometown and in her own place of residence. The situation was still problematic for her children, particularly the youngest, who was still being harassed. The day after the interview, the child moved back to Nuuk to stay with family and continue school there; the mother felt safe about that. The child who had been in therapy was doing a little better.

Another mother we knew from our field work was Simigaq (a pseudonym), who was well known in the homeless environment in Nuuk. She was married, and she and her husband had been homeless for eight or nine years. They were jewellery craftsmen and living a rough life where alcohol played a significant part through escapist drinking. In the interview, which was originally reported in a Danish newspaper,[55] Simigaq disclosed some of her experiences. In relation to being a mother she explains: "I have not seen my kids in six years. Before I left [her hometown], I gave my kids to my ex-husband, I have not been back since 2007." On her relationship, she disclosed: "It is tough being a homeless couple. When you are married. Maybe I give it more thought because

---

55 Rasmus Flindt Pedersen, "Den Onde Cirkel: Uden Bolig, Intet Job – Uden Job, Ingen Bolig" [The vicious circle: Without housing, no job – no job, no housing], *Ekstrabladet*, 3 May 2013.

I am a woman and once in a while I become depressed, but we have to take it like it is."

We met Simigaq on the street again in summer 2018. She and her husband had recently returned to [her hometown]. She looked happy. However, they both talked about dire circumstances for people experiencing homelessness, and longed to return to Nuuk, where it was easier to be homeless.

Another woman, Arnaq (also a pseudonym), had been described as living rough by NGO workers and others in service positions in the homeless environment and by health care professionals. In the health care system, she was known as a problem child, even though she was in her fifties. She sometimes visited the hospital with friends and stole hand sanitizer or rectified spirits (pure alcohol) from the medical ward. She also drank clandestinely in the back of the Salvation Army (known for its strict temperance), and afterwards was thrown out, and so on. During the prolonged fieldwork, it was rare to catch Arnaq in a sober moment. When under the influence, she fluctuated between being mild and calm and then becoming very angry with a short fuse. When she visited the day shelter, everyone knew to be on the lookout for potential trouble. Nobody had ever observed another side of her. Then, a year later, we spotted Arnaq accompanying a blind man for a walk around town. They were having a good time and talking together. The problem child was more than she let on.

A Discussion of the Empirical Findings

Safety, care, and mobilization are three elements that run through the empirical findings around women experiencing homelessness in Nuuk. Safety is a theme that occurred throughout the interviews and observations in Greenland as in northern Canada. In the chapter's opening quote from 1975, there are clear references to safety and security. The Christian NGO worker connected the women's search for faith with safety as well. The mother who was experiencing homelessness set her personal wishes aside; it was about the children first and foremost. She aimed at avoiding a "helter-skelter" life. This was a safety she no longer expected the Greenlandic public system to provide, so she was seeking this out in the private sphere. A woman often handles this by finding a boyfriend or by getting married. The relationship with a man becomes her channel for safety and security. The NGO worker noted that the women she sees are in a relationship with a man. The social security system lends little alternative in Greenland, unlike in northern Canada, where it is possible to seek out secure and safe privacy in a shelter for women. In Greenland, women who navigate spaces or situations of safety do so through relationships with men.

Care or caring is a theme related to children, if any. Many of the women we met during the fieldwork had children. In contrast to the nursing mothers in Nuuk's cafés or the Facebook of the middle class, they don't talk about their children. It is a commonality that the children are not living with them, having been removed to foster care due to histories of violence and/or abuse. When children are put into foster care in Greenland, it is usually in another city away from their parents. Greenland basically consists of fly-in or sail-in communities over great distances, making it expensive to visit one's children – in Simigaq's case, her ex-husband and their children were 600 kilometres away. The mother who had to leave her and her children's hometown to move to Nuuk had to come to an understanding about her boys' need to move back to Nuuk again and stay with family and continue school there. The narratives around care were coupled to experiences of neglect and loss. Care was also revealed in glimpses during the fieldwork, as when Arnaq was accompanying a blind man around town. Care becomes a compassionate dimension that refers to another world in contrast to abuse and misfortune. Our meetings and talks with men rarely revealed anything about their having children unless asked directly, and then they would give factual statements about their role as a father, or grandfather for that matter, but they rarely went into details. Occasionally we observed men conducting video chats with their children in the day shelter, but this was not commonplace. The men's statements often revolved around their financial situation, work, and a place to live. In this instance, homelessness was not a stigma: there was warmth and real caring among the group in Nuuk who were experiencing not having a place of their own. The group was not encapsulated by monotonous concepts such as marginalized, homeless, or have-nots, but was breaking away from these stigmatizing concepts.

The theme of the mobilization of marginalized women concerns empowerment strategies. In its original form, empowerment comes from within or from a bottom-up approach, meaning it is something a group sorts out on its own – for example, by establishing a common set of goals and plan of action. It is building up a capacity to have a unified voice that speaks to the concerns of Greenlandic women who are not heard. One mother told us that the municipality "*did not do a damn thing*," a statement that stayed with us after the field study. Sometimes, aspects not captured when the interviews were transcribed are the lingering silences after some sentences had been uttered. As an interviewer, one feels how the person across the table must be thinking. The person might be recalling a vulnerable time – you can almost hear the despair as you realize that opposite you is a citizen, a woman, a mother, in need of help. During one interview, a mother did pay attention to the fact that she herself was a citizen or a woman, but she was first and foremost a mother – the self-sacrificing mother in need of help. She had set everything else aside: *"for me it was about the kids."* In this case, it was the woman who was our focus, because she was the mother, the primary caregiver. But it was also she who did not have a voice loud enough to be heard by the public system, and it was she who resigned, finally withdrawing to her hometown with unresolved social issues.

Conclusion

Our interviews and other empirical observations are a testimony to the vacuum in the Greenlandic women's movement, which needs to understand advocacy as a technique of mobilization, to be used as a counter pressure against acceptance of the status quo. Using an expression from the Marxian tradition, we could be talking about the suppression of an authoritarian relationship. Power is shown through a lack of public understanding and lack of political focus when it comes to marginalized women, who then become invisible in the social system. In Greenland, the more joyful side of feminism – pride parades and the legalizing of same-sex marriages – might have outshone more traditional and radical feminism, where debates around equal rights are still ongoing. Women in Greenland still have a great deal to fight for, and need find a voice for their concerns, agendas, and issues.

In combating domestic violence, Greenlandic men need to help break certain social conventions – it is a majority issue and a social problem that women are abused and living in misery. And for it to have a long-term effect, men should be outspoken in addressing this issue. To have a one-sided understanding that women need to solve women's social problems, even if men are the cause, is problematic and one point where some versions of radical feminism might be counterproductive. Men should be included, and men with resources need to be first in line in ending domestic violence.

One profession that has women's issues as a central focus is social work. When looking at the curriculum for social workers' education in Greenland, however, there is nothing about feminism or gender research, central themes that should be mandatory. There is a great deal of written academic material on feminism in general and in the Arctic, but students have not been introduced to it. Ethically, social workers have a responsibility to advocate on behalf of socially marginalized groups in society.[56] If we look at social work as an example, then history is a testimony to a thoroughgoing social professional feminism that earlier on was embedded in the work of Jane Addams's social work with Hull House in Chicago in the 1800s.[57] During her time, social work aimed at women; that tradition could be introduced in Greenlandic social work. Part of Greenland's public social system then would be trained and accustomed to working with and looking at women's situations from their point of view.

On a final note, social policies play an important role of bringing women's issues into focus. Policies in northern Canada are examples of how programs such as transitional housing programs could focus on women experiencing homelessness.[58] In Canada, there are houses for mothers with children. In Greenland, under normal circumstances, a mother would lose the right to keep her children if she lost her home, and we often saw a connection between the removal of a child to foster care and women's homelessness.[59]

A lack of political solutions for domestic violence means that women are forced to put up with abuse in a violent home. Greenland's social policy in this area needs to ensure that this is not happening, by providing temporary living arrangements in the form of shelters for women and children who are fugitives on the run from domestic abuse.

In conclusion, Greenland's welfare system has severe challenges in providing for women who are experiencing homelessness. What is needed now is action to implement strategies to address these challenges.

---

56 International Association of Schools of Social Work, *Ethics in Social Work, Statement of Principles* (2004), www.iassw-aiets.org/archive/ethics-in-social-work-statement-of-principles/.
57 Jane Addams, "Democracy and Social Ethics," in *The Citizen's Library of Economics, Politics, and Sociology*, ed. Richard T. Ely (New York: Macmillan, 1992).
58 One such program, called Lynn's Place, was launched in Yellowknife in 2017; see "Transitional Housing," *YWCA NWT* (2021), https://www.ywcanwt.ca/transitional-housing.
59 Julia Christensen, "Indigenous Housing and Health in the Canadian North: Revisiting Cultural Safety," *Health & Place* 40, no. 1 (2016): 83–90, https://doi.org/10.1016/j.healthplace.2016.05.003.

11 Welfare Colonialism and Geographies of Homelessness in Nuuk, Greenland

JULIA CHRISTENSEN, STEVEN ARNFJORD,
AND MARIE-LOUISE AASTRUP

On a June 2018 evening in Nuuk, Greenland, with the Arctic summer sun still gleaming, we stood on Steven's balcony overlooking downtown Nuuk. "One, two, three, four...," we counted the cranes scattered across the skyline. "Five, six, seven, eight...nine!" From the vantage point of Steven's townhouse, we were able to count almost two hands' worth of cranes, busily assembling new residential high rises and government buildings across the Nuuk skyline. The total number of cranes we counted that evening was only a fraction of those we saw in Nuuk over the course of that summer. A local newspaper ran the headline "Bygge-Boom" (building boom) across its front page, an image that it then featured in poster promotions all summer long. In a participatory photography workshop with adult men and women experiencing homelessness, which we held as a part of our ongoing research on housing and homelessness in Nuuk, the topic of rapid development in the city was frequently discussed. Nothing was the same, and yet so much was: the rural-urban disparities driving the most recent wave of urban development was a familiar reflection of resettlement policies that have framed settlement geographies in Greenland since the earliest days of Danish colonization.

Nuuk is a city undergoing incredible expansion, building up and out at a pace that is almost impossible to track. The fervent push behind this rapid development, however, is not only to meet the needs of people who currently call the city home, but also the thousands of Greenlanders from rural settlements that Sermersooq, the municipality in which Nuuk is located, and the Greenlandic government plan to resettle in the capital city in the coming years. Twenty minutes from central Nuuk, a new Sermersooq subdivision – Siorarsiorfik – will be the largest urban development project ever in Greenland, designed to address significant population growth and persistent housing need in the municipality, as well as to draw young Greenlanders living abroad back to the country's capital. As we explore in this chapter, this latest urban expansion plan is part and parcel of a very long historical trajectory of (re)settlement and urbanization in Greenland. This trajectory has been a core element in Danish colonial policy in Greenland, and has thus rendered urban and colonial forms and processes largely inextricable. In contemporary Greenland, however, an ever-sharpening urban focus has become central to the government, and in this way resettlement and urbanization have become entangled as key strategies towards self-determination, decolonization, and, ultimately, total independence from the Danish state.

During the early to mid-twentieth century, the Danish state actively pursued the centralization of previously nomadic Indigenous peoples in Greenland.[1] Although (re)settlement policies were enacted to promote Greenlandic participation in the wage economy and facilitate administration by the colonial state, there were profound social and spatial implications as well. One of the key tools to promote settlement was the expansion of social welfare services, including the implementation of public health programs, education, public housing, and income support. The intention was to bring Greenlanders into the administration and culture of the Danish state – including language and culturally rooted practices of home, health, family, and social organization. Indigenous languages, customs, and cultures were actively undermined through policies such as "Danification" (Danish: *Danisering*), meant to erode Greenlandic language and even to remove "promising" youth to boarding schools in Nuuk or to foster families in Denmark. These practices disrupted and dislocated Greenlandic homes, health, family, and community – the effects of which are ongoing today in what scholars articulate as the intergenerational effects of colonialism – namely, negative effects on mental and physical health, family, and community relations, sense of place, and cultural identity. Furthermore, these practices effectively produced the condition of chronic housing need that underlies the emergence of hidden and visible forms of homelessness in Greenland today.

Greenland has Self Rule – that is, although Greenland is still part of the Kingdom of Denmark, the country has autonomy over its central governmental activities, including social policy, education, health, economy,

1 Jens Dahl, "Identity, Urbanization and Political Demography in Greenland," *Acta Borealia* 27, no. 2 (2010): 125–40, https://doi.org/10.1080/08003831.2010.527528; Frank Sejersen, "Urbanization, Landscape Appropriation and Climate Change in Greenland," *Acta Borealia* 27, no. 2 (2010): 167–88, https://doi.org/10.1080/08003831 .2010.527533.

and housing, while relying on Denmark for defence and foreign policy. Greenland has universal health care and is considered a welfare society following the Scandinavian model, meaning that taxpayers pay close to half their income in taxes in exchange for a wide spectrum of publicly administered services. At the same time, Greenland does receive considerable subsidies from Denmark to support its economy. Greenland's 56,000 inhabitants are settled in seventeen towns and some sixty smaller settlements (Danish: *bygder*) primarily along the west coast, which since 2009 have been administratively organized into four municipal regions. Notably there is no national road system, and therefore transportation between settlements is primarily by helicopter, small airplane, or boat. Not surprisingly, transportation is expensive, which further limits mobility between communities. About 90 per cent of Greenland's population is ethnically Greenlandic (Inuit); the remainder is mainly Danish.[2]

The population is highly urbanized, with well over 30 per cent of Greenlanders living in the capital city, Nuuk, and over 85 per cent living in the four largest settlements combined. Thus, towns and cities play a significant role in the lives of Greenlanders.[3] Although Greenland's towns and cities are not large in population relative to urban centres elsewhere in the world, its largest settlements constitute important administrative, political, economic, educational, and social centres. "The definition of a town in Greenland," according to Frank Sejersen, "is thus not only related to its size, but moreover to its importance as a centre."[4] The trend towards urbanization in Greenland is only growing, with urban populations rising while the number of rural dwellers is on the decline.[5] This is due in part to the fact that Greenlandic towns have been singled out as drivers of the kind of social change sought after by the Self Rule government.[6] In a referendum in 2008, roughly 75 per cent of the Greenlandic population voted yes to a law giving more self-rule to Greenland – a self-rule that was later approved by the Danish parliament to be implemented in 2009. This move necessitated an aggressive and clearly defined approach to self-determination and independence. At the same time, in order to finance greater independence from Denmark, the Self Rule government largely looked to industrialization

---

2 Central Intelligence Agency, "The World Factbook: Greenland," https://www.cia.gov
   /the-world-factbook/countries/greenland/.
3 Sejersen, "Urbanization, Landscape Appropriation."
4 Ibid., 167.
5 Klaus Georg Hansen, Søren Bitsch, and Lyudmila Zalkind, *Urbanization and the Role of
   Housing in the Present Development Process in the Arctic* (Stockholm: Nordregio, 2013).
6 Sejersen, "Urbanization, Landscape Appropriation."

to lessen its dependency on the annual block grant from Denmark.[7] The effects of climate changes have led Self Rule to speculate about the potential for industrial development due to the country's strategic position globally vis-à-vis oil and gas development and the shipping industry.[8] Despite what was traditionally a pessimistic and anti-urban attitude in Greenland, the Greenlandic way of life is no longer seen as incompatible with life in towns or cities.[9]

Yet, while the Self Rule government plods ahead with its Sermersooq expansion plans in Nuuk, we were interested in what continued rural-urban migration, urbanization, and resettlement mean for Greenlanders experiencing housing insecurity and, ultimately, forms of homelessness. We also sought to explore how the concept of welfare colonialism can be used to interpret the Danish colonial focus on resettlement in order to facilitate the extension of social welfare programs into Greenlandic lives, how social welfare here was intended as a main driver in cultural assimilation and "Danification," and ultimately how the shifting geographies of welfare colonialism underlie homeless (im)mobilities in Greenland. Much of the literature on Arctic rural-urban migration has identified this phenomenon as motivated by the pursuit of educational and employment opportunities. Yet, in our work on housing insecurity and homelessness in Alaska, the Canadian North, and Greenland, we see that a second migration stream is also occurring among those who are marginalized from educational and employment opportunities, and are reliant upon institutionalized health and social services. This has had a particular impact in recent years on Greenlandic youth, who are increasingly represented among those living without secure housing in Nuuk.[10] Finally, we argue in this chapter that, in the pursuit of modernization and independence through urbanization, without adequate social policy responses to chronic housing needs and increasing visible

---

7 Mark Nuttall, "Self-Rule in Greenland: Towards the World's First Independent Inuit State?," *Indigenous Affairs* 8, no. 3–4 (2008): 64–70, http://citeseerx.ist.psu.edu /viewdoc/download?doi=10.1.1.458.5032&rep=rep1&type=pdf.

8 Joan Nymand Larsen, "Climate Change, Natural Resource Dependency, and Supply Shocks: The Case of Greenland," in *The Political Economy of Northern Regional Development*, ed. Gorm Winther (Copenhagen: TemaNord, 2010), 205–18.

9 Bo Wagner Sørensen, "Perceiving Landscapes in Greenland," in *Nordic Landscapes: Region and Belonging on the Northern Edge of Europe*, ed. Michael Jones and Kenneth R. Olwig (Minneapolis: University of Minnesota Press, 2008), 106–40.

10 Julia Christensen et al., "Homelessness across Alaska, the Canadian North and Greenland: A Review of the Literature on a Developing Social Phenomenon in the Circumpolar North," *Arctic* 70, no. 4 (2017): 349–64, https://www.jstor.org /stable/26387309.

homelessness in Nuuk, a significant number of Greenlandic citizens continue to be marginalized through resettlement. Although policies and political powers have shifted over the years, the Self Rule government today has done very little to improve or plan for the housing and social welfare needs of socially marginalized Greenlanders.

The uneven geographies of social welfare institutions have a critical presence in Arctic homeless pathways, and Greenland is no exception.[11] Those at particular risk of homelessness include low-income Greenlanders who face compounding life challenges, framed in large part by chronic housing need, poor mental health (including trauma), developmental disabilities, addictions, and breakdowns in intimate, family and community relationships, risk factors that are tied indelibly to the sociocultural and material legacies of colonialism and modernization in the Arctic.[12] The absence of key health and social supports in rural settlements and their concentration in urban centres is an important outcome of resettlement and one that directly affects the (im)mobility of Greenlanders experiencing housing insecurity and homelessness. It is critical to acknowledge, however, that the condition of homelessness itself is produced and reproduced through the absence of housing – accessible, affordable, adequate housing that meets the needs of Greenlanders who might be living with a combination of the factors mentioned here.

Yet, while Nuuk experiences rapid expansion, accounts of housing insecurity and homelessness are also abundant in local media coverage and public discourse. In 2017, a man identified as homeless was found alive after seventeen days in a warehouse, where he had tried to find shelter but found himself locked in and unable to get out. Local media coverage of housing concerns and the plight of Greenlanders experiencing homelessness has increased steadily alongside the fervour surrounding municipal expansion. Indeed, anecdotal reports from housing advocates and support providers in the city indicate the number of people experiencing acute, or visible, homelessness in Nuuk is on the rise. What we see today in the city, and what we wish to explore

11 Julia Christensen, "Homeless in a Homeland: Housing (In)Security and Homelessness in Inuvik and Yellowknife, Northwest Territories" (PhD diss., McGill University, 2011); Knud E. Hansen and Hans T. Andersen, *Hjemløshed i Grønland* [Homelessness in Greenland] (Aalborg, Denmark: University of Aalborg, Statens Byggeforskningsinstitut, 2013).
12 Peter Bjerregaard and Tine Curtis, "Cultural Change and Mental Health in Greenland: The Association of Childhood Conditions, Language, and Urbanization with Mental Health and Suicidal Thoughts among the Inuit of Greenland," *Social Science & Medicine* 54, no. 1 (2002): 33–48, https://doi.org/10.1016/S0277-9536(01)00005-3.

in this chapter, is the confluence of (re)settlement, urbanization, and acute housing need in the form of visible homelessness. Urbanization, through various programs and since the Second World War, has come to characterize Greenlandic social, cultural, economic, and political landscapes, and passive and overt forms of urbanization policy effectively frame the geographies of housing insecurity and homelessness that we explore in our work. We are interested in examining here how the trajectory of housing need and homelessness over time interconnects with the trajectory of resettlement and urbanization, and how both parallel developments can be understood as part and parcel of the welfare colonial experience in Greenland. In other words, we seek to illustrate the ways in which homelessness in Nuuk does not emerge out of nowhere, but rather must be situated within the broader context of colonialism and urban development in Greenland.

This chapter emerges from our larger study aimed at understanding the social dimensions of homelessness in Nuuk, Greenland, which began in 2015. We begin with a brief overview of the history of colonialism, resettlement, and urbanization in the Greenlandic context, with a particular focus on the capital city of Nuuk. We also introduce the concept of welfare colonialism and its fundamental role in shaping these geographies. The colonial experience in Greenland has been facilitated through the social welfare state, a process that involved significant manipulation of the ways in which Indigenous peoples organized themselves spatially and socially while simultaneously implicating them in the affairs, desires, and decision making of state powers in Denmark and then the emerging Greenlandic elite. Thus, the processes of urbanization cannot be disentangled from the larger context of welfare colonialism and its effects on the health and social geographies of the Greenlandic people. We conclude with a discussion of key themes from our research in Nuuk to illustrate the ways in which welfare colonialism and passive and overt urbanization policies intertwine with the absence of social policy on housing and homelessness to exacerbate homelessness in the capital city.

Colonialism, Resettlement, and Urbanization in Greenland

Early Colonization and Settlement

Greenland was first colonized by Denmark in 1721. Yet despite Danish presence in Greenland, their influence was deliberately at arm's length. Historically, Greenlandic people lived largely nomadic lives, moving according to the seasons, the physical and spiritual bounds of their territories, and the availability of the animal and plant resources upon which their lives depended.[13] At the beginning of the colonial period, trade was based primarily on whaling, but by the closing of the eighteenth century, the Royal Greenland Trade Company, a Danish state company formed in 1776, had established a large number of small trading posts along the west coast.[14] The Company offered basic provisions to Greenlandic hunters in exchange for skins and furs. The Danish state favoured this decentralized settlement pattern at the time, believing it supported a high level of self-sufficiency and facilitated trade in hunting products by still encouraging traditional subsistence lifestyles, something Nils Ørvik called a "a northern model of development without modernization."[15]

Although a Danish-Greenland relationship had been ongoing for over two centuries, it was the Second World War that brought about the most profound transformation for Greenland. Similar to experiences in Alaska and the Canadian North, the period around and following the Second World War thrust Greenland into the global spotlight and inspired renewed and intensified interests from the colonial (Danish) state. During the war, Greenland was entirely cut off from Denmark, and the United States and Canada established relationships with the colony, which was positioned strategically between North America and Europe. After the war came to its conclusion, Denmark signed a new constitution that changed Greenland's status as a colony of Denmark to that of a Danish province, and gave Danish citizenship to all Greenlanders. As Marianne Stenbæk explains, this shift in the relationship led many Danes to believe that Greenlanders (or "northern Danes") and Greenland should be remade into a northern Denmark – a social, spatial, and indeed cultural reflection of the state of Denmark.[16] As such, "a pseudo-blueprint of Danish society – its institutions, its architecture, its educational system, etc. – should be impressed on Greenland."[17] A shift in ideology thus occurred during and following the war as the Danish state saw the economic, administrative, and geopolitical advantages of

---

13 Sejersen, "Urbanization, Landscape Appropriation."
14 Jørgen Viemose, *Dansk Kolonipolitik i Grønland* [Danish colonial policy in Greenland] (Copenhagen: Demos, 1977).
15 Nils Ørvik, *Sikkerhets-Politikken, 1920–1939; Fra Forhistorien til 9. april 1940* [The policy of security, 1920–1939; From prehistory to 9 April 1940] (Oslo: Johan Grundt Tanum Forlag, 1960), 68.
16 Marianne Stenbaek, "Forty Years of Cultural Change among the Inuit in Alaska, Canada and Greenland: Some Reflections," *Arctic* 40, no. 4 (1987): 300–9, https://www.jstor.org/stable/40510637.
17 Ibid., 301.

centralization and the assimilation of Arctic peoples into Danish cultural practices and modes of social organization. The Second World War became "the threshold between the old and the new" in Greenland.[18]

Resettlement, Modernization, and Urbanization

The most aggressive resettlement and modernization period occurred from the 1950s to the 1970s under consecutive reform schemes launched in 1950 and 1964, respectively.[19] These two parliamentary reports – the Report of the Commission for Greenland, published in 1950 and later referred to as G50, and the Report of the Greenland Committee of 1960, published in 1964 and referred to as G60 – were authorized by the Danish government to review the possibilities for development in Greenland. Danish and Greenlandic politicians believed the industrialization of fish production to be an efficient way to improve Greenlandic standards of living. In order to improve the level of welfare, education, living standards, and the labour market, movement to a handful of chosen towns along the west coast was encouraged by Danish authorities. Although families initially were invited to relocate through promises of new housing and better economic prospects, many communities were closed down outright, or investments withheld to encourage a concentration of the population in centres of industrial development, where modern educational, social, and health establishments were centralized.[20]

Under G60, economic development in Greenland was concentrated in four towns – Nuuk, Sisimiut, Paamiut, and Maniitsoq.[21] Between 1952 and 1963, approximately three thousand households, including families and extended families, were moved from smaller coastal settlements of roughly one to two hundred inhabitants each, to these fast-growing towns as part of this modernization process. Substantial investments were channelled into infrastructure, housing, production facilities, and education, as well as health institutions.[22] Towns became centres of construction work on a previously unknown scale, resulting

---

18 Ibid.
19 These development schemes also included the controversial *fødestedskriterie* (place of birth criterion), which "made Greenlanders so angry that it became a catalyst for political and cultural change because of its inherent discrimination" (ibid.).
20 Ibid.
21 Lawrence C. Hamilton et al., "Outmigration and Gender Balance in Greenland," *Arctic Anthropology* 33, no. 1 (1996): 89–97, https://www.jstor.org/stable/40316397.
22 Jes Barsøe Adolphsen and Tom Greiffenberg, *The Planned Development of Greenland 1950–1979* (Aalborg, Denmark: Aalborg Universitet, Institut for Samfundsudvikling og Planlægning, 1998).

in abrupt changes to their physical layout, with the building of factories and concrete apartment buildings, as well as roads and other
infrastructure.

Although improvements to Greenlandic social welfare were the
stated objective, this rapid resettlement had the effect of alienating
people from their culture and livelihoods, imposing living conditions
that people were not used to and not culturally prepared for, and led
to the increasing prevalence of health and social problems.[23] Housing
needs were calculated as the total required to cover renewal, migration, and population increase.[24] The new apartment units built in the
coastal towns were very small, and were designed primarily for small
or nuclear families, a practice that continues today, despite the fact
that many Greenlandic families lived (and continue to live) in multigenerational settings. Part and parcel of these resettlement strategies were the promises of housing and employment, including block
housing projects in Nuuk. One of the infamous symbols of this period,
these high-density apartment buildings, lined in rows in the centre of
Nuuk's downtown, were built to house the hundreds of families that
were resettled from outlying settlements. The new housing and development plans emphasized high-density housing programs in regional
centres alongside the expansion of social welfare services, which
included the implementation of public health programs, education,
and income support. These housing projects – modern (by the standards of that era) apartment blocks with sanitation, electricity, central
heating, and larger indoor spaces – were part of a broader modernization project in Greenland from 1950 to 1980.[25] The apartments were
designed for families engaged in modern employment, and established
by Danish-organized political committees with little appreciation for
the needs and wants of Greenlandic society. For example, the housing
was not suitable for traditional subsistence activities such as butcher-
ing a seal, although they had modern facilities such as running water
and electricity. Meanwhile, massive resettlement actually resulted in
limitations on the employment and housing opportunities promised
by the state, as migration increased competition for the limited supply

---

23 Marie-Louise Deth Petersen, "The Impact of Public Planning on Ethnic Culture:
   Aspects of Danish Resettlement Policies in Greenland after World War II," *Arctic
   Anthropology* 23, no. 1–2 (1986): 271–80, https://www.jstor.org/stable/40316115.
24 Ibid.
25 Tupaarnaq Rosing Olsen, *I Skyggen af Kajakkerne: Grønlands Politiske Historie 1939–79*
   [In the shadow of kayaks: Greenland's political history 1939–79] (Nuuk, Greenland:
   Atuagkat, 2005).

of both.[26] However, no strategies were in place to deal with the negative consequences of the resettlement, homelessness included. At this time, Greenland experienced what has been described as the period of its most direct colonial oppression, even though it was no longer legally considered a colony of Denmark, as the welfare system developed and Danish intervention was at its highest.[27] Towns became the symbolic, as well as concrete, manifestation of Danish cultural and political dominance and the arena for the assimilation of Greenlanders into a Danish way of thinking and behaving.

Contemporary Resettlement and Urbanization

The 1950s to 1970s brought about significant and unprecedented change to Greenlandic settlement patterns – prioritization of the urban and encouragement of rural-urban resettlement that persist today. More recent examples can be seen in the 2002 public housing tenants reform (*huslejere reform*) and the municipal expansion in Nuuk. When Home Rule was introduced in 1979, a financial and political focus was temporarily placed on a decentralized settlement structure, with an emphasis on a return to small places to compensate for years of negligence by the Danish state.[28] However, efforts to manage the mounting challenges of an aging housing stock and at the same time bolster efforts towards increased independence from Denmark led to renewed resettlement and urbanization efforts.

Centralization now continues through both passive and overt policies meant to disincentivize rural life and encourage urbanization, which has a particular impact on Greenlanders who are marginalized through a lack of education or employable skills or the presence of chronic health conditions such as addiction or trauma. Although the social welfare state has allowed small settlements to persist, the lack of sustainable local economies has meant that, when services and

---

26 Deth Petersen, "Impact of Public Planning."
27 Robert Paine, "The Path to Welfare Colonialism," in *The White Arctic: Anthropological Essays on Tutelage and Ethnicity* (St. John's: Memorial University of Newfoundland, Institute of Social and Economic Research, 1977), 7–28; Axel Kjaer Sørensen, *Danmark-Grønland i det 20. Århundrede – En Historisk Oversight [Denmark-Greenland in the 20th century – a historical oversight]* (Copenhagen: Nyt Nordisk Forlag Arnold Busck, 1983).
28 Jens Dahl, *Saqqaq: An Inuit Hunting Community in the Modern World* (Toronto: University of Toronto Press, 2000).

investment are pulled back, there is little reason for local residents to stay.[29] This kind of tactic has been employed time and again in Greenland in an effort to encourage migration to its largest centres, with little attention given to those who do not have the skills, resources, or social support to thrive in an urban economy. The promotion of an uneven geography of key health and social welfare services on the part of the Danish government, and now the Self Rule government, is, we argue, a passive form of resettlement policy. Moreover, the *bygge-boom* in Nuuk, with its emphasis on private rental and owned housing, makes clear that urban life is not envisioned for all Greenlanders, but only those who can access such housing. A remarkable irony can indeed be found in a *bygge-boom* that does not include a diversification of the housing spectrum in order to better meet the needs of all Greenlanders. In a country where public participation in policymaking has been underlined,[30] it is clear that this participation does not include Greenlanders who are experiencing acute housing need and homelessness. The increasingly punitive nature of housing policy, as we discuss in this chapter, further illustrates this point.

Conceptualizing Welfare Colonial Geographies of Homelessness

The social welfare state and its uneven spatialization has been central to resettlement efforts in Greenland, and indirectly to urban homelessness. Attending to the socio-spatial consequences of this geography is central to understanding the contemporary geographies of housing insecurity and homelessness. To explain the effects of resettlement on marginalized Greenlanders – namely, support service dependencies, which are entangled in the complex rural-urban geographies of social welfare (through welfare colonialism), and institutionalization – three conceptual bodies are at work. The first is the concept of welfare colonialism.[31] Danish colonial attitudes in the mid-twentieth century established a relationship between Indigenous peoples and the state that can be understood as welfare colonialism, a concept first articulated by Robert Paine to describe the uneven political and economic landscape of Indigenous peoples in the Canadian North.[32] Since then, the term

---

29 See Kåre Hendriksen, *Grønlands Bygder: Økonomi og Udviklingsdynamik* [Greenland's settlements: Economic and development dynamics] (Aalborg, Denmark: Aalborg Universitet and Danmarks Tekniske Universitet, 2013).
30 Christensen et al., "Homelessness across Alaska, the Canadian North and Greenland."
31 Paine, "Path to Welfare Colonialism."
32 Ibid.

has been taken up to describe more widely the policies and practices through which liberal democratic (settler) governments both recognize the citizenship of Indigenous peoples vis-à-vis access to welfare benefits and effectively deny their citizenship by nurturing their dependency on the state.[33] Through the workings of welfare colonialism, an unequal relationship of dependency is established, through which social welfare programs are then rationalized and used to equalize the material conditions of Indigenous peoples while serving to preserve and uphold the dominant, state-driven ideological framework. Of course, the workings of social welfare colonialism have been enacted in different ways across colonial contexts, and are also uneven in their effects within and between Indigenous communities. Those whose lives have been altered most significantly by way of these relations have experienced, and continue to experience, these dynamics of dependency in particular ways.

Second, institutionalization is the management of the social and health outcomes of colonialism and the direct result of culturally and contextually inappropriate social welfare programs that fail to address effectively the actual roots of the problems they seek to remedy.[34] Institutionalization therefore interacts directly with the intergenerational effects of colonialism, and particularly the effects of trauma, which play a significant role in factors contributing to homelessness among Indigenous peoples. Individual lived experiences of homelessness that were shared with us over the course of this research revealed that social welfare institutions such as the child welfare system, the criminal justice system, and income support play key roles in the lives of Greenlanders living homeless, the significance of which is deeply embedded in the uneven and persistent effects of trauma from rapid socio-cultural change.

Third, service dependency provides a geography of institutionalization in the sense that it serves to explain the socio-spatial consequences of institutional change and unevenness – namely, that of the rural-urban migration of Greenlanders most vulnerable to homelessness. The concept of service dependency speaks specifically to the relationships among poverty, health and social support needs, and mobility. In the

---

33 William Tyler, "Postmodernity and the Aboriginal Condition: The Cultural Dilemmas of Contemporary Policy," *Australian and New Zealand Journal of Sociology* 29, no. 3 (1993): 322–42, https://doi.org/10.1177/144078339302900303.

34 See Julia Christensen, "Indigenous Housing and Health in the Canadian North: Revisiting Cultural Safety," *Health & Place* 40, no. 1 (2016): 83–90, https://doi .org/10.1016/j.healthplace.2016.05.003; Julia Christensen, *No Home in a Homeland: Indigenous Peoples and Homelessness in the Canadian North* (Vancouver: UBC Press, 2017).

past, academic interest in service dependency focused on the phenomenon of "service-dependent population ghettos" – spatial concentrations of welfare populations and the facilities designed to assist them – in North American inner cities.[35] The concept, however, offers potential for understanding homelessness and urbanization in the Arctic as well. Urban centres such as Nuuk, Iqaluit, and Yellowknife act as areas of concentrated services for people in these communities, as well as those from smaller, outlying settlement communities. In this way, service dependency facilitates an examination of the social and institutional factors that contribute to rural-urban migration among those at risk of homelessness, as well as the rising visibility of homelessness in Arctic urban centres.

Passive and Overt Centralization

The extension of the social welfare state to Greenland following the Second World War was a key strategy in what was effectively an ongoing Danish colonial interest in Greenland. The centralization of key health and social services in Greenlandic towns and cities produced an uneven institutional geography across the country – one that is particularly important to the lives of marginalized Greenlanders who are at high risk of housing insecurity and forms of homelessness. In Greenland today, the state facilitates urbanization through deliberate policies. The most important change in this direction was probably the merging of eighteen municipalities into four large urban places in 2009 and the consequent gathering of most public administration and associated jobs in those cities. There has also been a significant centralization of post-secondary education, public housing, and health and social services.[36] For example, the sixteen former health districts were reorganized into five health regions, resulting in the closure of district hospitals and the centralization of health care services in the five largest centres, a move justified by economic advantages and administrative arguments that it would improve the quality of health care.

Along with the concentration of important social welfare functions in a few municipalities, a policy of simultaneous "real costs" has also played a key role in encouraging rural-urban movement. Kåre Hendriksen has argued that the social welfare state previously

35 Michael J. Dear and Jennifer R. Wolch, *Landscapes of Despair: From Deinstitutionalization to Homelessness* (Princeton, NJ: Princeton University Press, 2014).
36 See Hendriksen, *Grønlands Bygder*.

facilitated small settlements through subsidy programs, particularly the uniform price system, for electricity, heating, and water.[37] Since 2002, however, the uniform price system has been gradually clawed back to increase prices in the smaller communities that reflect "real costs" – a reform geared to benefit the economic dynamics in the towns and to promote a rural-to-urban transfer of population.[38] As a result, the high cost of living in the smaller communities has disincentivized rural life; the isolation of rural Greenlanders has been compounded by changes in the transportation structure and pricing system.

Framing the landscape of housing insecurity and homelessness in Greenland are the country's historical and contemporary dimensions of resettlement and rural-to-urban mobility. Although the resettlement plans of the mid-twentieth century were enacted to promote Greenlanders' participation in the wage economy and to facilitate administration by the colonial state, they also had profound social and spatial implications.[39] In an interview, a public housing provider in Nuuk highlighted the ways in which homelessness is a by-product of social and spatial transformations: "homelessness in Greenland has existed as long as the wage economy has, because along with the wage economy came the introduction of modern housing and rents and the idea that housing was something you needed to be able to pay for, to afford." Centralization policies then put into motion a distinct rural-urban geography, one that frames the emergence of visible forms of homelessness in Greenlandic urban centres. The shifting spatial dynamics of the Greenlandic social welfare state have had particular consequences for those without adequate education or are dependent on health and social services. The very institutions that are key in the lives of Greenlanders living with housing need or homelessness are precisely those that are increasingly centralized in urban Greenland: public housing, emergency shelters, the child welfare system, and the spectrum of health services.

37 Ibid.
38 Gorm Winther, ed., *The Political Economy of Northern Regional Development* (Copenhagen: TemaNord, 2010).
39 See Dahl, "Identity, Urbanization and Political Demography"; Anthony J. Dzik, "Settlement Closure or Persistence: A Comparison of Kangeq and Kapisillit, Greenland," *Journal of Settlements and Spatial Planning* 7, no. 2 (2016): 99–112, https://doi.org 10.19188/01JSSP022016/; Sejersen, "Urbanization, Landscape Appropriation."

Housing and Homelessness in Greenland

Homelessness as a Greenlandic social phenomenon is, with few exceptions, presented as predominantly urban, and largely Nuuk-centred.[40] A 2013 report cited an estimate of six hundred people living homeless in Greenland as a whole.[41] This number included shorter homeless periods ranging from days to a few weeks, but the report said little about homelessness as a more chronic situation. In fact, the absence of a standardized definition of homelessness in Greenland makes it difficult to assess who is homeless, to draw meaningful comparisons between rural and urban communities, or to determine the scale and scope of homelessness as a whole. Moreover, there is anecdotal evidence of significant numbers of people living homeless who are actually invisible to the system because they lack formal municipal registration. In Nuuk, a conservative estimate of people living in a more permanent state of homelessness is between one and two hundred,[42] but our research uncovered anecdotal evidence from non-governmental organization (NGO) support providers that the number is upwards of three hundred.[43] Moreover, we found that four main experiences of homelessness are most prominent: 1) men over age thirty who struggle with substance abuse; 2) youth with family, social, or economic problems who migrate from small settlements to larger centres in hope of new opportunities; 3) women who either are single or no longer have custody of their children, and who have often been victims of domestic violence (see Arnfjord and Christensen in Chapter 10); and 4) men and women over age fifty-five who have been evicted from their housing after failing to pay rent.[44] It is predominantly the second and third groups whose experiences of homelessness are framed by the kinds of passive and overt resettlement policy we describe in this chapter.

---

40 Media reports on homelessness in Greenland first appeared in the 1990s; however, they remained largely focused on Nuuk. See P. Kleist, *Hjemløs Beder om Hjælp* [The homeless ask for help] (Nuuk, Greenland: Atuagagdliutit, 1997); Steven Arnfjord and Julia Christensen, "Understanding the Social Dynamics of Homelessness in Nuuk, Greenland," *Northern Notes* 45 (Spring/Summer 2016), http://iassa.org/images /newsletters/Northern-Notes-Issue-45-Spring-Summer-2016.pdf.
41 Hansen and Andersen, *Hjemløshed i Grønland*, 24.
42 Greenland, Ministry of Family and Health, *Hjemløs i Grønland: Et Skøn over Samtlige Kommuners Hjemløse* [Homelessness in Greenland: An estimate of homelessness by municipality] (Nuuk, Greenland: 2008); Hansen and Andersen, *Hjemløshed i Grønland*.
43 Arnfjord and Christensen, "Understanding the Social Dynamics of Homelessness."
44 Ibid.

The Urban Housing Landscape

Efforts by the Self Rule government to promote resettlement to urban centres have included a steady decline in funding for housing in smaller settlements and the redirection of those funds towards public housing in the larger urban centres, mainly Nuuk.[45] Public housing in the Greenlandic context, however, does not necessarily mean it is housing for low-income Greenlanders. In Greenland, housing is viewed as a matter of public responsibility and consists mainly of public housing. Thus, the bulk of rental housing in Nuuk, and in Greenland as a whole, is public with a private housing stock in 2010[46] of 7,173 units compared with public housing stock of 13,650.[47] Rental housing in Greenland, in other words, is largely administered in one of two ways: through public housing or through public sector employment. To access public housing, which is administered by Greenland's public housing authority, INI (Greenlandic: *Inatsisartut Inissiaatileqatigiifik*), one can add one's name to the housing list starting at age eighteen. These waiting lists, however, can be incredibly long. In Nuuk, for example, it can take upwards of fifteen years to get an apartment of one's own. Meanwhile, certain jobs within the public sector, such as teachers, nurses, and university professors, come with apartment assignments. As long as one maintains the post, one gets to keep the assigned rental apartment. Previously it was not uncommon to have employment-related apartment assignments, where rent was covered as part of one's salary, but this changed with the introduction of the "real cost" reform.[48]

Meanwhile, the challenge of maintaining an adequate public housing stock in Nuuk and other regional centres has led to the adoption of more punitive housing policies. For example, Knud Hansen and Hans Andersen show an increase in evictions from public housing between 2005 and 2013, due largely to increasing enforcement of rent and housing rules in light of a diminishing housing stock. At the same time, evicted tenants might face great financial punishments not only due to unpaid arrears but also because the financial

45 See Hendriksen, *Grønlands Bygder*.
46 Official statistics on housing have been discontinued since 2010.
47 Greenland Statistics, "Dwellings by Ownership, Time and Place [BOE004]," *Statbank Greenland*, 1 August 2019, http://bank.stat.gl/pxweb/en/Greenland/Greenland__BO__BO99/BOX004.px/table/tableViewLayout1/?rxid=8309ba64-0f86-4e8c-ab3a-672e1bd5cc7d.
48 Hansen and Andersen, *Hjemløshed i Grønland*.

burden of repairs and renovations fall upon tenants, a direct result of the Self Rule government's lack of a restoration budget.[49] This financial burden was emphasized in an interview with a public housing provider, who expressed frustration with the absence of such funds:

> We have to make sure that every time a rent is paid, thirty to forty per-cent is put aside for major maintenance work, so that there is money at all times to cover expenses. We have always had the goal that we should avoid getting into the same situation as self-government that the money that should be set aside ... We make sure there is money present, put aside every single year, so to speak, so that we do not lack money for ongoing maintenance.

Thus, public housing tenants subsidize the cost of building mainte-nance through the rents they pay, which results in higher rents and greater financial strain on the tenants themselves.

Alternatives to the public housing waiting list include getting an education in order to find a job with an assigned apartment or pur-chasing a private house or apartment, which tend to be both expen-sive and in short supply. Thus, the housing landscape can be highly problematic for Greenlanders who do not have a high degree of edu-cation or sustainable employment prospects. Although Greenlandic is the country's official language, Danish is also widely spoken and is the primary language of operation in the professional world, pub-lic administration, and post-secondary education[50] – another remnant of Danish welfare colonialism in Greenland that leaves marginalized people behind. As several scholars have found, there is a distinct rural-urban disparity to Danish literacy, education levels, and employment outcomes,[51] leaving those who migrate from small settlements to the larger centres at a significant disadvantage in the employment and housing markets.[52]

Factors contributing to homelessness in Greenland are not only a matter of unemployment, material poverty, or housing insecurity; they

49 Ibid.
50 Central Intelligence Agency, "World Factbook: Greenland."
51 Hansen, Bitsch, and Lyudmila Zalkind, *Urbanization and the Role of Housing*.
52 Hansen and Andersen, *Hjemløshed i Grønland*; Hendriksen, *Grønlands Bygder*; Rasmus Ole Rasmussen, *Mobilitet i Grønland: Sammenfatning af Hovedpunkter fra Analysen af Mobiliteten i Grønland* [Mobility in Greenland: Summary of main points from an analysis of mobility in Greenland] (Nuuk, Greenland: Mobilitetsstyregruppen, 2010).

tightly intersect with trauma and other psychological issues, addiction, domestic violence, and other forms of abuse.[53] Hansen and Andersen have documented the existence of great social issues connected to homelessness in Greenland, such as abuse, problematic upbringing, poor social resources, unemployment, and so on.[54] Uneven rural-urban geographies, intergenerational impacts of welfare colonialism, institutionalization, and service dependency are directly related to critical social issues visible in Greenlandic welfare society today, including a rise in the number of children facing social problems and in violence against women.[55] Underneath these immense challenges is the escalation in homelessness. In fact, as Arnfjord and Christensen suggest in Chapter 10, housing insecurity has been identified as a critical element in violence against women in Greenland, exacerbating substance abuse, poor mental health, and intimate partner violence.[56] Yet curiously, neither violence against women nor homelessness is prioritized as a social political issue in Greenland.

There is also a critical link between chronic housing need and the emergence of homelessness. For example, Greenland's housing stock consists mainly of public housing, some of which is in poor condition or located in communities where employment, educational, and cultural opportunities are in decline.

---

53 Greenland, Ministry of Family and Health, *Hjemløs i Grønland*.
54 Hansen and Andersen, *Hjemløshed i Grønland*.
55 Ibid.; Torben M. Andersen et al., *Vores Velstand og Velfærd – Kræver Handling Nu* (Nuuk, Greenland: Skatte og Velfærdskommissionen, 2011); Cecilia Petrine Pedersen and Peter Bjerregaard, *Det Svære Ungdomsliv – Unges Trivsel i Grønland 2011: En Undersøgelse om de ældste Folkeskoleelever* [The difficult life of youth – The wellbeing of youth in Greenland 2011: A survey of the oldest high school students] (Copenhagen: Statens Institut for Folkesundhed, 2012); Jonas Fievé and Paarnaq Hansen, "Flere Kvinder Søger Hjælp" [More women are seeking help], *KNR*, 25 November 2016, https://knr.gl/en/node/181892; Mariekathrine Poppel, "Citizenship of Indigenous Greenlanders in a European Nation State: The Inclusionary Practices of Iverneq," in *Reconfiguring Citizenship: Social Exclusion and Diversity within Inclusive Citizenship Practices*, ed. Mehmoona Moose-Mitha and Lena Dominelli (London: Routledge, 2016), 127–36; Raadet for Socialt Udsatte [Council for socially marginalized people], *Udsatte Grønlandske Kvinder i København – En Undersøgelse af Kvindernes Livssituation, Problemer, Ressourcer og Behov* [Marginalized Greenlandic women in Copenhagen – a survey of women's life situations, problems, resources and needs] (Copenhagen: Raadet for Socialt Udsatte, 2016).
56 Mariekathrine Poppel, "Kvinder og Velfærd i Grønland" [Women and welfare in Greenland], in *Kvinder og Velfærd i Vestnorden* [Women and welfare in the West Nordic region], ed. Guðbjörg Linda Rafnsdóttir (Copenhagen: Nordisk Ministerraad, 2010), 39–68.

Rural-Urban Geographies of Homelessness

The literature on Greenlandic homelessness, though sparse, touches on the dynamics of social marginalization, but very little explicitly conceptualizes homelessness within its specific geographical, cultural, and social contexts. For example, research suggests that rural-to-urban and Greenland-to-Denmark migration is a significant factor in Greenland's homeless geographies, yet the dynamics of rural-to-urban mobility and their role in Greenlandic homelessness have not been well explored.[57] Rasmus Rasmussen surveyed a representative 1,550 people on the motivations behind their rural-to-urban move. Top responses included education and employment, living conditions, social network, leisure opportunities, and access to public services.[58] Furthermore, the majority of Greenlanders moving from rural to urban were young people between the ages of fifteen and twenty-five, which reflects a similar observation by Hansen and Andersen that youth at risk of homelessness were likely to engage in such a move.[59]

With the lack of investment in economic and educational opportunities in many small settlements, young people in these communities are forced to seek these opportunities in regional urban centres or beyond. Our research echoes the findings of Hansen and Andersen, revealing a growing trend of youth migration to the cities, particularly Nuuk, without any secure housing arrangements in place. This results in unsustainable temporary housing solutions, such as staying with friends or family.

Another strategy is for people to leave the country entirely to seek opportunities elsewhere. This typically means travelling to Denmark, where Greenlanders hold citizenship, and where more than fourteen thousand Greenlanders currently reside.[60] Yet such a move does not always mean a brighter future. In 2016, the Danish Council of Social Marginalization released a report on Greenlandic homelessness in Denmark.[61] The report describes problematic conditions, such as the language barrier, issues with access to education and employment, and

---

57 See Hansen and Andersen, *Hjemløshed i Grønland*.
58 Rasmus Ole Rasmussen, "Why the Other Half Leave: Gender Aspects of Northern Sparsely Populated Areas," in *Demography at the Edge: Remote Human Populations in Developed Nations*, ed. Dean Carson et al. (Farnham, UK: Ashgate, 2011), 237–54.
59 Rasmussen, *Mobilitet i Grønland*; Hansen and Andersen, *Hjemløshed i Grønland*.
60 Siddhartha Baviskar, *Grønlændere i Danmark: En Registerbaseret Kortlægning* [Greenlanders in Denmark: A census-based mapping] (Copenhagen: SFI, 2015).
61 Raadet for Socialt Udsatte, *Udsatte Grønlandske Kvinder i København*.

disempowered social networks, as well as Danish support staff who have limited understanding of Greenlanders' experiences and support needs. There has been little joint effort by Greenland and Denmark to offer public help for homeless Greenlanders in Denmark, leaving them instead in the care of local Danish NGOs.[62]

This somewhat mirrors the situation in Greenland, where the continued lack of engagement by the public sector on homelessness issues has been enabled in some sense by the active engagement of the non-profit sector, which has sought to fill the gap in programs and services for the housing insecure and homeless. In fact, these new forms of urban community and caring organizations are a positive outcome of the trends towards an increasingly urban Greenland. Local NGOs collaborate with one another to provide services to people living homeless in Nuuk, and they also express a common agenda to empower people living under homelessness and provide facilities for people within the environment to voice their concerns.

NoINI,[63] Kofoeds Skole,[64] and the local chapters of the Røde Kors (Red Cross) and Frelsens Hær (Salvation Army) are filling the gaps in public sector support. Particularly interesting and problematic here is that much of the funding is provided through foreign sources, local fundraising, and limited short-term packets of funding from the municipal government. If the headquarters of these international organizations determined different priorities and refocused their funds elsewhere, the consequences would be disastrous for Nuuk and for Greenland as a whole. Already, the NGOs cannot provide a full slate of support services – for example, Frelsens Hær and NoINI offer a soup kitchen only one night a week. Furthermore, these NGOs are run by dedicated but overworked staff and volunteers, making the landscape of support for urban Greenlanders experiencing homelessness even more precarious.

---

62 Steven Arnfjord, *Sociale Udfordringer Hos et Mindretal af Grønlandske Kvinder i DK Skal Håndteres i (Rigs) Fælleskab* [Social challenges concerning a minority of Greenlandic women in Denmark need to be handled within the Realm] (Copenhagen: Socialpolitisk Forening, 2016).
63 NoINI (established 2012) is a Nuuk based volunteer-run non-profit whose primary activity is a weekly soup kitchen targeted at people experiencing homelessness in Greenland.
64 Kofoeds Skole (established 1925 in Copenhagen, 2016 in Nuuk) is a non-profit initiative founded on Christian and humanitarian principles. Kofoeds Skole provides a wide range of different services to socially vulnerable and marginalized students of all ages.

Resettlement, Urbanization, and Homelessness

Several themes emerge to illustrate the ways in which resettlement and urbanization policies have, over time, laid the foundation for visible homelessness in Nuuk. In stark contrast to policy attention to the encouragement of rural-urban movement stands the total absence of social policy on homelessness. There is currently no homelessness strategy in existence at the municipal or national level in Greenland. The limitations of the ideological belief that housing is a public responsibility are revealed in the absence not only an official definition of homelessness, but also of social policy directed towards Greenlanders who are experiencing homelessness. A principle in Greenland's democratic welfare society is that the people affected by political decisions are given a chance to voice their concerns through public forums. In recent years, however, there has been a shift in the political climate towards the kinds of neoliberal, market-oriented policies seen in Alaska and increasingly in the Canadian North, and decision making about housing policy is evolving within the political environment with no public hearings. Even though Greenland does have a small organization of homeless people, people living under homelessness are rarely included in the development of policy, such as the one that governs the daily operations of the public shelter in Nuuk, leaving them with little agency over the realities of their lived experiences.[65]

At the same time, we observed the making of significant class divisions in Greenland, as public housing is largely accessible through education or employment. Meanwhile, a multitude of push-and-pull factors, many of them caused or exacerbated by the centralization policies of the Danish and then the Greenlandic state, encourage the movement of Greenlanders to urban centres.

Several signs suggest that homelessness in Nuuk is set to increase over the coming years. The intensified centralization since 2011 of health and social services and facilities in Nuuk and the next four largest Greenland centres as well as the urban concentration of employment and educational opportunities make the regional centres a draw for all Greenlanders, including those at risk of homelessness. Meanwhile, the municipality of Sermersooq, which includes Nuuk, is allocating more resources, including land, for housing, but not for

---

65 See B. Rørdam, "Mange Hjemløse i Grønland" [Many homeless in Greenland], *Hus Forbi* 20, no. 1 (2016): 5–6.

low-income groups, which suggests that ensuring a diverse housing spectrum is not a political priority. Yet, although the Self Rule government's urban focus is not limited to the facilitation of the wage economy, but also includes the administration of health and social services, it has not implemented a social policy strategy to manage the consequences of centralization on marginalized Greenlanders. As a result, understanding homelessness as a distinctly urban issue becomes self-fulfilling or reinforcing.

The rural-urban migration patterns of people living without secure housing in Nuuk are bound up in key institutional geographies – themselves significant in the lives of people experiencing homelessness through the complex dynamics of the intergenerational effects of welfare colonialism. In particular, we heard stories from youth who had been released from foster or boarding homes without housing in Nuuk, men and women who had been sent to Nuuk for psychiatric or hospital care and then released without housing, men sent to jail but then released without housing, and women who had migrated to Nuuk to escape violence at home, only to encounter tremendous difficulty in accessing housing once in Nuuk.

The lack of a social policy response to homelessness in Nuuk has resulted in a holding pattern for those who find themselves without suitable, secure shelter. There is only a very limited number of beds in the municipal shelter; in 2017, a few shipping containers were renovated into single-adult apartments for rental, with no emphasis on transitional or supportive housing and associated programs. These apartments were located next to a dump in an inaccessible area of the city. By and large, adults living without housing in Nuuk survive by sleeping in the heated stairwells or furnace rooms of large apartment buildings in the city. This creates a highly precarious living situation, entirely dependent on the tolerance of apartment residents and housing administrators, and is not a long-term, sustainable solution. All told, these geographies reflect the reframing of intergenerational social and health effects of rapid sociocultural change and ongoing colonialities as sites for institutional intervention.

Significantly, there is very little funding and policy direction from the national government. This is a big concern because housing and other social supports are delivered by municipalities, but with little to no coordination or follow-up among them. In the absence of more leadership from the Self Rule government, the onus falls on the municipalities, rather than reflecting the national geography of homelessness. This has resulted in the increasing involvement of the non-profit sector in issues around homelessness, particularly in Nuuk.[66]

To understand and ameliorate visible forms of homelessness in Nuuk, we must expand our focus outside urban bounds to include the significance of rural-urban dynamics. Nuuk is enmeshed in rural-urban, Greenland-Denmark dynamics that extend beyond northern bounds, particularly along historical or contemporary (welfare) colonial-administrative relations. The Greenland-Denmark ties are incredibly significant when examining the mobility of Greenlanders who are experiencing homelessness. Yet there is no integration of service delivery between the two countries or a coordinated policy approach to homelessness in general.

Conclusion

In examining the historical and contemporary dimensions of resettlement in Greenland, we find ourselves questioning the agency of Greenlanders in contemporary patterns of rural-urban migration, given the forms of passive and overt incentivization that the Danish and Greenlandic states have imposed over time. In particular, we are troubled by the contemporary ways in which the social welfare state has been spatialized unevenly, resulting in a manipulation of vulnerabilities entrenched through welfare colonial forms. These vulnerabilities are particularly significant among those Greenlanders who are experiencing homelessness, and they are woven throughout the narratives of homelessness shared with us in our research. In this way, the ongoing legacies of (re)settlement are evident, as the intergenerational effects of early resettlement policy and institutionalization underlie the service dependency of those Greenlanders experiencing housing insecurity and homelessness in Nuuk today. At the same time, resettlement and urbanization are representative of the welfare colonial process as Denmark sought to transform Greenland into a northern image of itself. As Nuuk continues to expand at a fervent pace and an urban Greenland is promoted to local and international audiences, there is an urgent need for social policy that directly addresses homelessness

---

66 Research on the collective actions of Nuuk NGOs is still at an early stage, but see Steven Arnfjord, "Social Udsathed og Tuberkulose i Nuuk" [Social marginalization and tuberculosis in Nuuk], *Tikiusaaq* 2, no. 23 (2015): 20–4.

at a national scale – one that recognizes the historical geographies that underlie what is commonly understood to be a contemporary phenomenon. In fact, housing insecurity and homelessness in Greenland today cannot be extricated from the broader historical, welfare colonial context. State efforts to encourage resettlement to Nuuk must include comprehensive and robust efforts to ensure the inclusion of all Greenlanders in its urban self-image.

Conclusion

Urbanization in the circumpolar North is a nascent yet growing field of study. In the North, where limited and prohibitively expensive housing stock is the norm across a relatively small population base spread out across vast landscapes, housing insecurity and homelessness provide an important lens on the social dimensions of northern urbanization. Together, the chapters in this book have sought to bring this lens into focus by exploring how the factors contributing to housing insecurity and homelessness in the urban North intersect with social policy. All told, this volume brings to the fore key considerations in the development of effective social policy for the urban and urbanizing North. By comparing experiences across the Canadian North, Alaska, and Greenland, we aimed to draw critical connections between homelessness, urbanization, and social policy in the North. Further, as these chapters collectively demonstrate, social policy development benefits from acknowledging and considering the qualitatively unique experiences of housing insecurity, homelessness, and urbanization in northern contexts.

The authors in this volume have attended to the ways northern urban places provide new forms of community building, health and social service provision, and inclusion for people experiencing homelessness. The northern urban centres we examined are places of opportunity, innovation, and collaboration. For example, Travis Hedwig (Chapter 8), Lisa Freeman and Julia Christensen (Chapter 1), and Christensen, Steven Arnfjord, and Marie-Louise Aastrup (Chapter 11) collectively illustrate how, across the Canadian North, Alaska, and Greenland, those in the non-profit sector are an incredibly important resource as providers of support, services, and housing, and as advocates and fundraisers who are doing so much and often with so little. It is the lack of sufficient governmental, financial, and infrastructural supports, however, that necessitates such a widespread need for non-profit response in the first place.

Although the three northern regions display significant differences in terms of governance, scale, settler-Indigenous relations and social welfare, a cross-contextual comparison does provide useful insight into a unique social geography that connects all of these places and illuminates ways to move forward with housing through improved social policy. By exploring experiences with housing insecurity and homelessness across these three geographic contexts, we can advance a more nuanced, robust understanding of the social dimensions of urbanization in the North, in its diverse, yet patterned, forms. Moreover, although the research presented in this volume has emerged from three different countries, each containing many distinct landscapes, rural and urban spaces, populations, and cultures – and although the authors represent many different disciplines – some broad, yet interconnected, themes emerge. Urbanization in northern North America is occurring within a unique social geography of rural-to-urban networks spread across vast landscapes. The contributors to this volume have called particular attention to the ways this northern geography affects governance and social organization, as well provides the social networks within which individuals build linchpin relationships. The chapters in this volume have exposed and explored several broad themes. In this conclusion, we briefly summarize these themes in order to identify common threads connecting homelessness and urbanization across distinct northern geographies.

The Unique Geography of Northern Homelessness

By and large, the contributors to this book present a collective picture of a unique northern geography of homelessness visible across the Canadian North, Alaska, and Greenland. Although a cold climate is a reality in all these contexts, adding increased urgency and risk to the experience of sleeping rough, other similarities also frame cross-contextual comparisons in important ways. In particular, homelessness in these northern regions is tied indelibly to their respective settlement and colonial histories, as well as to the contemporary landscape of remote rural settlements, hub towns, and larger urban centres. Northern settlement, both its historical roots and its contemporary layout, have shaped the factors that produce and reproduce homelessness in the urban North in significant ways. In Chapter 11, Christensen, Arnfjord, and Aastrup describe the ways in which colonial resettlement policy in Greenland acts as a starting point of a trajectory towards the emergence of visible homelessness in Nuuk. In Chapters 1 and 2, Freeman and Christensen, and Nick Falvo, collectively suggest that chronic housing need in small, settlement communities is an important backdrop to the kinds of socio-economic and health factors that frame contemporary homelessness in Yellowknife. The history of northern settlement, and the role that settlement and housing programs have played in cultural assimilationist efforts by the state, is also an important consideration in Frank Tester's Chapter 6. Thus, northern settlement geographies both established the rural-urban network that northern residents depend upon for the flow of resources, culture, and people, and contributed to the persistent social and health inequities that often contribute to contemporary experiences of homelessness.

As the authors acknowledge, although not everyone experiencing homelessness in the North is Indigenous, Indigenous experiences with homelessness are unique, and require further research and explicit policy and funding attention to articulate and contextualize homelessness in light of intergenerational trauma and contemporary forms of colonial violence and racialized discrimination. Northern settlement geographies that have disadvantaged Indigenous peoples both politically and economically, intergenerational effects of colonialism, discrimination against Indigenous peoples in housing and employment markets, and social determinants of ill health all contribute to homelessness among northern Indigenous peoples. Christensen, Arnfjord, and Aastrup (Chapter 11) write that, in Greenland, homelessness is a phenomenon that clearly affects Greenlanders more than it does the more transient Danes, who often have social and economic resources at home in Denmark. In Chapter 4, Carol Kauppi, Michael Hankard, and Henri Pallard detail the ways in which social, economic, and infrastructural inequalities, combined with legacies of colonialism, have particularly implicated Indigenous communities in northern Ontario in rural-urban homeless geographies. In Chapter 5, Joshua Moses expands on the notion of Indigenous homelessness, showing the ways dispossession from homelands through colonial interventions have reproduced multi-scalar experiences of homelessness among Indigenous peoples.

What "Counts" as Homelessness? Definitional Challenges

Definitions of homelessness differ in the Canadian North, Alaska, and Greenland, which exacerbates the challenge of comprehensively assessing the scale and scope of northern homelessness across expansive rural-urban networks. The absence of an agreed-upon definition of northern homelessness not only prevents accurate cross-contextual comparisons; it also leads to disconnections between policy and real, lived experiences. Discrepancies in the definition of homelessness employed by policymakers, non-governmental organizations, and various levels of government make it exceedingly difficult to draw a clear picture of the number of people living homeless and the extent of homelessness across the North, or to compare regional demographics.

There are also significant difficulties in defining homelessness to include important cultural and socio-structural dynamics. For example, the prevalence of hidden homelessness, including couch surfing and overcrowding, is a wide-reaching part of the overall northern homelessness spectrum, the gendered nature of which Arnfjord and Christensen highlight in their examination of women's homelessness in Nuuk (Chapter 10). Tester (Chapter 6) points to the significance of hidden forms of homelessness in Inuit experiences of housing, and suggests that an Inuit definition of homelessness would include a much broader range of culturally mediated housing experiences. The contribution of chronic housing need to northern homelessness, and the ways it renders northern homelessness qualitatively distinct, cannot be overstated.

The challenge in defining homelessness in northern contexts is compounded by difficulties in adequately quantifying homelessness. These difficulties are exacerbated by northern settlement geographies that place communities at a significant physical distance from one another. Chronic housing need and compounding issues such as limited employment and educational opportunities and social determinants of ill health in northern settlement communities are all inextricably linked to the factors contributing to homelessness in northern urban centres. Yet, as Falvo (Chapter 2) describes, Point-In-Time counts and other efforts to quantify homelessness in northern urban locales largely neglect the significance of rural-urban network dynamics in northern homeless geographies.

Rural-Urban Mobility and Migration as Shapers of Northern Homelessness Geographies

One contemporary manifestation of northern settlement histories is a geography of disparity between rural and urban communities. Northern urban centres such as Yellowknife, Anchorage, and Nuuk act as administrative, economic, political, and social hubs, and have long been draws for northerners in search of employment, education, and other opportunities. These urban centres are also ethnically and culturally diverse, including people who have moved to northern urban centres from more southerly locales or from other countries, as well as people from small northern settlements who have never lived in a town. Thus, northern urban centres become significant meeting places of people from diverse backgrounds, yet the urban North is not necessarily a place of opportunity for everyone. Indeed, the past few decades have seen a rise in urban homelessness and housing insecurity across the Canadian North, Alaska, and Greenland.

Passive and overt urbanization policies are also present in these regions. In Greenland, an aggressive urbanization plan is expanding Nuuk (Chapters 10 and 11). The plan, however, does not include low-cost housing for Greenlanders who lack employment or student status. Efforts to make rural settlement life less affordable, such as the real costs program Christensen, Arnfjord, and Aastrup describe in Chapter 11, also come with consequences in the form of greater rural-urban migration. Meanwhile, the urban concentration of health and social services, the criminal justice system, emergency shelters, economic opportunities, and friendship and kinship networks on which people at risk of homelessness are particularly dependent, all shape the rural-to-urban migration of northerners who experience homelessness. Christensen, Arnjord, and Aastrup conceptualize the concentration of key support services and the ways in which this frames the rural-urban mobility of Greenlanders at risk of homelessness as a matter of service dependency. Moreover, they suggest, the specific services upon which northerners living with homelessness rely can be understood as the outcome of institutionalization. In Chapter 5, Moses illustrates how contemporary geographies of northern resource extraction further drive a concentration of opportunities in northern urban centres – a geography, he argues, that is particularly significant for northern youth.

Yet, as Alex Nelson suggests in Chapter 3, the urban North has become the de facto space where key policy and governance decisions are made. At the same time, as argue in the Introduction to this volume, it is in the urban North that homelessness is visible – where homelessness is seen as being in place and therefore becomes the principal site of service delivery. Meanwhile, as many of the contributors note, northern homelessness emerges through a complex network of rural and urban experiences and mobilities. As Nelson illustrates, the urban North is in fact not a distinctly bounded place, but one that comes into being as the nexus of urban, rural, and northern spatial and social politics.

Limited (and expensive) transportation routes in the North mean that such mobility is usually a one-way move to the town or city. In Chapter 4, Kauppi, Hankard, and Pallard describe what is all too often the reality for northerners who move from small, rural communities to northern urban centres in search of work and access to housing: for those without employable skills or education, life is just as hard, if not harder, in the city. The authors also examine the significance of social relationships and how, in many cases, a breakdown in important familial and community relationships at home can result in the desire or need to relocate. On the other hand, some rural-urban migrants follow family and friends to the city in an effort to stay connected to important social networks.

Significantly, several chapters also demonstrate that regional centres are not the only urban locales important to northerners at risk of homelessness. Larger urban centres elsewhere in the United States, Canada, or, in the case of Greenland, Denmark are also inextricable nodes within the broader geography of northern homelessness. In Chapter 11, Christensen, Arnfjord, and Aastrup suggest that colonial relationships between Denmark and Greenland persist through ongoing social and institutional connections that are apparent in the mobility patterns of Greenlanders experiencing homelessness in both Greenland and Denmark. These relationships, however, are not acknowledged through social policy or integrated service delivery. Thus, not only is there no homelessness strategy or social policy framework in Greenland, but there are also no coordinated efforts to address homelessness of Greenlanders in Denmark either.

It is clear that the experience of homelessness is significantly gendered in all three northern regions, but the attention paid to the ways gender frames not only the factors contributing to homelessness but also women's encounters with support services and other resources varies significantly according to context. Arnfjord and Christensen (Chapter 10) suggest that, in Nuuk, a social policy focus on families – and therefore on women with children in their custody – has led women who are experiencing homelessness as a result of intimate partner violence to fall through the cracks. How gender plays a role in a distinct northern geography of homelessness is often related to high rates of overcrowding and housing insecurity, higher rates of intimate partner violence, and rural-urban disparities in support resources for women. Women leaving intimate partner violence outside urban centres often require a rural-to-urban move in order to access shelters for victims of domestic violence, follow children who have been apprehended by the child welfare system, access housing and employment options, or gain access to required resources to support health and well-being.

Urban Geographies of Welfare Colonialism

The legacies of welfare colonialism reveal themselves in myriad complex ways through the chapters in this volume. Yet, although Indigenous northerners disproportionately experience homelessness and chronic housing insecurity, these inequities are represented in distinct ways across the three regions. For example, in Alaska, where there has been a high degree of migration and settlement in the state, and a significant degree of ethnic diversity, Indigenous experiences of homelessness are found alongside those of veterans, recent immigrants, and other groups who are also prominently represented in homeless populations in southern US cities. In the Canadian North, the overrepresentation of Indigenous peoples among northerners experiencing homelessness is more apparent, although, as the Canadian contributors to this volume caution, these experiences need to be situated within the overall context of colonialism in northern Canada. In Greenland, however, the dynamics of settler colonialism are perhaps less overt in the overrepresentation of Greenlanders among those experiencing homelessness, although they become more obvious when considering the rising number of Greenlanders experiencing homelessness in Denmark (see Chapter 11).

Across all three northern regions, the historical and contemporary realities of northern settlement frame Indigenous experiences of housing insecurity and homelessness is critical ways. In Chapter 5, Moses draws important connections between the dispossession of, and displacement from, Indigenous homelands – historically, through modern land claims, and through resource extraction – and the ways in which Indigenous homelessness is experienced. In particular, he argues that these geographies of dispossession lie at the heart of northern rural-urban disparities, often leaving Indigenous youth with little choice but to follow the services and the (perception of) opportunity in northern urban centres, where little is in fact in place to house and support them. Freeman, Christensen, Falvo, and Tester each acknowledge in different ways how the spatial legacies of northern settlement, and the economic, political, and social prioritization of the urban North have disadvantaged rural Indigenous communities in significant ways. In Greenland, Arnfjord, Christensen, and Aastrup (Chapters 10 and 11) also illustrate how policies of settlement and urbanization have been particularly harmful for Greenlanders living in rural communities. Indeed, the urban North becomes the place where chronic housing need, economic underdevelopment, and lack of appropriate health and social supports in smaller northern communities become visible.

Several chapters present contemporary Indigenous homelessness in the urban North as a direct result of earlier colonial social policy that viewed housing as a means towards cultural assimilation. Ultimately, these approaches to northern housing meant that other cultural values and ideals were imposed on northerners through housing design and policy. In other words, the values, ideals, and needs of Indigenous northerners were not considered but simply left out of early northern housing programs. The same could be said today, as Freeman and Christensen (Chapter 1), Tester (Chapter 6), Hedwig (Chapter 8), and Christensen, Arnfjord, and Aastrup (Chapter 11) all describe ways in which contemporary homelessness arises through policies and programs that are either ill-adapted to northern cultures and contexts or aim specifically to impose ideals (such as nuclear family living, wage employment) on housing tenants.

In Chapter 6, Tester looks at the persistent dynamics of welfare colonialism in the ways housing is conceptualized in the context of Nunavut. Since its inception, northern housing policy, he argues, has wilfully ignored Inuit perspectives on home and shelter, instead using housing (designed after Euro-Canadian norms) as a means towards cultural change. The state's refusal to recognize Inuit conceptualizations of home and kinship obligations or to develop housing programs and policies that reflect, rather than seek to destroy, these relations allows for the reproduction of colonial models.

Yet, welfare colonialism is apparent not just in state-sanctioned social policy for housing and homelessness, but also in public discourse. As Clare Dannenberg explores in Chapter 9, northern urban publics also often impose their own expectations on people living homeless, seeking to both distance and "protect" themselves from people who are not adequately homed. Discourses of who belongs and who does not in northern urban centres are palpable in many of the chapters, while consideration of all the chapters together provides cross-contextualization of these discourses. Rather than viewing the town or city as the appropriate place to provide supports for northerners experiencing homelessness, the urban North is widely viewed as a place that is incongruous to homelessness. As Dannenberg describes, the uproar in Anchorage around homelessness is fuelled by narratives of threat and fear. The work of Sally Carraher and Travis Hedwig in Anchorage (Chapter 7) shows, however, that it is possible to bring housed and homeless community members together to create new discourses that prioritize social inclusion and recognize the importance of giving people experiencing homelessness room to speak on these issues in their own ways. Public feedback from their work demonstrates that many of the stereotypes housed community members have about the homeless can be challenged when people with lived experience of homelessness are given meaningful space and opportunity to participate and share their knowledge in public discourse.

Northern Urban Landscapes of Housing and (Im)Mobility

The high rates of chronic homelessness in the North reflect northern housing insecurity, limited transitional housing options, and lack of adequate or appropriate supports for people with issues of mental health or substance use. Northern regions need housing strategies that specifically aim to add stock at various critical points along the housing spectrum – an idea that has gained some footing in Alaska and the Canadian North through Housing First and transitional or supportive housing programs. Yet these options are concentrated in larger urban centres and limited in both number and the spaces available for occupants. Furthermore, as Hedwig describes in Chapter 8, Housing First programs have become reinterpreted, and their original intent manipulated, in the context of Anchorage. In other words, fidelity to the original intent of Housing First has been weakened in the face of funders' disinterest in harm reduction or, in the case of Yellowknife, encouraging quick transitions out of transitional housing (see Freeman and Christensen, Chapter 1). Meanwhile, Christensen, Arnfjord, and Aastrup (Chapter 11) describe a shipping container housing project in Nuuk that was publicly declared as Housing First but came with no corresponding wraparound supports.

The implementation of Housing First and other supportive or transitional programs in northern urban centres has also revealed the need to adapt such programs to the specific contexts and cultures of northern communities. Freeman and Christensen (Chapter 1) describe instances where housing residents have wanted to stay in transitional housing long term, but whose desires have clashed with funders' emphasis on "graduation." Yet, even for those who do finish a support program or graduate out of a transitional home, where are they to go? Urban locales in all three regions display a very limited housing spectrum that is not diversified enough to meet the complex and differing needs of low-income northerners. Surrounding this void is a palpable absence of social policy to coordinate housing with other social and health service needs, which leaves an overburdened non-profit and charity-based sector to compete for limited pots of funding amid growing need. Corresponding and compounding geographies of immobility are found in the narratives presented by Moses (Chapter 5), who sets the lives of Labrador youth against a backdrop of land claims, resource extraction, and an intensifying focus on the town of Happy Valley-Goose Bay as the only place to build a future.

Social Administration, not Social Policy

Across the Canadian North, Alaska, and Greenland, policy approaches to homelessness are largely guided by definitions applied in more urban, southern settings, which tend to neglect the ways in which northern social, cultural, economic, and settlement geographies contribute to homelessness.

Yet, it is clear across the chapters in this volume that a unique geographic context frames urbanization and homelessness in the North. Several chapters help to trace the roots of this context to common experiences across the three regions vis-à-vis historical settlement policy and historical (and contemporary) welfare colonial social policy, by and large administered by governments and decisionmakers far removed from day-to-day northern life. What also becomes clear from several chapters is that current governance and organizational challenges rely too heavily on southern models for social and housing policy and also fail to adapt such models to recognize and promote the unique strengths of northern cultures and contexts.

The close-knit nature of northern urban communities provides both strength and vulnerability, as these chapters reveal. In Chapter 9, Dannenberg suggests that successful practices and programming for homelessness in the urban North rely on community partnership and shared stakes. In her work, she highlights the challenges that non-profit organizations and support providers have had in building bridges to individual community members in Anchorage and the need for this broad political support to advance new programming. Freeman and Christensen (Chapter 1) illustrate the ways in which positive relationships between the non-profit sector, the territorial government, and private rental housing providers in Yellowknife have allowed for the implementation of transitional housing and Housing First programs in the community. And yet, they argue, the long-term sustainability of these programs is threatened when it relies on specific, positive, working relationships among key individuals who might not be in those same positions long term. There is thus a critical need to find ways to build stronger interagency collaboration in order to provide the foundation for positive relationships between organizations.

Across the urban North, we see to varying degrees a trend towards neoliberal or punitive housing policies, reduced government spending on public or social housing, social policies that prioritize urban areas, and insufficient or ineffective mental health and addiction services, all of which exacerbate northern conditions that contribute to homelessness. This shift might be contributing to the development of more punitive housing policies, noted by Freeman and Christensen (Chapter 1) and Falvo (Chapter 2), something that Kauppi, Hankard, and Pallard (Chapter 4) warn will increase social exclusion, which itself is connected to the systemic and structural conditions of homelessness. Additionally, although homelessness is a reflection of inadequate social programs, the implementation of new programs results in arguments that addiction and dependency are being facilitated. In Greenland, housing is viewed as a matter of public responsibility. The limitations of this responsibility, however, are revealed by Christensen, Arnfjord, and Aastrup (Chapter 11), who detail the absence of housing policy directed specifically towards the Greenlandic homeless population. Indeed, they write, the absence of a policy is, in effect, the policy: managing homelessness through a threadbare patchwork of services largely provided by the non-profit sector, and largely neglected by the Self Rule government.

The increasing reliance on the non-profit sector for social support also indicates a shift in the scope of social policy. As Freeman and Christensen describe (Chapter 1), the non-profit sector is the only supportive housing provider in Yellowknife, although it relies heavily on government funding. This funding, however, is doled out annually, making it difficult for NGOs to plan long term, a stress that gets downloaded onto housing clients. At the same time, efforts to lobby government for increased funding place the non-profit sector in an awkward position. Housing providers are, in effect, housing advocates, creating a "bite the hand that feeds you" scenario that does not sit well with supportive housing providers.

Meanwhile, in Nuuk, the non-profit sector is not just the only provider of supportive programs for people living homeless; it does so on very little government funding. Here, the non-profit sector relies heavily on charitable donations, locally as well as internationally, leaving the landscape of support programs for people living homeless incredibly vulnerable. Finally, the significance of the non-profit sector to programs and services for northerners living homeless sheds important light on the urban geography of support provision. Small northern settlements often do not have the non-profit sector one finds in northern towns and cities, meaning that the downloading of programs and services to that sector further concentrates supports for the homeless in northern cities.

Understanding the Urban North through Homelessness

In exploring the geographies of northern homelessness, the urban North reveals itself as a place made through relationships: between rural and urban, North and South, public and private housing providers, and among support providers. Homelessness itself is an experience that is made visible in northern urban centres, but that also implicates rural settlements in significant ways. Indeed, for many northerners experiencing homelessness, rural-urban (im)mobility is part and parcel of their efforts to cope with housing, social, and health support needs. The urban North needs to be understood, therefore, as enmeshed in complex regional and North-South networks.

The chapters in this book have explored how housing insecurity and homelessness reflect broader social issues related to urbanization, marginalization, and social policy in the northern context. They have examined the connections and intersections between structural causes of homelessness in the urban North, with the goal of identifying opportunities for the development of effective social policy. As the contributors have collectively articulated, effective social policy to address northern housing insecurity and homelessness needs to be contextually and culturally rooted. This collection demonstrates that programs and policies developed in the South do not necessarily translate as suitable for the North. An understanding of housing insecurity and homelessness in the North as qualitatively distinct is, thus, a necessary first step in the development and implementation of policies and strategies to mitigate the challenges faced by northern communities.

Alongside the unique challenges posed by housing insecurity and homelessness in the urban North are unique strengths and opportunities. Several chapters have explored the significance of relationships of northerners who are experiencing homelessness, highlighting the importance of social networks for survival. Other chapters have described the ways in which the non-profit sector provides important support and care for those living with housing insecurity, homelessness, or other forms of crisis. These relationships should be recognized for the strengths that they are, and supported through social policy and funding to ensure their sustainability.

Finally, the contributors to this book have shown that there is much to learn from northern communities that are attempting to address the complex challenges of housing, homelessness, and urbanization. Rather than turn to the South for ideas on social policy and programming, we need to turn to northerners for ideas on how to respond effectively to the factors that contribute to homelessness in the urban North. Just as local relationships are essential in delivering supportive programs for northerners experiencing housing crisis, so too should be relationships across northern regions in developing contextually and culturally appropriate definitions, enumeration, programming, and policymaking. It is our hope that this book makes a significant contribution towards the growth of a pan-northern community of housing and homelessness advocates.

Epilogue: Homelessness across the Arctic in the Shadow of COVID-19

In 2018, a group of residents, community leaders, government workers, service providers, advocates, and academics from northern Canada, Alaska, and Greenland came together in Yellowknife, Northwest Territories, to discuss experiences of homelessness in the urban North. The chapters in this volume are the result of that meeting. After that productive and eye-opening experience, we each travelled back to our homes to reflect, write, revise, and submit these chapters for peer review. The culmination of this effort reflects what we knew about homelessness, the northern housing crisis, and social policy immediately preceding the emergency of the COVID-19 pandemic. The editors thus felt that an epilogue was needed as a way of reflecting on how the pandemic and society's responses to it are affecting homelessness in the North right now. This is a difficult task, as we are actively living through the moment, and we do not yet have the wisdom of hindsight.

To date, the infection has spread to some northern regions and communities, but not others.[1] The fear of COVID-19 and its potential spread is palpable throughout the North, as evident in the pandemic responses in each northern region where travel, schooling, businesses, and public events have been closed or cancelled. Rural settlements in particular are feeling the impact of global trade interruptions and shortages of basic goods. The result is that even communities without any known cases of infection are still affected. Furthermore, shelter-in-place orders designed to reduce the transmission of COVID-19 are difficult to implement in small rural settlements, where a lack of adequate housing stock results in crowded living conditions that put the most medically vulnerable

---

1 At the time of writing, a second wave of COVID-19 is active in northern Canada. This has resulted in lockdowns in Nunavut and travel advisories across the North.

family members at higher risk should any member of the household become infected. In a short time, the pandemic has profoundly changed everyone's day-to-day life while we wait for the infection to stop spreading, either naturally or perhaps sooner with the development and mass production of a viable vaccine.

What is readily apparent now, however, is that the pandemic, like major historic epidemics before it, is further exposing the social inequities and structural violence built into our social systems and policies. In fact, we find that some of the themes highlighted throughout these chapters scream louder to us now: that, in the North, there is indeed a unique rural-urban geography through which funding, resources, and people move unevenly, with opportunities pooling in urban centres and not flowing out to rural and remote settlements.

The legacies of welfare colonialism that first created the housing stock crisis in the North now leave northern populations more vulnerable to COVID-19. Many northern communities, particularly those outside urban centres, have little to no access to local health facilities equipped to deal with this severe respiratory and circulatory disease. These same rural and remote communities are also more vulnerable to interruptions in the commercial food supply chain. Although much of the work in this volume has highlighted the ways in which homelessness is experienced similarly across the urban North, the current pandemic has also revealed how our respective nations differ in governance and social policy with respect to health care. There is a notable inverse correlation between the level of government action to "flatten the curve" and the resulting prevalence of COVID-19 in each region. Below, we briefly share our reflections on how the pandemic is interacting with and reshaping the housing crisis and different types of homelessness in the North. We close with some comments on how social policy might be affected by the pandemic, and where we feel future work should be done.

Alaska

News that the epidemic caused by the COVID-19 in China was about to spread to the Americas and elsewhere, and that it was indeed becoming a pandemic, came in mid-March 2020. Alaska reported its first confirmed case – a foreign national who developed symptoms shortly after arriving in Anchorage – on 12 March. The Municipality of Anchorage gave the order to "hunker down": businesses shuttered, public gatherings cancelled, schools converted to online learning. The working class suddenly found itself reshuffled into three categories: "essential workers" who provide groceries, gasoline, medical care, and other essential services to the public; workers who could pivot to working remotely; and the single-largest group of unemployed Alaskans since the height of the 1980s oil recession. Although everyone is affected in some way, essential workers are at greatest risk of exposure to the infection, while many are also precariously employed and lack protections such as paid sick leave.

Anchorage is one of the busiest air cargo hubs in the United States, and the point of entry for seasonal workers from around the world who travel to work in fisheries and extractive industries throughout the state. Lack of public health guidance, compounded by politicization of responses and misinformation surrounding available evidence, has worsened the problem. Self-quarantine and testing requirements of travellers entering the state are not enforced. Conglomerate living facilities, including group homes, assisted-living facilities, detox and treatment centres, homeless shelters, and transitional living facilities have become hotspots for community transmission.[2] Although extensive contact tracing training programs are under way in Anchorage, tracking movement within the state – especially of people who might only be passing through Anchorage en route to a smaller community for work – is extremely challenging. Coupled with lack of testing facilities, there is no accurate case count for the state and no information about the potential extent of asymptomatic transmission. Additionally, since almost all of the state's intensive care unit bed capacity exists in Anchorage, access to care is bottlenecked, and already-limited supplies of personal protective equipment and medical technology such as ventilators have been further diminished.

Like much of the United States, Alaska has been reluctant to enact universal guidelines to help prevent or slow the spread of COVID-19. Some see this as a positive thing, emphasizing the diverse needs and different levels of risk for urban and rural communities. Others criticize this as a failure of the governor and/or local communities to do enough to flatten the curve – especially more recently, as Alaska has been seeing a surge in infections since June 2020. Contributing to this, messages in late spring and summer 2020 from the state and the Municipality of Anchorage concerning phased reopening and mask wearing have been

2 Aubrey Wieber, "Feds to help manage Anchorage's COVID-10 outbreak among the homeless," *Anchorage Daily News*, 12 September 2020, https://www.adn.com/alaska -news/anchorage/2020/09/11/feds-to-help-manage-anchorages-covid-19-outbreak -among-the-homeless/.

contradictory and confusing. The governor declared in May that Alaska would "fully reopen" before Memorial Day weekend, a time traditionally filled with large crowds and family outings. In order to do so, it was announced that the state would move into Phase 3 and Phase 4 of its pandemic response plan simultaneously.[3] After sending an official memo to state employees in Anchorage that the city's mask mandate did not apply within state buildings in the municipality, the governor reversed course.[4] At the time of writing, there is still no statewide mask mandate. Restrictions are left for individual settlements to implement locally (or not), even though frequent travel continues between towns on the same highway. Although Alaska has fared better than the Lower 48, with a relatively low number of infections and deaths in the first half of 2020, its COVID-19 response mirrors the inadequacies and lack of coordination between national, state, and local governments that is evident at the national level. Similarly, like the rest of the United States, Alaska has seen a surge in COVID-19 infections throughout fall 2020: on 24 and 25 October, the state had its top two highest daily case counts of 355 and 526, respectively.[5]

Compared to the Canadian North and Greenland, Alaska has a much higher total of active infections, resulting in community transmission[6] throughout the state. All of this has happened within just four short months, with the greatest rise in transmission beginning around 22 June 2020. A mid-summer uptick followed the relaxation of some pandemic

3 Aubrey Weiber and Margan Krakow, "Gov. Dunleavy to lift most coronavirus restrictions on Alaska businesses Friday," *Anchorage Daily News*, 19 May 2020. https://www.adn.com/alaska-news/2020/05/19/dunleavy-to-lift-all-coronavirus -capacity-restrictions-on-alaska-businesses-friday/; James Brooks, "Alaska's governor and attorney general say Anchorage's mask mandate doesn't apply to state offices. the city disagrees," *Anchorage Daily News*, 29 June 2020, https://www.adn.com /alaska-news/anchorage/2020/06/29/alaskas-governor-and-attorney-general-say -anchorages-mask-mandate-doesnt-apply-to-state-offices-the-city-disagrees/.
4 Rashah McChesney, "Dunleavy announces new health mandates," *Alaska Public Media*, 22 July 2020, https://www.alaskapublic.org/2020/07/22/dunleavy-announces-new -health-mandates/.
5 Lex Treinen, "Official appeal to Alaskans for help as state reports 526 COVID-19 cases Sunday," *Alaska Public Media*, 25 October 2020, https://www.alaskapublic .org/2020/10/25/alaska-we-need-your-help-officials-appeal-for-precautions-as -state-reports-526-COVID-19-cases-sunday/.
6 Community transmission is when an epidemic infection is spreading significantly within a population and contact tracing can no longer determine who has become infected after being exposed to people who first brought the infection into a community; cluster transmission is when the infection is concentrated in a limited locality and it is easier to identify the chain of infection.

restrictions and reopening of businesses and public gatherings. Additionally, a significant number of non-resident cases of COVID-19 have resulted from seafood industry workers travelling to Alaska from other jurisdictions. Several remote settlements near commercial fishing work sites have shuttered their communities and restricted travel by non-residents in an attempt to prevent the spread of the infection to local populations. It is likely that the primary reason Alaska has relatively fewer cases than the rest of the United States is its lower population density. A surge of infections in fall 2020, however, has led three communities in rural southwest Alaska to impose their own lockdowns.[7] It seems the advantage of a geographically dispersed population is starting to evaporate.

Since the beginning of the pandemic, debate about how COVID-19 might affect those experiencing homelessness – and what "should be done" about homelessness in general – has been vigorous and tense. For the homeless, exclusion from urban public spaces has become even more severe, as shelters, day kitchens, libraries, stores, cafes, and parks have been closed under "hunker down" orders. In April 2020, a temporary "socially distant" shelter was opened in the Ben Boeke and Sullivan Arenas in midtown Anchorage, where cots were placed in squares spaced six feet apart, marked by tape on the floor. This space was to help relieve some of the cramping of limited indoor shelter in town while low temperatures made it dangerous to sleep outdoors. Additionally, the Municipality of Anchorage submitted a formal request to the Alaska National Guard for its "help" with the "homelessness problem" in the city, using federal COVID-19 relief funds. Some of these funds were to be used to hire the National Guard to patrol the temporary arena shelters and to have National Guard personnel patrol "high-volume homeless areas" such as around Fairview and both the Chester Creek and Campbell Creek multiuse trails, where people often camp. The request was denied, however, on the basis that "homeless camps were pre-existing to the pandemic."[8]

The pandemic has also brought the status quo of Alaska's inadequate shelter system into harsher relief and reignited the "not in my

7 Anna Rose MacArthur, "COVID-19 put 3 southwest Alaska villages into lockdown," *Alaska Public Media*, 9 October 2020, https://www.alaskapublic.org/2020/10/09/COVID-19-puts-3-southwest-alaska-villages-into-lockdown/.
8 Paul Dobbyn, "Anchorage's request for National Guard help with homeless camps is rejected," *Anchorage Daily News*, 15 April 2020, https://www.adn.com/alaska-news/anchorage/2020/04/15/anchorages-request-for-national-guard-help-with-homeless-camps-is-rejected/.

back yard" fervour of some non-homeless residents in Anchorage. For example, heated public testimony before the Anchorage Assembly took place in July 2020 on a possible vote to allow a rezoning ordinance for four midtown buildings to be purchased and developed into shelter and other services for the homeless. This anti-homeless effort calls itself "Save Midtown" and "Save Anchorage," revealing how the group perceives people living homeless both as a threat and as "others," rather than as fellow community members. This resistance is ramping up even as winter approaches, with dropping temperatures and reduced daylight, as several Save Anchorage advocates protesting the use of the hockey arena as a temporary homeless shelter, citing their children's rights to be able to play hockey as more important.

Canada

When the first cases of COVID-19 appeared in Canada, the concern was immediately palpable in northern communities. A persistent housing crisis, along with existing inequities in health care access, significantly increased northerners' vulnerability in the face of the global pandemic. Indigenous leaders and public health officials across northern Canada warned that a prevalence of compounding factors, including high rates of diabetes, asthma, tuberculosis, and other respiratory illnesses, likely would compound the impact of the pandemic on northern communities. For example, Nunavut's Chief Medical Officer of Health warned that the impact of the virus on the territory could be especially harsh due to a combination of housing need and the prevalence of respiratory illness. Inuit children experience the highest rates of chronic respiratory disease in the world, and have a tuberculosis rate that is three hundred times that of non-Indigenous Canadians. Similarly, a survey completed by the Dene Nation found that one-fifth of its membership were at increased risk of severe complications if infected with COVID-19, due to compounding factors including chronic housing need and high rates of chronic illness.

The strategies employed to slow the spread of the virus in much of southern Canada were, and remain, privileges not enjoyed by many northern communities. Overcrowded and inadequate housing makes physical distancing or self-isolation virtually impossible. Water insecurity poses a challenge for frequent hand washing or cleaning hard surfaces, while the high cost of living and logistical challenges complicate access to necessities such as soap, hand sanitizer, and disinfectant. Fortunately, northern Canada implemented many of the earliest, boldest public health restrictions to fight COVID-19, including a series of travel restrictions and self-isolation requirements implemented at various scales. On 20 March 2020, the Northwest Territories shut its borders to non-essential travel to control the spread of the virus, and also implemented mandatory fourteen-day self-isolation for all travellers, to be completed in one of the four largest communities before onward travel to smaller settlements would be permitted. A few days later, the Nunavut government released the tightest travel restrictions in Canada, with a travel ban for everyone except residents and critical workers, as well as mandatory fourteen-day pre-boarding self-isolation. Indigenous governments such as Dene Nation have responded by encouraging members to head out on the land to distance themselves from COVID-19.

Moreover, federal efforts to help northern and Indigenous communities through the pandemic have recognized their elevated and often-contextualized vulnerability. The Indigenous Community Support Fund, announced by the federal government on 18 March 2020, constituted a $305 million aid package for Inuit, First Nations, and Métis to prepare for, and react to, the spread of COVID-19. The federal government also provided a further $25 million to Nutrition North Canada, enabling the subsidy program to expand the range of nutritious food items accessible in isolated northern communities. An additional $129.9 million specifically for Yukon, Nunavut, and the NWT was allocated to bolster health care systems throughout the northern territories and support their COVID-19 response. This funding also provided financial support for northern airlines and other businesses.

Yet a rise in visible homelessness over the past two decades on the streets of northern capital cities and regional centres such as Yellowknife, Whitehorse, and Iqaluit made acute housing need increasingly apparent. Many northerners opted to follow the directives to self-isolate by sheltering in place or heading out on the land, but both of these strategies were out of reach for a significant number of northerners who lacked access to housing or other necessary resources to wait out the pandemic safely. As in Alaska, the COVID-19 pandemic illuminated the many ways in which people experiencing homelessness in northern Canada are particularly vulnerable to communicable disease, especially when few shelters allow clients to stay during daytime hours. Closures of local businesses, office buildings, libraries, and other gathering places in response to the pandemic also highlighted the importance of such spaces for people with nowhere to go to stay warm during the day in northern cities with minimal indoor public space. Moreover, the longstanding practices of releasing people on bail into northern capital cities and of banishing people on bail/probation from home communities have come under increased scrutiny amid the pandemic, as they leave people stranded in cities where they have no housing.

The early response to the effects of COVID-19 on northerners experiencing homelessness by the federal, provincial, and territorial governments demonstrated that quick action is possible. In April 2020, the NWT government announced a $5 million relief package to create temporary housing so that those with vulnerable or precarious housing situations could have a place to stay during the pandemic. The funds were directed towards emergency self-isolation programs in Yellowknife and to 130 self-isolation units in other NWT communities.

The NWT government also took the step early on to remove from standard social assistance calculations[9] both the Canada Emergency Response Benefit and the Canada Emergency Student Benefit – emergency income assistance measures intended to help millions of Canadians cope with the financial impacts of loss of employment during the pandemic. This move protected low-income NWT residents from the kinds of clawbacks Canadians on social assistance experienced in other provinces, which ultimately resulted for many in the inability to pay rent.[10]

In downtown Yellowknife, the day shelter was turned into an emergency shelter-in-place program for thirty adults experiencing homelessness in the territorial capital. The NWT Disabilities Council, which ran the day shelter program, said that turning the facility into a home for those thirty people would help ensure that they were not exposed to COVID-19 during the ongoing pandemic. Although the decision to limit access to the day shelter was highly controversial, the director of programs for the council stated that "with controlled distribution of alcohol and no access to illegal drugs, the people we support are telling us how they feel healthier than they have [in] years." In early May 2020, the Yellowknife Women's Society began operating the former Arnica Inn as an isolation space for people at risk of severe illness if they were to contract COVID-19, especially those facing homelessness. The facility's managed alcohol and cannabis program attempted to build on the success of the programming at the city's day shelter. The intention

---

9   Emily Blake, "NWT extending income assistance Covid-19 relief," *Cabin Radio*, 22 July 2020, https://cabinradio.ca/41798/news/nwt-extending-income-assistance -covid-19-relief/.
10 Bonnie Allen, "Landlords say poor tenants who received CERB can't make rent after losing social assistance," *CBC News*, 22 November 2020, https://www.cbc.ca/news /canada/saskatchewan/landlords-tenants-cerb-rent-1.5810230.

was eventually to turn the space into a transitional housing program. Interestingly, the project initially was stalled due to lack of cooperation between the territorial and municipal governments, but differences were quickly set aside in the wake of the pandemic.

Finally, in late May 2020, the NWT housing minister revealed that the 130 housing units set aside for self-isolation in smaller communities would be repurposed as public housing. These new units would reduce overcrowding, making communities less vulnerable to any second wave of the COVID-19 pandemic.

In Iqaluit, the beginning of the pandemic underscored existing concerns of overcrowding in the city's shelter spaces. In April 2020, city councillors approved the allocation of $351,200 to three local organizations helping with the city's ongoing COVID-19 homelessness response. These funds constituted the bulk of a $600,000 commitment to the City of Iqaluit under the federal $82 billion COVID-19 Economic Response Plan announced in March 2020. That nationwide economic response plan included an allocation of $157.5 million to Reaching Home, which supports community-based programs aimed at preventing and reducing homelessness. Additional funding under the Reaching Home program was provided to support an isolation shelter at the Uquutaq Men's Shelter in Iqaluit as well as to help sustain the shelter's regular programming. The YWCA Agvvik women's shelters received $105,000, including $90,000 for additional isolation space and $15,000 for supplies.

Greenland

To stop the spread of COVID-19 in Greenland, the government closed the borders and stopped all international and domestic flights and boat traffic in March 2020.[11] With a total population of 56,000, Greenland had just thirteen infections and no deaths as a result of the pandemic. Closing Greenland meant locking down the capital, Nuuk, which was the epicentre of the virus outbreak. The lockdown lasted throughout March and April and affected shops, public services, schools, and NGOs that form the core of service providers for vulnerable populations in the country. Closing these NGOs cut vital services to people experiencing homelessness.

---

11 Elements of the section on Greenland were published as "Greenland's Emerging Social Conscience: Voluntary Food Delivery to People Experiencing Homelessness in Nuuk," *Qualitative Social Work* 20, no. 1–2 (2021): 433–8, https://doi.org/10.1177/1473325020973209.

During times of crisis, shortfalls in social policy become visible, which was the case with Greenland's non-existent focus on social marginalization prior to the pandemic. During the lockdown, the public administration failed to make an emergency relief plan for people dependent on public services for food and everyday care. The lockdown meant the closing of social services and, thereby, of social work. Essentially, the shutdown meant that many already marginalized people experienced food insecurity and the risk of infection and spreading the virus. People experiencing homelessness are a high-risk group because many have existing chronic health conditions and live in densely packed shelters. Studies have found that this group is more vulnerable to tuberculosis than other social groups,[12] while recent research on COVID-19 has similar findings.[13] Diseases spread easier among people who lack access to sanitary facilities and the ability to maintain social distancing.

A local NGO in Nuuk, NoINI (meaning No Room) facilitates a weekly soup kitchen operated year-round and run by a few volunteers. The group uses a kitchen in the local Salvation Army and receives funding from the Greenlandic Red Cross. While NoINI continued to serve warm meals every Wednesday as usual during the lockdown, a solution for the rest of the week was required. By reaching out, NoINI received offers of volunteer and financial help from the Red Cross, and local restaurants volunteered to donate hot meals. NoINI established teams of three to receive the donated food, repack it in takeaway boxes, and distribute it to those in need through an open window every day for five weeks. In total, eighteen people volunteered to help NoINI with the food distribution program. Normally NoINI expedites around forty servings during the weekly soup kitchen; during the five weeks of lockdown, the volunteers distributed between sixty and ninety meals per day. It is assumed that the recipients also received help from families, informal networks, or through other means.

The food distribution initiative demonstrated Greenlandic society's social conscience. It was powerful and showed signs of real social responsibility. Uniquely, the volunteers who came forward were atypical and new to the voluntary sector in Nuuk, but this ad hoc social work still surpassed that of the public sector.

---

12 Kevin Patterson, "TB: The Patient Predator," *Mother Jones* 28, no. 2 (2003), https://www.motherjones.com/politics/2003/03/patient-predator/.

13 Jack Tsai and Michal Wilson, "COVID-19: A Potential Public Health Program for Homeless Populations," *Lancet Public Health* 5, no. 4 (2020): e186–7, https://doi.org/10.1016/S2468-2667(20)30053-0.

The emergency shelter was also shut down and, three weeks later, a tent camp was set up on the outskirts of Nuuk using rented Arctic tents from the mining sector. Although sanitary and providing a roof over people's heads, images in the media resembled that of a refugee camp. Residents of the camp were generally very positive, however, and one long-term result is that there is now finally a plan to facilitate proper housing programs aimed at people experiencing homelessness.[14] Nonetheless, the plan is representative of the social welfare system's very reactive approach in Greenland. The proposed housing initiative is being formed within the municipality and without any real national sanctioned legislation. It is still a wish for the future to see legislation that allows for definitions and preventive measurements aimed at setting up action plans and bringing down the numbers of Greenlandic homeless.

Conclusion

At the time of writing, both Canada and the United States are experiencing the second wave of the pandemic, with confirmed cases reaching record numbers. By November 2020, Nunavut, which had managed to get through the first wave without a single confirmed case of COVID-19, faced what everyone had been fearing: an outbreak of the virus in the community of Arviat, one of the hardest hit by overcrowding and poor housing conditions. Cases in the community of roughly 2,500 had exceeded one hundred by December 2020. Throughout northern Canada, case numbers were slowly increasing. Much of this surge has been linked to rotational workers travelling from southern Canada to extractive industry operations across the region. In Alaska, the second wave began in early fall 2020, and the state became ranked as one of the hardest hit in the country. The highest numbers of daily cases are found in the large urban centres of Anchorage and Fairbanks, but a significant number of outbreaks have occurred in rural and remote communities. Although Greenland's case numbers remain low, the country is only at the beginning of what is likely to be a long and challenging winter.

What the pandemic will mean for the North and for northerners experiencing homelessness will depend on how governments respond both in the short and long term. We have seen numerous examples of

---

14 "Kommunalbestyrelsen vedtager nyt hjemløsecenter" [The municipal council adopts a new homeless shelter], *Kommuneqarfik Sermersooq*, 8 July 2020, https://sermersooq .gl/da/nyheder/2020/7/8/Kommunalbestyrelsen-vedtager-nyt-hjemloesecenter-.

action on the part of local, state, provincial, and national governments to address what this public health crisis means for the housing insecure, but these actions by and large have been packaged as short-term, emergency responses. Little discussion is taking place in any of the three countries as to how these responses could be sustained and even expanded in a post-COVID world. In an effort to alleviate permanently the inequities that have heightened vulnerability to the pandemic for all northerners, particularly those in rural or geographically remote communities, policy discussions that steer us away from a return to the status quo are critical.

The COVID-19 pandemic has underscored, in no uncertain terms, the importance of home and housing to health. Before the pandemic, people without housing in northern cities were largely left to wander the streets, looking for a warm place to hang out and to use the washroom. Such places were becoming increasingly hard to come by as tensions increased among some local business owners and the public. The pandemic has also demonstrated that governments and citizens can be swift, bold, and resourceful in their reactions to crisis. Yet it remains to be seen what lasting change will come from the pandemic in addressing the northern housing crisis, including both hidden and visible forms of homelessness. It also remains to be seen what lies ahead for the harm-reduction measures, supportive housing programs, and expanded funding that have been dedicated to assisting northerners who have nowhere safe to shelter in place.

Contributors

Marie-Louise Aastrup holds a PhD in geography from Memorial University of Newfoundland and is currently executive director of NatureNL. An expert in mixed methods and community engagement, Dr. Aastrup also works as a private consultant in diverse community-university research collaborations.

Steven Arnfjord is an associate professor at the University of Greenland (Ilisimatusarfik) and Director of Ilisimatusarfik's Centre for Arctic Welfare. He has published extensively on the Greenlandic welfare society, with a focus on social policy, social work, poverty, and homelessness.

Sally Carraher is an applied medical anthropologist. She studies health and illness experiences among the peoples of Alaska and the Canadian North. Much of her work is community based and multidisciplinary, bringing community members together with health providers, scientists, and policymakers to do research that leads to real-world action. Dr. Carraher emphasizes research to help improve health and wellness *as envisioned by community members for themselves*. Dr. Carraher also works as the Ethnographic Fieldwork Lead for the Canadian North *Helicobacter pylori* (CANHelp) Working Group and is a long-time volunteer with Bean's Cafe in Anchorage, Alaska. Her current research focuses on the socio-cultural aspects of *H. pylori* bacterial infection in the Arctic and homelessness in Alaska.

Julia Christensen is an associate professor in the Department of Geography and Planning at Queen's University. A former Canada Research Chair in Northern Governance and Public Policy, Dr. Christensen has published extensively on northern social policy, housing, and homelessness. She leads the pan-northern research partnership At Home in the

North, which includes Indigenous, community, and regional representation from across the territorial and provincial Norths. Dr. Christensen is the author of numerous research articles and books, including *No Home in a Homeland: Indigenous Peoples and Homelessness in the Canadian North*.

Clare J. Dannenberg specializes in issues of language use and identity, and she has done extensive work with Native American, Appalachian, and African American varieties of English, investigating the rates and trajectory of language change in the face of language loss and cultural encroachment. Using both critical discourse and language variation theories, Dr. Dannenberg examines language variables at both the descriptive and theoretic levels of analysis in order to better understand the role of language change and identity construction around issues of language sustainability and policy. Principally, her work has concentrated in the southeastern region of the United States, where she had the opportunity to work with the Lumbee Tribe of North Carolina. Dr. Dannenberg has conducted research in Alaska on the maintenance of ethnic language varieties with the investigation of Central Yup'ik varieties of English within the Anchorage region in order to better understand the negotiation of language boundaries in multicultural contexts.

Michael Hankard is an associate professor and chair of the Department of Indigenous Studies at the University of Sudbury. He is the author of *Access, Clocks, Blocks and Stocks: Resisting Health Canada's Management of Traditional Medicine* and *We Still Live Here: First Nations, Alberta Oil Sands, and Surviving Globalism*.

Nick Falvo has a PhD in public policy from Carleton University and is one of Canada's most prominent researchers in affordable housing and homelessness. He is editor-in-chief, North America, of the *International Journal on Homelessness*, and is the 2021 winner of the President's Medal for Outstanding Housing Research – the highest honour given by Canada Mortgage and Housing Corporation.

Lisa Freeman is an adjunct professor in urban studies at Simon Fraser University. She is an interdisciplinary scholar whose research and teaching intersects in the fields of socio-legal studies, human geography, and urban planning. Her research focuses on the questions of law and regulation in the city, the relationship between gentrification and the suburbanization of poverty, and the role of municipal government in regulating low-income housing.

Travis Hedwig is an applied medical anthropologist and an associate professor of health sciences in the Division of Population Health Sciences, University of Alaska Anchorage. His research addresses social determinants of health inequality by engaging communities to identify solutions that are responsive to several related areas of vulnerability, including impairment/disability and fetal alcohol spectrum disorders, housing and homelessness, mental and behavioural health, and substance misuse. Dr. Hedwig has a long history of collaboration with communities across the circumpolar North and has worked on several multiyear applied public health projects in areas of child welfare, adolescent health and wellness, criminal justice, housing and employment support, and community-engaged approaches to alcohol and substance misuse prevention. He is passionate about teaching and learning, and enjoys the challenge of translating research into action in collaboration with communities.

Carol Kauppi is the director of the Centre for Research in Social Justice and Policy and professor in the School of Social Work at Laurentian University, and she served as the MSW program coordinator for several years. Dr. Kauppi's research interests have focused on homelessness and housing in a vast area of northeastern Ontario, including rural and remote communities in the James Bay lowlands, as well as urban centres in the region.

Joshua Moses is an associate professor of anthropology and environmental studies at Haverford College. He has worked with Nunatsiavut Inuit communities in northern Labrador on inequality, dispossession, community well-being, migration and identity in the context of recent land-claim settlements, and large-scale resource extraction. He has also conducted research in the Northwest Territories on migration, housing, and homelessness. Dr. Moses's focus on action research, collaborative research methods, and community-engaged research has led him to work with a number of Philadelphia-area community and environmental organizations, with a particular focus on youth.

Alex Nelson (pronouns they/them) is a PhD candidate in anthropology at Western University. Alex's research explores gender, homelessness, and housing policy, and specifically looks at the ways in which gender-diverse people with lived experience of homelessness mobilize their experiences to reform policy. Alex's academic research and community involvement is deeply informed by their lived experience of homelessness and involvement in the child welfare system, as well as their experiences at the intersection of queerness and disability.

Henri Pallard is a professor at the Department of Law and Justice at Laurentian University. Since 1993, he has led the Person, Culture and Law project, an international research team in the field of human rights. In 2008, he became director of the International Centre for Interdisciplinary Research in Law at Laurentian University, which supports and encourages research on law, democracy, human rights, cultural diversity, and more. Dr. Pallard has published extensively in several legal fields, as well as in the legal geographies of migration, homelessness, and health in northern Ontario.

Frank Tester is Emeritus Faculty in the School of Social Work at the University of British Columbia, and an advocate, researcher, and consultant on environmental issues, especially in Canada's Arctic. He focuses on the social and environmental history of the eastern Arctic. He has expertise in Canadian social policy, environmental and cultural issues, and Inuit social history.

www.ingramcontent.com/pod-product-compliance
Lightning Source LLC
Chambersburg PA
CBHW030236030426
42336CB00009B/125

* 9 7 8 1 4 8 7 5 5 2 8 9 3 *